AGAINST INTELLECTUAL MONOPOLY

"Intellectual property" – patents and copyrights – has become controversial. We witness teenagers being sued for "pirating" music, and we observe AIDS patients in Africa dying because of their lack of ability to pay for drugs that are expensively priced by patent holders. Are patents and copyrights essential to thriving creation and innovation? Do we need them so that we all may enjoy fine music and good health? Across time and space the resounding answer is: No. So-called intellectual property is in fact an "intellectual monopoly" that hinders rather than helps the competitive free market regime that has delivered wealth and innovation to our doorsteps. This book broadly covers both copyrights and patents and is designed for a general audience, with its focus on everyday examples. The authors conclude that the only sensible policy to follow is to eliminate the patent and copyright systems as they currently exist.

Michele Boldrin is Joseph G. Hoyt Distinguished Professor of Economics in Arts and Sciences at Washington University in St. Louis. He is a Fellow of the Econometric Society and a Research Fellow at the Center for Economic Policy Research (London) and at Fundación de Estudios de Economía Aplicada (Madrid). He is an associate editor of *Econometrica*, an editor of *Review of Economic Dynamics*, and an advisory editor of *Macroeconomic Dynamics*, published by Cambridge University Press. His research interests include growth, innovation, and business cycles; intergenerational and demographic issues; public policy; institutions; and social norms. He is the coauthor or coeditor of four books and has published in leading journals such as *American Economic Review*, *Econometrica*, *Review of Economic Studies*, *Journal of Political Economy*, *Journal of Economic Theory*, *Review of Economic Dynamics*, *Journal of Monetary Economics*, and *Journal of Economic Dynamics and Control*.

David K. Levine is John H. Biggs Distinguished Professor of Economics in Arts and Sciences at Washington University in St. Louis. He is a coeditor of *Econometrica* and *NAJ Economics*, president of the Society for Economic Dynamics, a Fellow of the Econometric Society, and a research associate of the National Bureau for Economic Research. Author with Drew Fudenberg of *Learning in Games* and editor of several conference volumes, his research interests include the study of intellectual property and endogenous growth in dynamic general equilibrium models; the endogenous formation of preferences, institutions, and social norms; and the application of game theory to experimental economics. Levine has published in leading journals such as *American Economic Review*, *Econometrica*, *Review of Economic Studies*, *Journal of Political Economy*, *Journal of Economic Theory*, *Quarterly Journal of Economics*, and *American Political Science Review*.

Against Intellectual Monopoly

MICHELE BOLDRIN

Washington University in St. Louis

DAVID K. LEVINE

Washington University in St. Louis

CAMBRIDGE UNIVERSITY PRESS

Cambridge, New York, Melbourne, Madrid, Cape Town, Singapore, São Paulo, Delhi

Cambridge University Press

32 Avenue of the Americas, New York, NY 10013-2473, USA

www.cambridge.org

Information on this title: www.cambridge.org/9780521879286

First published 2008

Printed in the United States of America

A catalog record for this publication is available from the British Library.

Library of Congress Cataloging in Publication Data

Boldrin, Michele, 1956–
Against intellectual monopoly / Michele Boldrin, David K. Levine.
p. cm.
Includes bibliographical references and index.
ISBN 978-0-521-87928-6 (hardback)
1. Intellectual property – Economic aspects. 2. Competition.
3. Monopolies. I. Levine, David K. II. Title.
K1401.BB65 2008
346.04′8–dc22   2007053007

ISBN 978-0-521-87928-6 hardback

Contents

Acknowledgments

Above all we are grateful to our families, Emanuela and Niccolò, Joyce, and Milena, for putting up with us while we wrote this – not to speak of reading and criticizing parts of it.

A great many people contributed to our ideas and knowledge of "intellectual property" expressed in this book – though many of them no doubt would disagree with our sentiments and some of our conclusions. We are particularly grateful to Nicholas Gruen, Doug Clement, Jim Schmitz, Tim Sullivan, and Scott Parris for their continued support and advice. Toward Scott Parris, our editor at Cambridge University Press, we have accumulated a particularly large debt for his infinite patience, careful reading of an endless sequence of versions, and very professional handling of our repeated mishaps.

Many people advised us about particular issues. We are grateful for Preston McAfee's analysis of the Rambus case; Alessandro Nuvolari's advice, especially about steam power; Ivan P'ng's example of the wheeled suitcase; Eric Rasumussen's analysis of marketing and copyright; Jean-Laurent Rosenthal's leads on the history of copyright; and George Selgin and John Turner's corrections to our story of James Watt.

Many people contributed examples, comments, and references, especially Serguey Braguinski, Tim Erickson, Jack Hirshleifer, Bronwyn Hall, Andrea Moro, G. Moschini, Ed Prescott, Paul Seabright, Malik Shukayev, Robert Solow, William Stepp, Stefano Trento, and Edward Welbourne.

We learned an immense amount from our fellow bloggers at http://www.againstmonopoly.org: John Bennett, Andrea Moro, Michael Perelman, Sheldon Richman, and William Stepp.

We are grateful also to the Slashdot Web site (http://slashdot.org) and its many contributors for a set of detailed comments on an early version of some of the chapters. Many other people contributed thoughts, ideas, examples, and discussion: Larry Ausubel, David Backus, Kyle Bagwell, Sandip Baliga, Gary Becker, Robert Becker, James Bessen, William Brock, Andres Bucio, Jorge Capapey, V. V. Chari, Pierre-Andre Chiappori, Eddie Dekel, Drew Fudenberg, John Gallup, Richard Gilbert, Mike Golosov, Clara Graziano, Dan Hite, Hugo Hopenhayn, Chad Jones, Larry E. Jones, Boyan Jovanovic, Nobu Kiyotaki, Lennart Krantz, Timothy Lee, Jay Lepreau, Bob Lucas, Mike Masnick, Salvatore Modica, Enrico Moretti, Roger Myerson, Paul Romer, Mark Sattherwaite, Rob Shimer, Nancy Stokey, Juan Urrutia Elejalde, Ivan Werning, Freddy Williams, Asher Wolinsky, Curtis Yarvin, and Alejandro Zentn. Our student and research assistant, Fanchang Huang, read the whole manuscript and corrected an endless list of typos, poorly assembled references, and other kinds of errors. He did a great job and we are most grateful to him. We are likewise grateful to Tenea Johnson, who copyedited the manuscript. We are sure some errors can still be found, and it is all our fault.

Earlier in the project, Chinese University of Hong Kong and the University of Pennsylvania IER/Laurence Klein Lecture provided opportunities to present our work to broad audiences, and for this and the many comments that resulted we are grateful.

A great many attendees at conferences and seminars listened patiently to variations on our analysis: the economic departments of Arizona State University, Beijing University, European University Institute, Florence, New York University, Oxford University, Purdue University, SUNY Buffalo, University of California, Los Angeles, Universidad Autónoma, Madrid, Venice International University, University of Wisconsin–Madison, and Wuhan University; theory and/or macroeconomics workshops at Brown University, Carlos III, City University of Hong Kong, Columbia University, Cornell University, Harvard University, Humboldt University of Berlin, Indiana University, Iowa State University, London School of Economics, Northwestern University, Rochester University, Stanford University, Universitat Pompeu Fabra, University of Toulouse, University of Alabama, University of California, Berkeley, University of Chicago, and University of Kansas; and conferences and seminars including American Economic Association meetings in Atlanta, Carnegie Rochester Conference, Federal Reserve Bank of Dallas conference on globalization, Federal Reserve Bank of Richmond, Fundación Urrutia Elejalde Conference, Madrid, Innocenzo Gasparini Institute for Economic Research, Milan, Instituto Tecnológico Autónomo de México, Mexico City, Loyola University, Chicago, Rochester University Wegmans Conference, Society for Economic Dynamics Conference, Paris, World Bank–Pompeu Fabra conference, and Yale University's Cowles Commission.

ONE

Introduction

In late 1764, while repairing a small Newcomen steam engine, the idea of allowing steam to expand and condense in separate containers sprang into the mind of James Watt. He spent the next few months in unceasing labor building a model of the new engine. In 1768, after a series of improvements and substantial borrowing, he applied for a patent on the idea, which required him to travel to London in August. He spent the next six months working hard to obtain his patent. It was finally awarded in January of the following year. Nothing much happened by way of production until 1775. Then, with a major effort supported by his business partner, the rich industrialist Matthew Boulton, Watt secured an act of Parliament extending his patent until the year 1800. The great statesman Edmund Burke spoke eloquently in Parliament in the name of economic freedom and against the creation of unnecessary monopoly – but to no avail.[1] The connections of Watt's partner Boulton were too solid to be defeated by simple principle.

Once Watt's patents were secured and production started, he devoted a substantial portion of his energy to fending off rival inventors. In 1782, Watt secured an additional patent, made "necessary in consequence of . . . having been so unfairly anticipated, by [Matthew] Wasborough in the crank motion."[2] More dramatically, in the 1790s, when the superior Hornblower engine was put into production, Boulton and Watt went after Jonathan Hornblower with the full force of the legal system.[3]

During the period of Watt's patents, the United Kingdom added about 750 horsepower of steam engines per year. In the thirty years following Watt's patents, additional horsepower was added at a rate of more than 4,000 per year. Moreover, the fuel efficiency of steam engines changed little during the period of Watt's patent; however between 1810 and 1835 it is estimated to have increased by a factor of five.[4]

After the expiration of Watt's patents, not only was there an explosion in the production and efficiency of engines, but also steam power came into its own as the driving force of the Industrial Revolution. Over a thirty-year period, steam engines were modified and improved as crucial innovations such as the steam train, the steamboat, and the steam jenny came into wide usage. The key innovation was the high-pressure steam engine – development of which had been blocked by Watt's strategic use of his patent. Many new improvements to the steam engine, such as those of William Bull, Richard Trevithick, and Arthur Woolf, became available by 1804: although they had been developed earlier, these innovations were kept idle until the Boulton and Watt patent expired. None of these innovators wished to incur the same fate as Hornblower.[5]

Ironically, Watt not only used the patent system as a legal cudgel with which to smash competition, but the very same patent system he used to keep competitors at bay hindered his own efforts to develop a superior steam engine. An important limitation of the original Newcomen engine was its inability to deliver a steady rotary motion. The most convenient solution, involving the combined use of the crank and a flywheel, relied on a method patented by James Pickard, which prevented Watt from using it. Watt also made various attempts to efficiently transform reciprocating motion into rotary motion, reaching, apparently, the same solution as Pickard. But the existence of a patent forced him to contrive an alternative, less efficient mechanical device, the "sun and planet" gear. It was only in 1794, after the expiration of Pickard's patent, that Boulton and Watt adopted the economically and technically superior crank.[6]

The impact of the expiration of his patents on Watt's empire may come as a surprise. As might be expected, when the patents expired "many establishments for making steam-engines of Mr. Watt's principle were then commenced." However, Watt's competitors "principally aimed at . . . cheapness rather than excellence." As a result, we find that, far from being driven out of business, "Boulton and Watt for many years afterwards kept up their price and had increased orders."[7]

In fact, it is only after their patents expired that Boulton and Watt really started to manufacture steam engines. Before then, their activity consisted primarily of extracting hefty monopolistic royalties through licensing. Independent contractors produced most of the parts, and Boulton and Watt merely oversaw the assembly of the components by the purchasers.

In most histories, James Watt is a heroic inventor, responsible for the beginning of the Industrial Revolution. The facts suggest an alternative interpretation. Watt is one of many clever inventors who worked to improve steam power in the second half of the eighteenth century. After getting one step ahead of the pack, he remained ahead not by superior innovation but also by superior exploitation of the legal system. The fact that his business partner was a wealthy man with strong connections in Parliament was not a minor help.

Was Watt's patent a crucial incentive needed to trigger his inventive genius, as the traditional history suggests? Or did his use of the legal system to inhibit competition set back the Industrial Revolution by a decade or two? More broadly, are the two essential components of our current system of "intellectual property" – patents and copyrights – with all of their many faults, a necessary evil we must put up with to enjoy the fruits of invention and creativity? Or are they just unnecessary evils, the relics of an earlier time when governments routinely granted monopolies to favored courtiers? Those are the questions we seek to answer.

In the specific case of Watt, the granting of the 1769 and especially of the 1775 patents likely delayed the mass adoption of the steam engine: innovation was stifled until his patents expired, and few steam engines were built during the period of Watt's legal monopoly. From the number of innovations that occurred immediately after the expiration of the patent, it appears that Watt's competitors simply waited until then before releasing their own innovations. This should not surprise us: new steam engines, no matter how much better than Watt's, had to use the idea of a separate condenser. Because the 1775 patent provided Boulton and Watt with a monopoly over that idea, plentiful other improvements of great social and economic value could not be implemented. By the same token, until 1794, Boulton and Watt's engines were less efficient than they could have been because Pickard's patent prevented anyone else from using, and improving on, the idea of combining a crank with a flywheel.

Also, we see that Watt's inventive skills were badly allocated: we find him spending more time engaged in legal action to establish and preserve his monopoly than in the actual improvement and production of his engine. From a strictly economic point of view, Watt did not need such a long-lasting patent; it is estimated that by 1783 – seventeen years before his patent expired – his enterprise had already broken even. Indeed, even after their patent expired, Boulton and Watt were able to maintain a substantial premium over the market by virtue of having been first, despite the fact that their competitors had had thirty years to learn how to make steam engines.

The wasteful effort to suppress competition and obtain special privileges is referred to by economists as rent-seeking behavior. History and common sense show it to be a poisoned fruit of legal monopoly. Watt's attempt to extend the duration of his 1769 patent is an especially egregious example of rent seeking: the patent extension was clearly unnecessary to provide incentive for the original invention, which had already taken place. On top of this, we see Watt using patents as a tool to suppress innovation by his competitors, such as Hornblower, Wasborough, and others.

Hornblower's engine is a perfect case in point: it was a substantial improvement over Watt's, as it introduced the new concept of the compound engine with more than one cylinder. This, and not the Boulton and Watt design, was the basis for further steam engine development after their patents expired. However, because Hornblower built on the earlier work of Watt, making use of his separate condenser, Boulton and Watt were able to block him in court and effectively put an end to steam engine development. The monopoly over the separate condenser, a useful innovation, blocked the development of another equally useful innovation, the compound engine, thereby retarding economic growth. This retardation of innovation is a classic case of what we shall refer to as intellectual property inefficiency (or IP inefficiency).

Finally, there is the slow rate at which the steam engine was adopted before the expiration of Watt's patent. By keeping prices high and preventing others from producing cheaper or better steam engines, Boulton and Watt hampered capital accumulation and slowed economic growth.

The story of James Watt is a damaging case for the benefits of a patent system, but we shall see that it is not an unusual story. New ideas accrue almost by chance to innovators while they are carrying out a routine activity aimed at a completely different end. The patent comes many years after that, and it results more from a mixture of legal acumen and abundant resources available to "oil the gears of fortune" than anything else. Finally, after the patent protection is obtained, it is primarily used as a tool to prevent economic progress and to hurt competitors.

Although this view of Watt's role in the Industrial Revolution may appear iconoclastic, it is neither new nor particularly original. Frederic Scherer, a prestigious academic supporter of the patent system, after going through the details of the Boulton and Watt story, concluded his 1965 examination of their story with the following illuminating words:

Had there been no patent protection at all, . . . Boulton and Watt certainly would have been forced to follow a business policy quite different from that which they actually followed. Most of the firm's profits were derived from royalties on the use of engines rather than from the sale of manufactured engine components, and without patent protection the firm plainly could not have collected royalties. The alternative would have been to emphasize manufacturing and service activities as the principal source of profits, which in fact was the policy adopted when the expiration date of the patent for the separate condenser drew near in the late 1790s. . . . It is possible to conclude more definitely that the patent litigation activities of Boulton & Watt during the 1790s did not directly incite further technological progress. . . . Boulton and Watt's refusal to issue licenses allowing other engine makers to employ the separate-condenser principle clearly retarded the development and introduction of improvements.[8]

* * *

The Industrial Revolution was long ago. But the issue of "intellectual property" is a contemporary one. At the time we wrote this, U.S. District Judge James Spencer had been threatening for three years to shut down the widely used Blackberry messaging network – over a patent dispute.[9] And Blackberry itself is not without sin: in 2001 Blackberry sued Glenayre Electronics for infringing on its patent for "pushing information from a host system to a mobile data communication device."[10]

A similar war is taking place over copyright – the Napster network was shut down by a federal judge in July 2000 in a dispute over the sharing of copyrighted files.[11] Emotions run high on both sides. Some civil libertarians promote the anticopyright slogan "information just wants to be free." On the other extreme, large music and software companies argue that a world without "intellectual" property would be a world without new ideas.

Some of the bitterness of the copyright debate is reflected in Stephen Manes's attack on Larry Lessig:

According to Stanford law professor and media darling Lawrence Lessig, a "movement must begin in the streets" to fight a corrupt Congress, overconcentrated media and an overpriced legal system. . . . Contrary to Lessig's rants . . . "Fair use" exceptions in existing copyright law . . . are so expansive that just about the only thing cut-and-pasters clearly can't do legally with a copyrighted work is directly copy a sizable portion of it.[12]

Certainly Lessig is no friend of current copyright law. Yet, despite Stephen Manes's assertions to the contrary, he does believe in balancing the rights of producers with the rights of users: his book *Free Culture* speaks repeatedly of this balance and how it has been lost in modern law.[13]

Like Lessig, many economists are skeptical of current law – seventeen prominent economists, including several Nobel Prize winners, filed a brief with the U.S. Supreme Court in support of Lessig's lawsuit challenging the extension of the length of copyright. Also like Lessig, economists recognize a role for "intellectual property": where lawyers speak of balancing rights, economists speak of incentives. To quote from a textbook by the two prominent economists Robert Barro and Xavier Sala-i-Martin: "It would be [good] to make the existing discoveries freely available to all producers, but this practice fails to provide the . . . incentives for further inventions. A tradeoff arises between restrictions on the use of existing ideas and the rewards to inventive activity."[14] Indeed, while many of us enjoy the benefits of being able to freely download music from the Internet, we worry as well how musicians are to make a living if their music is immediately given away for free.

Although a furious debate rages over copyrights and patents, there is general agreement that some protection is needed to secure for inventors and creators the fruits of their labors. The rhetoric that "information just wants to be free" suggests that no one should be allowed to profit from his or her ideas. Despite this, there does not seem to be a strong lobby arguing that, though it is OK for the rest of us to benefit from the fruits of our labors, inventors and creators should have to subsist on the charity of others.

For all the emotion, it seems both sides agree that "intellectual property" laws need to strike a balance between providing sufficient incentive for creation and the freedom to make use of existing ideas. Put differently, both sides agree that "intellectual property" rights are a "necessary evil" that fosters innovation, and disagreement is over where the line should be drawn. For the supporters of "intellectual property," current monopoly profits are barely enough; for its enemies, currently monopoly profits are too high.

Our analysis leads to conclusions that are at variance with both sides. Our reasoning proceeds along the following lines. Everyone wants a monopoly. No one wants to compete against their own customers, or against imitators. Currently patents and copyrights grant producers of certain ideas a monopoly. Certainly, few people do something in exchange for nothing. Creators of new goods are not different from producers of old ones: they want to be compensated for their effort. However, it is a long and dangerous jump from the assertion that innovators deserve compensation for their efforts to the conclusion that patents and copyrights, that is, monopoly, are the best or the only way to provide that reward. Statements such as, "A patent is *the* way of rewarding somebody for coming up with a worthy commercial idea"[15] abound in the business, legal, and economic press. As we shall see, there are many other ways in which innovators are rewarded, even substantially, and most of them are better for society than the monopoly power that patents and copyright currently bestow. Because innovators may be rewarded even without patents and copyright, we should ask, Is it true that "intellectual property" achieves the intended purpose of creating incentives for innovation and creation that offset its considerable harm?

This book examines both the evidence and the theory. Our conclusion is that creators' property rights can be well protected in the absence of "intellectual property," and that the latter does not increase either innovation or creation. They are an unnecessary evil.

* * *

This is a book about economics, not about law. Or, put differently, it is not about what the law is but rather what the law should be. If you are interested in whether you are likely to wind up in jail for sharing your files over the Internet, this is not the book for you. If you are interested in whether it is a good idea for the law to prevent you from sharing your files over the Internet, then this book is for you.

However, although this book is not about the law, some background on the law is necessary to understand the economic issues. We are going to examine the economics of what has, in recent years, come to be called "intellectual property," especially patents and copyright. In fact, there are three broad types of "intellectual property" recognized in most legal systems: patents, copyrights, and trademarks.

Trademarks are different in nature from patents and copyrights: they serve to identify the providers of goods, services, or ideas. Copying, which would be a violation of copyright, is quite different from lying, which would be a violation of trademark. We do not know of a good reason for allowing market participants to steal identities or to masquerade as people they are not. Conversely, there are strong economic advantages in allowing market participants to voluntarily identify themselves. Although we may wonder whether it is necessary to allow the Intel Corporation a monopoly over the use of the word *inside*, in general there is little economic dispute over the merits of trademarks.

Patents and copyrights, the two forms of "intellectual property" on which we focus, are a subject of debate and controversy. They differ from each other in the extent of coverage they provide. Patents apply to specific implementations of ideas – though in recent years in the United States there has been decreasing emphasis on specificity. Patents do not last forever: in the United States, patents covering techniques of manufacture last twenty years, and fourteen years for ornamentation. Patents provide relatively broad protection: no one can legally use the same idea, even if he or she independently rediscovers it, without permission from the patent holder.[16]

Copyrights are narrower in scope, protecting only the specific details of a particular narrative – though as with the case of patents, the scope has been increasing in recent years. Copyright is also much longer in duration than patents – the life of the author plus fifty years for the many signatory countries of the Berne Convention, and – in the United States since the Sonny Bono Copyright Term Extension Act – the life of the author plus seventy years.[17]

In the United States, there are limitations on copyright not present in patent law. As Stephen Manes correctly points out in his attack on Larry Lessig, the right of fair use allows the purchaser of a copyrighted item limited rights to employ it, make partial copies of it, and resell them, regardless of the desires of the copyright holder. In addition, certain derivative works are allowed without permission: parodies are allowed, for example, while sequels are not.

In the case of both patents and copyright, from the point of view of economics, there are two ingredients in the law: the right to buy and sell copies of ideas, and the right to control how other people make use of their copies. The first right is not controversial. In copyright law, when applied to the creator, this right is sometimes called the right of first sale. However, it extends also to the legitimate rights of others to sell their copies. It is the second right, enabling the owner to control the use of "intellectual property" after sale, that is controversial. This right produces a monopoly – enforced by the obligation of the government to act against individuals or organizations that use the idea in ways prohibited by the copyright or patent holder.

In addition to the well-known forms of "intellectual property" – patents and copyright – there are also lesser-known ways of protecting ideas. These include contractual agreements, such as the shrink-wrapped and click-through agreements that you never read when you buy software. They also include the most traditional form of protection – trade secrecy – as well as its contractual and legal manifestations, such as nondisclosure agreements. Like patents and copyright, all of these devices serve to help the originator of an idea maintain a monopoly over it.

We do not know of any legitimate argument that producers of ideas should not be able to profit from their creations. Although ideas could be sold in the absence of a legal right, markets function best in the presence of clearly defined property rights. We should protect not only the property rights of innovators but also the rights of those who have legitimately obtained a copy of the idea, directly or indirectly, from the original innovator. The former encourages innovation; the latter encourages the diffusion, adoption, and improvement of innovations.

Why, however, should creators have the right to control how purchasers make use of an idea or creation? This gives creators a monopoly over the idea. We refer to this right as "intellectual monopoly," to emphasize that it is this monopoly over all copies of an idea that is controversial, not the right to buy and sell copies. The government does not ordinarily enforce monopolies for producers of other goods. This is because it is widely recognized that monopoly creates many social costs. Intellectual monopoly is no different in this respect. The question we address is whether it also creates social benefits commensurate with these social costs.

* * *

The U.S. Constitution allows Congress "to promote the progress of science and useful arts, by securing for limited times to authors and inventors the exclusive right to their respective writings and discoveries."[18] Our perspective on patents and copyright is a similar one: promoting the progress of science and the useful arts is a crucial ingredient of economic welfare, from solving such profound economic problems as poverty to such mundane personal nuisances as boredom. From a social point of view, and in the view of the founding fathers, the purpose of patents and copyrights is not to enrich the few at the expense of the many. Nobody doubts that J. K. Rowling and Bill Gates have been greatly enriched by their "intellectual property" – nor is it surprising that they would argue in favor of it. But common sense and the U.S. Constitution say that these rights must be justified by bringing benefits to all of us.

The U.S. Constitution is explicit that what is to be given to authors and inventors is an exclusive right – a monopoly. Implicit is the idea that giving this monopoly serves to promote the progress of science and useful arts. The U.S. Constitution was written in 1787. At that time, the idea of copyright and patent was relatively new; the products to which they applied, few; and their terms, short. In light of the experience of the subsequent 219 years, we might ask, Is it true that legal grants of monopoly serve to promote the progress of science and the useful arts?

Certainly common sense suggests that they should. How are musicians to make a living if the moment they perform their music, everyone else can copy and give it away for free? Why would the large corporations pay small inventors when they can simply take their ideas? It is hard to imagine life without the Internet, and today we are all jet-setters. Is not the explosion of creativity and invention unleashed since the writing of the U.S. Constitution a testimony to the powerful benefit of "intellectual property"? Would not the world without patent and copyright be a sad, cold world, empty of new music and of marvelous new inventions?

So, the first question we will pose is, What might the world be like without intellectual monopoly? Patents and copyrights have not secured monopolies on all ideas at all times. It is natural, then, to examine times and industries in which legal protection for ideas has not been available to see whether innovation and creativity were thriving or were stifled. It is the case, for example, that neither the Internet nor the jet engine was invented in hopes of securing exclusive rights. In fact, we ordinarily think of *innovative monopoly* as an oxymoron. We shall see that when monopoly over ideas is absent, competition is fierce – and that, as a result, innovation and creativity thrive. Whatever a world without patents and copyrights would be like, it would not be a world devoid of great new music and beneficial new drugs.

You will gather by now that we are skeptical of monopoly – as are economists in general. Our second topic will be an examination of the many social costs created by copyrights and patents. Adam Smith – a friend and teacher of James Watt – was one of the first economists to explain how monopolies make less available at a higher price. In some cases, such as the production of music, this may not be a great social evil; in other cases, such as the availability of AIDS drugs, it may be a very great evil indeed. However, as we shall see, low availability and high price is only one of the many costs of monopoly. The example of James Watt is a case in point: by making use of the legal system, he inhibited competition and prevented his competitors from introducing useful new advances. We shall also see that because there are no countervailing market forces, government-enforced monopolies such as intellectual monopoly are particularly problematic.

Although monopoly may be evil, and although innovation may thrive in the absence of traditional legal protections such as patents and copyrights, it may be that patents and copyrights serve to increase innovation. The presumption in the U.S. Constitution is that they do, and that the benefits of more entertainment and more innovation outweigh the costs of these monopolies. Certainly the monopolies created by patents and copyright may be troublesome – but if that is the cost of having blockbuster movies, automobiles, and flu vaccine, most of us are prepared to put up with it. That is the position traditionally taken by economists, most of whom support patents and copyright, at least in principle. Some of them take the view that intellectual monopoly is an unavoidable evil if we are to have any innovation at all; other simply argue that at least some modest amount of intellectual monopoly is desirable to provide adequate incentive for innovation and creation. Our third topic will be an examination of the theoretical arguments supporting intellectual monopoly, as well as counterarguments about why intellectual monopoly may hurt rather than foster creative activity.

It is crucial to recognize that intellectual monopoly is a double-edged sword. The rewards to innovative effort are certainly greater if success is awarded a government monopoly. But the existence of monopolies also increases the cost of creation. In one extreme case, a movie that cost $218 to make had to pay $400,000 for the music rights.[19] As we will argue at length, theoretical arguments alone cannot tell us whether intellectual monopoly increases or decreases creative activity.

In the final analysis, the only justification for "intellectual property" is that it increases – de facto and substantially – innovation and creation. What have the last 219 years taught us? Our final topic is an examination of the evidence about intellectual monopoly and innovation. Is it a fact that intellectual monopoly leads to more creativity and innovation? Our examination of the data shows no evidence that it does. Nor are we the first economists to reach this conclusion. After reviewing an earlier set of facts in 1958, the distinguished economist Fritz Machlup wrote, "It would be irresponsible, on the basis of our present knowledge of its economic consequences, to recommend instituting [a patent system]."[20]

Because there is no evidence that intellectual monopoly achieves the desired purpose of increasing innovation and creation, it has no benefits. So, there is no need for society to balance the benefits against the costs. This leads us to our final conclusion: intellectual property is an unnecessary evil.

Comments

We are grateful to George Selgin and John Turner, of the University of Georgia Terry College of Business, for pointing out a number of factual mistakes and imprecisions in our rendition of the James Watt story, as it had appeared in earlier versions of this chapter and in our 2003 Lawrence R. Klein Lecture. In a recent article, Selgin and Turner also take issue with our interpretation of the facts and add a few additional ones that, in their view, contradict our vision of James Watt as a primary example of an intellectual monopolist. It seems clear, even from the references quoted by Selgin and Turner, that many students of the Industrial Revolution shared our view – or more properly, we share theirs.[21]

Selgin and Turner's argument and facts do not, however, address the issues we raise about Boulton and Watt. Take their discussion of the hypothetical "Watt sans patent." Obviously Boulton and Watt loved their patents, obviously they wanted and fought for them, and obviously they claimed they would have gone broke and the world would have come apart without their patents. Our point is another: could they have made enough money to compensate their opportunity cost without the patent? All the evidence, including that reported by Selgin and Turner, suggests this is the case. In fact, they make our case quite convincingly: to quote Scherer[22], they assert that seventeen years before the second patent expired they, Boulton and Watt, were already breaking even. In economics, *breaking even* means that your opportunity costs have been paid, and your capital has received the risk-adjusted, expected return – and Frank Scherer is a distinguished economist. Whatever profits Boulton and Watt made after that, it was all extra rents from monopoly power and, economically, not needed to pay their opportunity costs. So, we all agree that, at least for the final seventeen years, the patent was not serving a useful economic purpose; hence, it was damaging because it created monopoly distortions.

Notes

1. Lord (1923), p. 5–3.
2. Carnegie (1905), p. 157.
3. Much of the story of James Watt can be found in Carnegie (1905), Lord (1923), and Marsden (2004). Information on the role of Boulton in Watt's enterprise is drawn from Mantoux (1905). A lively description of the real Watt, as well of his legal wars against Hornblower – and many others – and of how he subsequently used his status to alter the public memory of the facts, can be found in Marsden (2004). That the patent on the Wasbrough mechanism (apparently also invented independently by Pickard) was unjust is also the view of Selgin and Turner (2006), who, like Watt, do not seem to provide any evidence of why it was so.

   As both the Lord and Carnegie works are out of copyright, both are available online at the very good Rochester site on the history of steam power, http://www.history.rochester.edu/steam (accessed February 23, 2008). Later drafts of this chapter benefited enormously from the arrival of Google Book Search, which allowed us to check many original historical sources about James Watt and the steam engine we would have never thought possible before.
4. Lord (1923) gives figures on the number of steam engines produced by Boulton and Watt between 1775 and 1800, and *The Cambridge Economic History of Europe* (1965) provides data on the spread of total horsepower between 1800 and 1815 and the spread of steam power more broadly. However, Kanefsky (1979) has largely discredited Lord's numbers, which is why we use figures on machines and horsepower from Kanefsky and Robey (1980).

   Our horsepower calculations are based on 510 steam engines generating about 5,000 horsepower in the United Kingdom in 1760. During the subsequent forty years, we estimate that about 1,740 engines generating about 30,000 horsepower were added, which leads to our estimate that the total increased at a rate of roughly 750 horsepower each year. For 1815, we estimate about 100,000 horsepower – that is, the average of the figures Kanefsky and Robey (1980) give for 1800 and 1830. This, together with the 35,000 horsepower we estimate for 1800, leads to our estimate that the total increased at a rate of roughly 4,000 horsepower each year after 1800.

   Data on the fuel efficiency, or "duty," of steam engines is from Nuvolari (2004b).
5. Kanefsky and Robey (1980), together with Smith (1977–78), provide a careful historical account of the detrimental impact of Newcomen's, first, and of Watt's patents,

later, on the rate of adoption of steam technology. Apart from the books just quoted, information about Hornblower's engine and its relation to Watt's are widely available through easily accessible Web sites, such as Encyclopaedia Britannica, Wikipedia, and so on. Some details of Hornblower's invention may be of interest. It was patented in 1781 and consisted of a steam engine with two cylinders, significantly more efficient than the Boulton and Watt design. Boulton and Watt challenged his invention and won, claiming infringement of their patent because the Hornblower engine used a separate condenser. With the 1799 judicial decision against him, Hornblower had to pay Boulton and Watt a substantial amount of money for past royalties, while losing all opportunities to further develop the compound engine. His principle of the compound steam engine was not revived until 1804, by Arthur Woolf. It became one of the main ingredients in the efficiency explosion that followed the expiration of Boulton and Watt's patent.

Watt's low-pressure engines were a dead end for further development; history shows that high-pressure, noncondensing engines were the way forward. Boulton and Watt's patent, covering all kinds of steam engines, prevented anyone from working seriously on the high-pressure version until 1800. This included William Murdoch, an employee of Boulton and Watt, who had developed a version of the high-pressure engine in the early 1780s. He named it the "steam carriage" and was legally barred from developing it by Boulton and Watt's successful addition of the high-pressure engine to their patent, though Boulton and Watt never spent a cent to develop it. For the details of this story, readers should see the Web site Cotton Times, at http://www.cottontimes.co.uk/ (accessed February 23, 2008), or Carnegie (1905), pp. 140–1. The "William Murdoch" entry in Wikipedia, at http://en.wikipedia.org/wiki/William_Murdoch (accessed February 23, 2008), provides a good summary. More generally, various researchers directly connect Murdoch to Trevithick, who is now considered the official inventor (in 1802) of the high-pressure engine. Quite plainly, the evidence suggests that Boulton and Watt's patent retarded development of the high-pressure steam engine, and thus economic development, by about sixteen years.

6. The story about Pickard's patent blocking adoption by Watt is told in von Tunzelmann (1978).
7. Thompson (1847), p. 110, and quoted in Lord (1923).
8. Scherer (1984), pp. 24–25.
9. NTP, Inc. v. Research in Motion Ltd., Civil Action Number 3:01CV767-JRS.
10. U.S. Patent No. 6,219,694 (filed May 29, 1998).
11. *In re Napster, Inc.* (9th Cir.).
12. Manes (2004).
13. Lessig (2004).
14. Barro and Sala-i-Martin (1995), p. 290.
15. The Economist (2001), p. 42 (italics added).
16. Information on U.S. patent law can be found at the U.S. Patent Office Web site (http://www.uspto.gov/main/patents.htm accessed February 23, 2008). In addition to utility and design patents, there is also a third class of patent, the plant patent. Like a utility patent, a plant patent lasts twenty years.
17. The Sonny Bono Copyright Extension Act can be found online at http://library.thinkquest.org/J001570/sonnybonolaw.html (accessed February 28, 2008), and the

Berne Convention on Copyright can be found at http://www.law.cornell.edu/
treaties/berne/overview.html (accessed February 28, 2008). A useful discussion of
fair use, including parodies, is Gall (2000).

18. U.S. Constitution, art. 1, sec. 8. The U.S. Constitution, not being copyrighted, is
found online at various places, such as http://www.law.cornell.edu/constitution.

19. The $218 movie was *Tarnation* and the information, from BBC News, is at
http://news.bbc.co.uk/2/hi/entertainment/3720455.stm.

20. Machlup (1958), p. 80. He nevertheless concluded that we should keep the patent
system. We discuss his position further in our conclusion.

21. For the 2003 Lawrence R. Klein lecture, see Boldrin and Levine (2004b). See also
Selgin and Turner (2006).

22. Scherer (1965).

TWO

Creation under Competition

The basic conclusion of this book is that intellectual monopoly – patents, copyrights, and restrictive licensing agreements – are unnecessary. Always beware of theorists bearing radical ideas – most ideas are bad, and most theories are wrong. This book may be yet another entry in that long list of confused and confusing dreams.

Therefore, we must first and foremost convince you that our ideas are firmly grounded in facts and practice. Most innovations have taken place without the benefit of intellectual monopoly. Indeed, the system of intellectual monopoly as it exists today is of recent vintage – some parts of the current system are only a few years old, and their damaging effects are already visible and dramatic.

No gardens of utopia, then, but the fertile fields of practical experience, as illustrated by thriving markets without intellectual monopoly – that is what this and the next chapter are about.

Software

In spite of being all around us, facts are often invisible because we look at them with wrong-shaded glasses. Look closely at the computer on your desk. You see a mouse, a keyboard, and, on your screen, a bunch of different overlapping windows with word processors, spreadsheets, instant messengers, and a Web browser through which you can access a vast array of information on a great diversity of subjects. At the end of the Second World War – sixty years ago – digital computers did not exist, nor, of course, did the software that makes them work. In few industries has there been such extensive innovation as in the software industry – and few technologies have changed our way of life as much. Will it surprise you to learn that virtually none of the innovations in this industry took place with the protection of intellectual monopoly? Our tour of the hidden world where innovation flourishes under competition starts here, in the software industry.

We read about Amazon suing Barnes and Noble for patent infringement – and being sued by IBM for the same – and we do not know whether to laugh or to cry. We find Microsoft hinting that it will sue us for patent infringement if we use GNU/Linux instead of Windows.[1] It seems as if no industry is as hemmed in with intellectual monopoly as the software industry. But it was not always like this. It turns out that over the past two decades, the software industry has "benefited" from massive changes in the law, legislated by that duly elected body, the U.S. Supreme Court. Indeed, prior to the 1981 U.S. Supreme Court decision in *Diamond v. Diehr*, it was not possible to patent software at all, and the current craze to patent every click of the mouse originates in the subsequent extension of patents to software products in the 1994 federal circuit court ruling *In re Alappat*.

Did this judicial legislation bring forth an explosion in software innovation? We mentioned Amazon suing Barnes and Noble over purchasing online with just "one click." Some might wonder how difficult and innovative this invention is, so it may seem a straw man. Whatever the merits are of one click, there are certainly many software inventions that we all agree are important and innovative. There are all the graphical user interfaces; the widgets such as buttons and icons; the compilers, assemblers, linked lists, object-oriented programs, databases, search algorithms, font displays, word processing, and computer languages – all the vast array of algorithms and methods that go into even the simplest modern program. These innovations not only are all difficult and important, but also the fact is that every single one of these innovations is used and is necessary to make the one click, or for that matter two clicks, work.

We do not mention any of these significant inventions as a consequence of patents on software innovation for one simple reason. Each and every one of these key innovations occurred prior to 1981 and so occurred without the benefit of patent protection. Not only that, had all these bits and pieces of computer programs been patented, as they certainly would have in the current regime, far from being enhanced, progress in the software industry would never have taken place. According to Bill Gates – hardly your radical communist or utopist – "if people had understood how patents would be granted when most of today's ideas were invented, and had taken out patents, the industry would be at a complete standstill today."[2]

Not only did patents play no role in software innovation, but also copyrights played only a limited role. Although computer programs were often copyrighted, in the early years of the PC industry, copyright was seldom respected or enforced. Consumers would purchase programs and use them on a variety of computers in violation of license agreements. People bought and sold computer programs and created new ones by using bits and pieces, modules and ideas, from existing programs. Although copyright may have limited the widespread copying of software by other publishers, it was not enforced in the draconian way that it is today.

The software industry is a leading illustration of one of the subthemes of this book. Intellectual monopoly is not a cause of innovation, but rather an unwelcome consequence of it. In a young, dynamic industry full of ideas and creativity, intellectual monopoly does not play a useful role. It is when ideas run out and new competitors come in with fresher ideas that those bereft of them turn to government intervention – and intellectual "property" – to protect their lucrative old ways of doing business.

If we examine the efforts of Microsoft to prevent "piracy" of their software, we find that it made little effort, either legal or technical, to protect its "intellectual property" in their early creative days. It is now, in the twenty-first century, that it invests its time and energy in the prevention of copying. However, if we compare releases of Microsoft operating systems or word processors over the past five or even ten years, it would be difficult to detect much innovation. What is Microsoft's greatest innovation since 1994? No doubt, the Web browser Internet Explorer. But who invented the Web browser? Not Microsoft, but a small group of creative competitors from whom, later on, Microsoft took the idea and then acquired most of the basic code: the first popular version of a browser, NCSA Mosaic, appeared in March 1993, but it was only in August 1995 that Microsoft released Internet Explorer 1.0.[3]

Try to imagine how the economic and social history of the past fifteen years would have to be rewritten if the creators of Mosaic had Microsoft's deep pockets and, in anticipation of Amazon patenting the one-click concept, had managed to patent the idea of the Web browser. Would we all have been better served by such an application of the doctrine of "intellectual property"?

Open-Source Software

The best evidence that copyright and patents are not needed and that competition leads to thriving innovation in the software industry is the fact that there is a thriving and innovative portion of the industry that has voluntarily relinquished its intellectual monopoly – both copyright and patent. This striking example of creation under competition is the open-source software movement. Often this software is released under a license that is the opposite of copyright – in many cases forcing those who wish to sell it to allow their competitors to copy it. This "copyleft" agreement is a voluntary commitment by software producers to avoid intellectual monopoly and to operate under conditions of free competition.[4]

It is an amazing testament to the benefits of competition that firms and individuals choose to voluntarily subject themselves to it. How, you ask, can it be in the economic self-interest of a firm or individual to voluntarily relinquish a monopoly? The answer is that it provides an important assurance to purchasers. For example, a new entry into the software market may find its market limited by the fact that potential customers are concerned about the long-term viability of the firm. Purchasers do not wish to become locked into proprietary software, only to see the sole legal supplier disappear. For obvious reasons, firms and individuals also have a preference for purchasing software where they expect to benefit from future competition. In some cases, the income from being first to market is sufficiently high that it is worth voluntarily giving up a future monopoly to be able to enter the market.

In the case of open-source software, the startling fact is how widespread it is, a fact our wrong-shaded glasses often prevents us from noticing. If you browsed the Web today, then it is virtually certain that you used open-source software. Although you probably think of yourself as a Windows user or a Mac user, the fact is that you are also a Linux user: every time you use Google, your request is processed by the open-source software originated by Linus Torvalds.

In addition to Windows and Mac, there are three other widely used operating environments: Solaris, Linux, and FreeBSD. Solaris, Linux, and FreeBSD are all open source, and so is a good chunk of the Mac code. In the server market, Google is scarcely exceptional – it is estimated that the Linux operating system has a 25 percent market share.[5] Not only Google uses Linux – so does the widely used TiVo digital video recorder. Even in desktops, Linux is estimated to be passing Mac in popularity.

A great deal of the data you find on the Internet – for example, that amusing blog about the shenanigans of Washington politicians you are reading – is stored in databases. There are six major databases: Oracle, DB2, SQL Server, Sybase, MySQL, and PostgreSQL. Two are open source, and the odds are that the blog you are reading uses the open source MySQL database – along with the open-source scripting language PHP. MySQL, by the way, is developed and supported by a private, for-profit company, as is the scripting language PHP. In addition, PHP has recently supplanted the open-source Perl language as the premier scripting language for the

World Wide Web, and four of the other widely used scripting languages, Lua, Python, Ruby, and Tcl, are also open source. Only the Microsoft ASP language is proprietary.

Open source dominates the Internet. Whatever you are viewing on the Web – we hesitate to ask what it might be – is served up by a Web server. Netcraft regularly surveys Web sites to see what Web server they are using. In December 2004, Netcraft polled all of the 58,194,836 Web sites it could find on the Internet, and found that the open-source Web server Apache had 68.43 percent of the market, Microsoft had 20.86 percent, and Sun had only 3.14%. Apache's share is increasing; all others' market shares are decreasing. So again, if you used the Web today, you almost certainly used open-source software.[6]

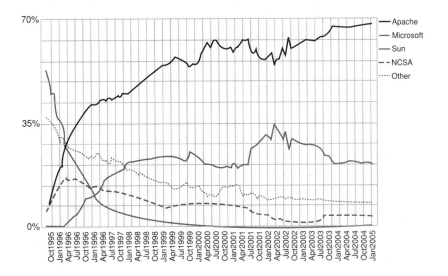

Even on the desktop, open source is spreading and not shrinking. Ten years ago there were two major word-processing packages, Word and Word-Perfect. Today the only significant competitor to Microsoft for a package of office software that includes word processing is the open-source program OpenOffice.

Thousands of productive and highly paid programmers voluntarily choose to produce and market software products that are distributed freely to end users and to other developers. This must surely lead one to question the common assumption that – without copyright and patents – the information technology revolution would have not come about, or that it will die in the years to come.

Why has the software market worked so well under competition and without intellectual monopoly? The wide use of free software licenses has unleashed the great collaborative benefit of competition. Open-source software makes available the underlying source code from which the computer programs are compiled. Of particular importance is the free software movement, pioneered by Richard Stallman and others. Free software not only is open source but also is released under a license such as the GNU General Public License (GPL),which allows modifications and distribution only when the source code to those modifications is made available under the same license. It should be understood here that the word *free* here means (according to the motto of the GNU project) "free as in freedom, not free as in beer." Although free software is often distributed without charge, it is the freedom of the user to make use of the software that distinguishes free software, not the price at which it is sold. The free software license serves as a commitment for those who wish that their contribution also be freely available, and as a guarantee to users that they will have access to the source code in the future, if they so wish.

These free software licenses have allowed most open-source software to be written by large and loosely organized teams of programmers, each of which contributes small pieces of code and all of which benefit from the sharing of information and ideas. Because of the commitment to make public all the ideas and code, each individual collaborator expects to benefit from the advances made by his or her colleagues, and so has strong incentive to share ideas and code. Moreover, individuals who may not actually be part of the "formal" team often contribute ideas and expertise – also assured that they will ultimately benefit from the innovation triggered by their information.

It is striking to us that a Washington conservative think tank figure such as Ken Brown, president of the Alexis de Tocqueville Institution, an extremely vocal proponent of the great benefits of the free enterprise system, would argue against public licenses such as the GPL.[7] Brown apparently feels that this private institution is some form of government socialism. Although there is a strong case for eliminating or deregulating intellectual monopoly such as copyright and patents – which are inimical to free enterprise and capitalism – there is also a strong case for preserving copyleft contracts such as the GPL, which strengthen free enterprise and the system of competitive markets.

The success of open-source software is not some strange miracle, unrepeatable under normal circumstances. On the contrary, it is the ever-repeating pattern in innovating and growing industries. Later we will learn about an identical episode, which took place in England about 150 years earlier: the development of the Cornish steam power engine, without which the Industrial Revolution would have been a shadow of what it turned out to be. Too bad we do not have time to write an entire encyclopedia of competitive innovations. We could tell of similar wonders in the American automobile industry, the Swiss and German chemical industries, the worldwide oxygen steelmaking industries, the Italian textile and fashion industries, the Swiss watch industry, the wine farms of Europe and California, the Czech and Venetian glass industries, and so on and so forth.[8]

"Pirating" Software

The idea that a software producer – say, Microsoft – could earn a profit without copyright protection always puzzles people. Without copyright protection, wouldn't "pirates" step in and sell cheaper imitations, putting Microsoft out of business? Although this is an interesting theory of how markets work, it is not one supported by the facts.

Again, we turn to open-source software and the Linux computer operating system. Because it is open source, Linux may be resold commercially, but only if the source code is made freely available, including any modifications made to the original program. For example, Red Hat is a company that sold a modified and customized Linux system with easy installation and many other useful features. Although Ret Hat obtains the underlying Linux system for free, the customization and testing that Red Hat conducts is costly. Using prices quoted on the Internet on July 10, 2002, Red Hat charged $59.95 for a package containing its system. Because it is based on the underlying Linux system, Red Hat must also make available its code to competitors. As a result, anyone who wishes to can sell his or her own "Red Hat" system. And, in fact, there were at least two companies, HCI Design and Linux Emporium, that did exactly this. For example, on July 10, 2002, HCI Design offered for sale Red Hat Linux 7.2 for a price of $16, about one-third of the price charged by Red Hat. The Web site Linuxemporium.co.uk offered a similar deal.

So how does Red Hat stay in business? For starters, it turns out that Red Hat sold many more $59.95 packages than HCI Design and Linux Emporium sold $16 packages. Moreover, Red Hat is a large, well-known company, while no one has ever heard of the other two, nor does it appear that they ever represented a dangerous market threat to Red Hat.[9] How could this be? Or more accurately, how could this not be? Have you ever used software that worked properly? If you had a problem with software you bought, and had to call the seller for advice, who would you prefer to call: the people who wrote the program or the people who copied it?

The story is not over yet; please bear with us. Taking years in writing a book chapter is not proof of high productivity, but there is a silver lining. On December 24, 2006, we went back to the Internet to see what happened to these three companies. All three of them still exist, and many other have joined the game. After years of having all its innovations mercilessly "pirated," Red Hat is still the market leader, has a worldwide web of offices, sells lots of Linux-based software products while also giving away lots of others for free, and its revenues are soaring. HCI Design, in spite of the advantage of being a legal "pirate," does not seem to have done very well; it is still there, but it is selling very few products and all Linux-based products are now off its shelves. Linux Emporium had a more interesting life. After either changing its name to or having been acquired by ChyGwyn, it is back in business under the original name and it is thriving. Indeed, it has pioneered an entire new line of business: it sells at positive prices software that is downloadable for free from the original companies, by claiming it sells "high class software for the cognoscenti." The power and creativity of competitive markets sometimes surprise even us!

Copyrightables: Books, News, Movies, and Music

Copyright has traditionally been used for literary works and for media ranging from newspapers to music and movies. Large media firms, such as Disney, and industry associations, such as the Recording Industry Association of America (RIAA) and the Motion Picture Association of America (MPAA), argue loudly and vociferously for ever-increasing control of their "intellectual property." So, you might imagine that creative activity is low and artists are poor when and where copyright is weak. Needless to say, nothing could be further from the truth.

Fiction and Literature

People find it hard to wrap their heads around the concept that ideas can be rewarded without a copyright or patent. Without a copyright, how will the author of a novel get paid? Consider the facts.

Start with English authors selling books in the United States in the nineteenth century. "During the nineteenth century anyone was free in the United States to reprint a foreign publication"[10] without making any payment to the author, besides purchasing a legally sold copy of the book. This was a fact that greatly upset Charles Dickens, whose works, along with those of many other English authors, were widely distributed in the United States, and "yet American publishers found it profitable to make arrangements with English authors. Evidence before the 1876–8 Commission shows that English authors sometimes received more from the sale of their books by American publishers, where they had no copyright, than from their royalties in [England],"[11] where they did have copyright. In short, without copyright, authors still got paid, sometimes more without copyright than with it.[12]

How did it work? Then, as now, there is a great deal of impatience in the demand for books, especially good books. English authors would sell American publishers the manuscripts of their new books before their publication in Britain. The American publisher who bought the manuscript had every incentive to saturate the market for that particular novel as soon as possible, to avoid the arrival of cheap imitations soon after. This led to mass publication at fairly low prices. The amount of revenues British authors received up front from American publishers often exceeded the amount they were able to collect over a number of years from royalties in the United Kingdom. Notice that, at the time, the U.S. market was comparable in size to the U.K. market.[13]

More broadly, the lack of copyright protection, which permitted the U.S. publishers' "pirating" of English writers, was a good economic policy of great social value for the people of United States, and of no significant detriment, as the 1876–8 Commission report quoted above and other evidence confirm, for English authors. Not only did it enable the establishment and rapid growth of a large and successful publishing business in the United States, but also, and more important, it increased literacy and benefited the cultural development of the American people by flooding the market with cheap copies of great books. As an example, Dickens's *A Christmas Carol* sold for $.06 in the United States, while it was priced at roughly $2.50 in England. This dramatic increase in literacy was probably instrumental to the emergence of a great number of U.S. writers and scientists toward the end of the nineteenth century.

But how relevant for the modern era are copyright arrangements from the nineteenth century? Books, which had to be moved from England to the United States by clipper ship, can now be transmitted over the Internet at nearly the speed of light. Furthermore, although the data show that some English authors were paid more by their U.S. publishers than they earned in England, we may wonder how many, and if they were paid enough to compensate them for the cost of their creative efforts. What would happen to an author today without copyright?

This question is not easy to answer – because today virtually everything written is copyrighted, whether or not intended by the author. There is, however, one important exception – documents produced by the U.S.

government. Not, you might think, the stuff of best sellers, and hopefully not fiction. But it does turn out that some government documents have been best sellers. This makes it possible to ask in a straightforward way, How much can be earned in the absence of copyright? The answer may surprise you as much as it surprised us.

The most significant government best seller of recent years has the rather off-putting title *The Final Report of the National Commission on Terrorist Attacks Upon the United States*, but it is better known simply as the *9-11 Commission Report*.[14] The report was released to the public at noon on Thursday, July 22, 2004. At that time, it was freely available for downloading from a government Web site. A printed version of the report published by W. W. Norton simultaneously went on sale in bookstores. Norton had signed an interesting agreement with the government.

> The 81-year-old publisher struck an unusual publishing deal with the 9/11 commission back in May: Norton agreed to issue the paperback version of the report on the day of its public release.... Norton did not pay for the publishing rights, but had to foot the bill for a rush printing and shipping job; the commission did not hand over the manuscript until the last possible moment, in order to prevent leaks. The company will not reveal how much this cost, or when precisely it obtained the report. But expedited printings always cost extra, making it that much more difficult for Norton to realize a profit.
>
> In addition, the commission and Norton agreed in May on the 568-page tome's rather low cover price of $10, making it that much harder for the publisher to recoup its costs. (Amazon.com is currently selling copies for $8 plus shipping, while visitors to the Government Printing Office bookstore in Washington, D.C. can purchase its version of the report for $8.50.) There is also competition from the commission's Web site, which is offering a downloadable copy of the report for free. And Norton also agreed to provide one free copy to the family of every 9/11 victim.[15]

This might sound like Norton struck a rather bad deal – one imagines that other publishers were congratulating themselves on not having been taken advantage of by sharp government negotiators. It turns out, however, that Norton's rivals were, in fact, envious of this deal. One competitor in particular – the *New York Times* – described the deal as a "royalty-free windfall,"[16] which does not sound like a bad thing to have.

To be clear, what Norton received from the government was the right to publish first, and the right to use the word *authorized* in the title. What it did not get was the usual copyright, the right to exclusively publish the book. Because it is a U.S. government document, the moment it was released, other individuals, and more important, publishing houses, had the right to buy or download copies and to make and resell additional copies – electronically or in print, at a price of their choosing, in direct competition with Norton. In other words, after the release of the book on

July 22, the market became a conventional competitive market. And the right to compete with Norton was not a purely hypothetical one. Another publisher, St. Martin's, in collaboration with the *New York Times*, released its own version of the report in early August, about two weeks after Norton, and this version contained not only the entire government report but also additional articles and analysis by *New York Times* reporters. Like the Norton version, this version was also a best seller.[17] In addition, it is estimated that 6.9 million copies of the report were (legally) downloaded over the Internet. Competition, in short, was pretty fierce.

Despite this fierce competition, the evidence suggests that Norton was able to turn a profit. We do not know, unfortunately, how much it would have paid up front to the "author" had the rights to go first been put out to bid. But we do have some idea of how much it made after the fact. First, we know that Norton sold about 1.1 million copies, and that it charged between $1 and $1.50 more than St. Martin's did.[18] Other publishers also estimated that Norton made on the order of $1 of profit on each copy. Assuming that St. Martin's has some idea of how to price a book to avoid losing money, this suggests Norton made, at the very least, on the order of $1 million. We also know that its contract with the government called upon the publisher to donate its "profits" to charity – and we know that it did, in fact, "donate $600,000 to support the study of emergency preparedness and terrorism prevention."[19] Because the entire Hollywood movie industry has managed by creative accounting to avoid earning a profit during its entire history, we can be forgiven if we suspect that Norton earned a bit more than the $600,000 it admitted to.

We have already mentioned that it took us a few years to revise this book for final publication. The delay was probably bad for our reputation as professional book writers, but the three years that passed between the first draft and the revised edition allowed for a number of our wild conjectures to be tested by facts. Just recently a second natural experiment, similar to that of the *9-11 Commission Report*, has taken place. The Iraq Study Group, also known as the Baker-Hamilton Commission, was appointed on March 15, 2006, by the U.S. Congress. Its task was to carry out a bipartisan evaluation of the situation in Iraq following the United States–led invasion and subsequent occupation, and to make policy recommendations about how that dramatic situation could be improved.

The United States Institute of Peace (USIP) provided support for the Iraq Study Group, whose final report was released on the USIP Web site on December 6, 2006, for free downloading. Vintage Books, a division of Random House, published the same report and put it on sale at bookstores and Internet sites around the world on the same day. We have been unable to find evidence of how much Vintage Books paid for the right to access the manuscript before it was freely downloadable, but it is probably not zero. Recall that the report cannot be copyrighted, and any other publisher may, and probably will, get in on the fray without having to pay Vintage a single penny. We checked the Web, and the book is widely available at prices that range between about $9 and $11. It quickly made Amazon's top twenty-five best sellers list and, on December 25, 2006 (the last day we have data for), Amazon ranked it as No. 191 for total sales under the category "books," meaning among all books Amazon had available. Not bad for a document that anyone can also download for free, in about thirty seconds, from the UISP and many other Web sites.[20]

What, then, do these facts mean for fiction without copyright? By way of contrast to the *9-11 Commission Report*, which was in paperback and, including free downloads, seems to have about 8 million copies in circulation, the initial print run for *Harry Potter and the Half-Blood Prince* was reported to be 10.8 million hardcover copies.[21] So, we can realistically conclude that if J. K. Rowling were forced to publish her book without the benefit of copyright, she might reasonably expect to sell the book to a publishing house for several million dollars – or more. This is certainly quite a bit less money than she earns under the current copyright regime. But it seems likely, given her previous occupation as a part-time French teacher, that it would still give her adequate incentive to produce her great works of literature.[22]

News Reporting

The distribution of news on the Internet makes an interesting contrast to the distribution of music. While the RIAA has used every imaginable legal (and in some cases illegal) strategy to keep music off the Internet, the news reporting industry has embraced the Internet. Most major news agencies have a Web site where news stories may be viewed for, at most, the cost of a free registration. Far from discouraging the copying of news stories, most sites invite you to "e-mail a copy of this story to a friend." In fact, news is available so freely over the Internet that it is possible to create an entire newspaper simply by linking to stories written by other people. An example of such a "newspaper" is the site run by Matt Drudge, which consists almost entirely of links to stories on other sites. Yet the incentive to gather the news has not disappeared. According to intellectual monopolists' preaching, this should be impossible: to report from the Sudan requires the huge cost of going there in person, but copying that same report is as cheap as it can possibly get. So, why are highly paid journalists traveling to the Sudan to get the news?

The fact is that, prior to the advent of the Internet, the news industry was already a relatively competitive one, with many hundreds of news organizations employing reporters to gather news and write stories on the same subjects. Copyright has never provided a great deal of protection, and the copying of news stories is endemic to this industry: the enterprising reporter who manages to get his helicopter over the car chase first is not rewarded with the exclusive right to fly helicopters over the site. Copyright protects specific words, but not the news itself – and new reports of the form "the AP is reporting that the government of Pakistan has just captured Osama Bin Laden" are perfectly legal and not a violation of copyright at all. Because the news industry has been thriving, profitable, and highly competitive for a long while, the advent of the Internet scared off only a few incompetent fellows.

Still, everyone wants a monopoly, and the news industry is scarcely immune to greed. The arrival of innovative technologies and creative competitors drives the temptation to use existing copyright legislation to preserve or gain monopoly power particularly hard to resist. In fact, the impression one gets from a cross-country comparison is that the less competitive and more inefficient the news industry of a country is, the stronger is the demand for monopolistic protection from new entrants. Consider the example of Spain, a country where very few publishers, about five, control most of the national market, with one of them, Grupo Prisa, the grateful darling of every socialist government since 1982, acting as the undisputed leader. In 2002, the four largest Spanish publishing companies began lobbying for the creation of an industry cartel that would mandate a complete monopolization of the news distribution industry. This would be accomplished through the creation of a national agency, Gedeprensa, owned and managed by the same publishing companies, and entrusted with the right and duty to oversee the distribution of news through all kinds of media. News would be licensed and a "user fee" collected whenever it was "used," something analogous to the royalties that music monopolies collect whenever a tune is played in public. According to plans released by the lobbying group, this fee-collecting activity would range from the Internet to the photocopied press clips and news briefs distributed for internal usage in large organizations.

How the monopolies backing the Gedeprensa initiative planned to monitor and enforce exclusive proprietorship of the news escapes our imagination, but the proposal is a fact. Unfortunately for the would-be monopolists, on May 12, 2004, the Spanish Tribunal de Defensa de la Competencia firmly denied the requested authorization to proceed with the Gedeprensa project. One wishes the Supreme Court of the United States had shown the same understanding of basic economics, and the same concern with preserving market competition and improving social welfare, when ruling in the *Eldred v. Ashcroft* case that a monopoly that lasts forever lasts only for a limited time. Alas, it did not.[23]

How would the news industry operate in the complete absence of copyright? Obviously local newspapers would no longer feel the need to license stories from the Associated Press and Reuters. Most likely, the big news services would sell first to a few impatient and highly motivated customers, for whom getting the news an hour earlier than other people is highly valuable. Among the very impatient customers of Reuters, we might find the *Washington Post* and the *New York Times*, and maybe other news replicators, who then give away the replicas of the Reuters story with a few hours' delay and at a substantially lower price. It is possible that, depending on technology, speed of replication, and stratification of the market for news, a third or fourth layer of Reuters replicators would appear.

If this does not sound like a Star Trek story to you, it is simply because we already witness a very similar arrangement in the market for financial and most other valuable news. Here, highly impatient customers pay substantial fees to purchase from Bloomberg, Moody's, or Reuters the real-time news and quotes. The news and quotes then trickle down from Web sites to cable televisions, to national newspapers, and so on, until, often a whole day later, the New York Stock Exchange quotes are published in most newspapers around the world. In fact, just click on the Yahoo site, or the Reuters site, or the CNN site before you go to sleep at night. What do you get? You get the main ingredients of the articles you will read tomorrow morning from your beloved newspaper. The only difference with the financial news is that, for "normal" news, people's degree of impatience is a lot lower, which does not allow Reuters or CNN to charge you a high fee for feeding the news online before the newspapers publish it. Reuters and CNN, then, must get by with the revenues they collect from advertisers, or with the smaller fees they charge other professional news organizations. Still, the news gets collected, written and distributed, and most journalists, apparently, seem to find the salary they make in this competitive industry a reasonable compensation for their creative effort.

Similar considerations apply to the parroted questions about the highly paid author, the sleek imitators, and the money-losing publisher standing stupidly in the middle: the latter would stop standing stupidly in the middle and would get smart. This is not to say that authors might receive only a modest amount for their work – for example, Stephen King might not spend weeks and weekends writing his latest great work if he could sell it for only a grand total of $19.95. But as we have seen, the evidence of the *9-11*

Commission Report suggests he would command a rather higher price than this.

The Modern American Newspaper

The very form in which the news is currently distributed is itself a triumph of competitive innovation. The innovation was that of Benjamin Day, who in September 1833 started publishing the New York daily *Sun*, which he managed to sell at a penny while other newspapers sold at $.05 or $.06.[24] His low price came from two simple innovations: he collected lots of advertising instead of relying on subscriptions, and his paper was sold on street corners by armies of newsboys.

In the current parlance, these are "innovative business methods" and today they would be patentable. Fortunately for the American newspaper sector and for millions of American readers, they were not patentable in 1833; Day's innovation spread like fire to the whole country, including in New York City itself. Yet, despite the competition from his imitators, Day became one of the most important publishers in the United States and, by 1840, the *Sun* and its direct competitor, the *Herald*, were the two most popular dailies.

Notice that Day's innovations were very costly, as he had to change completely the whole distribution chain for the newspaper and set up and train an entirely new sales force to acquire advertisements. At the same time, copying him was only apparently easy: the idea was quite straightforward, but implementing it was not so cheap. It involved roughly the same set up costs that the *Sun* had to face in the first place.

"And this is where your anti-intellectual property stance is revealed to be just anti-business!" would-be Bill Gateses are thinking at this point – but, equally probably, not Bill Gates himself, as our earlier quote of his own words suggests. You see, without any "intellectual property" protection, brave inventors will try out expensive new things, while parasitic imitators will sit out, letting the experiments run their course, and then imitate only successful practices. In this way, as the RIAA constantly reminds us on its antipiracy Web site, "The thieves . . . go straight to the top and steal the gold,"[25] bringing the recording company to economic ruin.

This argument may sound smart and "oh-so-commonsense" right when you hear it the first time – but pause for a minute, and you will realize that it makes no business sense. Picking only winners means waiting until it is clear who is a winner. Well, try it: try getting somewhere by imitating the leaders only after you are certain they are the leaders. Try ruining the poor pop star by "pirating" her tunes only once you are certain they are big hits! Excuse us, we thought that "being a hit" meant "having sold millions of copies." Try competing in a real industry by imitating the winners only when they have already won and you have left them plenty of time to make huge profits and establish and consolidate their position – and probably have not left much of a market for you, the sleek imitator.

The World Before Copyright

Movies and news, not to speak of software code, are relatively new products. Music and literature go back to the dawn of civilization. For at least three thousand years, musical and literary works have been created in pretty much every society, and in the complete absence – in fact, often under the explicit prohibition – of any kind of copyright protection. For the economic and legal theories of "no innovation without monopolization," this plain fact is as inexplicable a mystery as the Catholic dogma of *virginitas ante partum* is for most of us.[26] To see the actual impact of copyright on creativity, let us start with some history. Copyright emerged in different European countries only after the invention of the printing press. Copyright originated not to protect the profits of authors from copyists or to encourage creation, but rather as an instrument of government censorship. Royal and religious powers arrogated to themselves the right to decide what could and could not be safely printed. Hence, the right to copy was a concession of the powerful to the citizenry to print and read what the powerful thought proper to print and read; Galileo's trial was nothing more than an exercise in copyright enforcement by the pope of Rome.

Later on, and mostly in the eighteenth century, in parallel with the diffusion, for the same purpose, of royal patents, copyright concessions began to be used as tax instruments. Selling a copyright, exactly like selling a patent, amounted to giving monopoly power to someone in exchange for bribing the royal power. The creation, in the United Kingdom, of the Stationers' Company, with virtual monopoly over printing and publishing, is probably the best-known example of such practice. There is no evidence, from the United Kingdom or from other European countries, such as the Republic of Venice, which adopted similar laws, that they provided any particular boost to either literary creation or the spread of literacy.

The Statute of Anne, adopted in England by 1710, is considered the first piece of legislation that, in the modern spirit, separates the censorship function from that of the personal ownership of the literary product, allocating to authors, or to the lawful buyers of their manuscripts, an exclusive right of publication that lasted for fourteen years. Notice the number: fourteen, not as it is today, the life of author plus seventy-five; William Shakespeare had found incentives for writing his opus even without those fourteen years, and yet no Shakespeare appeared after 1710.

It took almost a century of controversial ups and downs for the copyright legislation to be fully accepted in England, and to spread to the rest of Europe.[27] Around the time of the French Revolution, and under the label of *propriété littéraire*, the idea that the works of art, literature, and music belonged to their authors who could sell or reproduce them at will, without royal authorization, became popular. The fight for *propriété littéraire* was not a fight for monopoly but, instead, a request to abolish a particularly hideous royal monopoly: that over ideas and their expression. The institutional arrangements surrounding eighteenth-century French publishing in the absence of copyright is also of some interest. Books were copied frequently and quickly. There were no royalties and authors were paid in advance. Many small firms were organized just to publish a single book. In short, books were published, authors were paid, and all without the benefit of copyright.

We have already mentioned, early in this chapter, the very particular form in which literary copyright was introduced in the United States in 1790 and how the absence of copyright protection for foreign writers favored the diffusion of literacy in the country. In Germany, it was the monopoly-friendly Otto von Bismarck who, in 1870, introduced a uniform copyright legislation, modeled along the British lines; Goethe and Schiller, Kant and Hegel, did not profit from it. It is only in 1886 that the Berne Conference and the signing of the first international copyright treaty began to bring a degree of uniformity to copyright throughout the Western world.

Literature and a market for literary works emerged and thrived for centuries in the complete absence of copyright. Most of what is considered "great" literature and is taught and studied in universities around the world comes from authors who never received a penny of copyright royalties. Apparently the commercial quality of the many works produced without copyright has been sufficiently great that Disney, the greatest champion of intellectual monopoly for itself, has made enormous use of the public domain. Such great Disney productions as *Snow White and the Seven Dwarfs*, *Sleeping Beauty*, *Pinocchio*, and *Little Hiawatha* are, of course, all taken from the public domain. Quite sensibly, from its monopolistic viewpoint, Disney is reluctant to put anything back in the public domain. However, the economic argument that these great works would not have been produced without an intellectual monopoly is greatly weakened by the fact that they were.

How New Is Napster?

It is tempting to think that everything under the sun is new. For example, the Napster phenomenon is surely new and cries out for new laws and regulation; surely, the music industry cannot survive the advent of widespread copying. Or can it?

At the turn of nineteenth century, the music industry was different from the one we are familiar with today. No CDs, no mass concerts, and no radio or television. The core source of revenue was the sale of printed sheet music, which was carried out worldwide and on a very large scale. We learn, for example, that in Britain alone about 20 million copies were printed annually. The firms carrying out this business were not large multinationals as today, but family-owned companies, such as Casa Ricordi in Milan, which, nevertheless, managed to reach also foreign countries. Apparently these "majors" managed to collude quite efficiently among themselves. The records show that the average script sold in the United Kingdom for about a fourteen pence. Then "piracy" arrived, as a consequence of two changes: the development of photolithography and the spread of "piano mania," which increased the demand for musical scripts by orders of magnitude. "Pirated" copies were sold at two pence each.[28]

Naturally the "authorized" publishers had a hard time defending their monopoly power against the "pirates," enforcement costs were high, and the demand for cheap music books was large and hard to monitor. Music publishers reacted by organizing raids on "pirate" houses that were aimed to seize and destroy the "pirated" copies. This started a systematic and illegal "hit and destroy" private war, which led, in 1902, to the approval of a new copyright law. The latter made violation of copyright a matter for the penal code, putting the police in charge of enforcing what, until then, was protected only by the civil code.

The *South Park* portrayal herein of the "copyright police" storming the house to arrest children for sharing files exaggerates the current situation. In the early twentieth century, however, the hit squads of the authorized publishers did indeed burn down entire warehouses filled with "pirated" copies of sheet music – so perhaps *South Park* should remind us of what might be if Congress continues in its current direction.

At least in the case of sheet music, the police campaign did not work. After a few months, police stations were filled with tons of paper on which various musical pieces were printed. Being unable to bring to court what was a de facto army of illegal music reproducers, the police stopped enforcing the copyright law.

The eventual outcome? The fight continued for a while, with "regular" music producers keen on defending their monopoly and restricted sales strategy, and "pirates" printing and distributing cheap music at low prices and very large quantities. Eventually, in 1905, the king of the "pirates," James Frederick Willett, was convicted of conspiracy. The leader of one of the music publishers' associations, and the man who had invented the raids, launched the Francis, Day & Hunter's new sixpenny music series. Expensive sheet music never returned.[29]

The Birth of the Movie and of the Recording Industries

A fact not heavily advertised by the MPAA is that the Hollywood film industry was built by "pirates" escaping the heavy hand of intellectual monopoly.[30] After a long period of competitive fighting, in 1908, the major producers of film and movie equipment – including the Edison Film Manufacturing Company and the Biograph Company – formed a cartel in the form of the Motion Picture Patents Company (MPPC). Through this instrument, they demanded licensing fees from all film producers, distributors, and exhibitors. They vigorously prosecuted "independent" filmmakers who refused to pay royalties. In 1909, a subsidiary of the MPPC, the General Film Company, tried to confiscate equipment used by the unlicensed companies, disrupting their operations.

To avoid the legal battles and royalty payments, the independents responded by moving from New York to California.

California was remote enough from Edison's reach that filmmakers like Fox and Paramount could move there and, without fear of the law, pirate his inventions. Hollywood grew quickly, and enforcement of federal law eventually spread west. But because patents granted their holders a truly "limited" monopoly of just 17 years (at that time), the patents had expired by the time enough federal marshals appeared. A new industry had been founded, in part from the piracy of Edison's creative property.[31]

Roughly during the same period of time, the recording industry grew out of a similar kind of "piracy." In fact, the 1909 legislation that gave the MPCC the right to charge licensing fees to all moviemakers also began regulating the recording industry by introducing statutory licensing for recorded music. By doing so, Congress struck a compromise between composers, who wanted complete monopoly over the performance of their pieces, and recording artists, whose trade had grown briskly and competitively during the previous two or three decades. Between 1878, when Edison's first tinfoil phonograph was patented, and 1889, when the Columbia Phonograph Company started to market the treadle-powered Graphophone, recording music to be sold for commercial purposes became possible. The development, following Henry Fourneaux's prototype, of the player piano also greatly facilitated recording of music that would, otherwise, require an expensive ensemble to be performed. Although composers had exclusive rights to control sheet music and public performances, there was no clear right to control over recordings of music – something that had not previously existed. This ended in 1909, when Congress extended copyright to recordings but imposed statutory licensing; the recording industry grew – all on the basis of recordings "pirated" from composers.

Ironically, these parallel and contemporaneous stories teach us something about the principles guiding the fight for or against the enforcement of "intellectual property rights." The reader may have already noted, in fact, that Thomas Edison was sitting on both sides of the fence in this period. When it came to movies, because he was holding strong patents on the main tools used to tape and show movies, Edison had to favor a strong enforcement of "intellectual property." At the same time, though, his interests in the recorded music industry argued against an extension of copyright protection. Demand for Edison's phonograph obviously increased as cheaper and more abundant recordings of music became available, which was facilitated by a weak enforcement of the composers' monopoly power.

Encrypted versus Unencrypted Sales

The book, recorded music, and movie industries have been heavily influenced by the Napster experience, in which music has been given away for free over peer-to-peer networks. Consequently these industries have made a strong effort both to encrypt their products and to lobby the government to mandate encryption schemes. The Digital Millennium Copyright Act, for example, makes it a federal crime to reverse-engineer encryption schemes used to protect copyright. When it comes to competitive markets, the Napster experience is deceptive – the product distributed on Napster-like networks is not only cheaper than the commercial product but also is also better. An unencrypted song in a standard MP3 format can easily and readily be played on and transferred to many devices. Music in the chosen format of the major labels can be played inconveniently and only by a small number of devices. So, the experience of music on Napster begs the question of the performance of a market without copyright: will a good product sold at a reasonable price be widely distributed for free?

Within the book industry there is considerable evidence with which to answer this question, because, while most publishers have released electronic editions only in encrypted form, a few have sold unencrypted editions. Moreover, many books are currently available on peer-to-peer networks, and there have been lawsuits by a number of authors attempting to prevent this. So, we might expect relatively few sales of unencrypted electronic books because they will immediately appear for free on peer-to-peer networks, while encrypted books will sell better because they are not subject to "piracy." Strikingly, the data shows exactly the opposite.

The case of Fictionwise.com is an especially instructive natural experiment because, depending on the publisher and author, the site sells some books in encrypted form and others in unencrypted form. The encrypted books tend to be by the best-known authors. When we collected data on September 1, 2002, for example, the most highly rated book (by purchasers) was encrypted. Both types of books sell for a similar price – about $5 for a novel. However, Fictionwise.com also provides some sales data: it lists the top twenty-five recent best sellers and the top twenty-five best sellers for the past six months. On the randomly chosen date of September 1, 2002, no encrypted e-book appeared on either list. Almost three years later, on August 10, 2005 – stop laughing, it took us a while to revise this book – the situation has changed somewhat in favor of encrypted books but not dramatically so. Ranging through the same categories, one observes that the market is now about 50-50 between encrypted and not. Interestingly, the prices seem to be the same, signaling that either the unencrypted books are systematically a lot better than the encrypted ones or that the impact of "piracy" on the demand for legitimate products is quite negligible.

Data prior to the advent of Fictionwise tells the same story. At that time there were many outlets, including most of the major publishers, for encrypted e-books, and only one, Baen, for unencrypted e-books. Here is a report from author Eric Flint on the success of unencrypted "Webscriptions," compared to other encrypted e-book enterprises:

Webscriptions, unlike all other electronic outlets I know of, pays me royalties in substantial amounts. As of now, I've received about $2,140 in electronic royalties from Baen Books for the year 2000. . . . That sum is of course much smaller than my paper edition royalties, but it can hardly be called "peanuts." Every other electronic outlet I know of, in contrast, pays royalties – if at all – in two figures. My friend Dave Drake has given me permission to let the public know that his best-earning book published by anyone other than Baen, in one reporting period, earned him $36,000 in royalties for the paper edition – and $28 for the electronic edition. And that's about typical for even a successful book issued electronically [in encrypted form].[32]

Interestingly, searching the Gnutella peer-to-peer network on September 1, 2002, and on a number of subsequent occasions, the keyword *e-book* turns up several books released by Baen in electronic form. But they are legal copies of books given away by Baen for free – we found none of the books that Baen sells.

In the end, it is difficult to avoid the conclusion that it is the unpopularity of the music industry with its customers, combined with the inferiority of the "legitimate" product, that has led to the widespread giving away of MP3s for the cost of personal time and bandwidth. In the case of products sold in a superior form at a reasonable price, there appears to be little effort to trade them on peer-to-peer networks – so much so that the unencrypted product outsells the encrypted version.

Pornography

What would the entertainment industry look like without copyright? As a model, we might examine the segment of the industry for which copyright is not so important. Although the pornography industry is nominally protected by copyright, it does not receive the type of social approval that other industries have, and as a result, the industry has not focused on using the legal system to protect its intellectual monopoly. When we read of the FBI seizing illegal DVDs in raids in Hong Kong, it seems that they seize illegal copies of *The Sound of Music*, not illegal copies of *Debbie Does Dallas*, though we suspect that "pirated" copies of the latter are widely sold.

Despite social disapprobation, in most relevant respects the pornography industry is similar to that of so called legitimate movies and recordings. Producing and distributing a pornographic movie or magazine is technically and economically no different from producing and distributing a legitimate movie or magazine – so we can gain considerable insight into how those industries might operate in the absence of copyright by examining the pornography industry. In an earlier era, with the large overhead of producing movies and glossy magazines, the pornography industry operated much as the legitimate industry operates. However, the tenuous legal status of the industry has made it difficult for it to use copyright laws to inhibit competition, and so as technology has changed, pornography has become a cottage industry with many competing small-scale producers. It is perhaps not so difficult to imagine that in the absence of copyright, the legitimate industry would have been forced to adopt the same model, so we may see the current stage of the pornography industry as a model of the legitimate industry without copyright.

If we turn the clock back to the 1960s, when the legal pornography industry first became widespread in the United States, we find that publishing costs were high and a few giants, most notably *Playboy* and *Penthouse*, dominated the industry. However, unlike the legitimate industry, these large monopolists were not able to inhibit entry through the manipulation of the legal system, the abuse of copyright law, or political favoritism. The consequence has been that, as technology has changed, there have been frequent entries and constant innovation in this industry. Still, as long as the main technology for the reproduction and distribution of pornographic materials consisted of glossy magazines and movies circulating through the chain of X-rated movie theaters, the threat of competition and imitation was weak, and the big houses thrived.

All through the 1980s and then, at a much faster pace, the 1990s, technologies such as videotapes and the Internet became available and were quickly adopted. Indeed, it is arguable that the replication and distribution of pornographic materials was one of the reasons for the early explosive growth of the Internet between 1994 and 1999. The thousands of Internet sites distributing pornographic materials around the globe are, most of the time, imitators of the main initial producers, most often in violation of copyrights and licensing restrictions. Online pornographers are usually among the first to exploit new technologies – from video streaming and fee-based subscriptions to pop-up ads and electronic billing. Their bold experimentation has helped make porn one of the most profitable online industries, and their ideas have spread to other legitimate companies and become the source of many successful and highly valuable imitations.

Notice that if intellectual monopoly were a necessary requisite for sustained innovation, the circumstances we are describing should have brought the porn industry to a commercial standstill, halted innovation, and greatly reduced the amount of pornographic materials available to consumers. We are all well aware that exactly the opposite has happened. The consequence of the tremendous reduction in the cost of copying and redistributing visual materials, and the advent of peer-to-peer networks, has not brought about any reduction in the quantity of new pornography available to consumers – indeed, it seems to have expanded considerably – nor are we aware of complaints about a reduction in quality. There has, however, been an extremely adverse impact on the monopolies that originally dominated the industry – with *Penthouse* filing for Chapter 11 protection, and *Playboy* and *Hustler* dramatically losing profitability and market share. When we wrote this section, during a visit to Hong Kong in March 2004, the local newspapers announced the shutting down of the Asian edition of *Penthouse,* yet the newsstands in Kowloon and Hong Kong were bursting with pornographic materials, all from the many competitive imitators of those fading monopolies.[33]

If we compare the pornographic movie and entertainment industry to its legitimate counterpart, we find an industry that is more innovative, creates new products and adopts new technologies more quickly, and for which the reduction in distribution cost has resulted in more output at lower prices and a more diverse product. We also find an industry populated by many small producers and no dominant large firms capable of manipulating the market either nation- or worldwide. European intellectuals and politicians, obsessively fearing colonization by American movies and music, should take note: strengthening copyright protection, as you are all advocating, may just make you a couple of euros richer and a lot more intellectually colonized.

Finally, in pornography we find an industry in which "stars," be they actresses and actors or directors, earn a good living but are far from accumulating the fabled fortunes of the stars of its monopolistic counterparts. The evidence shows that porn stars make many more movies and earn between one and two orders of magnitude less, overall, than regular stars. In other words, they work more and make less money. This may seem a bad feature of the nonprotected industry, but from a social point of view it need not be. Indeed, it is the other side of the fact that more and cheaper porn movies are available. The stars of the porn movie industry are simply a lot closer to earning their "opportunity wage" – economic parlance for what they would be earning, given their skills and prevailing market conditions, in their best alternative occupation – than are the stars of the legitimate movie industry.

Organizing markets and industries in such a way that goods and services are provided while factors of production, either labor or capital, earn no more than their opportunity cost is what a socially desirable policy should aim to achieve. Now, on the basis of the available evidence, we cannot rule out the possibility that Ms. Sharon Stone or Mr. Brad Pitt – unlike Ms. Tera Patrick and Mr. Rocco Siffredi – have such lucrative alternative occupations that they would have given up Hollywood had they not earned the tens of million of dollars per movie that copyright laws allowed them to earn. Still, we cannot help but wonder if many legitimate actors and actresses would leave the industry if intellectual monopoly protection evaporated. Although it is clear that the dominant firms and the big players in the legitimate industry might fear such an outcome, there is certainly no reason for the consumers of these products, legitimate or not, to do so.

Comments

Nobody, unfortunately, has yet written a historical book on competitive creation, but any survey of literature and writing will enable readers to gather an idea of how much creation took place, over two thousands years, absent intellectual monopoly.

Notes

1. Hints that Microsoft might sue GNU/Linux users have been widespread since it announced in May 2007 that GNU/Linux infringes on 235 Microsoft patents. The announcement and reactions have been widely covered in the press.
2. Bill Gates, "Microsoft Challenges and Strategy," memo, May 16, 1991.
3. Extensive discussion of the role of copyright and patents in the software market can be found in Bessen and Hunt (2003). The first browser and Web server were written by Tim Berners-Lee, of the European Organization for Nuclear Research (known widely as CERN), who was also instrumental in persuading his superiors at CERN to keep the code and protocols free and open. NSCA Mosaic was the first popular browser and provided the source code for both Netscape and Internet Explorer. The original Internet Explorer was based on code licensed from Spyglass, the commercial arm of NSCA Mosaic. See, for example, http://www.blooberry.com/indexdot/history/browsers.htm (accessed February 23, 2008).
4. Note that copyleft, as it works today, uses copyright law to force the release of source code for derivative works. One consequence of abolishing copyright would be to eliminate also the GPL and similar agreements that restrict the right of downstream users and innovators to keep their source-code secret. One could argue in favor of "negative copyright" disallowing copyright that serves collusively to inhibit competition but allowing copyright such as the General Public License (GPL) that serves to enhance it. However, we think that the government trying to enforce antisecrecy agreements such as the GPL makes little more sense than its enforcement of secrecy agreements. Moreover, we doubt in practice that, in the absence of copyright, source code secrecy would prove an important practical problem.

5. The estimate of Linux's 25 percent share of the server market is from http://news.zdnet.co.uk/software/0,1000000121,2122729,00.htm (accessed February 23, 2008).

6. Statistics on the popularity of Web servers can be found at http://www.netcraft.com (accessed February 23, 2006). Updated information about the Netcraft Web server survey, reporting that as of January 2007 Apache stands at 60 percent of the market and Microsoft a distant second at 30 percent, can be found at http://news.netcraft.com/archives/web_server_survey.html (accessed February 20, 2007).

7. Brown (2005).

8. A fairly complete, but short enough to be readable, story of the open-source software movement, drawing interesting and clear parallels with two nineteenth-century episodes of collective invention in the complete absence of intellectual monopoly that we also often quote – for example, the Cleveland blast furnace and the Cornish steam power engine – can be found in Nuvolari (2005).

9. Information about the viability of the Red Hat approach to producing and distributing open-source software can be found, for example, in Gilbert (2005), which reports that Red Hat revenues were growing at a rate of 46 percent a year in mid-2005, and in Flynn and Lohr (2006), who describe the details of a deal between Novell and Microsoft through which the latter would ensure that Novell's version of Linux could operate together with Windows in the corporate environment.

10. Plant (1934), p. 172.

11. Plant (1934), p. 172.

12. The earnings of English authors from American publishers is discussed in Plant (1934). His perspective on intellectual property is similar to ours.

13. In 1850, the U.S. population from the census was 23.2 million; in 1851, the U.K. population from the census was 27.5 million. During those same years, per capita gross domestic product, in 1996 U.S. dollars, was roughly $1,930 in the United States and $2,838 in the United Kingdom. Literacy rates in both countries were roughly 85 percent. Thus our conclusion that the market for books was of similar size in the two countries.

14. The story of the *9/11 Commission Report* is from several sources, primarily Koerner (2004) and Wyatt (2004).

15. Koerner (2004), p. 1.

16. Wyatt (2004).

17. That the St. Martin's version was a best seller is reported in the *Washington Post* (2004), with the Norton version at No. 1 and the St. Martin's version at No. 8.

18. May (2005).

19. Associated Press (2005).

20. Details about the Iraq Study Group report and its sale performances are widely available on the Web, e.g. at http://www.cnn.com/2006/SHOWBIZ/books/12/07/us.iraq.book.ap/index.html (accessed December 25, 2006).

21. The initial print run of *Harry Potter and the Half-Blood Prince* was widely reported; see, for example, http://www.veritaserum.com (accessed February 23, 2008).

22. Information on J. K. Rowling's previous occupation is from an online biography at http://www.essortment.com/jkrowlingbiogr_reak.htm (accessed February 23, 2008).

23. The same Spanish newspapers involved in the Gedeprensa project have been quite eager to publish editorials by one of us and fellow Spanish economist Juan Urrutia on

a wide variety of economic subjects. Not surprisingly, they have refused to publish editorials by the same authors criticizing the Gedeprensa proposal. In case you are interested, the editorials are at the Web site http://lasindias.com/articulos/grandes_firmas/gedeprensa.html (accessed February 23, 2008).

24. The story of Benjamin Day is taken from Surowiecki (2003), available at http://www.newyorker.com/archive/2003/07/14/030714ta_talk_surowiecki (accessed February 24, 2008.) who correctly notes: "This is how American business worked until very recently. Innovators came up with new ways of selling products, handling suppliers, running organizations, or managing information. If the ideas were good, the innovators got rich, but they also got imitated, which made them less rich than they might have been. It was great for everyone else, though. The competition lowered prices and increased quality; the new ideas spread and were improved upon. The mail-order catalogue, the moving assembly line, the decentralized corporation, the frequent-flier mile, the category-killer store - none of these radical ideas were patented." The ultimate monopolistic fate of the American publishing industry is discussed in the excellent historical review by Hesse (2002).

25. http://www.riaa.com/issues/piracy/default.asp (accessed, June 10, 2007).

26. Should our passing reference to Catholic dogmas make the reader curious about *virginitas ante partum, in partu,* and *postpartum,* http://www.answersingenesis.org (accessed February 23, 2008) is a starting point for delving into the doctrine.

27. That in the nineteenth century literacy was higher in England than anywhere else in Europe, with the possible exception of the kingdom of Prussia, we learned from Cipolla (1969).

28. Almost all the facts reported here we have learned from Coover (1985), which we discovered thanks to Mann (2000) and Johns (2002), who, apart from the information contained in Coover, seems to have also checked a number of original references.

29. See Johns (2002), pp. 70–71.

30. The stories of Hollywood and of the origin of sound recording are from Lessig (2004).

31. Lessig (2004), p. 54.

32. Flint (2002), p. 1.

33. Reporting of *Penthouse*'s financial problems, and indications that they are due to the advent of the Internet, are widespread in the press. See, for example, Carr (2002). Our main source of information about the pornography industry was Swartz (2004).

THREE

Innovation under Competition

We have just seen numerous examples showing the frenetic pace of creation in the absence of copyright. Of course, people love to create stories, music, movies – and even news. So, perhaps you agree that copyright is not such a big deal, and even that it is not such a good idea. However, although we may hope to live lives free of boredom in the absence of intellectual monopoly, what about invention, the driving force of economic growth and prosperity? Would we benefit from all of the machines, drugs, and ideas that surround us if not for the beneficent force of patent law? Can we risk the foundation of our prosperity and growth by eliminating patents? In fact, the evidence shows that the invention of marvelous machines, drugs, and ideas does not require the spur of patents. If anything, the evidence shows, it is the other way around: patent protection is not the source of innovation, but rather the unwelcome consequence that, eventually, tames it.

We have already looked at the computer software industry: at its inception and during its most creative decades, the industry was essentially free of patents and made almost no use of copyright protection to prevent entry by competitors. As creativity slowed down, consolidation took place, and a few large monopolists emerged (one in particular), the demand for copyright first and patents later grew. Nowadays copyright and patents stand at the core of the software industry, which has become both monopolized and substantially less innovative than in the past.[1] Innovation and creativity come from the competitive fringe, which has great difficulty hiding behind "intellectual property" protection. Neither Google nor YouTube nor Skype is the golden egg of the patents' chicken, and in fact they do not use patents to retain their competitive advantage. By contrast, Microsoft would have had a hard time imitating and then catching up with Netscape had the latter managed to patent the idea of a browser, something it could do today.

These are the facts: the great role of patents in giving us modern software is unadulterated fantasy.

We shall see now that the story of software is far from unique. Most successful industries have followed the same pattern: "intellectual property" plays little role at the pioneering stage when new innovations and better and cheaper goods are pouring in. Then, when the creative reservoir runs dry, there is the desperate scramble for the pork that "intellectual property" provides. Because this is true for every well-established sector, from cars to electricity, from chemicals and pharmaceuticals to textiles and computers, and because this is widely documented in every decent history of such industries, we will not bore readers by going through these most traditional, if economically crucial, sectors. Instead, in keeping with our odd tradition of looking where our arguments have fewer chances of holding water, we will try to make our point by looking at some less obvious industries – for example, where imitation is cheap and there is lots of fierce competition.

World without Patent

Historically, very few ideas and innovations have been rewarded with government protected monopolies. Although the Venetians introduced limited patent protection to "accutissimi Ingegni, apti ad excogitar et trouar varij Ingegnosi artificij"[2] in 1474, this was an exceptional provision aimed at attracting particularly skillful artisans and merchants from other states. Such it remained for about a century and a half, with kings, princes, and doges giving or taking away exclusive privileges as they saw fit either to promote the economic vigor of the state or, more often, to promote the financial well-being of their purse.

It was English Parliament that, in 1623, pioneered patent law in its modern version with the aptly named Statute of Monopolies. At the time, the euphemism "intellectual property" had not yet been adopted – that a monopoly right and not a property right was being granted to innovators no one questioned. Moreover, the act of Parliament introducing the statute did not create a new monopoly. It took the power of granting monopoly away from the monarchy (represented at the time by King James I) and lodged it instead with Parliament. This basic fact is often missed in discussions over the role of patents in the economic development of the United Kingdom. Before the statute was enacted, the royal power to sell monopolies (on either new or old products, it did not matter: think of the salt monopoly) went completely unchecked and its use aimed at maximizing royal revenues. The economic incentives of innovators or, more generally, of entrepreneurs were nobody's concern in issuing letters of patent.

The statute, therefore, replaced the super-monopolistic power of expropriation and arbitrary grants of monopoly the Crown had enjoyed until then, with the milder temporary monopoly actual inventors would receive from Parliament. This, no doubt, represented progress in terms of private property rights and incentives to private economic initiative. Further, the range of products to which patent protection could and would be given was greatly reduced, as it was restricted to actual inventions (that is, forget the monopoly of salt) that satisfied the tight requirement that "they be not contrary to the law nor mischievous to the state by raising prices of commodities at home, or hurt of trade, or generally inconvenient."[3] Last but not least:

All Monopolies and all Commissions, Grants, Licenses, Charters and Letters Patent heretofore made or granted or hereafter to be made or granted to any Person or Persons, Bodies Politic or Corporate whatsoever, of, or for the sole Buying, Selling, Making, Working or Using any Thing within this Realm . . . or of any other Monopolies, or of Power, Liberty or Faculty . . . are altogether contrary to the Laws of this Realm, and so are and shall be utterly void and of none effect and in no wise to be put into use or execution.[4]

In current parlance, the Statute of Monopolies amounted to a gigantic liberalization or deregulation of the British economy, which came together with a strengthening of private property rights, a reduction of royal power, and the establishment of restrictive – by current standards, extremely restrictive – criteria for patent grants. These historical facts are worth keeping in mind vis-à-vis the frequent claims that the introduction of patent privileges in seventeenth-century England played a crucial role in spurring the subsequent Industrial Revolution. The statute did not replace intellectual competition with intellectual monopoly, as we are often led to believe, but an indefinite and broad government monopoly with a definite and restricted private monopoly. The second is a much lesser evil than the first, as it provides the innovator with both protection and economic incentives, whereas before there was nothing but royal arbitrium and widespread monopoly.

The Statute of Monopolies, in any case, defined the basic concept of patents and allowed for the possibility of a fourteen-year monopoly provided that "they be not contrary to the law nor mischievous to the state by raising prices of commodities at home, or hurt of trade, or generally inconvenient." The Statute of Anne, in 1710, extended and revised the law, while also introducing copyright. Until these formal laws were introduced, patents and copyright were nonexistent, were used as a form of governmental extortion through the sale of economic privileges, or were a tool for harassing scientists and philosophers, as Galileo and many others across Europe were forced to learn. Insofar as the British system of patent was helpful in inducing the Industrial Revolution, it is likely that the limitation it placed on the arbitrary power of government to block and monopolize innovation was the most important factor.

After the British legislative innovations of 1623–4 and 1710, imitation proceeded rather slowly in the rest of Europe: for good or ill, the transmission of ideas always takes time. A patent law was enacted in France in 1791; because it was based on the principle that no examination of any kind was required, it amounted to no more than a registry of inventions, often with very many duplicates, variations, and so on. It was also quite costly to get a patent, and the latter was declared void if the inventor tried to patent the invention also in another country, a small detail revealing the mercantilist foundation of "intellectual property," something that, as we argue later, remains essential to current legislation. As a consequence of all this, the French system did not introduce much monopoly until it was reformed in 1844.

It is only towards the end of the nineteenth and the beginning of the twentieth century that countries such as France, Germany, Italy, and Spain came to adopt fairly comprehensive "intellectual property laws." By this time, innovation, rule of law, and ownership of ideas in these countries were widespread, and the introduction of "intellectual property" laws served to create private monopolies rather than to limit the arbitrary power of government. Germany enacted a comprehensive patent law, introducing for the first time the principle of mandatory examination, only in 1877. Still, German patent law was mostly restricted to processes, not products; in particular, chemical products did not become patentable until much later. A number of significant holdouts remained until around the First World War; for example, Switzerland and the Netherlands and, to a lesser extent, Italy.

As for the United States, the adoption of "intellectual property" laws started with the Patent Act of 1790 and extended progressively to more and more areas of business. The first U.S. patent was granted in 1790 to Samuel Hopkins of Philadelphia for "making pot and pearl ashes," a cleaning formula used in soap making. Since then, the applicability of patent law has increased steadily, with new industries and areas of invention being added one after the other. The length of patent terms has also increased, as the courts' rulings have leaned more and more in favor of patent holders.

There have been a few temporary setbacks to this trend, and they have been associated either with renewed antitrust efforts or with situations of national emergency, such as the First World War and, especially, the Second World War. This fact, by itself, is revealing and noteworthy: that patents could or could not be used in one area of research or in a whole industry has never been the outcome of a spontaneous, well-informed, and well-reasoned decision by the legislative branch. It has always happened in bits and pieces by mixing court rulings with small legislative changes, and always upon request from the industry that "needed" to be monopolized – oops, protected. It would take another book to spell out the fascinating political economy account of how one mature industry after another patentability grew over time because of lobbying by would-be monopolists that had run out of steam for inventing and were too afraid of newcomers or foreign competitors. Various historical episodes (the 1870s, and the 1970s–1980s, especially) give the impression that slow productivity growth favors extensions of patentability, as all three branches of government gave in to the pressure of incumbent firms trying to preserve profitability by increasing monopoly power instead of competing harder.

The crucial fact, though, is that the following causal sequence never took place, either in the United States or anywhere else in the world. The legislature passed a bill saying, "Patent protection is extended to inventions carried out in the area X," where X was a yet-undeveloped area of economic activity. A few months, years, or even decades after the bill was passed, inventions surged in area X, which quickly turned into a new, innovative, and booming industry. In fact, patentability always came after the industry had already emerged and matured on its own terms. A somewhat stronger test, which we owe to a doubtful reader of our work, is the following: can anyone mention even one single case of a new industry emerging as a result of the protection of existing patent laws? We cannot, and the doubtful reader could not either. Strange coincidence, is it not?

During the last twenty-five or thirty years, the "everything should be patented" trend has set in, especially in the United States, with the European Union, as always, barking at the heels. Even in the United States, business practices and financial securities were not subject to patent prior to 1998, and software code was not patentable until 1981. In most of the rest of world they still cannot be patented.

As is transparent from our cursory survey of the countries and sectors to which patent laws have applied, the list of industries that were born and grew in the absence of "intellectual property" protection is almost endless. Services were not covered by patent laws until the late 1990s, and then only in the United States and in some particular sectors. The mechanical and metallurgical industries are those in which patent laws were most broadly applied, whereas the chemical industry was originally only partially affected by intellectual monopoly provisions. In Italy, pharmaceutical products and processes were not covered by patents until 1978; the same was true in Switzerland for processes until 1954, and for products until 1977. Agricultural seeds and plant varieties could not be effectively patented in the United States until 1970, and they still cannot be in most of the world. All kinds of "basic science," from mathematics to physics (and even economics, but no longer finance), have never been and cannot be patented, even if a rapidly growing number of observers alarmingly point out that, at least in the United States, the "going upstream" tendency in patenting has started to seriously affect the results of very basic research, especially in the biological and life sciences.

We are not alone among economists in noticing these facts; George Stigler, writing in 1956, cites a number of examples of thriving innovations under competition:

When the new industry did not have such barriers [patents and other contrived restrictions on entry], there were an eager host of new firms – even in the face of the greatest uncertainties. One may cite automobiles, frozen foods, various electrical appliances and equipment, petroleum refining, incandescent lamps, radio, and (it is said) uranium mining.[5]

He provides further elaboration in the case of the mail-order business:

There can be rewards – and great ones – to the successful competitive innovator. For example, the mail-order business was an innovation that had a vast effect upon retailing in rural and small urban communities in the United States. The innovators, I suppose, were Aaron Montgomery Ward, who opened the first general merchandise establishment in 1872, and Richard Sears, who entered the industry fourteen years later. Sears soon lifted his company to a dominant position by his magnificent merchandising talents, and he obtained a modest fortune, and his partner Rosenwald an immodest one. At no time were there any conventional monopolistic practices, and at all times there were rivals within the industry and other industries making near-perfect substitutes (e.g. department stores, local merchants), so the price fixing power of the large companies was very small.[6]

Since 1955, sticking to the merchandising and distribution sector, we can add to this list such modern innovations as Ray Kroc's fast-food franchise (better known as McDonald's), the twenty-four-hour convenience store, home delivery of precooked food, the suburban shopping mall, franchise everything (from coffee to hairdressing), the various steps that make up the delivery business of UPS, FedEx, and DHL, and, obviously, online commerce. That is, pretty much each and every innovation that, during the last half century, has had any lasting impact in the retail and distribution sector was not spurred or protected by patents.

However, these all seem rather obvious, if not stereotypical, examples. A less obvious but nevertheless familiar form of innovation is emigration. The first English, Dutch, Irish, or Somali immigrant to the United States was no less innovative than the inventor of the airplane, and emigrants are constantly discovering new countries and business opportunities without any need for intellectual monopoly. Indeed, emigration and the formation of new communities is both a prototypical example of the fundamental role played by competitive innovation in the development of human civilization and a reminder of the fact that the forces of monopoly are always and almost inescapably at work after every great competitive leap forward.

The first immigrant faces a large cost: he or she must cross the ocean, or desert, or mountain range. He also faces a high risk of failure: who knows what is waiting over there and what living conditions will be like? The cost is much smaller and less risky for imitators – seldom if ever are unsuccessful immigrants imitated. Followers of early settlers already know that the newfound land is hospitable and fertile – and the pioneers are available to inform newcomers about job opportunities and local laws and customs. Yet the common association of "early settlers" with "old money" or "political influence," or both, suggests that there is still a substantial advantage to being first.

Sadly, as in other industries, after years have gone by and the number of new opportunities for immigrants diminishes, pressure from early entrants for monopoly protection emerges. Such rent-seeking legislation in the immigration industry we call immigration and naturalization restrictions or quotas. Although economists doubt that these restrictions provide much benefit for the early entrants, there is no doubt that protection from competition from new immigrants is much sought after.

The history of emigration carries also some broader messages about innovation. It shows that free entry and unrestricted imitation characterize the most successful experiences, whereas monopolistic restrictions on immigration are often associated with subsequent poor economic performances. One example is the contrasting experiences of the Portuguese and Spanish settlements of Central and South America, respectively, and that of the English settlements of North America. The first was limited to small bands of politically connected adventurers; the second was open even to politically unpopular groups such as the Puritans. The economic consequences speak for themselves.

In a similar way, successful new industries are almost invariably the product of innovation-cum-imitation-cum-cutthroat competition, and many potential successes have been thwarted from the start by the adoption of monopolistic arrangements favoring the very early innovators. It is also true that the more mature and economically successful a country is, the stronger is the internal pressure to introduce monopolistic restrictions to immigration. So it is also at the end of the industry life cycle that wealthy, mature, and technologically stagnant firms are the breeding ground of monopolistic restrictions purchased through the constant lobbying of politicians and regulators.

The Industrial Revolution and the Steam Engine

It has been argued that the Industrial Revolution took place when it took place (allegedly, sometime between 1750 and 1850) and where it took place (England) largely because patents giving inventors a period of monopoly power were first introduced by enlightened rulers at that time and in that place. The exemplary story of James Watt, the prototypical inventor-entrepreneur of the time, is often told to confirm the magic role of patents in spurring invention and growth. As we pointed out in the introduction, this is far from being the case.

The pricing policy of Boulton and Watt's enterprise was a classical example of monopoly pricing: over and above the cost of the materials needed to build the steam engine, they would charge royalties equal to one-third of the fuel cost-savings attained by their engine in comparison to the Newcomen engine. Notice two interesting properties of this scheme: it allows for price discrimination, and it is founded on the hypothesis that, thanks to patent protection, no further technological improvement will take place. It allows for price discrimination because, given the transport technology of the time, the price of coal – and horses, the alternative to the Newcomen engine being horses – varied substantially from one region to another. It assumes that technological improvement will be stifled, because it is based on the idea that only the Watt engine could use less coal than the Newcomen engine. No surprise, then, that Boulton and Watt spent most of their time fighting in court any inventor, such as Jonathan Hornblower, who tried to introduce a machine either superior to theirs or, at least, superior to the Newcomen engine. It will also come as no surprise to our readers that, in the Cornwall region, where copper and tin were mined and coal was expensive, a number of miners took to "pirating" the engine. This naturally brought about a legal dispute with Boulton and Watt, which ended only in 1799 with the symbolic victory of the two monopolists. Symbolic, because their patent expired a year later.

The episode that interests us here, though, lies in the pace and nature of innovation after the expiration of the Boulton and Watt patents. In 1811, after the Boulton and Watt patents had expired "a group of mine... managers decided to begin the publication of a monthly journal reporting the salient technical characteristics, the operating procedures and the performance of each engine."[7] Their declared aims were to permit the rapid individuation and diffusion of best-practice techniques and to introduce a climate of competition among the various mines' engineers. The publication enterprise continued until 1904.

One year later, in 1812, and in the same region, the first high-pressure engine of the so-called Cornish type was built by Richard Trevithick. Interestingly enough, Trevithick did not patent his high-pressure pumping engine and allowed anybody who wanted to copy it.[8] Trevithick's engine happened to be as efficient as Watt's, but much more amenable to improvement. This triggered a long and extremely successful period of competitive-collaborative innovation in which different firms made small, incremental changes to the original design of the Cornish engine. Such changes were neither patented nor kept secret, thereby spreading rapidly among other firms in the Cornwall area, allowing, and at the same time forcing, new improvements from competitors.

As a measure of the social value of competition versus monopoly, consider the following facts. The duty of steam engines (a fundamental measure of their coal efficiency) that, during the twenty-five years of the Boulton and Watt monopoly (1775–1800), had remained practically constant improved by roughly a factor of five between 1810 and 1835.

This successful collaborative effort to improve the Cornish engine illustrates the genius of the competitive market. Because of uncertainty in coal mining, a modest number of investors engaged in mutual insurance by each owning shares in a broad cross-section of mines. As is the case with shareholders in publicly traded companies, this means that each investor was able to capture the benefit of innovation, regardless of which particular firm or engineer made the improvement. Indeed, the employment contracts of engineers reflected these incentives. Engineers were employed on a contract basis by particular mines to improve engines, with the understanding that they would publish their results. Investors captured the common gains to all mines from each innovation, while engineers, having signed away the right to monopolize their invention, profited instead from their fees and from the advertising value of publicizing their innovations. Indeed, in many respects, this early-nineteenth-century competitive-collaborative mine engine-improvement system is similar to the modern-day open-source software system.[9]

The period of the Industrial Revolution is, when one looks at it without bias-shaded glasses, a mine of examples, both of patents hindering economic progress while seldom enriching their owners and of great riches and even greater economic progresses achieved without patents and thanks to open competition. Of the many anecdotes, the story of Eli Whitney is particularly instructive. Born in Westborough, Massachusetts, in 1765, Whitney graduated from Yale College in 1792. The following year he designed and constructed the cotton gin, a machine that automated the separation of cottonseed from the short-staple cotton fiber. Very much like Watt's engine in the coal districts of England, the cotton gin was enormously valuable in the South of the United States, where it made Southern cotton a profitable crop for the first time. Like James Watt, Eli Whitney also had a business partner, Phineas Miller, and the two opted for a monopolistic pricing scheme not dissimilar from Boulton and Watt's. They would install their machines throughout Georgia and the South and charge farmers a fee to do the ginning for them. Their charge was two-fifths of the profit, paid to them in cotton. Not surprisingly, farmers did not like this pricing scheme very much and started to "pirate" the machine. Whitney and Miller spent a lot of time and money trying to enforce their patent on the cotton gin, but with little success. Between 1794 and 1807, they went around the South bringing to court everyone in sight, yet received little compensation for their strenuous efforts. In the meanwhile, and thanks also to all that "pirating", the Southern cotton-growing and cotton-ginning sector grew at a healthy pace.

Ironically, Eli Whitney did eventually become a rich man – not through his efforts at monopolization, but through the wonders of competitive markets. In 1798, he invented a way to manufacture muskets by machine, having developed the idea of interchangeable parts and standardized production. Having probably learned his lesson, he did not bother to seek patent protection this time, but instead set up a shop in Whitneyville, near New Haven. Here he manufactured his muskets and sold them to the U.S. Army. So it was not as a monopolist of the cotton gin, but rather as the competitive manufacturer of muskets, that Whitney finally became rich.

Agriculture

Among economists the reaction to the idea that economic progress is the fruit of competition is varied. Those belonging to the theoretical variety, interested in matters of pure economic theory and logic, tend to quickly agree and then yawn away the rest of the seminar, as the conclusion seems straightforward. Specialists working in the areas of innovation, economic growth, and industrial organization, long steeped in the conventional wisdom that there is no innovation without monopolization, are often certain that the opposite idea cannot possibly be correct, even if they are uncertain as to why. There are, however, the specialists in agricultural economics, who react with neither boredom nor rage. Steeped not in the myths of theory, but versed in the facts of agricultural innovation, these specialists point out that, until the early 1970s, animal and plant species innovation flourished without much in the way of protection from intellectual monopoly. Breeders would develop a new plant variety, the initial seeds of which were sold to farmers at relatively high prices. Farmers were then free to reproduce and resell such seeds on the market and compete with the initial breeders, without the latter bringing them to court because those bushels of, say, Turkey Red wheat were illegal copies of the Turkey Red wheat variety they held a patent on.[10]

A sizable chunk of innovation in agriculture revolves around plants and animals. Neither the 1793 original nor the 1952 revised version of the U.S. patent code mentioned the possibility of patenting different forms of life, be they animal or vegetable. The issue did not arise during most of the nineteenth century, but a precedent against patenting was established in 1889, when the U.S. commissioner of patents rejected an application for a patent to cover a fiber identified in the needles of a pine tree. The commissioner wisely pointed out that patenting some newly found form of life would be tantamount to attributing monopoly power (and de facto ownership) to all copies of that form of life to be subsequently found, which struck him, as it strikes us, as "unreasonable and impossible."

The story of agriculture, however, like that in other industries, is also the story of the intellectually bankrupt seeking protection for their old ideas. The discovery of the economic potential of Mendel's law – imagine a world in which Gregor Mendel had managed to patent applications of his law, no longer an impossibility these days – started a long series of attempts to subvert the 1889 doctrine. The National Committee on Plant Patents, created and financed by U.S. breeders, was the leader of an intense lobbying campaign arguing that, now, contrary to before, a "new" plant or animal could, in principle, be exactly identified and that its "creation" was equivalent, therefore, to the invention of a new mechanical tool. Note an important detail: during the many decades it took to buy monopoly protection from Congress, the breeding industry was, literally, blossoming and grow-ing under conditions of competition and without intellectual monopoly protection. In fact, it had prospered so much that its economic power and ability to influence Congress and the public opinion increased to the point that it was able to eventually have the law changed.

Once again we are faced with the basic pattern noted earlier. Innovative and dynamic industries emerge either because intellectual monopoly is not present or because it can easily be bypassed. They grow rapidly because competition and imitation allow and force their firms to innovate or perish. In fact, in the early stages, agricultural innovators often would provide their customers with incentives to copy and reproduce their seeds, as a tool to spread their use. However, as the industry grows more powerful and opportunities for further innovation diminish, the value of monopoly protection for the insiders increases, and lobbying efforts multiply and most often succeed.

In the case of the breeding industry, a partial victory was first achieved during the Great Depression, with the Plant Patent Act of 1930. The vic-tory was only partial because, mostly as a result of issues of enforceability, patents were allowed only for plants that could reproduce asexually. The act explicitly excluded tuber and sexually reproducing plants. For these crops, the scientific knowledge of the times made it impossible to satisfy the patent law requisite that a patentable invention be disclosed specifically enough to be identically reproducible.

As the reader may imagine, this limitation did not please the American Seed Trade Association, which had greatly contributed to the lobbying effort. Although it was a useful precedent, the 1930 act was too weak and covered too few plants; hence, it did not really provide breeders with the extensive monopoly power they sought. Such weakness revealed itself in the fact that, while agricultural innovations continued at a substantial pace, only 911 plant patents were assigned in the period until the early 1950s. In the meanwhile, lobbying by potential monopolists did not go away; instead it intensified as new and powerful interest groups joined the clan. The discovery of the DNA code, and the subsequent development of biological engineering, would, eventually, come to rescue the monopolist's demand for full protection.

To summarize, (1) before 1930, only some mechanical and chemical inventions related to agriculture could be patented. (2) In 1930, the Plant Patent Act offered patent protection to asexually reproduced plants. (3) In 1970, the Plant Variety Protection Act extended such protection to plants that are sexually reproduced. (4) Between 1980 and 1987, patent protection was extended to the products of biotechnology. One would expect this progressive extension of "intellectual property" protection to bring about a dramatic acceleration in useful innovation, at least since the early 1970s.

One measure of useful innovation is what economists call total factor productivity (TFP): how much output (of food, for example) can be produced from given inputs (labor and land, for example). So, we might expect that the growth rate of TFP in the agricultural section accelerated in response to all this additional patentability. This is not the case, as the historical data clearly show: in the United States, agricultural TFP has been growing at a remarkably constant pace since the end of the Second World War.[11] More precisely, the average growth rate from 1948 to 1970 was essentially the same as from 1970 to 1992 – that is, about 50 percent – and it seems to have marginally slowed down after that. Oscillations in TFP have certainly increased in size, which is hardly a good thing besides being hard to interpret. Some argue that it is still too early to tell, an argument we find pretty hard to understand and to debate: if more than thirty years is not a long-enough period for increased "intellectual property" protection to bring about its benefits for society, then why bother with patents?

US Agricultural TFP 1948-2002

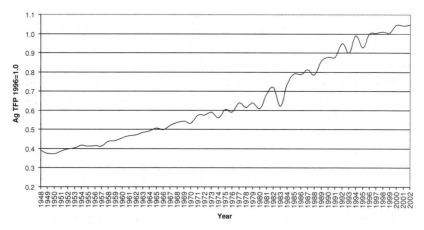

But, perhaps, agricultural TFP is too broad a measure of productivity to reveal the impact of extended patentability in agriculture. To mark the progress of innovation in agriculture, one may want to focus on specific species of plants, in which case corn, as a common and important crop, may be a useful case study. We show in the subsequent figure crop yields for U.S. corn, averaged by decade.[12]

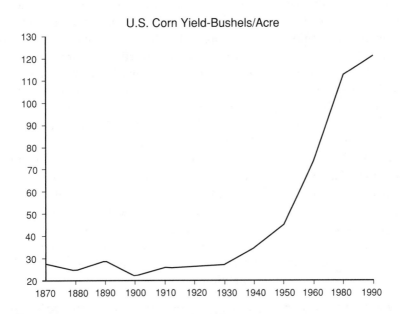

Up until the 1930s, yields did not change much – as the specialized literature we mention in the notes explains, this turns out to have little to do with lack of innovation. It is primarily because as agriculture moved west, into poorer climates and soil, continuous innovation was required just to maintain crop yields. As the area under cultivation stabilized, beginning in the 1930s and especially in the 1950s, crop yields exploded. The primary innovations underlying this explosion were the introduction of improved hybrid varieties that are more responsive to heavy fertilization.

The key point is that the bulk of the growth in yield took place when patents on plant life were impossible or rare and certainly did not apply to corn, which is not asexually reproduced. Indeed, patents on corn hybrids became widespread only after DNA-based research began. Pioneer-Hi-Bred International recorded the first such patent on corn in 1974, after most of the growth in yield reported in the figure had already taken place.[13] The large surge in the patenting of corn varieties occurred in the period

1974–84 – substantially after the revolution in crop yield was well under way. In fact, the growth rate in corn yield seems to have decreased since the 1980s!

Spanish *Hortalezas* and Italian *Maglioni*

Introducing high-tech greenhouse to grow fruits and vegetables in Almería, Spain, in the early 1960s (the "hortalezas" of the title) was as much an economic innovation as the development of the 286 microprocessor in California two decades later. It took place through the effort of a large number of completely unknown farmers and in the absence of any patent protection of the business methods and production techniques they created or adopted.[14]

In 1963, Almería was such a poor and desert area that Sergio Leone went there to shoot his spaghetti westerns. The area was no less desolate than are Arizona and Southern Utah, but the region was so poor that it was a lot cheaper to make a film there. Shortly after that, the first greenhouse, a simple and low-cost pergola-type structure, gave birth to the so-called Almerían miracle. The consequences of this innovation are so profound that the results can even be seen from space: the NASA satellite images herein, show Almería before and after the miracle.[15] (See color plate on next page.) A picture is really worth more than a thousand words: we cannot imagine a better way to show how innovation under competition can improve in a short period of time people's economic conditions.

A similar, if less visually stunning, revolution happened at about the same time in the area around Treviso, Italy, when the members of the Benetton family introduced the ready-to-color sweater (maglione) production process and adopted creative franchising techniques that in a couple of decades transformed a large segment of the clothing sector.[16] Both their original production process and their marketing and distribution methods were rapidly imitated, and improved, first by competitors from the same area and then by competitors from all kinds of faraway places. The megastores of Zara and H&M, which attract hordes of shoppers everywhere in the world, are, until now, the most recent stage of the innovation-cum-imitation process that Benetton started forty years ago in a poor area of the Italian Northeast.

Each of these economic innovations was costly, took place without "intellectual property," and was quickly imitated; thus, the innovations not only brought fortune to their original creators but also led to widespread economic changes in the geographical areas and the economic sectors harboring the initial innovation. In the cases of Almería and Treviso, the innovation-cum-imitation process was so deep and so persistent that it spilled over to other sectors, leading to a continued increase in productivity that, in a few decades, turned two relatively underdeveloped areas into some of the richest provinces of Spain and Italy, respectively. Indeed, the social value of an innovation is maximized when it spreads rapidly, and by spurring competition, it induces further waves of innovation. Current legislation seems designed to prevent this from happening, thereby greatly reducing the social value of innovative activity.

Financial Markets

When you hear the phrase "judge-made law," you probably think of controversial areas, such as abortion and privacy. But the greatest changes in the legal system made by judges, without legislative review or approval, have occurred in the area of patent law. The extension of patent protection to computer software is one example; another is the patenting of financial securities. Prior to 1998, investment bankers and other firms selling financial securities operated without the "benefit" of "intellectual property." The rapid pace of innovation in financial securities prior to 1998 is well documented, for example by Tufano.[17] Tufano estimates that roughly 20 percent of new security issues involve an innovative structure. He reports developing a list of some 1,836 new securities over a twenty-year period and remarks:

> [This] severely underestimate[s] the amount of financial innovation as it includes only corporate securities. It excludes the tremendous innovation in exchange traded derivatives, over-the-counter derivative stocks (such as the credit derivatives, equity swaps, weather derivatives, and exotic over-the-counter options), new insurance contracts (such as alternative risk transfer contracts or contingent equity contracts), and new investment management products (such as folioFN or exchange traded funds.)[18]

Three features of this market particularly deserve note. The first is that innovating in the financial securities industry is very costly, as those that create new securities are highly paid individuals with Ph.D.'s in economics, mathematics, and theoretical physics. The second is that competitors quickly imitate financial innovations. The third is that there is a pronounced advantage of being first, with the innovator retaining a market share between 50 percent and 60 percent even in the long run. Accounts in the popular press of investment banking in the 1980s, such as Lewis's vivid portrayal, also document that innovation was widespread, despite the complete lack of intellectual monopoly. We are all well aware that, for good or for bad, but mostly for the first, the investment banking industry grew tremendously between the late 1970s and the late 1990s, bringing economic growth to the whole of the nation and increased welfare to millions of consumers. And all of this happened in the complete absence of any form of intellectual monopoly.

This story, sadly, is now over. On July 23, 1998, in *State Street Bank & Trust Co. v. Signature Financial Group, Inc.*, the U.S. Court of Appeals for the Federal Circuit held patentable Signature's data-processing system for hub-and-spoke financial services configuration. Prior to this ruling, methods of doing business and mathematical algorithms could not be patented. After this ruling, at least insofar as they are embodied in computer code, business methods and algorithms are patentable; in particular, it is now possible to patent financial securities: there are now tens of thousands of patented "financial inventions." By this remarkable act of judicial activism, the courts extended government-granted monopolies to thriving markets, such as those for financial securities, where innovation and competition had gone hand in hand for decades. Should this trend not be reversed, we expect that within a decade or so, economists studying the U.S. financial securities industry will be pondering a productivity slowdown and wondering what on earth may have caused it. At the current time, about eight years after patents were introduced in the financial and banking sectors, there are no signs that this reallocation of property rights has spurred any wave of new innovations and unprecedented economic growth.

Design

For historical and practical reasons, neither fashion design nor design at large (architecture, furniture, lighting, and so forth) are – or better said, were, until the other day – effectively protected by patents and copyrights. To be sure, design patents exist, they are carefully and scrupulously described in voluminous manuals, and hundreds of design patent applications are filed with the U.S. Patent and Trademark Office every month. However, it is quite clear from everyday experience that, in design, imitation is as widespread and common as sand in the Sahara Desert.

General design concepts, and even quite particular and specific ones, are de facto not patentable. On the one hand, too many features of the design of a useful object are dictated by utilitarian concerns; on the other hand, even very minor ornamental variations are enough to make a certain design different from the original one. Practically speaking, what this means is that car companies imitate one another in shaping and styling their cars; architects and engineers do the same with buildings and bridges, not to speak of university halls; furniture makers copy one another's beds, sofas, and coffee tables; lamp makers are continuously coming up with yet another variation on the design of Artemide's Tizio; all *tailleurs* are copycats of Chanel – and so on and so forth.

Although design is not all that there is in a coat or in a sofa, it is more and more the factor around which a competitive edge is built. Even the most casual of observers can scarcely be unaware of the enormous innovation that occurs in the clothing and accessories industry every three to six months, with a few top designers racing to set the standards that will be adopted by the wealthy first, and widely imitated by the mass producers of clothing for the not-so-wealthy shortly after.[19] And "shortly after," here, means really shortly after. The now-worldwide phenomenon of the Spanish clothing company Zara (and its many imitators) shows that one can bring to the mass market the designs introduced for the very top clientele with a delay that varies between three and six months. Still, the original innovators keep innovating and keep becoming richer.

The pace of innovation, the lack of artificial intellectual monopoly, and the speed and ease of innovation in the fashion design sector is well documented by Kal Raustiala and Chris Sprigman. Once again, a picture is worth a thousand words.

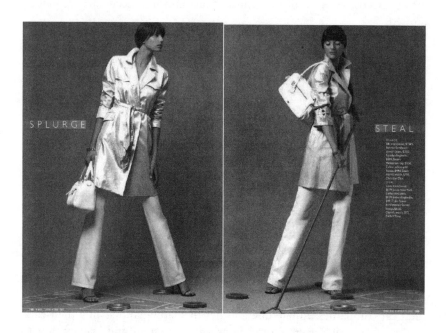

What may be hard to read in the picture is the text of the "Steal" ad: it advertises both its own price and the "Splurge" price. The splurge trench coat, for example, costs $1,565 and the steal only $159.

Similarly, in the fine arts, while individual works can be protected by copyright, methods, techniques, styles, and concepts cannot be patented. Varnedoe provides vivid documentation of the enormous inventive activity in the modern figurative arts – and the equally rampant imitation that occurred in that field – all in the complete absence of intellectual monopoly.[20] His discussion of widespread experimentation and imitation – by a variety of artists – on the use of perspective is but one example. Finally, consider the enormous growth of the contemporary stepbrother of the fine arts, advertising and marketing. The economic impact of advertising and marketing are one or two orders of magnitude greater than that of the traditional fine arts sector (though the borders have become more and more blurred during the course of the past century). Also, in this sector, neither patents nor copyrights play a relevant role. Still, and almost by definition, if there is a sector of economic activity for which innovation and novelty are the key factors, advertising is certainly the prime candidate.

Sports

When examining the social merit of public institutions, a useful question to ask is whether the same institutions are used in the private sector. For example, government bureaucracies are widely thought to be inefficient. Yet we observe, for example, in the very competitive information technology industry, that IBM's internal bureaucratic structure has survived, and indeed thrived, over many years. Hence, we have to conclude that it is likely that bureaucracies do achieve some socially desirable goals.

We can ask the same question about intellectual monopoly. If intellectual monopoly is a good idea in the public sector as a way to encourage innovation, is it used in the private sector for that purpose? A case in point is sports leagues. Typically, these leagues have near-absolute power over an entire sport and the rules by which it is played; they also have full control of the commercial part, and stand to benefit from anything that increases demand for their product. Innovation is also important in sports, with such innovations as the Fosbury flop in high-jumping, the triangle offense in basketball, and of course the many new American football plays that are introduced every year, serving to improve performance and provide greater customer satisfaction. Indeed, the position of the sports leagues with respect to innovation in their own sport is not appreciably different from that of the benevolent social planner invoked by economists in assessing alternative economic institutions.

Given that sports leagues are in the position of wishing to encourage all innovations for which the benefits exceed the cost, they are also in the position to implement a private system of "intellectual property," should they find it advantageous. That is, there is nothing to prevent, say, the National Football League from awarding exclusive rights to a new football play for a period of time to the coach or inventor of the new play. Strikingly, we know of no sports league that has ever done this. Apparently, in sports, the competitive provision of innovation serves the social purpose, and additional incentive in the form of awards of monopoly power do not serve a useful purpose.

As always, there is an ironic footnote to this triumph of competition: some legal analysts in the United States now argue that the government should enforce patents on sports moves.[21]

Profits without Patents

Patenting is high and growing by historical standards. The number of total U.S. patents granted yearly has increased by 78 percent, to 113,834 between

1983 and 1995, after which it peaked at 187,015 in 2003 to reach the somewhat lower level of 157,717 in 2005, the last year for which data are available. Similar, albeit quantitatively less pronounced, patterns apply to the European Union and Japan. Yet it turns out that businesses do not regard patents as a significant factor in their decisions to innovate. There are two surveys of research and development directors in which this clearly emerges. This first is the Yale Survey taken in 1987, and the second is the Carnegie Survey done in 2000.[22] We focus on the more recent and more detailed Carnegie Survey, but the same facts emerge from the earlier Yale Survey.

The Carnegie Survey reported in 2000 that it received responses from 1,118 firms for product innovations and 1,087 for process innovation. The firms were asked whether particular methods were effective in appropriating the gains from an innovation. The table here shows the percentage of firms indicating that the particular technique was effective. The numbers in parentheses are the corresponding figures for the pharmaceutical and medical equipment industries respectively: these are the two industries in which the highest percentage of respondents indicated that patents are effective.

	Product	Process
Secrecy	51.00% (53.57%, 50.97%)	50.59% (68.13%, 49.24%)
Lead time	52.76% (50.10%, 58.06%)	38.43% (35.52%, 45.15%)
Complementary manufacturing	45.61% (49.39%, 49.25%)	43.00% (44.17%, 49.55%)
Complementary sales/service	42.74% (33.37%, 52.51%)	30.73% (25.21%, 32.12%)
Patents	34.83% (50.20% ,54.70%)	23.30% (36.15%, 34.02%)
Other legal	20.71% (20.82%, 29.03%)	15.39% (16.04%, 22.27%)

This strongly suggests that legal means, including patents, are regarded as the least effective method of appropriating rents. Only about one-third of respondents believed that patents are effective. Secrecy, lead time – the advantage of being first – and complementary manufacturing were rated as the most effective. Indeed, in the case of products, being first is viewed as the most effective means of appropriation. The two exceptional industries, which report a relatively high importance of patents, are the pharmaceutical and medical equipment industries. Indeed, these industries, especially the pharmaceutical industry, are often held up as examples of why it is essential to have patents. Yet even in these industries, only about half the respondents rated patents as an effective means of appropriation. Also striking is that in these industries, other means such as lead time, complementary manufacturing, and secrecy are regarded as about equally effective as in other industries. Hence, while patents are viewed as more effective in these industries, nonlegal means are still quite effective in appropriating rents.

Patent Pools

In addition to sports leagues, there is another significant and widespread example of private companies that voluntarily relinquish "intellectual property." These are the so-called patent pools.[23] A patent pool is an agreement, generally by a number of businesses in the same industry, to share patents. Although it is sometimes the case that when the pool is set up, a company that has few patents will make a payment to a company that has many patents, once the pool is operating, there is no payment among companies for patents. Any patent by any company in the pool is freely available to any other company in the pool. In some cases, patent pools take the form of cross-licensing agreements in which firms agree to automatically cross-license all patents that fall into certain categories.

Despite the apparent communistic nature (no "intellectual property" for the in-group) of these arrangements, patent pools have been widely used.

In the United States, in a number of industries, processes of "collective invention" were implemented by means of patent pools. Note that in some cases, patent pools were created after having experienced phases of slow innovation due to the existence of blocking patents. In the 1870s, producers of Bessemer steel decided to share information on design plants and performances through the Bessemer Association (a patent pool holding control of the essential patents in the production of Bessemer steel). The creation of this patent pool was stimulated by the unsatisfactory innovative performance of the industry under the "pure" patent system regime. In that phase, the control of essential patents by different firms had determined an almost indissoluble technological deadlock. Similar concerns over patent blockages led firms operating in the railway sector to adopt the same expedient of semi-automatic cross-licenses and knowledge sharing.[24]

At the current time, patent pools are generally mandatory for participants in recognized standard-setting organizations such as the International Telecommunication Union and the American National Standards Institute. Large microprocessor corporations, such as IBM, Intel, Xerox, and Hewlett-Packard, engage in extensive cross-licensing. Important computer technologies, including the MPEG-2 movie standard and other elements of DVD technology are part of a patent pool.

Given the widespread willingness of large corporations to voluntarily relinquish patent protection through cross-licensing and patent pools, you might wonder why eliminating patents would even be necessary. Unfortunately, although patent pools eliminate the ill effects of patents within the pool, they leave the outsiders, well, outside. If the existing firms in an industry have a patent pool, then the prospects of a newcomer entering are bleak indeed. So, although patent pools may give a strong indication that patents are not a terribly good idea, and that competition has many benefits, they unfortunately do not undo some of the most important harm of government-enforced monopoly – that of preventing entry into an industry.

In fact, the widespread existence of patent pools in industries with a well-established set of mildly competing insiders is wonderful, simultaneous evidence of two important things. First, patents are inessential to compensating individual firms for the fixed cost of invention. Second, patents are a powerful tool for establishing monopoly power and preventing entry by potential competitors.

Comments

A good, if dated, and relatively succinct survey of the history of technology is in Derry and Williams.[25] A quicker-to-find one is, as usual, the entry "history of technology" in Wikipedia. A classical account of the view that the Industrial Revolution would, at least, have been greatly retarded had patents not been available in England at the end of the eighteenth century can be found in North's book.[26] A recent, and quite balanced, rendition of this point of view is in the book by Gregory Clark,[27] which also contains various other references. One of the many extreme applications of this claim to contemporary issues is a U.N. Economic Commission for Africa report claiming that the Industrial Revolution missed Africa mainly because the latter did not adopt the European system of patents.[28]

Should the curious reader want to embark on a more complete survey of the history of patent laws, the Wikipedia piece on the Statute of Monopolies is as good, and free, starting point as any we know of outside the specialized literature. The technical literature on the life cycle of industries is very large, though still only a few authors seem to have paid attention to the correlation between competition and the degree of technological innovation on the one hand, and between obsolescence and demand for monopolistic restrictions on the other; a paper by Braguinsky, Gabdrakhmanov, and Ohyama[29] is one recent and excellent exception containing references to the few earlier authors that had mentioned aging industries' rent seeking as an explanation of patents and their dynamics.

Notes

1. The statement that the software industry is currently much less innovative than it was at its inception may appear odd to fans of *World of Warcraft* and of "major" innovations such as massive multiplayer online role-playing games (known as MMORPGs). Still, this is the very robust, if controversial, finding of most empirical studies carried out by the experts in this area. Incredulous readers should visit James Bessen's site at http://www.researchoninnovation.org/online.htm for starters, and then continue on with the references therein. Alternatively, all one needs to do is enter "software patents innovations" in Google and then click happily away.

2. Meaning "superior inventors, capable of discovering and finding many ingenious machineries." The text of this first patent is reproduced in many historical books, e.g. Kaufer (2002), p. 5.

3. Price (2006), p. 138; the complete text of the Statute of Monopolies can be found in the appendix to Price (2006).

4. Ibid, p. 135.

5. Stigler (1956), p. 275.

6. Ibid, p. 274. Stigler argues against the Schumpeterian view that monopoly is a good thing because it brings forth innovation. As indicated by the quotations in the text, his view, like ours, is that plentiful innovation occurs under competition.

7. Nuvolari (2004a), p. 354.

8. That Trevithick did not patent his invention is documented in Rowe (1953).

9. The Cornwall mining industry experience is studied in Nuvolari (2004a, 2004b), where data on the fuel efficiency, the "duty," of steam engines can be found. An analogous episode is that of Cleveland's iron producers – Cleveland, United Kingdom, not Ohio – deftly documented and discussed in Allen (1983). Around the middle of the nineteenth century, the iron producers managed to fiercely compete while allowing technical information on the development and improvements of the blast furnace to flow freely from one company to the other. Firms in industries involving iron and coal, apparently, are prone to practicing invention and innovations without patents and intellectual monopoly protection; Adams and Dirlam (1966) tells the story for the big-steel industry post–Second World War.

10. Historical analyses of the agricultural sector before the advent of patenting can be found in McClelland (1997) for the United States, and in Campbell and Overton (1991) for Europe. Detailed studies of the "nineteenth and early twentieth century . . . stream of biological innovations" in U.S. agriculture are, for example, those of Olmstead and Rhode (2002) for grain and cereals, Olmstead and Rhode (2003) for cotton, and Barragan Arce (2005) for fruit trees. Olmstead and Rhode (2003) also document how, in the cotton-farming sector, "inventors, during an early phase of the product cycle, actually encouraged consumers to copy and disseminate their intellectual property."

11. The estimates of agricultural TFP for 1948–2002 are taken from the U.S. Department of Agriculture, Table 1, at http://www.ers.usda.gov/data/agproductivity/ (accessed February 23, 2008).

12. Crop yield data is from the National Agriculture Statistics Service, online at http://www.nass.usda.gov/QuickStats/ (accessed February 23, 2008).

13. The information on patents of corn hybrids is from Urban (2000).

14. More detailed facts concerning Almería are in Costas and Heuvelink (2000). In case you doubt our statement that Almería's horticulture is probably the most efficient agricultural enclave in the world, check out http://edis.ifas.ufl.edu (accessed February 23, 2008). One of the many stories of innovation with imitation and competition we have not told, but that should be told, is that of the extremely successful Taiwanese machine-tool industry, an account of which is in Sonobe, Kawakami, and Otsuka (2003). Quoting only this, though, amounts to doing an injustice to so many others – but even books have limited capacity.

15. The satellite images of Almería are from NASA and are reproduced widely and in color, for example at http://www.iberianature.com (accessed February 23, 2008) or, courtesy of NASA, from http://visibleearth.nasa.gov/ (accessed February 23, 2008).

16. The history of *maglioni* in the Italian Northeast comes mostly from the first-hand experience of one of us; a chronology of Benetton is at www.museedelapub.org.

17. Innovation in the financial industry prior to patents is documented in two papers by Tufano (1989, 2003) and in a recent paper by Herrera and Schroth (2004). A less academic view of the investment banking industry can be found in Lewis (1989). The business-practices patent dates to the 1998 Court of Appeals for the Federal Circuit decision in *State Street Bank v. Signature Financial*. In one of the most dramatic examples of judicial legislation, the court held that there is no prohibition in U.S. law on patents for business methods as long as they are new, useful, and nonobvious. This is mentioned in Ladas and Parry (2003), who also provide a useful summary of key developments in U.S. patent law. The *State Street* case is also discussed at http://www.gigalaw.com (accessed February 23, 2008).

18. Tufano (2003); the quote is from page 7 of the original working paper available on line at the author's site, http://www.people.hbs.edu/ptufano/fininnov_tufano_june2002.pdf (accessed February 23, 2008).

19. The best empirical treatment of the fashion industry is Raustiala and Sprigman (2006), from whom we stole the wonderful photographs of splurge versus steal. The paper contains a great many similar examples and photographs. One of us just came back from a skiing vacation during which he could not help but notice one thing: the skiing industry innovates at a dramatic pace, essentially at the same pace as the fashion industry, and it is, like the latter, de facto free of any kind of effective patent protection. Do not get us wrong: each new gadget or shape or edge cut is duly patented by the firm that gets to the patent office first. Still, every year, the twenty or so companies that produce skis come up with new models and – they are all practically identical! Just think of the various generations of carving skis: can you tell which firm "invented" the idea of a carving ski? If the firm patented it – we could not find evidence either way – it clearly did not matter, as everyone copied it rather quickly. A patent (European Patent EP1208879) apparently sits out there, describing something that may result into a pair of carved skis if you already know what they are, but no one seems to care much. The same story applies to the dozen or so firms competing in the ski-boots sector.

    A theoretical treatment of the fashion cycle can be found in Wolfgang Pesendorfer (1995) whose model is perfectly consistent with competitive creation.

20. Varnedoe (1990).

21. A proposal for patenting sports moves is Kukkonen (1998). Although it may be that sports leagues do not give monopolies for fear that exclusive rights will give one

team too much of an advantage, they can also have optional or mandatory licensing to allow the good ideas to spread.

22. The Yale Survey is described in Levin et al. (1987) and Klevorick et al. (1995). The Carnegie Survey is described in Cohen, Nelson, and Walsh (2000).
23. Most of the information about patent pools is from Shapiro (2001).
24. Nuvolari (2004a), p. 360.
25. Derry and Williams (1960).
26. North (1981).
27. Gregory Clark (2007).
28. See Nwokeaba (2002).
29. Braguinsky, Gabdrakhmanov and Ohyama (2007)

FOUR

The Evil of Intellectual Monopoly

We hope by now to have convinced at least a few among you that there has been, there is, and there would be plentiful innovation in the absence of intellectual monopoly. We took this as our starting point because a widespread disbelief in the ability of competitive markets to reward innovators inhibits thinking about a functioning free market economy without intellectual monopoly.

After establishing that substantial amounts of money can be made, has been made, and is made by innovators in the complete absence of patents and copyright, the next fundamental doubt is, Is that money enough? It is quite a rhetorical question for the thousands of innovators who, absent legal monopoly, have nevertheless innovated: the money they expected to make must have been enough to motivate them. It is not necessarily such a rhetorical question, though, for potential innovators who chose not to innovate and for all those innovators who took advantage of intellectual monopoly in their activity. Because it is true that an innovator can generally earn more with a monopoly than without, so the profits made under competition may not be enough and some socially valuable innovations may not occur under competition. This – in principle – leaves room for government intervention to correct this market failure. Awarding intellectual monopoly is one possible form of intervention. Unfortunately, it is an especially pernicious form.

Economists and decent citizens alike are suspicious of monopoly. There are many good reasons for this. The traditional economic analysis of monopoly emphasizes the welfare triangle – the loss of efficiency due to the fact that monopolies create artificial scarcity to garner a higher price. More recent economic analysis emphasizes x-inefficiency – that monopolies use inefficient and excessively costly methods of production. The political economy literature emphasizes the rent-seeking nature of monopoly, especially of government-mandated monopoly: monopolies distort the political system by purchasing favorite treatment at the expense of everyone else, thereby wasting away a substantial fraction of the social surplus.

There is yet another reason to be wary of monopolies: to transfer wealth away from the rest of society and toward themselves they must prevent entry. The easiest way to achieve this is to stifle innovation. This blocks productivity growth, thereby reducing overall prosperity. It is a different and arguably more pernicious source of social inefficiency than the previous three, as it operates invisibly: how much innovation and productivity growth could have taken place in the software industry if Microsoft had not succeeded in stifling innovation is very hard to imagine, let alone quantify. This form of inefficiency is specific to the kind of monopoly power that patents and copyrights bring about. Being its "discoverers," we will christen it "IP-inefficiency" and illustrate its working by means of a few significant examples. The theory of why IP-efficiency comes about is rather simple: like every profit maximizing entrepreneur, monopolists are willing and able to do anything legally and technically feasible to retain their monopoly profits.

Later in the book, we talk about the Schumpeterian model of dynamic efficiency via creative destruction. This model dreams of a continuous flow of innovation due to new entrants overtaking incumbents and becoming monopolists until new innovators quickly take their place. In this theory, new entrants work like mad to innovate, drawn by the enormous monopoly profits they will make. Our simple observation is that, by the same token, monopolists will also work like mad to retain their enormous monopoly profits. There is one small difference between incumbents and outsiders: the former are bigger, richer, stronger, and much better connected. David may have won once in the far past, but Goliath tends to win a lot more frequently these days. Hence, IP-inefficiency.

Although the current tendency in economics is to argue that the welfare triangle is not large, in the case of innovation this is not always true. The example of AIDS drugs illustrates both the theory and the potential losses. Drugs for AIDS are relatively inexpensive to produce. They are sufficiently inexpensive to produce that the benefits to Africa in lives saved exceed the costs of producing the drugs by orders of magnitude. But the large pharmaceutical companies charge such a large premium over the cost of producing the drugs – to reap profits from sales in Western countries where those drugs are affordable – that African nations and individuals cannot afford them. They create artificial scarcity – excluding Africa from AIDS drugs – to garner a higher price for their product in the United States and Europe. Through "intellectual property" and international "free" trade agreements, they also prevent potential competitors (read: imitators) from entering the African or Latin American markets for such drugs. The welfare triangle – the net loss to society – from this policy is real and enormous. That is IP-inefficiency at work on a global scale.

We understand that the careful reader will react to this argument by thinking, "Well, the AIDS drugs may be cheap to produce now that they have been invented, but their invention did cost a substantial amount of money that drug companies should recover. If they do not sell at a high enough price, they will make losses, and stop doing research to fight AIDS." This argument is correct, theoretically, but not so tight as a matter of fact. To avoid deviating from the main line of argument in this chapter, we simply acknowledge the theoretical relevance of this counterargument and postpone a careful discussion until our penultimate chapter, which is all about pharmaceutical research. For the time being, two caveats should suffice. The key word in the former statement is "enough": how much profit amounts to "enough" profit? The second caveat is a bit longer as it is concerned with price discrimination, and we examine it next.

The example of AIDS drugs brings out another feature of monopolies – their desire to price discriminate. That is, competitors charge the same price to everyone, but monopolies try to extract a higher price from those who value the product more highly. Economists usually argue that this is a good thing because monopoly without price discrimination is even worse than monopoly with price discrimination. Price discrimination, they argue, enables lower-valued consumers to purchase a product that otherwise the monopoly would not sell to them. Relatively speaking – that is, relative to a world where the monopolist does not price discriminate – this is a correct statement. In the case of AIDS drugs, effective price discrimination would enable the large pharmaceutical companies to charge a low price to poor Africans without lowering the price they charge rich Westerners. A more successful example of price discrimination for drugs is the low price charged to poor Canadians against the high price charged to rich Americans.

In practice, however, it is both difficult and costly to price discriminate. Experience suggests that though it is relatively easy to find consumers who highly value a product and are willing to pay a high price, there is not much selling by monopolies at low prices to consumers who are only willing or able to pay a low price. Economic theory suggests two related reasons for this. In anonymous markets, the monopolist has a hard time telling which consumers value its product a lot and which value it little, as the former would pretend to be the latter when given a chance. The second reason, even more straightforward, is that selling to some consumers at a low price creates competition for the monopolist. It creates an incentive to buy at the low price and resell at a medium price that undercuts the high price charged by the monopolist to the highly valued consumers. In the case of Canada and the United States, the lower price charged to Canadians has led to a booming gray market for importing drugs from Canada into the United States – so much so that there have been efforts both to enshrine the right to import cheap Canadian drugs in U.S. law and to make it illegal entirely.

In the case of AIDS drugs, the pharmaceutical companies do not sell to Africa at a steep discount because they are afraid that a parallel market, reselling the cheap African product in the Western market, will undercut their profits. Do not let the pharmaceutical companies' laments confuse you. It is not by selling to the African market at a low price that they would record a loss, to compensate for which they would desperately need the U.S. and European profits. Because the cost of producing a larger quantity of AIDS drugs is very low, the pharmaceutical companies would make a profit also by selling cheaply to the African market. Their problem is the loss of monopoly profits in markets other than the African one. This example is, in fact, quite general: intellectual monopolists often fail to price discriminate because doing so would generate competition from their own consumers.

Effective price discrimination is costly to implement and this cost represents pure waste. For example, music producers love digital rights management (DRM) because it enables them to price discriminate. The reason that DVDs have country codes, for example, is to prevent cheap DVDs sold in one country from being resold in another country where they have a higher price. Yet the effect of DRM is to reduce the usefulness of the product. One of the reasons that the black market in MP3s is not threatened by legal electronic sales is that the unprotected MP3 is a superior product to the DRM-protected legal product. Similarly, producers of computer software sell crippled products to consumers in an effort to price discriminate and preserve their more lucrative corporate market. One consequence of price discrimination by monopolists, especially intellectual monopolists, is that they artificially degrade their products in certain markets so as not to compete with other more lucrative markets.[1]

So, monopoly has many bad consequences. Through a series of case studies, we use this chapter to document some of the more egregious problems in the case of patents. We discuss the problems of copyrights (or "copy-wrongs") in the next chapter.

The Cost of Patent

The second half of the 1990s witnessed an extraordinary increase in the number of new patents registered in the United States, and in the European Union as well. In the United States, the yearly number of patent applications reached about 345,000 by the end of the 1990s, rising more than threefold from a value that had oscillated at around 90,000 during the 1960s. In just four years, between 1997 and 2001, patent applications exploded by a spectacular 50 percent.[2] Part of the radioactive fallout from this explosion in patent applications was the increase in the membership of the "intellectual property" section of the American Bar Association, which went from 5,500 to almost 22,000.[3]

If patents beget prosperity and innovation, we might expect that this explosion in patenting coincided with a vast technological improvement. Of course, it did not. A common measure of technological improvement is the increase in total factor productivity (TFP) – as mentioned in the previous chapter, this measures how much additional output can be produced from a given combination of inputs by using those inputs better. Higher TFP means, for example, more and better cars from the same labor and using other factors such as metal and plastic. Rough-and-ready aggregate measures of TFP growth do not display a strong trend during the past fifty years. They increased during the 1950s and early 1960s, then decreased from the late 1960s until the late 1980s or even early 1990s, and then recovered, slightly, during the 1995–2000 period. After the 2001 recession, the same measures have kept growing at their long-term average. More sophisticated measures of TFP show that, on the one hand, the productivity slowdown in the late 1960s to late 1980s may be nothing but poor measurement on our part, while on the other hand, the 1990s TFP recovery either did not take place or is almost entirely due to the widespread adoption of information technologies. The latter, as we documented in Chapters 2 and 3, owe extremely little if anything to the presence of patents.

Similar findings apply to any member country of the Organization for Economic Co-operation and Development flying in the face of the claim that patents are a good measure of, let alone cause, true improvements in productivity. If they were, TFP should have increased remarkably, and its growth rate should keep increasing in proportion to the continuing increase in the number of patents. Neither happened.

The Patent Thicket

Part of the enormous increase in the number of patents is because patents beget yet other patents to defend against existing patents. The following statement is from Jerry Baker, senior vice president of Oracle Corporation:

Our engineers and patent counsel have advised me that it may be virtually impossible to develop a complicated software product today without infringing numerous broad existing patents.... As a defensive strategy, Oracle has expended substantial money and effort to protect itself by selectively applying for patents which will present the best opportunities for cross-licensing between Oracle and other companies who may allege patent infringement. If such a claimant is also a software developer and marketer, we would hope to be able to use our pending patent applications to cross-license and leave our business unchanged.[4]

Pundits and lawyers call this navigating the patent thickets, and a whole literature, not to speak of a lucrative new profession, has sprung up around it in the past fifteen years. The underlying idea is simple, and frightening at the same time. Thanks to the U.S. Patent and Trademark Office policy of awarding a patent to anyone with a halfway competent lawyer – and, as noted a moment ago, "intellectual property" lawyers have quadrupled – thousands of individuals and firms hold patents on the most disparate kinds of software-writing techniques and lines of code.[5] The numbers are mind-blowing, particularly in the information technology and software sectors: Nokia sits on twelve thousand patents, while Microsoft is adding at least one thousand a month to a mountain that is already more than twenty thousand patents strong, and so on and so forth.[6] As a consequence, it has become almost impossible to develop new software without infringing some patent held by someone else. A software innovator must, therefore, be ready to face legal action by firms or individuals holding patents on some software components. A way of handling such threats is the credible counterthreat of bringing the suitor to court, in turn, for the infringement of some other patent the innovative firm holds.

Do our readers need more evidence of the fact that large corporations are aware that both most of these patents are a social waste and are artificial legal devices in the sense that their number can be increased or decreased arbitrarily by purely legal means having nothing to do with actual innovations? Here you go: Mr. Bruce Sewell, from Intel, is reported as saying, "We have 10,000 patents – it's an awful lot of patents. Would I be happy with 1,000 patents rather than 10,000? Yes, provided the rest of the world did the same thing."[7] Mr. John Kelly (director of IBM's "intellectual property" strategy) points out, "Even though we have 3,000 patents [awarded annually in America] if we had to, I could make that number 10,000."[8] Moreover, how did Microsoft get into the patenting game? Here's the description:

In 2003, Bill Gates . . . faced a number of problems centered around intellectual property. First, the company found it was being sued for patent infringement more often and had to pay hundreds of millions of dollars in damages. Second, antitrust regulators were forcing Microsoft to open its technology to rival to allow different systems to work together. Third, the company recognised that its monopoly on its operating system and desktop software would be eroded over time, in part by open source alternatives, and wanted to delay that process. Lastly, Microsoft was spending around $5 billion a year on R&D and wanted some revenue to help offset that outlay.[9]

This anecdotal evidence is backed by hard data. Lanjouw and Lerner examined a sample of 252 patent suits. They find that their data is consistent with the hypothesis that preliminary injunctive relief is a predatory weapon in patent cases.[10]

This situation is akin to that of the cold war, when we used to hold thousands of expensive nuclear weapons for "defensive purposes." Here, firms are spending vast amounts of money to obtain and hold defensive patents. This leads to an equilibrium that is equally socially bad (because lots of resources are spent to build weapons that should never be used) but desperately more insane than the "threat of mutual assured destruction" was during the cold war. Then, at least, we were trying to protect ourselves from a real and external Communist threat we had not created. In the current defensive patents equilibrium, there is no external threat to our well-being – the threat is entirely one we have created by picking the wrong legislation.

In short, a vast expenditure in defensive patents is entirely a product of our "intellectual property" legislation. By allowing intellectual monopoly, and because the courts and patent office allow more and more outrageous claims, there is an enormous incentive for rent seekers of all kinds and shapes to waste resources in obtaining patents solely to blackmail innovative firms and extract rents from their creative activity. This is exemplified by Panip IP, LLC, a company formed to collect from small businesses using patent claims.[11] Consider the company's proposed interpretation of two patents that it holds:[12]

- U.S. Patent No. 5,576,951: Using graphical or textural information on a video screen for the purpose of making a sale.
- U.S. Patent No. 6,289,319: Accepting information to conduct automatic financial transactions via a telephone line and video screen.

Obviously, the company has contributed nothing of significance to either of these broad activities, but their lack of innovation has not prevented it from threatening numerous small businesses with lawsuits alleging patent infringement. Typically, the company sets the licensing fee sufficiently low so that it is less costly to pay the fee than to go to court.

It is often argued that, especially in the biotechnology and software industries, patents are a good thing for small firms.[13] Without patents, it is argued, small firms would lack any bargaining power and could not even try to challenge the larger incumbents. This argument is fallacious for at least two reasons. First, it does not even consider the most obvious counterfact: How many new firms would enter and innovate if patents were not around, that is, if the dominant firms did not prevent entry by holding patents on pretty much everything that is reasonably doable? For one small firm finding an empty niche in the patent forest, how many have been kept out by the fact that everything they wanted to use or produce was already patented but not licensed?

Second, people who argue that patents are good for small firms do not realize that, because of the patent system, most small firms in these sectors are forced to set themselves up as one-idea companies, aiming only at being purchased by the big incumbent. In other words, the presence of a patent thicket creates an incentive not to compete with the monopolist, but to simply find something valuable to feed it, via a new patent, at the highest possible price, and then get out of the way. Although this may be quite advantageous to the few lucky entrepreneurs who manage to be bought out by the monopolist at a good price, it is not the economic system that we, as a society, should want. It is not beneficial either to consumers, who keep living in a monopolized world paying high prices for crummy products, or to the average potential entrepreneur who, plain and simple, cannot enter and compete. This is IP-inefficiency at work.

If it were not for preventing even the minimum chance of competitive entry in its industry and for keeping all small firms at bay, why would Microsoft waste money applying every year for thousands of patents like No. 20,050,160,457, Annotating Programs for Automatic Summary Generation? Oh, sorry, we did not tell you what this great invention is about; here is the official abstract:[14]

Audio/video programming content is made available to a receiver from a content provider, and meta data is made available to the receiver from a meta data provider. The meta data corresponds to the programming content, and identifies, for each of multiple portions of the programming content, an indicator of a likelihood that the portion is an exciting portion of the content. In one implementation, the meta data includes probabilities that segments of a baseball program are exciting, and is generated by analyzing the audio data of the baseball program for both excited speech and baseball hits. The meta data can then be used to generate a summary for the baseball program.

Unfortunately, political and judiciary attitudes have shifted toward the use of patents as monopolist's tools. Oscillations in popularity are somewhat recurrent in the history of patents, but never before have the proponents of intellectual monopoly been so powerful in the political and judicial arena and in public discourse. By way of contrast, in the late 1970s, antitrust suits were fought and won against monopolists, and as late as 1997, the Justice Department spoke of the possible role of "intellectual property" in antitrust violations. Private companies also sued large monopolies sitting upon piles of unused inventions, such as in *Xerox v. 3Com*.[15] Today, sadly, the three branches of government have given up the fight against appropriating the fruits of other people's labor and the defensive patenting it begets.[16]

In addition to asking about the incentive to innovate, which we discussed in the previous chapter, the Carnegie Survey also examined why firms do and do not choose to patent, as the subsequent table shows.[17] The use of patents in negotiations and horse-trading among firms is higher (but not overwhelmingly higher) in complex industries than in simple ones.

	Product	Process
Measure performance	5.75%	5.04%
Licensing revenue	28.27%	23.25%
Use in negotiations	47.38%	39.96%
Prevent suits	58.77%	46.50%
Prevent copying	95.81%	77.61%
Blocking	81.81%	63.58%
Enhance reputation	47.91%	34.03%

Examining the table, we see an average rating of 88 percent to prevent copying or to block competitors, which may be loosely translated as "being a monopolist." We see an average rating of 53 percent for patents being used for negotiations or to prevent suits, which may be loosely translated as "wasteful rent seeking." This effort is not directed at innovation but is used as a legal and bargaining tool. The economically valuable uses of patents according to standard pro–intellectual property theories – that is, measuring performances and obtaining licensing revenues – are a meager 17 percent. If one recognizes, as we argue, that revenues from licenses are in large part due to wasteful monopoly power, the Carnegie Survey tells us that patents are employed for economically valuable uses only about 6 percent of the time.

There are other indications of the abuse of the patent system for legalistic reasons. The *Polaroid v. Kodak* settlement is widely credited as an important signal of the value of defensive patenting.[18] It is unclear what it is that society gained from that settlement, as all it did was restore monopoly in a relatively important consumer market and bring almost to bankruptcy an otherwise thriving company, Kodak. With the windfall payment it received, Polaroid neither created new innovations nor new employment and value-added; it just enriched its lawyers, its executives, and, albeit marginally, its shareholders. Similarly, we have the following statement from Roger Smith of IBM:

The IBM patent portfolio gains us the freedom to do what we need to do through cross-licensing – it gives us access to the inventions of others that are key to rapid innovation. Access is far more valuable to IBM than the fees it receives from its 9,000 active patents. There's no direct calculation of this value, but it's many times larger than the fee income, perhaps an order of magnitude larger.[19]

This recognizes that patents are just a trading tool among "big players." Instead of a competitive market for innovations, we have an oligopolistic market for patents structured around the patent-pool mechanism we discussed in the previous chapter. This use of cross-licensing of patents is not merely the innocuous sharing among existing firms in the industry. Nor, as Bessen points out, are patent pools merely a good tool for navigating the patent thicket. They are also a wonderful instrument for preventing new firms from entering the industry. New firms, not having a portfolio of defensive patents, and not participating in the patent pool, find that they cannot legally compete with the existing oligopoly.

Using Patents to Block Competition
First off, patents and "intellectual property" more generally are, by definition, aimed at blocking competition, as their main aim is to prevent others from competing with the innovator by producing the same thing either a little more cheaply or of a little better quality. Although this is trivial, and we have repeated it ad nauseam, it is good to keep the idea in mind. Now, let us move to the less obvious ways in which patents are strategically used to block competition.[20]

The idea, widely advertised in business courses and management textbooks, that cross-licensing, patent pools, and patents more generally can be used to block entry and enhance collusion has not escaped the notice of firms. Following the increased enforcement of the antitrust laws after the Second World War, the chemical and petrochemical industries pioneered the use of patent law as a legal method to collude and block entry. As the number of possible examples is long, and the general principle is rather clear, we will be brief. Here are some samples:

Both American Telephone and Telegraph and General Electric, for example, expanded their in-house laboratories in response to the intensified competitive pressure that resulted from the expiration of key patents. . . . Patents also enabled some firms to retain market power without running afoul of antitrust law. The 1911 consent decree settling the federal government's antitrust suit against GE left their patent licensing scheme largely untouched, allowing the firm considerable latitude in setting the terms and conditions of sales of lamps produced by its licensees, and maintaining an effective cartel within the U.S. electric lamp market. . . . Patent licensing provided a basis for the participation by GE and DuPont in the international cartels of the interwar chemical and electrical equipment industries. U.S. participants in these international market-sharing agreements took pains to arrange their international agreements as patent licensing schemes, arguing that exclusive license arrangements and restrictions on the commercial exploitation of patents would not run afoul of U.S. antitrust laws.[21]

In recent years, there have been innovative efforts to expand the use of patents to block competitors. For example, we find the following:

A federal trade agency might impose $13 million in sanctions against a New Jersey company that rebuilds used disposable cameras made by the Fuji Photo Film Company and sells them without brand names at a discount. Fuji said yesterday that the International Trade Commission found that the Jazz Photo Corporation infringed Fuji's patent rights by taking used Fuji cameras and refurbishing them for resale. The agency said Jazz sold more that 25 million cameras since August 2001 in violation of a 1999 order to stop and will consider sanctions. Fuji, based in Tokyo, has been fighting makers of rebuilt cameras for seven years. Jazz takes used shells of disposable cameras, puts in new film and batteries and then sells them. Jazz's founder, Jack Benun, said the company would appeal. "It's unbelievable that the recycling of two plastic pieces developed into such a long case." Mr. Benun said. "There's a benefit to the customer. The prices have come down over the years. And recycling is a good program. Our friends at Fuji do not like it."[22]

Once again, examples abound and we could go on forever, so let us close with a particularly important one. We mention later in this chapter how the Wright brothers used their patents to try to block the emergence of a U.S. aircraft industry. Interestingly, this pattern of behavior continued. In 1972, the U.S. government charged the aircraft industry with an antitrust violation, basically because it kept using its patent pool and cross-licensing to prevent entry. That is IP-inefficiency at its best.

Seeds, Animals, and Genes

A recent "innovation" in patent law has been the enormous expansion in the types of "ideas" that can be patented. A case in point is the patenting of plants and animals. We have previously examined how innovations in the agriculture sector were frequent and abundant, in the complete absence of any kind of patent protection, until the early 1970s. Plainly speaking, agriculture evolved, during a period of about 12,000 years, in the complete absence of patent protection. During these 120 centuries, agricultural productivity increased by a few orders of magnitude, making it possible to feed an enormously larger world population. Then, about thirty-five years ago, the U.S. Congress intervened.

The U.S. Plant Variety Protection Act (PVPA) of 1970 was the first step toward the complete "oligopolization" of the agriculture sector, first in the United States, then in the European Union, and more recently around the world. It allowed for a limited patent protection of sexually reproducing plants and animals. Alas, the appetite of potential monopolists is never satiated. Full protection came in the Supreme Court ruling of June 16, 1980, in the *Diamond v. Chakrabarty* case.[23] The case concerned the patentability of an oil slick–consuming bacterium that had been bioengineered by Ananda Chakrabarty, a biochemist working for General Electric. It extended the full protection of patent law to all kinds of engineered or engineerable products of nature, be they alive or not. The final nail in the coffin was set in 1985, when the U.S. Patent Office Board of Appeals ruled that sexually propagated seeds, plants, and cultured tissue could be protected by utility patents. Sadly, we read that this act seems to have done little for innovation:

The PVPA appears to have contributed to increases in public expenditures on wheat variety improvement, but private-sector investment in wheat breeding does not appear to have increased. Moreover, econometric analyses indicate that the PVPA has not caused any increase in experimental or commercial wheat yields. However, the share of U.S. wheat acreage sown to private varieties has increased – from 3 percent in 1970 to 30 percent in the 1990s. These findings indicate that the PVPA has served primarily as a marketing tool.[24]

This is not the odd conclusion of some antiglobalization green group. No, it is the practically unanimous verdict reached by an army of agricultural economists who have analyzed the socioeconomic impact of that tombstone of free competition known as the Plant Variety *Protection* Act. The word "protection" is most ironic, as in the hand of a few monopolistic and, unfortunately, mostly U.S.-based multinationals, this bill has become the single most dangerous tool against plant variety protection. We could go on for the rest of the book talking about this subject, which is of utmost importance for the future of not just hundreds of millions of farmers in developing countries, but also of us, the mostly nonfarmers living in developed countries. Still, this would take as too far astray from the IP-inefficiency topic that is the concern of this chapter; hence, we stop here.

Back to economic development. The agricultural sector is a small fraction of national income both in the United States and in the European Union, between 3 percent and 10 percent, depending on the country. As we already documented in the previous chapter, there is no evidence in the data that this enormous increase in patent protection lead to any measurable increase in the growth rate of TFP in the U.S. agricultural sector. But the tentacles of IP-inefficiency reach far outside national borders. In poor and developing countries, the share of agriculture in national income is an order of magnitude greater than in the United States, and its strategic role for future development is absolutely crucial. It is for these countries that agricultural patents are a deadly blow, as they manage to do two harms at once. On the one hand, by making new seeds and animal species prohibitively expensive, agricultural patents render farmers from poor countries unable to compete in the global agricultural market. One may wonder why this affects poor farmers more than rich ones, and the answer is trivial: credit constraints. New seeds are, on average, more efficient than traditional ones, but they also require a much higher up-front investment to be purchased. Because they cannot finance initial purchases of efficient seeds, poor farmers use less efficient ones, which means that the break-even price at which they can sell their products is higher, thereby making them uncompetitive. On the other hand, by monopolizing seeds and species that are and have been for centuries in the public domain, agricultural patents rob the same poor farmers of their capital.

The history of economic development, and of agricultural development in particular, is a history of imitation: catching up takes place because followers imitate the more advanced techniques of the leader. If a small group of companies from the leading countries prevent and prohibit imitation by monopolizing agricultural innovations around the globe, imitation and adoption of advanced techniques and seeds are retarded or altogether blocked. Furthermore, subtly and unjustly, this small group of monopolistic companies is slowly but surely expropriating the agricultural wealth of many developing countries. How? By taking traditional seeds and plants that have been grown and selected there for centuries, modifying/improving them genetically to a more or less relevant extent, and then grabbing a patent as broad as possible. Modified varieties are usually stronger or have a superior yield than the original variety, thereby displacing the latter quite rapidly. When this does not work fast enough, the broad patent is used, supported by an army of "intellectual property" lawyers and the "diplomatic" weight of the U.S. government, to claim property rights on the original varieties.

This sounds like one of those multinational conspiracy stories favored by lunatics and antimarket (but copyright-protected) snobs attending Parisian art shows while sipping patented California Chardonnay. Some stories of course are exaggerations, but many are both true and well documented. One such story is the example of Basmati rice.

The battle over who controls the world's food supplies has escalated dramatically with the Indian government launching a legal challenge in the United States against an American company which has been granted a patent on the world-renowned basmati rice. It is thought to be the first time a government in a developing country has challenged an attempt by a US company to patent – and thus control the production of – staple food and crops in what campaigners dub the "rush for green gold." Basmati rice, sought-after for its fragrant taste, was developed by Indian farmers over hundreds of years, but the Texan company RiceTec obtained a patent for a cross-breed with American long-grain rice. RiceTec was granted the patent on the basis of aroma, elongation of the grain on cooking and chalkiness. However, the Indian government last week filed 50,000 pages of scientific evidence to the US Patents and Trademarks Office, insisting that most high quality basmati varieties already possess these characteristics. The US Patent and Trademarks office accepted the petition and will re-examine its legitimacy. The patent – granted only in the [United States] – gives RiceTec control over basmati rice production in North America. Farmers have to pay a fee to grow the rice and are not allowed to plant the seeds to grow the following year's crops. India fears the patent will severely damage exports from its own farmers to the [United States]. In 1998, they exported almost 600,000 tonnes of basmati rice.[25]

Another surprising example of American intellectual over-reach is in – not so surprising – Iraq:

The American Administrator of [Iraq] Paul Bremer, updated Iraq's intellectual property law to "meet current internationally-recognized standards of protection." The updated law makes saving seeds for next year's harvest, practiced by 97% of Iraqi farmers in 2002, the standard farming practice for thousands of years across human civilizations, newly illegal. Instead, farmers will have to obtain a yearly license for genetically modified seeds from American corporations. These GM seeds have typically been modified from IP developed over thousands of generations by indigenous farmers like the Iraqis, shared freely like agricultural "open source." Other IP provisions for technology in the law further integrate Iraq into the American IP economy.[26]

The old Communists like Lenin used to argue that monopolistic capital breeds war because it needs the support of the imperialistic state to acquire new markets and grab economic resources. As a theory of wars and as an argument in favor of socialism, this is as dumb as it gets. It does no good to either capitalism or democracy, though, to have rent-seeking monopolists and their lawyers make dumb theories look reasonable to the alienated masses of poor people by following dumb policies.

Undoing Progress

Design

The "everything is patentable" virus seems to have also struck in the business of architectural design. The federal judges in the U.S. Court of Appeals for the Federal Circuit have never seen a competitive industry with lively innovation that they could not "improve" by allotting a little monopoly power here and there, and they recognize no judicial restraint on their ability to impose judge-made law. Certainly, they appear always ready to rule in favor of anyone who claims that their intellectual "property" has been violated by someone else's commercial success. Sadly, their conceit has penetrated also to the lower courts.

So it is that, as we write on August 10, 2005, Judge Michael B. Mukasey has ruled that there are enough similarities between David M. Child's 2003 design for the Freedom Tower to be erected at Ground Zero in New York City and a 1999 architectural student's project such that the student, Thomas Shine, may sue the architect.[27] Mukasey ruled that observers "may find that the Freedom Tower's twisting shape and undulating diamond-shaped facade make it substantially similar to Olympic Tower [the student's project at Yale School of Architecture], and therefore an improper appropriation" of copyrighted artistic expression. Never mind that, as he also pointed out, it is "possible, even likely, that some ordinary observers might not find the two towers to be substantially similar," and that Child's final project for the Freedom Tower will not make use of the so-called diagrid design that is here being debated (which, in case you live in Chicago, you can admire on the John Hancock building.) Never mind also that "in the late 1990's – around the time Shine was at Yale – there was a virtual tidal wave of twisting tower projects."[28]

Imagine, if you will, the same judicial logic applied to, say, the Modernista design patterns of Barcelona's Quadrat d'Or, or to the Renaissance buildings of Rome and Florence, or to the Doric column or to any other column's design for that matter. Imagine the city of Venice or the government of Egypt bringing Las Vegas hotels to court because their buildings imitate similar buildings in Venice, or Egypt, or Paris for that matter, as in Las Vegas we now have an imitation of the Eiffel Tower as well. Imagine the owners of eighteenth- or nineteenth-century Mediterranean-style villas in Naples or the Côte d'Azur suing the Hollywood "stars" for the blatant imitation of the originals in which they live, which they can afford only because of their copyright-induced monopoly rents! Oh, how sweet *that* would be. It seems to us that rather than releasing a string of judicial decisions into competitive industries – largely benefiting patent lawyers, litigation lawyers, and rent seekers with no inherent ties to industry creativity – common sense should prevail here.

Software

We have previously observed that, for a long time, the software industry was free of patent protection. The long-standing tradition of free competition and lack of intellectual monopoly began to crumble in 1981, with the Supreme Court decision in *Diamond v. Diehr,* and collapsed completely with the publication of new examination guidelines by the U.S. Patent and Trademark Office in 1996, which made computer programs fully and clearly patentable. This change in the property-rights regime in the software industry was relatively fast; it constitutes, therefore, an interesting case study to test competing hypothesis on the determinants of patents and their impact on productivity. After carrying out a careful econometric analysis of the microeconomic evidence from the software industry, Bessen and Hunt reach three interesting conclusions. The first is that the shift in legal standards for patenting software was a potent incentive to increase expenditure in patents. It may, in fact, be one of the key factors behind the dramatic increase in the number of patents we reported earlier in this chapter. As we noted, the increase in the number of patents in the U.S. economy was not accompanied or followed by an equally visible increase in TFP or in any other economic measure of effective innovation and productivity. The second finding by Bessen and Hunt supports and reinforces this assertion:

Thus, our analysis appears to decisively reject the incentive hypothesis during the 1990s. Software patents may have complemented R&D during the early [19]80s – when patenting standards were still relatively high – but they substituted for R&D during the 1990s. Regulatory changes increased the amount of patenting, but they are also associated with lower R&D. We can reject naïve arguments that more patents, relaxed standards, or lower patenting costs lead to more R&D.[29]

Notice, in particular, that patenting is found to be a substitute for research and development, leading to a reduction of innovation. In the authors' calculation, innovative activity in the software industry would have been about 15 percent higher in the absence of patent protection for new software. Finally, and most interestingly in our view, Bessen and Hunt point out that one of the channels through which relaxed patenting criteria and a judicial system more prone to entertain claims of patent infringement, negatively affect innovative activity is by increasing the risk of the return on innovations. Stephen P. Fox, associate general counsel and director of Hewlett-Packard highlights that "pervasive uncertainty about legal rights, both in terms of ability to enforce one's own patents and ability to avoid rapidly escalating exposures to infringement claims by others. And that uncertainty heightens risks surrounding innovation investment decisions."[30]

According to Cecil D. Quillen Jr., former general counsel at Eastman Kodak:

> If the uncertainties are such that you cannot be confident that your products are free and clear of others' patents you will not commercialize them, or a higher return will be demanded if you do to compensate for the additional risk. And this probably means you will not do the R&D that might lead to low return (or no return) products.[31]

Submarine Patents

A particularly egregious method of patent abuse is the submarine patent. Until recently, the length of patent term was measured from the time at which the patent was awarded; prior to the award, the existence of the patent is secret, and it is possible to continually defer the award of the patent by filing amendments. Although the patent term was measured from the date of award, prior art and the validity of the patent are measured from the day of submission. Hence, the submarine patent – the filing of a useless patent on a broad idea that might, one day, be useful. The existence of the filing is secret (thus, the term "submarine"), and the application process is dragged out until some actual innovator invests the time and effort to make the idea useful. At that time, the amendment filing stops, the patent is awarded, and the submarine surfaces to demand license fees.

This form of legal blackmail was pioneered by George Selden, who patented the idea of a "road engine" in 1895. He first applied for a patent in 1879 and used all possible legal means to delay approval for sixteen years. This took place while the American automobile industry was developing and the technology of the road engine was being widely adopted and improved. Once Selden's patent, No. 549,160, was awarded, it commanded royalties of 1.25 percent on the sale value of every automobile sold in the United States. Selden's monopoly power had a dramatic impact on the future of the U.S. automobile industry; it lead, de facto, to its reorganization under a much more oligopolistic structure than at the time Selden acquired its patent. We learn the following from Stuart Graham's doctoral dissertation chapter:

Selden had sold his patent 549,160 in 1899 to a syndicate for $10,000 and 20% of any royalties. Early manufacturers who had originally seen the Selden patent as a threat formed a cartel around the patent, the Association of Licensed Automobile Manufacturers, which limited membership and licenses to manufacture under the Selden patent.[32]

So, if you were wondering why the U.S. automobile industry developed so quickly into the oligopoly we know and hate, a fair share of the roots lie in bad "intellectual property" legislation and the intellectual monopoly it created.

In more recent days, Jerome Lemelson, who patented the "idea" of machine vision and related data-identification techniques, has probably matched Selden in this dubious ranking. Bringing lawsuits eighteen to thirty-nine years after initially filing for patents, it is estimated that Lemelson's submarines collected on the order of $1.5 billion, primarily by suing large end users such as Motorola and Ford. Although this is not an example of IP-inefficiency, the Lemelson case and hundreds of less-known ones are worth reflecting upon as a strange and socially inefficient consequence of our patent laws.

Jerome Lemelson was most certainly a man of genius and quite dedicated to his lifelong task of being an inventor. Anyone surfing the Web and reading about his career on the hundreds of sites celebrating his genius will realize that Lemelson invented and successfully patented dozens of interesting devices and ideas. The problem is that he invented them only "so to speak," so that where the patent applications may have run hundreds of pages, the useful information was quite generic and there is little evidence that the ideas contained in them led to useful devices. Most of the ideas or devices he invented never made it to the market, and those that did were developed by someone else – as far as we can tell, without having benefited from the original patented idea. Lemelson contented himself with either selling his patents to producers interested in that line of business or suing them, when someone else who was somewhere else, most often unaware of Lemelson's discovery and patent, was producing a useful tool that could more or less be related to the preexisting Lemelson patent. The issue here is not the often-debated issue of whether Lemelson was or was not in good faith making the claims he made. The issue is that what matters for social welfare are copies of ideas, that is, ideas that materialize into goods and services that are produced and that people use. Hence, Lemelson's contribution to social welfare was small, or even negative, as he cost at least $1.5 billions to firms that were inventing by themselves and then producing goods and services useful to consumers.[33]

Submarine patents are an especially egregious problem because by the time the claim is made, the cost of development is sunk, so there is no reason for the submarine to allow the innovator even to cover his or her own costs. The most recent extension of the patent term from seventeen to twenty years measures the patent term from date of application rather than date of award, which makes submarine patents more difficult. But as the case of Rambus shows, submarine patents are still a significant social problem.

Rambus is a "fabless" manufacturer of memory chips, meaning that it does not actually manufacture chips but designs them, and sublets the actual manufacture to other companies that have the large expensive "fabs" needed to produce chips. More recently, as its own designs have not turned out to be terribly successful, Rambus has switched to a new business model: trying to collect license fees from other chip makers that have successful designs. In the early 1990s, Rambus patented a number of memory chip–related ideas. The most significant among these was the "idea" of including on-chip phase-lock-loop (PLL) circuitry to control timing. It should be noted that PLL circuitry was already widely used to control timing on processor chips.

What happened next, according to the Federal Trade Commission (FTC), is a classic case of a submarine:

Rambus's anticompetitive scheme involved participating in the work of an industry standard-setting organization, known as JEDEC, without making it known to JEDEC or to its members that Rambus was actively working to develop, and did in fact possess, a patent and several pending patent applications that involved specific technologies proposed for and ultimately adopted in the relevant standards. By concealing this information – in violation of JEDEC's own operating rules and procedures – and through other bad-faith, deceptive conduct, Rambus purposefully sought to and did convey to JEDEC the materially false and misleading impression that it possessed no relevant intellectual property rights. Rambus's anticompetitive scheme further entailed perfecting its patent rights over these same technologies and then, once the standards had become widely adopted within the DRAM industry, enforcing such patents worldwide against companies manufacturing memory products in compliance with the standards.[34]

This hijacking of an industry standard is at once very profitable and socially costly. There are generally many similar designs for computer circuitry, and compatibility is often more important than the specific implementation. If, however, an "intellectual property" claim can be made against a standard after it has been implemented, the claimant can free ride on the "network externality" that arises because it is expensive to switch to a different standard.

In the end, the FTC charged Rambus with fraud. Although a lower court found that Rambus did indeed engage in fraudulent behavior, an appeals court subsequently overturned this decision. It now appears that all memory-chip makers – and consumers of memory chips – will have to pay an "intellectual monopoly tax" to Rambus, which contributed little of substance to the design of the memory chips that are to be taxed.

An indication of patent abuse is patents that are never used by the patentee or licensed. Such patents do not represent useful ideas, but are fishing expeditions, representing the hope that someone else will invest the time and effort to produce a commercially useful idea sufficiently related to the original so that royalties can be collected. Indeed, it is estimated that 40 percent to 90 percent of issued patents are not used or licensed by the patentee. One specific example: in 1991, Minolta was ordered to pay Honeywell $127.5 million in damages after a court ruled that Minolta had infringed Honeywell's autofocus camera patent. Yet it was also established that Honeywell was not actually using the idea.[35]

The Dilbert Factor

Monopoly has many costs. Some, like loss of social surplus and rent seeking, have been extensively studied by economists. A less well-known cost is that not all innovators and managers are the clever, intelligent individuals usually assumed in economic theory. In the history of innovation, examples abound of innovators who, far from maximizing their monopoly profits, have achieved closer to the minimum.

One exceptional example of innovators playing with a less than full deck is that of the Wright brothers. Despite their own rather modest contribution to the development of the airplane, in 1906, the Wright brothers managed to obtain a patent covering (in their view) virtually anything resembling an airplane. The application had been filed much earlier, meaning that between March 1903 and May 1906 they were capable of building an airplane or teaching other people how to do it, but they did not. Further, even after the patent was granted, rather than take advantage of their legal monopoly by developing, promoting, and selling the airplane, the Wright brothers kept it under wraps, refusing for a couple of more years to show it to prospective purchasers. However, while refusing to devote any effort to selling their own airplane, they did invest an enormous amount of effort in legal actions to prevent others, such as Glenn Curtiss, from selling airplanes. Fortunately for the history of aviation, the Wright brothers had little legal clout in France, where airplane development began in earnest about 1907.[36]

Another case in point takes place in England, also before the First World War. At that time, the Badische Chemical held a patent covering practically all chemical-based textile-coloring products. Levinstein and Co. developed a new and superior process to deliver the same product. Badische Chemical sued and obtained a court restraint, preventing Levinstein from using the new process to obtain the old product. Did Badische take advantage of this legal victory to introduce the new and superior process in its own business? No. In fact, Badische was apparently unable to figure out how the new process worked, and so did not make use of it. Levinstein, on the other hand, moved to the Netherlands, where the patent was not enforced. Badische was less fortunate, as competition from Levinstein eventually put the company out of business.[37]

Lest one take away the lesson that narrow-mindedness was prevalent among monopolists only prior to the First World War, because we know many monopolists today who aren't so circumscribed in their thinking, we draw attention to the recent behavior of the recording industry. The single most important innovation in the movie industry has been the videotape – today about 45 percent of all industry revenue is derived from the sale of recordings, and though the videotape is gone, current video-recording devices all evolved from that basic idea: record movies so that they can be watched at home. Far from embracing this lucrative new technology when it first appeared, the movie industry fought a long and costly legal battle against it. Shortly after Sony introduced the Betamax, Universal and Disney filed suit. Fortunately for them, when the court ruled in 1979, it ruled against them. Foolish to the end, Universal appealed the decision, and was "rewarded" in 1981 by an appellate court decision, overruling the original decision. After further speedy actions by the court system, the U.S. Supreme Court in 1984 finally reversed the appellate decision, finding that, as had the original court, "time-shifting" – that is, recording a program to watch later – constitutes fair use.

The music industry, in the form of the Recording Industry Association of America (RIAA), has also engaged in a series of legal blunders. In 1998, RIAA filed a lawsuit against a small, relatively unknown company, Diamond Multimedia Systems. Diamond's crime? It was engaged in selling a portable electronic device capable of playing music in a compressed format not widely known at that time – the MP3 format. RIAA not only managed to lose the lawsuit, but the attendant publicity was an important factor in popularizing the format among consumers. As newspapers gave the case enormous coverage, music aficionados rushed to their computers to convert their inconvenient old CDs into convenient MP3 collections.[38]

The massive conversion of CDs is largely responsible for the next chapter in the sad saga of the RIAA – the peer-to-peer network. With the advent of Napster in 1999, music lovers discovered that, especially with the advent of broadband connections, MP3-formatted songs could be conveniently shared over the Internet. RIAA lawyers sued Napster. The lawsuit did little to prevent the spread of the technology – though it may have helped publicize it. Court filings indicate that at that time Napster had fewer than 500,000 users. By mid-2000, driven by the enormous publicity over the case, Napster reported nearly 38 million users worldwide. By 2001, RIAA prevailed on appeal, and an injunction against Napster began the effective shutdown of the network. By 2002, Napster declared bankruptcy.[39] So effective has this shutdown been that it is now estimated that in the United States alone, there are more than 40 million people sharing files using peer-to-peer networks. [40]

"Being a monopolist" is, apparently, akin to going on drugs or joining some strange religious sect. It seems to lead to complete loss of any sense of what profitable opportunities are and of how free markets function. Monopolists, apparently, can conceive of only one way of making money, and that is by bullying consumers and competitors to put up and shut up. Furthermore, it also appears to mean that past mistakes have to be repeated at a larger, and ever more ridiculous, scale. Consider the ongoing controversy over the Google Print project, which is now relabeled Google Book Search and is fighting to survive the legal obstacles we summarize next. The Authors Guild filed a lawsuit about two years ago trying to stop the project; in the lawsuit, it accuses Google of violating fair use and of infringing upon its copyrights. Trying to prevent the very damaging effect that the lawsuits could have on its overall finances (Google has become a very rich company, in recent times), Google seems to be caving in to all kinds of incredible requests, modifying the Book Search product accordingly. Anyone who has used it both in 2004 and 2006 can appreciate the difference. The original Google Print was a wonderful tool for bibliographic research that made us purchase very many useful books; the current Google Book Search is an emasculated and frustrating program whose social value and marketability are unclear, to say the least.

Now, what did Google Print plan to do? It planned to scan all books in a number of large university libraries around the world and to allow people to search their content via the Internet in the usual "Google style." Once an item is searched and results are found, Google Print would have allowed the user to see about one or two paragraphs, sometime a few pages, from the scanned book in which the item is mentioned or referred. It would also have linked users to various sites where they could easily purchase the book.

That is all. Instead of spending hours going to the library trying to find out which books discuss the Dilbert factor, one can just enter "Dilbert factor" at http://books.google.com and find that dozens of interesting books discuss it.[41] On Google Book Search, one can, for example, find amusing little texts such as *When Did Ignorance Become a Point of View*, by Scott Adams, and purchase it from one of the many online bookstores linked to the same page, as we just did. Why? Partly to compensate the Authors Guild for the dramatic loss of revenue that our book will cause them, and partly because one of us got interested by Adams's proposal of a new way of making presidents of powerful countries accountable to their own people when using their mighty military power. Alternatively, one can avoid spending money purchasing bad books, such as *After the Y2K Fireworks*, by Bhuvan Unhelkar, reading one page of which was enough to convince us that there is more than one way to contribute to human understanding of the Dilbert factor. Finally, you may search Google Book Search for "Authors Guild" and spend an afternoon browsing tons of interesting books suggesting that it was once a society run by smart people and not a shill for Disney.

One can hardly think of a better advertising-cum-shopping tool for books. This service is to be offered, absolutely free of charge, to authors and publishers alike. Still, not to allow the motion picture industry to out-perform it in monopolistic blindness, the Authors Guild has sued and the publishers' lobby followed soon after.[42]

We have no reason to think that monopoly makes people unusually incompetent and hateful of others. So, the reader may wonder: why are incompetent monopolists more dangerous than, say, incompetent ham-burger flippers? Simply put, competition tends to weed out the incompetent. Beyond this, a relatively simple mathematical result known as Jensen's inequality shows that whereas one in ten firms in an industry run by an incompetent is short-term amusement for the rest of the industry, one in ten industries run by an incompetent is a social catastrophe.

Errors in Patenting

A man "has a right to use his knife to cut his meat, a fork to hold it; may a patentee take from him the right to combine their use on the same subject?" – Thomas Jefferson[43]

The private sector has no monopoly on time-wasting. Government bureau-crats are notorious for their inefficiency. The U.S. Patent Office is no excep-tion. Its incompetence increases the cost of getting patents, but this is a small effect, and, perhaps a good thing rather than a bad thing. It also issues many patents of dubious merit. Because the legal presumption is that a patent is legitimate unless proved otherwise, this is a substantial legal advantage to the patent holder, who may use it for blackmail or other purposes. Moreover, although some bad patents may be turned down, an obvious strategy is simply to file a great many bad patents in hopes that a few will get through. Here is a sampling of some of the ideas the U.S. Patent Office thought worthy of patenting in recent years.[44]

- U.S. Patent No. 6,080,436: refreshening bread in a toaster operating between 2,500°F and 4,500°F.
- U.S. Patent No. 6,004,596: the sealed, crustless peanut butter and jelly sandwich.
- U.S. Patent No. 5,616,089: "A method of putting features the golfer's dominant hand so that the golfer can improve control over putting speed and direction."
- U.S. Patent No. 6,368,227: "A method of swing on a swing is disclosed, in which a user positioned on a standard swing suspended by two chains from a substantially horizontal tree branch induces side to side motion by pulling alternately on one chain and then the other."
- U.S. Patent No. 6,219,045, from the press release by Worlds.com: "[The patent was awarded] for its scalable 3D server technology . . . [by] the United States Patent Office. The Company believes the patent may apply to currently, in use, multi-user games, e-Commerce, web design, advertising and entertainment areas of the Internet."[45] This is a refreshing admission that instead of inventing something new, Worlds.com simply patented something already widely used.
- U.S. Patent No. 6,025,810: "The present invention takes a transmission of energy, and instead of sending it through normal time and space, it pokes a small hole into another dimension, thus, sending the energy through a place which allows transmission of energy to exceed the speed of light." The mirror image of patenting stuff already in use: patent stuff that can't possibly work.

Comments

This chapter used to be much longer and was crammed full of additional examples of the patent system gone crazy. We decided to cut many of them, as we felt that readers did not need to be overwhelmed with horror stories to see the general point. Two of the expunged stories, though, are particularly amusing and one of us cannot resist the temptation to at least provide two quick additional examples. A very recent one has to do with a patent covering the idea of having breakfast by mixing various kinds of cereals and milk.[46] The second is much older and convoluted: to learn how the use and abuse of patents affected the improvement of that classical transportation tool called the bicycle.[47]

Notes

1. Intellectual monopolists are quite aware that their interest requires selling restricted products that are less useful for consumers, which is why they perceive the "darknet" – on which you and I can trade the things we purchase – as a major threat. Biddle et al. (n.d.) clearly, if unwillingly, documents this.
2. Detailed data on patents applications, approvals, country of origin, and so on and so forth are available online, for the period 1963–2005, at the site of the U.S. Patent and Trademark Office, at http://www.uspto.gov.
3. That in the 1990s the number of intellectual property lawyers grew even more than the number of patents is a very bad sign for all of us, we learned from an address by Richard Posner to the American Enterprise Institute, November 19, 2002. We read it at http://www.techlawjournal.com/intelpro/20021119.asp (accessed February 4, 2005).
4. Quoted in Bessen (2003), p. 1. Jerry Baker's statement was made at the U.S. Patent and Trademark Office (1994) hearings.
5. We inferred the "halfway competent" assessment about lawyers from the official approval rates for patent applications, which is at http://www.uspto.gov/web/offices/ac/ido/oeip/taf/us_stat.pdf (accessed February 24, 2008). Since the early 1960s, roughly 50 percent of applications are granted. Percentages are even higher for particular kinds of applications, such as those for designs and plants (see http://www.thestandard.com/article/0,1902,20543,00.html accessed February 24. 2008).
6. Much of the discussion of patents in the software industry is drawn from Bessen (2003) and Bessen and Hunt (2003), who give detailed references to the original judicial, legal, and factual sources.
7. *The Economist* (2005).
8. Ibid.
9. Ibid. In the same issue of that celebrated magazine we can find the story of Qual-Comm, the prototypical "IP company," the paean of which is sung so beautifully and in such revealing terms that we cannot help quoting, extensively, from pp. 8–9 of the previously mentioned special survey:

    Qualcomm created a technology called CDMA, which now forms the basis of third-generation wireless networks. Around one third of the company's revenues (and 60% of its profits) come from royalties on all equipment that uses the technology; the remainder comes from selling the chips that rely on that intellectual property, where it has a market share of over 80%. Because its technology underlies the third-generation mobile-phone standard, Qualcomm has become a toll bridge that all equipment-makers must cross.... The licensing practice began when Qualcomm was young and struggling in the early 1990s, helping its cashflow. At first, the company made the mobile phones as well as developing the underlying technology, but in 1999 it sold its handset division in order to focus on the less tangible – and more lucrative – part of the business. Today it spends almost $1 billion a year, or 19% of revenue, on R&D. . . . In August [2005] Qualcomm paid $600m for Flarion, a firm with little revenue but around 100 patents either issued or pending on a new generation of wireless technology. If all goes as planned, this will allow Qualcomm to dominate the next phase of high-speed mobile communications too.

10. Lanjouw and Lerner (1996).
11. The story of Panip IP is well documented in the press. See, for example, Pofeldt (2003).
12. Details of particular patent applications can be found at the U.S. Patent and Trademark Office Web site by entering the particular patent number, or by using Google Patent Search.
13. Two studies arguing that patents are good for small firms are Gans, Hsu, and Stern (2000) and Mann (2004). The first is particularly interesting, as it proves what we argue, only it reverses the value judgment; that is, it claims that competition is due to inefficiencies in the market for ideas. The authors call the cross-licensing between innovators and incumbents aimed at maintaining monopoly pricing for the cooperators "cooperative commercialization strategy," and conclude the following: "While a cooperative commercialization strategy forestalls the costs of competition in the product market and avoids duplicative investments in sunk assets, imperfections in the "market for ideas" may lead innovators to instead pursue a competitive strategy in the product market. . . . [F]irms who control intellectual property or are associated with venture capital financing are more likely to pursue a cooperative strategy" (p. 30).
    Notice what this says: IP facilitates collusive behavior and the persistence of monopoly. Competition and "creative destruction" come along only when IP rights are weak or nonexistent. To which we say, "Exactly, Sherlock."
14. Online at http://www.freepatentsonline.com/20050160457.html (accessed February 24, 2008).
15. The Federal Circuit Court Opinion in this case can be found at http://www.ll. georgetown.edu/federal/judicial/fed/opinions/00opinions/00-1464.html (accessed February 24, 2008).
16. For the views of the Justice Department on the relation between antitrust and intellectual property see Klein (1997). Also in 1997, Xerox sued 3Com, maker of the PalmPilot, over the "graffiti" handwriting recognition system. The Xerox patent covered the "idea" of using a variation on the Latin alphabet to aid the computer in recognizing the difference between different letters. Needless to say, Xerox never put the idea to any good use, and the Xerox "invention" does not seem to have assisted 3Com in any material way in designing a useful working system.
17. The Carnegie Survey is described in Cohen et al. (2000).
18. Polaroid Corp. v. Eastman Kodak Co., 866 F.2d 1415, 9 USPQ2d 1877 (Fed. Cir. 1989).
19. Quoted in Bessen (2003), p. 2.
20. Gilbert and Newbery (1982) develop a theoretical analysis of how and why strong patent protection makes monopolists' preemption of competitive entry viable and,

indeed, profitable. They conclude: "Indeed, a perfect market for R&D inputs [i.e., complete IP enforcement] gives the monopolist a credible threat that it would overtake any rival undertaking a competitive research program, which reduces the cost of preemption to nil and makes the preservation of his monopoly costless and hence doubly attractive" (p. 524).

This paper was written in the late 1970s, before the current IP craze began, and before the special Court of Appeals for the Federal Circuit was established, by the lobbying of IP lawyers, to handle IP cases. Its content, including its optimistic predictions that this kind of preemptive activity may not become socially too damaging because of the high cost of enforcing IP, sadly reads today as an unheard alert against the social losses that increasing legal and judicial IP protection was bound to bring on us.

21. Mowery and Rosenberg (1998), pp. 18–19. See also the original Mowery (1990).
22. *The New York Times*, August 3, 2004, Business Section.
23. Information about *Diamond v. Chakrabarty* and its implication for the patentability of biotechnology products is widely available on the Web. One possible starting point among many is Urban (2000). Two other judicial rulings that were instrumental in the process of extending patents to the agricultural and biotechnological sector are *Ex parte Hibbert* in 1985 and *Ex parte Allan* in 1987.
24. Alston and Venner (2000), Abstract. For a classical study of the diffusion of agricultural innovation in the US in the period before the PVPA bill made it a big monopolies feast, the technically inclined reader should consult Griliches (1957), who beautifully documents competitive innovation at work. The many sweeping statements we have made, here and in the previous chapter, in relation to the agricultural sector and the irrelevance of patents for its technological development, are based on the scientific research reported in Butler and Marion (1985), Campbell and Overton (1991), Griliches (1960), Kloppenburg (1988), McClelland (1997), among others.
25. June 25, 2000, article, available at http://www.biotech-info.net/basmati_patent.html (accessed February 24, 2008). Additional detailed information about the Basmati rice patent is widespread on the Internet. For example, http://www.american.edu/TED/basmati.htm (accessed February 24. 2008), reports detailed, precise information about this and a dozen other cases.
26. Slashdot, http://politics.slashdot.org/article.pl?sid=04/11/13/2023220 (accessed February 24, 2008). The story about the Provisional Authority imposing agricultural IP on Iraq farmers is also widely documented elsewhere.
27. The copyright lawsuit over the Freedom Tower is discussed in Sadeghi (2004).
28. The discussion and quotations are from "Suit Claiming Similarities in Tower Design Can Proceed" *New York Times* Region Section, August 11, 2005.
29. Bessen and Hunt (2003), p. 25. James Bessen, formerly an electronic publishing innovator, has become during the past few years a prolific researcher on the theme of software patents, with a particular attention to the empirical aspects of the problem. A number of other interesting papers, beside those we quote here, can be found at his site, http://www.researchoninnovation.org, and a substantial amount of technical news is at the blog Technological Innovation and Intellectual Property, found at http://www.researchoninnovation.org/WordPress/, which he edits.

    For more fun with software patents go to the site by the same name, at swpat. ffii.org/patents/effects/index.en.html, which defines itself as a "Collection of news stories and case studies showing how the granting, licensing and litigation of patents is affecting players in the software field." It makes for an entertaining and very educational reading.

30. Fox (2002), p. 2.
31. Quoted in Bessen and Hunt (2003), p. 27. Consistently similar arguments can be found in his writings and presentations collected at http://www. researchoninnovation.org/quillen/quillen.htm.
32. Graham (2002), p. 1. This valuable, if technical, dissertation is the source for our story of Selden and the cartelization of the American automobile industry. Graham also looks at the "strategic" usage of the continuation patent during the 1975–94 period. To make a long story short, "continuation" consists of a set of legal tricks, all supported by current legislation, allowing you to keep secrecy and make your patent last longer at the same time; a kind of "Duracell monopoly." It will certainly not surprise you that, since the middle 1980s, the share of continuation patents has been increasing rapidly and steadily.
33. A good discussion of Jerome Lemelson and his submarine patents is in Perelman (2002), but plenty of information can be found online by just entering the name in Google and following the links. Most sites are grossly apologetic, but they report the facts, and the facts speak by themselves.
34. From the FTC complaint, FTC (2002), p. 2. The story of Rambus is drawn from that complaint, available at http://www.ftc.gov/opa/2002/06/rambus.shtm (accessed Feburary 24, 2008).
35. The outcome of *Honeywell v. Minolta* was widely reported. See, for example, Mallory (1992).
36. The Wright's brothers patent can be found online at http://invention.psychology. msstate.edu/i/Wrights/WrightUSPatent/WrightPatent.html (accessed February 24, 2008). The story of Glenn Curtiss and the Wright brothers is from Shulman (2003). The evidence suggests that Curtiss not only contributed far more to airplane design than did the Wright brothers but also was far less inclined to use patents as a tool against competitors.
37. The story of Levinstein and Badische Chemical, together with the demise of the British coloring industry, is discussed by Penrose (1951), p. 106, and Gardner (1981), Chapter 28. See also http://www.colorantshistory.org/BritishDyestuffs.html.
38. Information about the *Diamond* lawsuit can be found at http://www.wired.com/ news/business/0,1367,16586,00.html (accessed February 24, 2008).
39. For information about Napster, go to http://www.grammy.aol.com/features/0130_naptimeline.html (accessed October 31, 2006).
40. The figure of 40 million current users is from http://www.usatoday.com/tech/ webguide/internetlife/2002–10-14-p2p-swapping_x.htm (accessed February 24, 2008).
41. If a search on Google Book Search does not bring you the information on Dilbert you crave, try visiting Dilbert's Web site, at http://www.unitedmedia.com/comics/ dilbert/ (accessed February 24, 2008).
42. The story of the Google Print project, its unfortunate transformation into the Google Book Search project, and the legal battles we mention are easily traceable at – well, Google Search, what else?
43. When we started writing this book, arguing that patents and copyright are bad for our economic system was thought to be a radical-fringe position. No longer.

Mainstream media, from the *New York Times* to the *Wall Street Journal,* from *Fortune* to *BusinessWeek,* are reporting regularly about the evident damages the patent epidemic is causing our free market economy. The irresistible, and more relevant than ever, quote from Jefferson we found in a *BusinessWeek* article (dated January 9, 2006) on yet another case of submarine patent affecting the car industry, the title of which was, in fact, "The Patent Epidemic."

44. In case our short list of insane patents amused you, and you need more of them for your weekend barbecue with friends, Jaffe and Lerner (2005) is a good source.
45. http://www.worlds.net/news/PressReleases/prn054.html (accessed April 30, 2006).
46. See http://freeculture.org/cereal/ (accessed February 24, 2008).
47. See http://velonews.com/news/fea/7550.0.html (accessed February 24, 2008).

FIVE

The Devil in Disney

Patents threaten our economic prosperity, we have argued, because of the many evils of monopoly and especially because of the evil we call IP-inefficiency. Copyright seems less threatening. Enriching without reason a few actors, singers, or book writers is not as bad as letting millions of people die because some monopolist is not producing enough anti-AIDS pills. The copyright industry itself is economically insignificant. The entire motion picture and recording industry has fewer employees than the IBM Corporation. If we consider all employment in copyright-connected industries, we find that industries such as fabricated metal production and transportation equipment manufacturing employ substantially more workers – the "copyright" industry is about on par with the furniture industry in terms of economic importance.[1]

In important respects, copyright law seems less threatening than patents. Although the length of copyright is excessively long, the scope of coverage historically has been narrow: in principle, only the expression of ideas is covered, not the ideas themselves. Again, in principle, this is less harmful to the downstream production of new ideas and the expression of ideas than is the much broader protection offered by patents. Certainly, in practice, if I want to write a Harry Potter–like book about child sorcerers I am free to do so. On the other hand, over time, copyright has grown in scope: I am not free to write a sequel in the Harry Potter series. In some respects, copyright increases competition, encouraging the production of similar but different works. From a social perspective, however, it may well be better to improve existing works rather than to create redundant similar works.

Despite the fact that copyright may seem to lack economic importance, in a classic case of the tail wagging the dog, the copyright industry manages to threaten our freedom and our culture. Copyrights are at least as inefficient, insulting, and unjust as patents are. They are as inefficient as patents, because it is painfully obvious from theory, historical facts, and current data that we would lose scarcely an iota of artistic and cultural productions if copyright were completely and instantaneously abolished. They are more insulting than patents, because the repeated retroactive extensions of copyright terms pushed by the Disney Corporation make a mockery – or a Mickey Mouse, if you like – of the U.S. Constitution's allowance of "limited times" for patents and copyrights. They are as unjust as patents, because the wealth of copyright-protected media stars cries in the face of the embarrassing quality of their products and their support for such causes as fighting pharmaceutical monopolies over AIDS drugs.

Everlasting Copyright

When we left the U.S. publishing industry, despite the limited copyright for U.S. authors, it was a thriving competitive environment. As is so often the case, the story has a sad continuation when the original innovators grew into fat, stagnant monopolists:

A critical shift in the political balance occurred in the 1880s as the older American publishing houses on the east coast began to see their profits eroding in the face of a new generation of mass penny-press publishers, expanding especially in the midwestern states, who undercut their costs and reached yet wider markets. In the face of this challenge the older houses reshaped their business strategies and their arguments about intellectual property. They now realized that they would be better positioned than the new generation of publishers to sign exclusive copyright agreements with foreign authors that would be enforceable within the United States. The signing of the Berne Convention in Europe in 1886 added further momentum to a shift in the views of major publishing houses like Harper's and Scribner, who recognized the advantage of the movement for American adherence to some form of international agreement, at least with England. American theologians, including the Reverend Isaac Funk, now denounced the "national sin of literary piracy" (which had allowed him to make his fortune on his pirated "Life of Jesus") as a violation of the seventh commandment. And their voices resounded on the floor of Congress. Although Congress refused to sign the Berne Convention on the grounds that American law did not recognize authors' natural rights, in 1891 an international agreement with England for reciprocal copyright protection was finally signed by Congress.[2]

This was the beginning of the everlasting expansion and increase in copyright. The monopolists put further screws to the public with another major revision of the U.S. Copyright Act in 1909. This broadened the scope of categories protected to include all works of authorship. The copyright term had been fourteen years with a possible renewal of fourteen years until 1831, when it was extended to twenty-eight years plus a fourteen-year renewal. The 1909 act further extended the renewal period to twenty-eight years. Today, the length of copyright term is ninety-five years for works for hire, and the life of the author plus seventy years otherwise. In addition to these increases in the length of copyright term, media lobbyists have succeeded in recent years in enormously increasing the penalties for copyright violations, now a criminal as well as a civil offense. Additional laws are being pushed, ranging from mandating hardware protection in general-purpose computing equipment – something we will later describe as a policy blunder – to allowing large media corporations to hack into computers without legal liability, which could better be described as criminal insanity.

We might well begin by asking how well the 1909 revision of copyright worked. Did it increase the rate at which books and other copyrightable new products were produced in the United States? Apparently not. Even abstracting from the general increase in literacy over the century, the increase in the registrations of literary works per population ratio is miniscule in the forty years following the 1909 act as shown in the table below.[3]

Year	Registrations/Population
1900	0.13%
1925	0.14%
1950	0.14%

Is this exceptional? No, it is not. Scherer's work on eighteenth- and nineteenth-century classical music, showed that the adoption of copyright did not increase and possibly reduced the output of classical music composers. Moreover, beginning in 1919, the length of copyright has been continually extended. At the turn of the century, it was twenty-eight years and could be extended for another fourteen. Prior to the Sonny Bono/Mickey Mouse Act of 1998, it was seventy-five years for works for hire, and the life of the author plus fifty years otherwise, its last major extension having been approved in 1976. So, the length of copyright term roughly doubled during the course of the century. If this approximate doubling of the length of copyright encouraged the production of additional literary works, we would expect that the per-capita number of literary works registered would have gone up. Here we present a graph of the number of literary copyrights per capita registered in the United States in the last century.[4] Apparently, economic theory works, whereas the theory according to which extending copyright terms boosts creativity in the long run does not. The various copyright extensions have not led to an increase in the output of literary work.

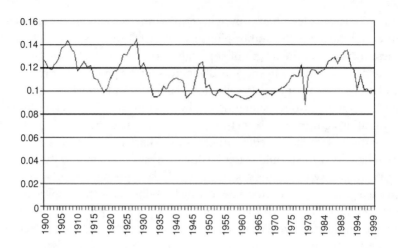

While vigorously defending their "property," the big media corporations are busily grabbing yours. The most recent copyright extension, the Sonny Bono Copyright Term Extension Act of 1998 (CTEA), is the biggest land grab in history. This remarkable piece of legislation extended the term of copyright not only by twenty years for new works but also retroactively to existing works. Copyright increased a hefty 40 percent in one quick legislative shot. Now, consider any normal economic activity, say, the amount of effort you put in your daily work. Try to imagine what would happen if your hourly wage went up substantially overnight. Our bet is that you would put a lot more effort in your work, and your company would witness a productivity explosion taking place at your desk. Did anyone notice an explosion of artistic and cultural creations in the United States during the past ten years? Did artists, writers, and musicians begin to migrate in flocks from everywhere else in the world to the United States, to reap the fantastic benefits of the CTEA? Strangely, if this amazing development took place, both the mainstream media and the underground media seemed to have missed it.

How is it possible that an extension of copyright terms by 40 percent could have zero impact on artistic production? The answer is simple, and you probably have already figured it out: those extra years come far in the future during the life of an author; hence, their economic value for the author is very small. In fact, a calculation in a legal brief prepared by a number of distinguished economists, including several with Nobel prizes, shows that, as far as living artists are concerned, those extra years are equivalent to increasing their expected revenues of a hefty 0.33 percent. As they explain:

The twenty years of copyright term added by the CTEA provide a flow of additional benefits that is very far into the future, and hence very small in present value. To illustrate, suppose that an author writes a book and lives for thirty more years. In this case, under the pre-CTEA copyright regime, the author or his assignee would receive royalties for eighty years. If the interest rate is 7%, each dollar of royalties from year eighty has a present value of $0.0045. Under the CTEA, this same author will receive royalties for one hundred years. Each dollar of royalties from year one hundred has a present value of $0.0012. In this example, the present value of total additional revenues under the CTEA can be calculated by adding up the present values of revenues from year eighty-one through year one hundred. Suppose that the work produces a constant stream of revenues, and assume once again that the interest rate is 7%. In this case, the present value of the total return from years eighty-one to one hundred is 0.33% of the present value from years one to eighty. Put differently, under these assumptions, the additional compensation provided by the CTEA amounts to a 0.33% increase in present-value payments to the author, compared to compensation without the twenty-year term extension.[5]

The question is, then, Why all this fuss over a bill that increased revenues for artists by just 0.33 percent? Why bother legislating if that is all that was achieved? And why are the European countries currently discussing a similar proposal of extending copyright term from fifty to about ninety years? We must have gone through all this trouble to make someone better off, right? Because living artists and creators are not the designated beneficiaries of such bounty and consumers of copyrighted products are not either, *Qui prodest*?

Those additional years are far in the future only if you are a living artist or creator. But imagine that you are a large media company that owns the copyright over some very lucrative character, or song, or movie produced long, long ago by a great artist who is now dead. This creation has been yielding huge royalties for many decades, a largesse you have grown accustomed to. Once the copyright expires, though, the flow of dollars will stop – making it difficult for the executives to pretend that the company is efficient and profitable and that they are highly creative professionals deserving every penny of the superstar salaries and bonuses the shareholders have become accustomed to approve. Once the copyright expires, these superstar executives may even have to work to try to produce new music, movies, and comic characters. Hence, investing a portion of that huge flow of dollars in lobbying the U.S. Congress is a wonderful investment.

Because both economic logic and the U.S. Constitution encourage copyright only to the extent that it promotes the production of literary and other copyrightable works, the rent-seeking nature of this kind of proposals is pretty self-explanatory. Extending the length of copyright for works that have already been produced can scarcely make them more likely to be produced. The goal of this legislation is, of course, not to increase creativity. What it means is that all the books, music, and movies that you purchased with your hard-earned money, and that you would have owned outright when the copyright expired, will instead continue to be owned by the big media corporations.

The U.S. Constitution allows copyright only for limited times, and then only to promote the progress of science and the useful arts, and the retroactive extension clearly violates both of these provisions. After the CTEA was passed, it was challenged in court on these constitutional grounds (in *Eldred v. Ashcroft*). Surprising to some, justices who have argued that they take the literal meaning of the Constitution seriously ruled that a limited time is in fact an unlimited time. During the lawsuit, interesting information about the social cost of the copyright extension emerged.

Some numbers will put this change in context. Between 1923 and 1942, there were approximately 3,350,000 copyright registrations. Approximately 425,000 (13%) of these were renewed. The Congressional Research Service (CRS) estimated that of these, only 18%, or approximately 77,000 copyrights, would constitute surviving works that continue to earn a royalty. The annual royalties for one segment of those surviving works, books, music, and film . . . will be, CRS estimates, approximately $317,000,000. . . . [B]ecause of CTEA, the public will both have to pay an additional $317 million annually in royalties for the approximately 50,000 surviving works, and be denied the benefits of those and 375,000 other creative works passing into the public domain in the first 20 years alone. (Today, the proportions would be far more significant, since there is no renewal requirement that moves over 85% of the works copyrighted into the public domain. Under current law, 3.35 million works would be blocked to protect 77,000.)[6]

Most of the arguments for retroactive copyright extension during the course of the congressional hearings were along the lines that offspring of great artists, such as Geroge Gershwin, were incapable of earning a living except by hawking the works of their great predecessor.[7] The only intellectual argument offered was that works under copyright will be more widely available than those that are not. From a theoretical point of view, this is a strange argument, because monopolies do not profit by making things more widely available.

Strange arguments abounded during the debate over the CTEA. An often-used one was that the U.S. media and entertainment industry needed the extension to keep up with the European one (never mind that the same companies are monopolizing both sides of the Atlantic Ocean), which had just obtained or was on the verge of obtaining such extension from various national parliaments. The argument is strange for many reasons, but one stands out: eight years later, the same media monopolists are wildly lobbying the European Parliament and the European Commission to extend copyright protection in Europe from fifty to ninety-five years – to keep up with U.S. legislation!

Forgive the digression, and let us go back to the theoretical argument saying that works under copyright will be more widely available than those that are not. We see no reason to limit ourselves to the theory. Edgar Rice Burroughs, the well-known author of *Tarzan*, wrote a number of lesser-known pulp fiction series. Depending on the dates, some are still under copyright, some not, so we can determine which are more widely available. The data in the subsequent table was gathered on September 3, 2002; it shows pretty clearly that a work being out of copyright is often more widely available, and in many more forms.[8] In case the very natural suspicion that we selected the work of Burroughs because it is one of the few that fits our viewpoint comes to your mind, we invite you to take advantage of the power of the Internet and repeat the same exercise with your preferred "on the fence" (of copyright term) author. If you find one for which the pro-copyright extension theory works, let us know. Contrary to the pro-copyright lobby, we value facts quite a bit.

Mars series out of copyright	Mars series under copyright	Venus series under copyright
#1 *A Princess of Mars* (1912) Available on Amazon.com, electronic version, original magazine version, illustrated HTML version.	#6 *The Master Mind of Mars* (1928) Out of print	#1 *Pirates of Venus* (1934) Available on Amazon.
#2 *The Gods of Mars* (1914) Available on Amazon.com, electronic version, original magazine version, illustrated HTML version	#7 *A Fighting Man of Mars* (1930) Out of print	#2 *Lost on Venus* (1935) Out of print
#3 *The Warlord of Mars* (1918) Available on Amazon.com, electronic version, original magazine version, illustrated HTML version	#8 *Swords of Mars* (1936) Out of print	#3 *Carson of Venus* (1939) Out of print
#4 *Thuvia, Maid of Mars* (1920) Available on Amazon.com, electronic version	#9 *Synthetic Men of Mars* (1940) Out of print	#4 *Escape on Venus* (1946) Out of print
#5 *The Chessmen of Mars* (1922) Available on Amazon, electronic version	#10 *Llana of Gathol* (1948) Out of print	#5 *The Wizard of Venus* (1963) Out of print

Why is it that old literary and musical works that are out of copyright are often more widely available than works of roughly the similar quality and age that are still copyrighted? This is a case study of IP-inefficiency that explains why we asserted before that the CTEA is the biggest land grab in history. To understand the underlying economic mechanism, one only needs to ask, Why did Disney and the big media corporations lobby so strenuously for the CTEA? The simple answer is this: because the copyright term of *a* few very successful titles was due to expire.

There was obviously no interest in reissuing the tens of thousands of books, movies, and music pieces produced during the previous fifty years, which had discrete success at the time, faded away from the top-seller list, and are now out of print and impossible to purchase. Many of these products of creativity are valuable artistic pieces that have a discrete but small demand, too small to be profitable for media giants. They may be an attractive product for small publishers or music companies, they may be valuable inputs for new artists and creators who could find in them inspiration for additional works, but they are not worth the effort or reissue for the likes of Disney corporation. Worse, reissuing a substantial portion of these titles would "crowd out" current products that the same media giants are heavily marketing. Hence, thanks to the CTEA extension, these tens of thousands of titles will remain copyrighted by the companies that originally acquired them, but they will not be made available to the public. This effect will be compounded by the phenomenon of orphan works, that is, works for which it is difficult or impossible to contact the copyright holder but that, as a result of the extension, are still legally copyrighted. Monopolists maximize profits by restricting supply, elementary economics teaches us, and a simple way to restrict supply of artistic work is to make sure that not too many equivalent western movies, adventure novels, comic novels, symphonic pieces, and so on, are available for purchase at any given point in time.

There lies IP-inefficiency and the gigantic land grab. Because of the way in which the law works, copyright extension must apply *erga omnes* (or "to everyone"), and not only to the few selected titles Disney cares about. So, to retain copyright protection on the few eternal hits – three hundred at most and a few dozen more likely – tens of thousands of works of human creativity have been kidnapped and will not be released to the public.

Wait a second, you might say, if a small publisher can make money by publishing the old classic for the market niche interested in it, why do you argue that the big publisher will not? Answer: because for the big publisher the old classic is more valuable unpublished than published! The cheap paperback version of a sixty-year-old spy story would, to some degree, reduce demand for the expensive hardback version of a brand-new spy story. So, the private value to, say, Eldred, of the old spy story is less than the private value of the very same story to, say, Random House. The latter would ask $100 to sell the rights, whereas the former would be able to only pay $90 and break even. Conclusion: the old spy story will remain out of print. To put it bluntly, after kidnapping, with the help of Congress and the Supreme Court, all the artistic creations of the past fifty years, the monopolistic kidnappers may well set the ransom too high for us, the public, to get them released. Talk about promoting the progress of science and useful arts!

The Economics of Music

The RIAA produces propaganda ranging from white papers to videos arguing that technological change makes it necessary for the government to intervene to prevent the "piracy" that is killing the industry. Certainly musicians should profit from their creations. But in the current system, does the money from the copyright monopoly go to the musicians, or to the seven major producers that act as intermediary and gatekeeper? Courtney Love, a musician, reports the following:

This story is about a bidding-war band that gets a huge deal with a 20 percent royalty rate and a million-dollar advance. (No bidding-war band ever got a 20 percent royalty, but whatever.) ... They spend half a million to record their album. That leaves the band with $500,000. They pay $100,000 to their manager for 20 percent commission. They pay $25,000 each to their lawyer and business manager. That leaves $350,000 for the four band members to split. After $170,000 in taxes, there's $180,000 left. That comes out to $45,000 per person. That's $45,000 to live on for a year until the record gets released. The record is a big hit and sells a million copies. So, this band releases two singles and makes two videos. The two videos cost a million dollars to make and 50 percent of the video production costs are recouped out of the band's royalties. The band gets $200,000 in tour support, which is 100 percent recoupable. The record company spends $300,000 on independent radio promotion ... which are charged to the band. Since the original million-dollar advance is also recoupable, the band owes $2 million to the record company. If all of the million records are sold at full price with no discounts or record clubs, the band earns $2 million in royalties, since their 20 percent royalty works out to $2 a record.[9]

The stylized story told here is important. With modern Internet distribution and laptop computer "recording studios," the cost of producing music is quite low. So, the allegedly large fixed cost to be recouped via monopoly profits is not due to the actual economic cost of producing and distributing the music, which modern technology has cut to a fraction of what it used to be. The large fixed cost that needs to be recouped via monopoly profits seems to be due to the very existence of the system of copyright and the large monopolies thriving on it. From there come the legal, agency, and marketing costs contemporary monopolized music faces, and passes on to consumers.

There is a second important fact buried in this story, indeed a fact most of us already know but that is often forgotten: in this case, the "successful" professional musicians are earning only about $45,000 per year from their CD sales, that is to say: from that portion of their activity that is protected by intellectual monopoly. Most likely they are earning about the same or more from live concerts, which are not protected by intellectual monopoly and do not benefit from it either. When creative effort takes place and yet the reward it collects via the "intellectual property" system is minor, the case for intellectual monopoly is weak. Evidently rock musicians do not need the prospect of multimillion dollar contracts to perform and record their music. Further, because they are satisfied with expected gross incomes from recording in the range of $100,000 to $150,000 thousand a year, evidently their opportunity cost of recording, as opposed to doing something else, is not all that high. Again, this substantially weakens the case for intellectual monopoly.

Indeed, with modern computers there are a great many creative innova-tors – lacking perhaps the physical skills and training to play an instrument, or even to read sheet music – who could modify, edit, and create great new music on their home computers at trivial cost. The greatest bar to this outpouring of wonderful new innovative music – if you haven't guessed already – is the copyright system itself. We cannot create great new music by modifying wonderful old music because all the wonderful old music is under copyright at least until the twenty-second century. If we were to abolish copyright today, we are confident that the most important effect would be a vast increase in the quantity and quality of music available.

Examples of individual creativity abound. An astounding example of the impact of copyright law on individual creativity is the story of the documentary *Tarnation*.

Tarnation, a powerful autobiographical documentary by director Jonathan Caou-ette, has been one of the surprise hits of the Cannes Film Festival – despite cost-ing just $218 (£124) to make. After Tarnation screened for the second time in Cannes, Caouette – its director, editor and main character – stood up.... A Texan child whose mother was in shock therapy, Caouette, 31, was abused in foster care and saw his mother's condition worsen as a result of her "treatment." He began filming himself and his family aged 11, and created movie fantasies as an escape. For *Tarnation*, he has spliced his home movie footage together to create a moving and uncomfortable self-portrait. And using a home computer with basic editing software, Caouette did it all for a fraction of the price of a Hollywood blockbuster like Troy. . . . As for the budget, which has attracted as much attention as the subject matter, Caouette said he had added up how much he spent on video tapes – plus a set of angel wings – over the years. But the total spent will rise to about $400,000 (£230,000), he said, once rights for music and video clips he used to illustrate a mood or era have been paid for.[10]

Yes, you read this right. If he did not have to pay the copyright royalties for the short clips he used, Caouette's movie would have cost a thousand times less.

This brings us to what the RIAA and the debate over "intellectual property" is all about. It is not about the right to the fruits of one's own labor. It is not about the incentive to create, innovate, or improve. It is about the "right" to preserve an existing way of doing business. In this, we agree with Robert Heinlein's fictitious judge:

There has grown up in the minds of certain groups in this country the notion that because a man or corporation has made a profit out of the public for a number of years, the government and the courts are charged with the duty of guaranteeing such profit in the future, even in the face of changing circumstances and contrary to public interest. This strange doctrine is not supported by statute or common law. Neither individuals nor corporations have any right to come into court and ask that the clock of history be stopped, or turned back.[11]

The business model that copyright has created not only is inefficient and unjust but is also corrupt. Naturally, every industry has its scandals, and competitive firms are not necessarily run by angels. The fact is, though, that monopoly power breeds bad habits, and nowhere more than in the music industry has corruption become essential and endemic. You have probably heard of "payola," a contraction of the words "pay" and "Pianola." It refers to the traditional payment of cash or gifts in exchange for airplay of music selections on the radio. The first payola case to be brought to court dates back to May 1960, when disc jockey Alan Freed was indicted for accepting $2,500 to play some tunes; he was fined and released. Forty-five years later, it is no longer a matter of small-time radio disc jockeys and symbolic fines. On July 26, 2005, New York Attorney General Eliot Spitzer (then the elected governor of New York State) indicted Sony BMG for bribing radio stations on a large and systematic scale to play the tunes Sony BMG wants to promote.

Sony BMG, apparently, has agreed to pay a $10 million settlement. How does corporate monopolist payola work? Here is a description, posted on the Web quite a while before Spitzer's indictment of Sony BMG:

There are ways around the laws. The newest one it to make a song an ad. Here is an example. The D.J. announces something like "Here is Avril Lavigne's Don't Tell Me, presented by Arista Records." That announcement makes the paid-for song an advertisement, and technically not a violation of any laws against payola. During just one week in May, WQZQ FM in Nashville played that song 109 times. On a single Sunday, WQZQ played that song 18 times, with as few as 11 minutes between airings of it. Garett Michaels, program director of San Diego rock station KBZT has said, "Basically, the radio station isn't playing a song because they believe in it. They're playing it because they're being paid." This is payola plain and simple. According to an article by Jeff Leeds of the Los Angeles Times, all five major record corporations have at least dabbled in the sales programs, industry sources said, with some reportedly paying as much as $60,000 in advertising fees to promote a single song.... Nothing has really changed. If you want your song played on the radio, you better cough up dough, and a lot of it. Once you stop paying, your song will be dropped from play lists.... It is yet another corrupt practice of the recording and radio industries that we are angry about. It exploits artists and shortchanges fans, but more than that, it is a waste, especially when there is another method of promotion that works just as well, if not better, and is free: File trading networks. To paraphrase today's youth: radio is old and busted, file trading is the new hotness.[12]

The Digital Millennium Copyright Act

The latest outrage of the large media corporations has been the Digital Millennium Copyright Act of 1998 (DMCA).[13] This resulted from a heavy lobbying effort in which these large corporations claimed, as usual, that they must run twice as fast just to stand still – and in particular that digital media, from which they earned no revenue at all twenty years earlier, are especially prone to "piracy."

The most offensive feature of the DMCA is section 1201, the anticircumvention provision. This makes it a criminal offense to reverse-engineer or decrypt copyrighted material, or to distribute tools that make it possible to do so. On July 27, 2001, Russian cryptographer Dmitri Sklyarov had the dubious honor of being the first person imprisoned under the DMCA. Arrested while giving a seminar publicizing cryptographic weaknesses in Adobe's Acrobat e-book format, Sklyarov was eventually acquitted on December 17, 2002.

The DMCA has had a chilling effect on both freedom of speech, and on cryptographic research. The Electronic Frontier Foundation reports on the case of Edward Felten and his Princeton team of researchers:

In September 2000, a multi-industry group known as the Secure Digital Music Initiative (SDMI) issued a public challenge encouraging skilled technologists to try to defeat certain watermarking technologies intended to protect digital music. Princeton Professor Edward Felten and a team of researchers at Princeton, Rice, and Xerox took up the challenge and succeeded in removing the watermarks.

When the team tried to present their results at an academic conference, however, SDMI representatives threatened the researchers with liability under the DMCA. The threat letter was also delivered to the researchers employers and the conference organizers. After extensive discussions with counsel, the researchers grudgingly withdrew their paper from the conference. The threat was ultimately withdrawn and a portion of the research was published at a subsequent conference, but only after the researchers filed a lawsuit.

After enduring this experience, at least one of the researchers involved has decided to forgo further research efforts in this field.[14]

The Electronic Frontier Foundation goes on to catalog a variety of abusive DMCA threats, largely by corporations eager to avoid having their dirty laundry aired in public, against various private individuals and organizations. One common use of the DMCA is to threaten researchers who reveal security flaws in products. Another notable use is that of the ink-jet printer makers, who use the DMCA to threaten rivals that make compatible replacement cartridges.

The second obnoxious feature of the DMCA is the "takedown" notice. The DMCA creates a safe harbor for Internet service providers (ISPs) whose customers post copyrighted material. To qualify for this safe-harbor provision, however, the ISPs must comply with takedown notices – basically claims from individuals who purport to hold a copyright over the offending material. Needless to say, such a provision may easily be abused and has a chilling effect on free speech. For example, from the Electronic Frontier Foundation we learn the following:

The Church of Scientology has long been accused of using copyright law to harass and silence its critics. The Church has discovered the ease with which it can use the DMCA to take down the speech of its critics. It has made DMCA claims against a popular search engine, Google, to bully the engine to stop including in its index any information about certain websites critical of the Church.[15]

The DMCA also allows large media corporations to issue subpoenas with only cursory oversight by a court clerk. These subpoenas have been used to identify individuals who are alleged to make copyrighted material available on peer-to-peer networks and are the basis for various lawsuits currently being brought by the RIAA against various thirteen-years-olds and their grandmothers. Needless to say, this type of subpoena power is also easily abused: one pornography site has used the subpoena provision in an effort to learn the identity of its customers so that it could blackmail them.

Finally, there is the Grokster case. A number of entertainment companies, led by MGM, brought a lawsuit against the makers of a large array of software products. Most important among them is Grokster, whose peer-to-peer software is widely used for all kinds of file sharing, including, obviously, the sharing of music and video files. MGM and its coconspirators argue that because the software used by Grokster is used to do something unlawful, Grokster should be directly held liable for such use. Imagine how this would work in the automobile industry. Ford makes cars, cars are sometime used to rob banks, and a lot more often to drive while drunk or intoxicated. Because both these, and other activities carried out using cars, are unlawful, Ford should be liable for such crimes. In its rulings, the courts have placed a great deal of weight on intent – do the makers of peer-to-peer software intend to encourage illegal use? Of course, we can raise the same issue with respect to automobiles. In the United States the highest speed limit is seventy-five miles per hour. Apparently, the only reason to build cars that can go faster than that must be to break the law. So, should automobile makers suffer the penalties every time that the speed limit is violated? It is extremely dangerous to innovation and prosperity to hold the distributor of a multipurpose tool liable for the infringements that may be committed by end users of the tool.

Until March 2005, MGM and its co-Torquemadas had not had much luck with our court system; then, unfortunately, our Supreme Court was brought into the picture, and things are now looking somewhat different. We quote from Wikipedia, which briefly and clearly summarizes the facts:

In April 2003, Los Angeles federal court judge, Stephen Wilson, ruled in favour of Grokster and Streamcast . . . against the Recording Industry Association of America and the Motion Picture Industry and held that their file sharing software was not illegal. On 20 August 2003, the decision was appealed by the RIAA and the MPPA. On 17 August 2004, the United States Court of Appeals for the Ninth Circuit issued a partial ruling supporting Grokster, holding "This appeal presents the question of whether distributors of peer-to-peer file-sharing computer networking software may be held contributorily or vicariously liable for copyright infringements by users. Under the circumstances presented by this case, we conclude that the defendants are not liable for contributory and vicarious copyright infringement and affirm the district court's partial grant of summary judgment."

In December 2004, the Supreme Court agreed to hear the case. . . . Oral arguments were held for *MGM v. Grokster* on 29 March 2005, and in June 2005, the Court unanimously held that Grokster could indeed be sued for infringement for their activities prior to the date of this judgement.[16]

Notice, and it is not a minor detail, that the Supreme Court has ruled that Grokster could be sued, not that it is to be held liable for the use of its software. The legal details of the ruling are, in this case, quite relevant, and interpreting, as someone did, the Supreme Court ruling as a final sentence against innovative software producers and in favor of the big monopolies is going a bit too far. More precisely, both sides were asking for a summary decision. MGM and friends wanted the Supreme Court to say that peer-to-peer applications were not protected by its previous decision in the Sony Betamax case. Grokster and the other peer-to-peer producers, on the other hand, were asking for a summary judgment saying that, because there are files available to share legally, the software-producing companies cannot possibly be liable for illegal use of their legally distributed products. To us, as you may expect, the latter is the only position that makes sense; but that is another story. The Supreme Court did not satisfy either request, and instead ruled as follows: "We hold that one who distributes a device with the object of promoting its use to infringe copyright, as shown by clear expression or other affirmative steps taken to foster infringement, is liable for the resulting acts of infringement by third parties."[17]

Meaning, if you can prove, in a lower court, that if Grokster and the other software producers are intentionally distributing their products to foster infringements of the law, then they are liable. When you put it this way, the Supreme Court ruling sounds reasonable and balanced. Unfortunately, the law never works that way. Mark Cuban, a media entrepreneur and owner of the Dallas Mavericks basketball team, summarizes the problem as follows:

It won't be a good day when high school entrepreneurs have to get a fairness opinion from a technology oriented law firm to confirm that big music or movie studios won't sue you because they can come up with an angle that makes a judge believe the technology might impact the music business. It will be a sad day when American corporations start to hold their US digital innovations and inventions overseas to protect them from the RIAA, moving important jobs overseas with them.... It doesn't matter that the RIAA has been wrong about innovations and the perceived threat to their industry, EVERY SINGLE TIME. It just matters that they can spend more then everyone else on lawyers. That's not the way it should be. So, the real reason of this blog. To let everyone know that the EFF and others came to me and asked if I would finance the legal effort against MGM. I said yes. I would provide them the money they need. So now the truth has been told. This isn't the big content companies against the technology companies. This is the big content companies, against me – Mark Cuban and my little content company. It's about our ability to use future innovations to compete [versus] their ability to use the courts to shut down our ability to compete. It's that simple.[18]

Some time has elapsed since we first wrote this part of the book. When visiting the URL http://www.grokster.com/ in November 2006, we found the following text on the tombstone of the now-defunct company:

The United States Supreme Court unanimously confirmed that using this service to trade copyrighted material is illegal. Copying copyrighted motion picture and music files using unauthorized peer-to-peer services is illegal and is prosecuted by copyright owners. There are legal services for downloading music and movies. This service is not one of them.

YOUR IP ADDRESS IS 70.238.155.121 AND HAS BEEN LOGGED. Don't think you can't get caught. You are not anonymous.

In the meantime, please visit www.respectcopyrights.com and www.musicunited. org to learn more about copyright.

Scary, don't you think? Ah, the Wikipedia entry on Grokster has also been updated. It now reads:

Grokster Ltd. was a privately owned software company based in Nevis, West Indies rendered extinct by a United States Supreme Court ruling against its mainstay product, a peer-to-peer file sharing program for computers running the Microsoft Windows operating system. The product was similar in look and feel to Kazaa which is marketed by Sharman Networks. . . . Grokster closed its site on November 7, 2005. A note on its home page cited a United States Supreme Court ruling that copying copyrighted material using "unauthorized peer-to-peer services is illegal" and while legal download services exist, "this service is not one of them." The site also claims to log the visitor's IP address but that is just to scare you. The company has said it hoped to establish a "legal" service soon, referencing a new URL: www.grokster3g.com.[19]

Have an interesting experience – try that URL.

Freedom of Expression

The DMCA is not just a threat to economic prosperity and creativity; it is also a threat to our freedom. The best illustration is the recent case of Diebold. Diebold makes computerized voting machines, now used in various local, state, and national elections. Unfortunately, it appears from internal corporate documents that these machines are highly insecure and may easily be hacked. Those documents were leaked, and posted at various sites on the Internet. Rather than acknowledge or fix the security problem, Diebold elected to send takedown notices in an effort to have the embarrassing "copyrighted" material removed from the Internet. Something more central to political discourse than the susceptibility of voting machines to fraud is hard to imagine. To allow this speech to be repressed in the name of copyright is frightening.

Perhaps this sounds cliché and exaggerated – a kind of "leftist college kids'" overreactive propaganda. In keeping with this tone here is a college story about the leaked documents, and how the Diebold and the DMCA helped to teach our future generations about the First Amendment:

Last fall, a group of civic-minded students at Swarthmore [came] into possession of some 15,000 e-mail messages and memos – presumably leaked or stolen – from Diebold Election Systems, the largest maker of electronic voting machines in the country. The memos featured Diebold employees' candid discussion of flaws in the company's software and warnings that the computer network was poorly protected from hackers. In light of the chaotic 2000 presidential election, the Swarthmore students decided that this information shouldn't be kept from the public. Like aspiring Daniel Ellsbergs with their would-be Pentagon Papers, they posted the files on the Internet, declaring the act a form of electronic whistle-blowing. Unfortunately for the students, their actions ran afoul of the 1998 Digital Millennium Copyright Act (D.M.C.A.). . . . Under the law, if an aggrieved party (Diebold, say) threatens to sue an Internet service provider over the content of a subscriber's Web site, the provider can avoid liability simply by removing the offending material. Since the mere threat of a lawsuit is usually enough to scare most providers into submission, the law effectively gives private parties veto power over much of the information published online – as the Swarthmore students would soon learn.

Not long after the students posted the memos, Diebold sent letters to Swarthmore charging the students with copyright infringement and demanding that the material be removed from the students' Web page, which was hosted on the college's server. Swarthmore complied.[20]

Well, the story did not end there, nor did it end that badly. The controversy went on for a while. The Swarthmore students held their ground and bravely fought against both Diebold and Swarthmore. They managed to create enough negative publicity for Diebold, and for their oh-so-progressive liberal arts college, that Diebold eventually had to back down and promise not to sue for copyright infringement. Eventually the memos went back on the Internet.

All's well that ends well? When the wise man points at the moon, the dumb man looks at the finger.

From Policy Error to Policy Blunder: Mandating Encryption

Some policies, such as the retroactive extension of copyright, are bad policies, because the social cost exceeds corresponding benefit. Other policies have potential benefits that are orders of magnitude smaller than their potential costs. We would describe these types of policies not as merely bad policies, but as policy blunders. Simply put, in the face of uncertainty, it is important that the potential losses from being wrong bear some sensible relationship to the potential gains from being right; when they do not, then you are not taking the chances of making a policy mistake, but rather you are taking your chances at a real policy blunder. To fix ideas, think of Iraq.

The various proposals that the government should require computer manufacturers to install a special chip to prevent the "piracy" of copyrighted material constitute a major policy blunder. Such a chip is sometimes called a Fritz chip in honor of Fritz Hollings, the Democratic senator from South Carolina (some would say from Disney), who repeatedly introduced legislation to this effect. It turns out that threatening the safety of the entire computing industry to, possibly, protect digital music and movies cannot be a good idea. It is, as we said, a policy blunder.

A flavor of these efforts is given by the preamble to one of the recent bills, known as the Consumer Broadband and Digital Television Promotion Act: "A BILL To regulate interstate commerce in certain devices by providing for private sector development of technological protection measures to be implemented and enforced by Federal regulations to protect digital content and promote broadband as well as the transition to digital television, and for other purposes."[21] Talk about the tail wagging the dog: the entire computer industry is apparently to be threatened for the important purpose of promoting broadband television. At least the BILL makes no bones about what it is about: as consumers are unwilling to pay for the devices needed to play media content in a form in which the content providers wish to supply it, the BILL will simply force them to do so. The key point is that these devices may not work as advertised – or worse yet, may malfunction and cause computers to lose data. The loss from such a malfunction bears no sensible relationship to the value of copyrighted content that is being "protected."

There are many foolish details in the various bills proposed so far, which will no doubt be replicated in yet further efforts at legislation. Although we do not believe that current copyright legislation, especially the length of term, makes sense, even if we did, would it make sense to mandate by law content protection on general-purpose computing devices?

Tape recorders and DVD players are single-purpose devices designed to play media content. Any harm done through content protection is largely limited to the value of the material that is supposed to be protected. That is, the harm of DVD players that do not work is limited to the economic value of DVDs. By way of contrast, if general-purpose computing devices fail to operate properly on account of content protection, the harm is potentially equal at least to the economic value of computers and the data they store – a value that greatly exceeds the value of the material that is supposed to be protected.

To get some idea of the importance of the "intellectual property" versus the computer industry, here are some numbers. According to the RIAA, the value of all CDs, live presentations, music videos, and DVDs in 1998 in the United States was $13.72 billion.[22] According to the Statistics of Income (SOI), in 1998, the business receipts of the computer and electronic product manufacturing industries, including both hardware and software, was $560.27 billion. In other words, the computer industry has an economic value more than 40 times as large as that of the "copyright" industry. Indeed, IBM's (worldwide) sales in 2000 alone were $88 billion – more than six times the size of the entire U.S. "copyright" market.

Notice, however, that although music market revenues are a reasonable indication of the value of music players, the potential loss of data from malfunctioning computers can greatly exceed the revenues of the industry. A recorded CD containing some music can hardly contain other materials, and its economic value is therefore equal to the value of the music it contains. A PC, not to speak of a business mainframe, stores the product of hundreds, or even tens of thousands, of valuable hours of work – personal records, programs, business accounts, personal software, and on and on. If a PC stops functioning, say, because its hard disk is wiped out by some malfunctioning content-protection device, the value of those thousands of hours of work is gone. Think of a mainframe for some large business company becoming dysfunctional even for a few hours or days. Millions of dollars of valuable services would be lost. It is this kind of comparison that should be kept in mind. Forcing the installation of content-protection devices on all our computers would force each of us, consumers and businesses alike, to live with the continuous threat of such gigantic loss. The music and movie industries, whose monopolistic interests the proposed piece of legislation aims to protect, are most certainly not willing or able to compensate us in case of such a disaster.

Let us examine the idea of content protection, also known as "digital rights management" (DRM) in more detail. There are two distinct types of content-protection schemes. One type of scheme is advisory in the sense that media is simply labeled as protected, and authorized players refuse to copy material that is protected. The Serial Copy Management (SCM) system mandated by law for digital audiotapes is an example of such a scheme, as is the more recent "broadcast flag" for television. Advisory schemes are easy to implement, but they are ineffective if not mandated by law, because there is no reason to buy software or hardware that respects the advice.

The second type of scheme encrypts content, and only software that knows the relevant algorithms and keys can unlock the encryption. An example of such a scheme is DVD encryption. Until the scheme was cracked, it was impossible to play a DVD without an authorized player. Encryption schemes do not require legal enforcement to be effective: media companies simply need to provide material in a format that cannot be played without a player that they authorize. Encrypted material can also be linked to a particular computer or device. Computer operating systems are sometimes linked in this way, as is the case with Windows XP. So, even trading encrypted material can be foiled by a carefully designed scheme. Notice also that under the DMCA it is already illegal to crack these schemes.

Encryption schemes are widely used for video-game players. They require special software that resides only on consoles (produced and commercialized by the same company that manufactures the games) to be played. When you buy one such game, you are aware that, without access to the specific additional tool, you will not be able to play it. The market for video games works well without any mandatory legislation. Those consumers who like video games enough to pay also for the console buy the latter; those who do not, do not. Some people buy a video game without owning a console or planning to buy one. Evidently, they rely on the kindness of acquaintances and friends to play the games on their borrowed machines. Should the federal government step into this market and mandate that anyone who buys a video game should also purchase the player to play it? This sounds insane, as we are all used to the current arrangement and understand that it works quite well. Obviously, there is no end to such insane possibilities for government regulation. For example – digital audiotapes are not selling very well, so why doesn't the federal government pass a law specifying that everyone who buys a CD player must also buy a digital audiotape recorder?

A key fact about legally mandating a content protection scheme is that it requires everyone to bear the cost, regardless of whether they would choose to do so. For example, businesses use a substantial fraction of all general-purpose computers, including all mainframes and supercomputers. It is hard to imagine that many businesses would voluntarily purchase expensive and unreliable devices for their computers so that employees could spend their time at work watching copyrighted movies. Clearly, it is economic nonsense to require them to do so.

Encryption schemes are pervasive and extremely common, despite that they are not mandated by law. In fact, some of them are so familiar to us that we do not even realize we are using them. So, for example, most rock bands sing in English and people in countries in which English is not the mother tongue have to learn English, at some cost, if they want to appreciate the lyrics. Nevertheless, the French government, for example, does not legislate that French consumers purchasing music with English lyrics should also pass a mandatory TOEFL test. They are intelligent enough to understand that, if their citizens are happy just listening to the music and mumbling some distorted English words, then they should be permitted to do so.

Academic economists, such as the authors of this book, are also producers of copyrighted materials and have, in fact, adopted an encryption scheme. We write our research articles in jargon, using a large amount of mathematical symbols and formulas. This encryption is very effective: the content of our research is accessible only to people who are willing to invest enough resources to acquire the skills needed to break the mathematical code. As a matter of fact, those skills can be acquired (in general) only by purchasing the services of academic economists, that is, by enrolling in and successfully completing a Ph.D. program in economics. Certainly, we would be most happy if the federal government decided to make a Ph.D. in economics mandatory for anybody who purchases an economic book or journal or downloads a paper from an academic site (why not?). Nevertheless, we very much doubt this would be in the national interest. Unfortunately, the American Economic Association is not, yet, as powerful a lobby as are the music and video industries, so it is unlikely that some benevolent congressperson will ever propose such a doubtful piece of legislation.

Despite the fact that encryption schemes work well without legal protection, the monopolist naturally prefers that the scheme be legally mandated. Otherwise profits are reduced by the cost of the device. However, the cost of the device is part of the social cost of producing music and movies. Without the device, the music will not be produced. Hence, by making the purchase of the device mandatory, we actually subsidize the monopolist by taxing the consumers. The latter must pay for the cost of the device, and still pay the monopolist the full value of the music they then purchase. The mandatory device results in a transfer to the monopolist from the consumers. This is the redistributional effect. This redistribution, by altering the price at which the monopolist can sell the music, also induces an economic inefficiency: music is now overpriced, and the monopolist has an incentive to overproduce it.

Overproducing a few songs and overrewarding a monopolist by subsidizing the cost of an encryption device may seem to be a small matter. However, the social cost of mandating a device is not merely the fact that too many songs are produced. More seriously, consumers for whom it is not socially optimal to purchase the device are forced to bear the cost of the device. This social cost may be very large: in the case of mandating protection for general-purpose computing devices, we would think of this as including the entire business market for computers. By way of contrast, the social benefit is fixed regardless of the social cost of mandating the device. Because the potential benefit (protecting the "copyright" industry) is quite small relative to the potential cost (destroying the forty-times-larger information technology industry), we would describe a legally mandating content-protection scheme as not merely a policy mistake, but as a policy blunder.

Even encryption schemes can be cracked. An example is the DVD encryption, which was cracked when an authorized but carelessly written piece of software revealed the encryption keys. It is also the case that the encryption schemes used by video-game players have been widely cracked. Sometimes hardware add-on devices – the so-called mod chips – are used to physically undo the encryption. In other cases, software flaws are exploited to hack into the device. This points out two important facts. First, no encryption works perfectly forever. Second, the video games are produced and sold profitably despite the fact that the encryption is eventually cracked. No matter how much the video game manufacturers may dislike it, their business is scarcely threatened by the mod chips.

Should encryption schemes be legally protected as with the DMCA? The substantial costs of the DMCA and the fact that occasional cracking of encryption scarcely poses a threat to the copyright industry argues it should not. Worse, the only really effective legal protection against cracking encryption schemes is a draconian legal mandate that prevents software from even examining encrypted material without authorization.

How would it be possible to prevent unauthorized software from even looking at encrypted material, given that it is transmitted over the Internet and stored on hard disks? It would not be easy, obviously. At a minimum, it would require a complete rewriting of operating systems, and it would require computers that would load only authorized operating systems. The reason is that the operating system would have to check every program loaded and make sure that the program is authorized to see encrypted data. The Microsoft Xbox uses such a scheme. The difficulty of implementing such a scheme can be seen in the fact that the scheme Microsoft implemented in its Xbox hardware has, in fact, been successfully cracked and has a number of known security flaws. The simple fact is that, though people prefer not to have their computer broken into by hackers and attacked by viruses, no one has yet produced an operating system immune to attack. No less a government agency than the National Security Agency is working on a secure system. The level of success attained may be judged by the fact that the agency is now proposing to set up a new network not connected to the Internet at all, solely for the use of secure government transactions.

So, if hardware and software, together with the eager cooperation of the computer user, have proved inadequate to protect content that the owner wants protected, what chance has a media company of protecting content on someone else's computer that the computer owner does not want protected? Indeed, this goes to the technical weakness of all content-protection schemes – at some point, the purchaser will want to see the music or watch the video. What human beings can hear or see, technology can record. So what is next? Mandatory content protection for microphones? If a microphone detects a special copyright watermark, will it refuse to record the offending material? So, then we can't make home movies if our neighbor is playing loud copyrighted music next door?

There are other problems worth noting. For example, government agencies ranging from intelligence agencies to the police will need to have the ability to crack codes. It is foolish to think that these agencies are immune to corruption. More generally, security must protect against the weakest link. The weakest link in many content-protection schemes is the human one: it is all too easy to bribe someone to bypass the protection; this has been the major source of newly released (or unreleased) movies leaking onto the Internet. Human error is a problem more broadly. Software can fail in its intended purpose. The DVD encryption scheme was cracked because of human error in the writing of software. The Xbox was cracked because of a bug in a game authorized and certified by Microsoft.

Finally, it is extremely likely that a legally mandated system would be abused. So far, large corporations have exhibited little regard for such concerns as consumer privacy and have accidentally given up such minor bits of information as people's credit-card numbers and Social Security numbers.

Rent Seeking and Taxes

Intellectual monopolists have many tricks to get the government and the public to pay their bills. In case you are still capable of being astounded by the greed and chutzpah of the media industry, we submit the following. Canada levies a tax on blank media such as CD-Rs and CD-RWs, using the proceeds of the tax to pay copyright holders for the presumed copying of their material on to these media. Toward the end of 2006, similar legislation had been approved in Spain and approval was pending in a number of European countries.

On January 1, 2001, the Canadian Copyright Board increased the tax from 5.2 cents to 21 cents per disc. Brian Cheter, a spokesperson for the board in Toronto, described the new tariff as a valuable measure that protects artists.

He described it as a preemptive measure to recoup losses from "piracy" and the peer-to-peer exchange of music. Notice the perversity: you tax a general-purpose item such as CDs, which have many functions beside storing copied music, to "enforce" some monopoly rents. Because the discs purchased in bulk cost only about 60 cents each (without the tax), the tax is pretty hefty. And now the chutzpah: the music producers are trying to prevent downloading of music in Canada, even as they collect the revenue from the tax designed to compensate them for this "piracy."[23]

Notes

1. According to the 1997 Economic Census (available online at http://www.census.gov/epcd/www/econ97.html accessed, February 24, 2008), the motion picture and sound-recording industries – which include not only motion picture and television production but also music and sound recording – employ 275,981 paid employees. In contrast, IBM alone employs more than 300,000 people. The publishing industry is quite a bit larger, with 1,006,214 paid employees, but many of these (403,355) are in newspaper publishing, which receives practically no protection from copyright. If we use the Motion Picture Association of America's exaggerated estimate that the motion picture industry employs 580,000 people and add in the entire publishing industry, we get 1,586,214 employees. Looking at manufacturing, we notice that the fabricated metal product manufacturing, computer and electronic product manufacturing, and transportation equipment manufacturing industries all employ more workers. Looking more realistically at the industries that benefit from copyright, we add the 275,981 workers in motion picture and sound recording to the 336,479 publishing workers who do not work for newspapers or publish software to get an estimate of 612,460 workers – this is a tiny fraction of the U.S. workforce, and about the same number of workers employed, for example, in the furniture industry.
2. Hesse (2002), p. 42.
3. The copyright data is from the annual registrations reported at http://www.copyright.gov/reports/annual/2000/appendices.pdf (accessed February 24, 2008). Since 1909, nonliterary works were also covered by copyright. However, the next appendix in the same source gives a breakdown of copyrighted works by category for the year 2000, at which time literary works are 46.3 percent of the total. Assuming that the number of nonliterary works increased linearly at a fraction of the total from 1909 to 2000 should provide a high degree of accuracy in the early and later parts of the century, and a decent estimate in the intervening midcentury. In 1976, the starting date of the fiscal year was changed. Hence, the four-month long fiscal "year" 1976 consists of a weighted average of 1976 and 1977, with weights 1.0 and 0.67, respectively. The strange decrease in registrations in 1976 is because the start date of the fiscal year was moved; the downward spike represents a "year" that is only four months long. Population data is from http://www.census.gov/population/estimates/nation/popclockest.txt (accessed February 24, 2008).
4. From http://www.copyright.gov/reports/annual/2000/appendices.pdf (accessed February 24, 2008).

5. Akerloff et al. (2002), p. 1.

6. Citation from http://eon.law.harvard.edu/openlaw/eldredvashcroft/cert-petition. html (which also features the full text of *Eldred v. Ashcroft*, accessed February 24, 2008).

7. As for George Gershwin and his (absent CTEA) impoverished heirs, you may find it somewhat entertaining to read the well-documented story of how Gershwin borrowed freely from a variety of existing (and uncopyrighted) musical sources and then copyrighted everything. In plain English, that is called stealing. The story is told in Arewa (2006).

8. The data on Edgar Rice Burroughs was accurate as of the date reported. Since that time, some of the copyrighted Mars series books have become available online through sellers of used copies. Hence, there is no longer much difference in availability between the copyrighted and uncopyrighted parts of the series, unless you are one of these rare individuals who likes to buy their books new. Our point is not, however, that copyrighted works are invariably less available than the uncopyrighted ones, but rather that they sometimes are, and never the other way around. The claim of copyright supporters according to which copyright increases the availability of old books is, therefore, plainly contradicted by the facts.

9. Speech by Courtney Love at the Digital Hollywood online entertainment conference in New York, on May 16, 2000, published by Salon.com and retrievable at http:// dir.salon.com/story/tech/feature/2000/06/14/love/index.xml (accessed August 13, 2007).

10. BBC News, May 18, 2004, Web site article by Ian Youngs, BBC News Online correspondent in Cannes http://news.bbc.co.uk/2/hi/entertainment/3720455.stm (accessed February 24, 2008).

11. Heinlein (1939), reprinted in *The Past Through Tomorrow: 'Future History' Stories* Putnam and Sons, 1967, p. 25.

12. http://www.dontbuycds.org/payola.htm.

13. Much of the discussion of the DMCA is drawn from the Electronic Frontier Foundation (2003).

14. Ibid., at http://www.eff.org/IP/DMCA/20030102_dmca_unintended_consequences. html (accessed February 24, 2008).

15. Ibid.

16. At http://en.wikipedia.org/wiki/Grokster on August 20, 2007. As Wikipedia's content is often modified, this exact text may not be there at a later date.

17. U.S. Supreme Court in *Metro-Goldwyn-Mayer Studios Inc. v. Grokster, Ltd.*, June 27, 2005. Page varies by source. Available onlines at http://w2.eff.org/IP/P2P/MGM_v_Grokster/04-480.pdf (accessed February 24, 2008).

18. From Mark Cuban's blog, at http://www.blogmaverick.com/entry/1234000230037801/ (accessed February 23, 2007).

19. At http://en.wikipedia.org/wiki/Grokster, on August 20, 2007.

20. Boynton (2004).

21. Senator Fritz Hollings's Consumer Broadband and Digital Television Promotion Act, S. 2048. Available at http://www.politechbot.com/docs/cbdtpa/hollings.s2048.032102.html.

22. Sales data on recorded music and DVDs is from http://www.riaa.com/pdf/md_riaa10yr.pdf (last accessed June 12, 2004). At one time, the RIAA regularly

published a useful account of industry data. Since it has become obsessed with piracy, it no longer does so, apparently fearing that it might undercut its own propaganda. George Ziemann has decided he is not going to let the propaganda go unchecked and properly debunked. At http://www.azoz.com, you can find abundant, and economically excellent, analysis of the RIAA sales, pricing, and revenue figures, separating the 99 percent propaganda from the 1 percent of facts.

23. And the cherry on top of the pie: the "patent epidemic" is quickly becoming also a "copyright epidemic." Even verbally expressed opinions are apparently copyrightable these days. The Off-Off-Broadway production of *Tam Lin* discovered this, in a rather costly way, during 2006, Green (2006) reports.

SIX

How Competition Works

Property is a good thing. Ownership of houses, land, automobiles, potatoes, and coffee contributes to our wealth and well-being. Property brings with it rights: you cannot take my property without my permission, but I may, if I wish, sell it to you. This provides incentives to produce, accumulate, and trade. In countries such as Zimbabwe, where property can be arbitrarily taken away by government action and theft, there is little reason to produce or acquire valuable property, which results in widespread poverty and even famine.[1] Without the ability to sell our property, there is little reason to specialize in the production of goods and services, and no mutually beneficial trades are possible.

If property is good for automobiles and potatoes, should it not also be true, as Michael Novak argues, of ideas as well? Intellectual monopoly supporters such as Novak have found it convenient to assert that there is a connection between "intellectual property" as enshrined in copyright and patent law and property rights in the ordinary sense.[2] Property in the ordinary sense is a good thing – and this is as true of ideas as of automobiles and potatoes. Ordinary property of a piece of land enables the owner to improve and sell it for a profit. Owning a piece of land is not equivalent to controlling all pieces of land: plenty other people also own land, which carries the right to improve it without asking for permission. Ordinary property involves the same set of rights when applied to copies of an idea: you may do whatever you like with your copy of an idea without preventing others from doing what they like with their copies of the same idea or with its derivatives. This is what property in the ordinary sense allows one to do both on pieces of land and with copies of an idea, which is quite different from what intellectual property allows one to do with copies of an idea. Intellectual property is the "right" to monopolize an idea by telling other people how they may, or more often may not, use the copies they own. In all of the innovative industries we looked at in previous chapters, it was the right to buy, sell, and improve on copies of ideas, not the prohibition against using them, that lead to innovation and prosperity.

Competition is a good thing. That is why the National Basketball Association and the Tour de France are so popular, and why we give our all at the annual interdepartmental basketball game. Competition is not just fun; it is also useful. History, practical experience, common sense, and economic theory all agree: economic competition is probably one of the greatest ideas humans ever came up with. When a bunch of people compete to achieve the same goal, great things seem to happen that otherwise would not. Things get done faster, cheaper, and better; new methods for lifting a weight or quenching a thirst are invented; the average guy ends up with more of the stuff he likes at a lower price than before. That is why, in the end, socialism collapsed like a rotten wall: it did not allow its people to compete, and as a result, it not only made their economic life miserable but also strangled their hearts and souls.

Most economists argue that property and competition are good in general, but only a few among them, such as George Stigler, have argued that if competition is good for the production of cellular phones and bananas, it should be equally good for the production of ideas and of their copies.[3] We agree with the few in the latter group: indeed, it is. In this chapter, we explain how competition works in the market for ideas and why it is beneficial. We will try to stick to English and not use the mathematics so favored by economists. The brave and the curious can find all the mathematics they want in the references listed in the final notes.

We are going to imagine a world similar to that in Switzerland or in the Netherlands in the late nineteenth century, in which there are no patents – and there are no copyrights as well. When an economically valuable idea comes to their mind, entrepreneurs can spare one another an insane race to the patent office, profitably invest the money that would otherwise go to lawyers, and get down to the business of selling to consumers the new thing they just invented. We have amply seen in Chapters 2 and 3 that a state of affairs in which patents and copyright are absent does not mean that innovation is a profitless enterprise conducted only by great altruists. Here, we see why this ought to be so even according to economic theory.

The Fruits of the Idea Tree

When innovators come up with an idea for a new product, they make copies of it to sell, and those copies are their property in the same way their socks are. The sale of ideas is all about copies – it is only copies of ideas that can be sold. I am even less able to sell "my idea" than to sell myself. In the presence of patents, when an inventor sells the exclusive rights to an idea, what is being traded is a copy of the idea plus the right (acquired by the buyer) to now prevent the original inventor from using her idea. Alternatively, when an inventor licenses the use of his idea, what is being sold are just copies of the idea, while the right of telling owners of such copies what to do with them remains with the original inventor. I either sell objects containing copies of my idea – books, CDs, how-to manuals, trousers with a low cut, multipurpose gadgets, you name it – or teach my idea to other people directly, and charge for that. Either way, I am selling copies of my idea. In the first case, the copies are contained in the objects; in the second case, the copies are contained in the minds of the people whom I have taught. When I write a book and publish 100,000 copies, it is 100,000 copies of my idea that I am trying to sell.

Once I willingly sell a copy of my idea to you – for example, a copy of this marvelous book – you become the owner of that copy and I retain my idea together with all the other copies I have printed and not yet sold. In the absence of "intellectual property" you can do what you want with your copy of my idea – the book you purchased from me – in the same way that you can do what you want with the ice grinder you bought yesterday from someone else. Without intellectual property there is something you can do that you cannot legally do in the world we currently live in: you can spend your time and your resources to make new copies of the book you purchased. If you were to change the title or the name of the author or engage in some other fraudulent deception, that would be plagiarism – which we are not in favor of. But if you change the cover, the quality of the paper, the fonts, the chain of distribution, or the media carrying the original text in an honest straightforward fashion – or even modify the text with a clear acknowledgment of the original contribution – in the absence of copyright, no property right would be violated. Obviously, if you elected to do so, your copies will compete with the copies I am trying to sell and, possibly, with the copies that other purchasers of the book may have decided to produce.

Do the innovators lose because of this? Probably, although there are circumstances in which not even this is true. The good news is that, in most circumstances, everybody else gains a lot more than the innovators lose. Good economic laws and institutions are designed not to make a few lucky people super wealthy, but to make the average consumer better off. Three desirable features of a world without intellectual property should be noted:

- The number of copies available to consumers is higher and the price is lower, thereby making consumers better off.
- The initial innovator still earns a substantial amount of money.
- The market functions whether there is one innovator or many – and socially beneficial simultaneous innovation is possible.

How can innovators make a substantial amount of money in the face of competition from all of their customers? Take this book. We own our original manuscript, which is necessarily the source of all future copies. Our original manuscript is, therefore, like a capital good such as a shoe factory, and its competitive price reflects the future profits it will generate. When a publisher buys the book from us, the price it is willing to pay reflects the fact that it will be able to make copies and sell them to other people, who can make copies in turn. Absent copyright, how much would have a publisher be willing to pay us for the manuscript? That would have depended upon its expectations about how many other publishers we could have sold the manuscript to, and how many copies of the book they would have brought to the market, as well as some estimate of the potential market size, obviously. Sometimes publishers' expectations are too optimistic, which leads to losses; some other times they are too pessimistic, which leads to exceptional profits. If one replaces the words "book" and "manuscript" with "plants" and "seeds," one gets a description of how the market for agricultural plants worked before patents were introduced. If one leaves those words where they are, one gets a description of how the market for English authors' manuscripts worked in the United States until roughly 1890.

So, while it is true that competition between publishers will eventually result in a lower market price of the book, it is not true that they can profit at our expense or we at theirs. The same is true for any other purchaser of the book, should she decide to get into the business of making additional copies by using the copy she lawfully bought. Whatever profit you could hope to earn from selling our book will be driven to zero as you and other purchasers compete with one another to pay us, the original writers, a price that reflects the market value of the book to you. Whether we make many copies of our manuscript and sell them directly to you, or whether we sell our manuscript to a publisher makes no economic difference, at least as long as the market for reproduction and distribution of books is more or less competitive. We own the manuscript, and under the standard definition of property – in the complete absence of copyright law – we can sell our manuscript at whatever price the market bears. If potential readers exist and reproducing and distributing copies of books is costly, our manuscript will fetch a positive price – in the same way that Wolfgang Amadeus Mozart's or Ludwig van Beethoven's uncopyrighted manuscripts fetched substantial amounts of money in the competitive markets for musical scripts of eighteenth- and nineteenth-century Europe.

Initial copies of an idea are owned by the innovators, and those initial copies are like roots of a tree from which all other copies will emerge like branches of the same tree. Hence, when private property holds, and in the absence of intellectual monopoly, competition lowers the price at which copies of the idea will sell now and in the future. However, because all competitors have to pay to obtain the idea directly or indirectly from the original innovator, when the original manuscript is the only necessary input, the original innovator collects all profits from the reproduction of copies of his idea. When other inputs are needed beside the original manuscript, the inventor collects a share of total profits. As the latter obviously is the most frequent case, we should dwell carefully with it, especially to understand when such share of profits is large enough to motivate the competitive innovator to go ahead with her idea and when it is not.

Economists refer to the net benefit to society from an exchange as "social surplus." With intellectual property, the innovator collects a share of the social surplus she generates; without intellectual property, the innovator collects a smaller share – this is the competitive value of an innovation. When such competitive value is enough to compensate the innovator for the cost of creation, the allocation of resources is efficient – neither too few nor too many innovations are brought about, and social surplus is maximized. One can show mathematically that, under a variety of competitive mechanisms, the private value accruing to an innovator increases with the social surplus: inventors of better gadgets make more money. This is true even when the private value becomes a smaller share of the social surplus as the latter increases.

Notice that we insist on a share of the social surplus, not the entire surplus. Contrary to what many pundits repeat over and over, there is nothing terrifying about this: even under intellectual monopoly innovators receive a less than 100 percent share of the social surplus from innovation, as the rest goes to consumers. Under competition for those innovations that are produced, both consumers and imitators receive a portion of the social surplus an innovation generates, and such portion is strictly larger than in the previous case. Confused pundits use the jargon "uncompensated spillovers" to refer to the social surplus accruing to those besides the original innovator. There is nothing wrong with such spillovers, however. That competitive markets do allow for social surplus to accrue to people other than producers is, indeed, one of their most valuable features, at least from a social perspective; it is what makes capitalism a good system also for the not-so-successful among us. The goal of economic efficiency is not that of making monopolists as rich as possible; in fact, it is almost the opposite. The goal of economic efficiency is that of making us all as well off as possible. To accomplish this, producers must be compensated for their costs, thereby providing them with the economic incentive of doing what they are best at doing. But they do not need to be compensated more than this. If, by selling her original copy of the idea in a competitive market and thereby establishing the root of the tree from which copies will come, the innovator earns her opportunity cost – that is, she earns as much or more than she could have earned while doing the second-best thing she knows how to do – then efficient innovation is achieved, and we should all be happy.

The garden of Eden portrayed until now – and through which we stroll until when, in a couple of sections, we will eat the apple of indivisibility and be forced out of the garden without even an evil snake to blame – follows from the fundamental principle that it is copies of ideas that have economic value, and that there can be many copies of the same abstract idea: your copy, my copy, my brother Jake's copy, Wilson Pickett's copy, and so forth. Copies of ideas are always limited, and it is always costly to replicate them, which is why they are valuable and why they should enjoy the same protection afforded to all kinds of property. They should not be taken away without permission, and the owner should have the legal right to sell them. Copyrights and patents are not needed to afford this ordinary level of protection. Copyrights and patents are the additional – and unnecessary – right to tell other people what they cannot do with the copies they have lawfully purchased. If ideas are afforded the ordinary protection of property, but not the extraordinary protection of intellectual property, would people still come up with valuable ideas and make copies of them to sell to other people? You bet they would! As we have just argued – more important, as the endless list of examples in Chapters 2 and 3 proves – people can make lots of money from selling copies of an idea under this competitive property right regime. In fact, we have already seen that most markets have functioned and still function this way, and people operating in those markets have created new ideas at a breakneck pace and have profitably sold them for centuries.

The image of an idea as the roots of a tree is more than just a metaphor; we have already seen that markets for plants and animals worked for centuries according to the principles we describe here. Competing breeders were able to sell the first exemplars of the new species at prices that were orders of magnitude greater than their cost because those exemplars were in very limited supply right after their introduction. By so doing, competing agricultural innovators captured a substantial share of the value of all future profits accruing to subsequent users of the new plant or animal. Sometimes the new variety of grain turned out to be particularly prolific; so, the innovator would learn, ex post, that she sold it at a "discount" to the theoretical price. Some other times the new variety of tomatoes turned out to be not nearly as resistant to bugs as the breeder and her clients had expected, so that she sold at a "premium" over its theoretical price. Nevertheless, to the extent that entrance in the breeders' market was not distorted, one would expect breeders to make an average profit in line with that of other, similarly risky, lines of business.

The average-profit aspect of our argument is often missed by people who are not familiar with economic reasoning, leading to an understandable, but incorrect, criticism of the theory of competitive innovation. Here is an "offspring of the great stallion" version of it:

The Boldrin-Levine paper makes a similar argument about copies of creative works. They suggest that because the first people to buy a creative work will capture value from copying that work, what they will pay for the first copy will be very high. Thus, copyright is not necessary. The owners of Seabiscuit did not need a copyright in order to capture the breeding value of their horse. If Seabiscuit, the horse, does not need a copyright, why do we need a copyright for Seabiscuit the book? My guess is that the publisher, Ballantine Books, could not be sure ahead of time whether Seabiscuit would be a winner or an also-ran. The book was available to be copied before this uncertainty was resolved. Without copy protection, another publisher could wait for Ballantine's full line-up of books to come out, observe how they sell, and then choose to copy only the popular titles. In contrast, the owner of the horse could wait until the quality of the horse was established before making the horse available to others to make copies. I can see how the Boldrin-Levine mechanism works for horses, but I have a hard time seeing it work for books.[4]

Observe, though, that waiting until Ballantine has saturated the market with its copies of *Seabiscuit* the book before producing your own cheap imitation is a business strategy that will fill Ballantine's coffers with money and not yours. We will discuss this point in greater detail in the section "Ideas of

Uncertain Value" later in this chapter. However, we observe that even the copyright protection that made him a multimillionaire seems unable to keep Mr. Costner from also producing monumental flops every few years or so.

Most critics, in any case, miss the fact that it is an empirical and not a theoretical issue to figure out whether the share of social surplus accruing to an innovator under competition covers his opportunity cost. Theory, per se, does not guarantee that the share of social value accruing to the holder of a patent will be enough to cover his cost of innovation either. Both mechanisms, the competitive and the monopolistic, allow the innovators to capture a share of the social surplus, which may be larger or smaller than the cost of innovating. The share accruing through the second mechanism is generally larger than the one through the first, but monopoly achieves it by introducing the unwelcome evils documented in Chapters 4 and 5. Such evils should and will be weighed against the extra innovation monopoly brings about in Chapters 8 and 9. In this and the next chapter, we stick to theoretical matters because critics appear to be forgetful of the way competitive industries work. Our first concern is the channels through which competitive innovators capture a share of social surplus, thereby earning positive rents, when a fixed cost is present.

Fixed Costs and Competition

The mythical inventor spends lots of time and resources to come up with a new product, a different way of doing things, a novel organizational form, or whatnot. Once the invention is completed, reproducing copies of it is a routine task that anybody can perform at low cost. Leave aside the fact that this mythical description probably applies to no more than a tiny fraction of innovations – that most of the useful things surrounding us are not the product of some great leap forward due to the imagination of a Promethean genius but are, instead, the outcome of a string of humble and mostly overlooked incremental improvements carried out by thousands of very normal human beings. In the mythical case, competition will force the invention to trade at the very low cost of reproduction, leaving the inventor with no compensation for the very high initial cost of invention. This has led many to believe that innovations are unbefitting of trading in competitive markets.

This is a powerful argument, so powerful, in fact, that it ought to apply to all industries. Take, for example, the shoe industry. A factory that produces shoes is expensive. Once the factory is built, shoes can be produced cheaply at a relatively low cost for each pair. If two shoe factories are built, competition between them will drive prices down to the cost of producing a pair of shoes, leaving the factory owners with nothing left over to pay for having built the shoe factories. Why, then, do we not consider shoes a special entity among economic goods, also unsuitable for competitive markets? Why not enact special shoe laws entitling the shoe manufacturer to special rights over the lives of shoe buyers and sellers? The same could be said of gasoline and many other industries: an oil refinery is most certainly a very expensive plant. Building a refinery costs orders of magnitudes more than producing a gallon of gasoline from that same refinery once it is in place; still, we are not troubled by the idea that the oil and refinery industry should be ruled by open competition.

What is it that makes us so confident that competition in shoes and gasoline is an obvious and good thing to have? A factory cannot produce an unlimited number of shoes, and oil refineries have limited capacity. If the shoe factory is small enough, relative to the size of the market, it will produce only a modest number of shoes, and consumers will be willing to pay a premium over marginal cost for the limited number of shoes available.

We can illustrate our story about shoe production in a diagram of supply and demand much beloved by economists. On the horizontal axis, we show the quantity Q of the number of pairs of shoes that are sold. On the vertical axis, we show the price P and the cost of shoes. The height of the grey horizontal line labeled MC is what economists call marginal cost. This is the cost of producing a pair of shoes after the shoe factory is built. But the factory – or the factories – can produce only so many pairs of shoes. This limited number is the capacity of the factory – or of the industry, when there are many firms producing similar shoes – which we represent by the dotted and dashed vertical lines, which show the cases of low and high capacity, respectively. The willingness of consumers to pay for the shoes is their demand, represented by the sloped line. The more pairs of shoes they buy, the less willing consumers are to pay for additional shoes, so the demand curve slopes downward. Take first the case of high capacity – the dashed vertical line. Under competition, we have the famous result that competitors will produce shoes until the price of shoes – represented by demand – falls to marginal cost. In economics jargon, the competitive equilibrium is at the intersection of the grey horizontal supply and sloping demand curves. Because each pair of shoes is sold for the marginal cost of producing a pair of shoes, the factory owners earn no profit – and so have nothing left over to pay for their factories. Realizing from the beginning that this will be the case, they would not build any factory and we would all go around barefoot.

Diagramatics of Capacity Constraints

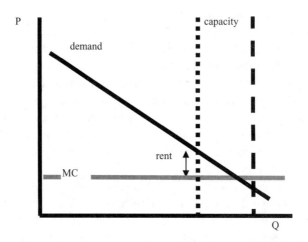

If shoe producers were foolish enough to build only large-capacity factories, or to build so many factories that total industry capacity always stands
at the dashed vertical line, this would be the end of the story. Suppose
instead that the factory is a low-capacity factory, represented by the dotted
vertical line. Even better, suppose the dotted vertical line corresponds to the
industry total supply obtained by adding up a bunch of reasonably sized
factories. It is no longer possible to supply enough shoes to drive price down
to marginal cost. The competitive equilibrium is now at the intersection of
the vertical capacity line and the sloping demand curve. Price is more than
marginal cost. The difference between the price and marginal cost is called
competitive rent.[5] This amount can be used by shoe producers to cover the
cost of building their factories. And indeed, in the competition to build factories, shoe producers will build just enough capacity that their competitive
rents cover the cost of building the factories. This is Adam Smith's invisible
hand – just the right number of factories of the appropriate size are built,
and social surplus is maximized.

What is true for shoes is also true for ideas. It is no more possible to flood
the world instantaneously with copies of an idea than it is to produce an
infinite number of shoes from a finite-sized factory. Because copies of ideas
are always limited, like shoes, they always command a positive price.

Nowhere is limited capacity more important than in a nascent industry.
The first entrants earn large rents, over and above the opportunity cost of

capital, for quite a while, until enough productive capacity is built up to push prices down toward marginal cost. The presence of large initial rents are the carrots for which innovators innovate, while the threat and arrival of imitators is the stick that forces capacity to grow until the rents are almost completely dissipated. The newcomers not only will try to replicate the leader, but also will probably try to go one better than her by cutting costs or improving the product, or both; and she will do the same to inhibit their arrival and keep her rents from falling. This is what, in everyday language, we call economic competition. It is this competitive process that rapidly improves new products and makes them cheaper, which makes all of us better off in the meanwhile.

Eventually the competitive process increases capacity and reduces competitive rents, but not to zero. This is true in both the shoe and the idea industries. To the extent that even the last entrant must build a costly plant, she will have to earn some rents on the price of shoes, to pay for the cost of the plant. Similarly for the imitator who is trying to compete with an innovator: as long as imitating an idea and learning how to make copies of it involves some fixed cost, a positive distance will remain between the market price and the marginal cost of reproduction. Hence, rents will be earned for a long while, and the rents earned by the innovator are commonly much larger than those earned by his imitators: the market shares of Aspirin, Coca-Cola, and Tide are still very large indeed.

An observation for the technically inclined reader. Nothing depends upon the fact that, in the previous graph, the MC line is a straight horizontal line, representing what economists call constant marginal cost. Imagine that, for given capacity, marginal cost was increasing, which means that the MC line would slope upward. Everything we said is still true, and the competitive rents are still there, as long as the dotted vertical line crosses the sloped line of demand *before* the MC curve does. What matters is that total installed capacity is not too large with respect to the size of the market, that is, demand. In the next section, "Indivisibility" we look at the case in which this does not happen and the initial productive capacity is too large.

When the innovation is particularly good and making copies particularly easy, many people will imitate the innovator. We have seen this happen over and again in new industries: too many people enter and too rapidly, too much capacity is built, and some firms, usually the least efficient, earn negative rents, which in the real world are called losses, and exit. Economists call this stage in the development of an industry the shakeout. Shakeouts happen in the market for shoes and in that for lollipops, so we expect them to happen in a competitive market for copies of ideas as well. You may recall when the last shakeout in a competitive market for ideas took place – it was the dot-com bust of 2000–1. Using the Internet to do business, from selling airline tickets to managing your financial portfolio, was a great, innovative idea that someone, perhaps Al Gore, had. Fortunately for us all, it was not yet patentable, and once the first dot-com business was created, other entrepreneurs started to make copies of this idea, and other dot-com companies were created. This was the boom to which the bust followed, and then the more stable but still fast growth we have witnessed during the past years. We would have not had an efficient dot-com sector without a boom and the following shakeout, and we would not have had either if intellectual monopoly had its way there.

Although entrepreneurs whose inefficient firms are forced to exit do not like to hear this, shakeouts are good and socially valuable events. It is a pity that all those ill conceived and inefficient companies are forced to shut down, but competition is not a gala dinner,[6] and getting rid of inefficient firms while allowing efficient ones to blossom is exactly what competition is supposed to accomplish. We all agree that this is good for the shoe industry. It is good also for the idea industry. We may have forgotten, but it was Xerox, not Microsoft or Apple that invented the graphical user interface based on manipulating icons on a graphic screen. Still, most of us would agree that it was socially beneficial that Microsoft imitated and outperformed the original innovators. Eventually, mature industries reach some kind of long-run equilibrium where there is roughly the correct amount of productive capacity, the rents earned by the marginal firm are just enough to pay for its fixed costs, and competitive equilibrium reigns – until, of course, some other innovator comes along with a new kind of shoe and steps over the placid equilibrium lake to create the socially beneficial waves of competitive innovation, which is the source of all progress.

Indivisibility

Our analogy between shoes and ideas has served us well so far, which is why it is the right time to drop it and examine the crucial difference between the economics of shoes and the economics of innovation. The fact that the innovator will earn a rent means that some ideas will be produced under conditions of competition. But it does not imply that every socially valuable idea will be produced: eating the fruit of the indivisibility tree will reveal to us the limits of competitive innovation.

Consider again the case of a shoe factory. The standard theory of competition asserts not only that shoe factories will be built but also that the socially desirable number of shoe factories will be built. The reason for this is that shoe factories are fairly divisible: we may build smaller or larger shoe factories. The builder of the first factory, when deciding how large a factory to build, will not build so large a factory that the rents from the fixed capacity of the factory will be less than the cost of building it. The builder – facing competition from imitators building other shoe factories – will wish to increase the size of his factory as long as the rents from a little more capacity exceed the cost of adding the capacity. Imitators will do likewise. This is exactly the condition for maximizing social surplus, and that is why economists do not argue that owners of shoe factories should be awarded government monopolies. This pleasant solution does not necessarily apply in the case of innovations.

In contrast to shoe factories, even with minimal installed capacity, the copies of a book that can be made over an extremely short period of time may be so many as to essentially flood the market, dropping the price to near marginal cost almost immediately. (We should note that the evidence suggests that this is not the case.) The resultant difference between price and marginal cost may be so small that, when multiplied by the number of copies, it yields an insufficient rent. The rent is insufficient because, say, the book is very complicated, and it took a long time to complete. There is no way to offset this combination of excess capacity and large fixed cost by producing a smaller book that is a good substitute for the complete book; this is something we can bear witness to. The presence of such an indivisibility in the innovation process and the fact that initial capacity may be large relative to the size of the market is a key fact about innovation under competition.

Most ideas are not divisible, and there are cases in which the cost required to come up with the first prototype of an idea is quite large compared to the size of the market for copies of that idea. Said differently, the capacity the innovator must install (more often, the capacity that is already installed) is so large, given the demand for the good, that one is not likely to earn any rent over marginal cost. In this case, a rational innovator understands that she cannot recover the initial fixed cost, and she does not even get started. For a given demand, when these two anomalies – large minimum capacity and large fixed cost – meet, competitive markets do not function properly. This is the heart of the economic argument for intellectual monopoly: that the additional profit achieved by a monopolist may, some of the time, lead to socially desirable innovations that would not be produced with unfettered competition. Let us be clear: as a theoretical argument this is a sound one and we would not dream of denying it. In fact, it is a special case of the very same model we have proposed both here and elsewhere. We are not arguing the case of large initial capacity and small market size cannot arise, just that it is far from being the only possible case. Determining which one is more frequent in the real world is an empirical problem, not a theoretical one. The theory of competitive innovation admits both the case in which the minimum size is small and the indivisibility irrelevant and the case in which it is relevant.

Is indivisibility a relevant practical problem? As we have already seen and as we shall see even more, available evidence suggests that it is not. Notice that, as a matter of both theory and facts, when the economy expands in size, the economic relevance of indivisibility is progressively reduced – so, too, as people become richer over time. Hence, economic progress makes competitive innovations easier and easier, and the economic justification for intellectual monopoly diminishes as time passes and the economy grows.

The Collaborative Advantage

Large advances are generally built out of many small innovations. The process of innovation is greatly enhanced when innovators share information, enabling other innovators to bootstrap off of their advances. Because under competition all competitors can imitate, and so benefit from the innovation of everyone else, the incentive to share information is strong. By sharing information, the innovator increases the chances that her competitors will make further innovations – and under competition the original innovator expects to benefit from the innovation she induces from her colleagues.[7]

The incentive to share information is especially strong in the early stages of an industry, when innovation is fast and furious. In these early stages, capacity constraints are binding, so cost reductions of competitors do not lower industry prices, as the latter are completely determined by the willingness of consumers to pay for a novel and scarce good. So the innovator correctly figures that by sharing his innovation he loses nothing but may benefit from one of his competitors leapfrogging his technology and lowering his own cost. The economic gains from lowering his own cost, or improving his own product, when capacity constraints are binding, are so large that they easily dwarf the gains from monopoly pricing. It is only when an industry is mature, cost-reducing or quality-improving innovations are harder to bring about, and productive capacity is no longer a constraint on demand that monopoly profits become relevant. In a nutshell, this is why firms in young, creative, and dynamic industries seldom rely on patents and copyrights, whereas those belonging to stagnant, inefficient, and obsolete industries desperately lobby for all kinds of intellectual property protections.

The collaborative advantage argument is often countered with the following:

Suppose one firm chooses not to spend anything on innovation. It gets the same amount of progress... as the other firms that do spend on innovation. Hence it gives its stockholders a higher return. Rational stockholders accordingly do their diversification across industries, but specialize in just that firm within the industry. Or, if you prefer, a rational takeover artist gets control of one of the firms acting as... described, cuts its R&D budget to zero, increases its profits, sees its stock rise, and makes a killing when he sells.[8]

The problem is that those who do not bother to spend on research and development (R&D) do not get "the same amount of progress... as the other firms that do spend on innovation." Those who are part of the collaboration benefit – bystanders do not. How much has your knowledge of writing a computer operating system benefited from all the hard work by the Linux kernel programmers? To obtain and use the "free" information contained in the other firms' R&D, you had better carry out R&D on your own. If you do not, you are unlikely to be able to understand and process the technical information that the rest of the industry is producing. So, too, the other industry players will probably not rush to aid you in your lack of understanding.

The First-Mover Advantage

Competitive rents are the least amount that an innovator can expect to earn in conditions of competition. Because the innovator initially is the only one to know the idea, there are many ways to profit from this first-mover advantage. As remarkable as the phenomenon of economists who believe that ideas are transmitted freely, while writing a voluminous literature on technology transfer and the cost of information, is the other phenomenon of economists who believe that innovators have no first-mover advantage, while writing a voluminous literature on the strategic advantages of being first. These strategic advantages are well documented: Fudenberg and Tirole's text on game theory is one example,[9] while Rudyard Kipling is a less obvious one:

> I knew – I knew what was coming, when we bid on the Byfleet's keel –
> They piddled and piffled with iron: I'd given my orders for steel!
> Steel and the first expansions. It paid, I tell you, it paid,
> When we came with our nine-knot freighters and collared the long-run trade!
> And they asked me how I did it, and I gave 'em the Scripture text,
> "You keep your light so shining a little in front o' the next!"
> They copied all they could follow, but they couldn't copy my mind,
> And I left 'em sweating and stealing a year and a half behind.[10]

The most striking implications of the first-mover advantage, may, however, lie elsewhere. They are captured by the observation first made by Jack Hirshleifer, that the innovator, by virtue of inside information, may be able to earn vastly more than the social value of the innovation.[11] To understand Hirshleifer's argument, consider the recent innovation of the Ginger scooter, now relabeled the Segway, which was said to revolutionize urban transportation, and grant that this unlikely prediction was actually true. How could the inventor, Dean Kamen, profit from this knowledge? There was a point in the development of the scooter at which Mr. Kamen was the only one to know that urban transportation is soon to be revolutionized, and that the automobile itself is soon to be obsolete. Rather than surround himself with patents, and hawk his knowledge to venture capitalists, as he did, he could simply have sold short automobile stock using whatever funds he had available to him and leveraged to the maximum extent possible. Then, rather than develop the scooter himself, he should simply have mailed the blueprints to the *New York Times*. As soon as the blueprints were published, the stock-owning public would naturally realize that the automobile industry is on the way out, and the price of automobile stocks would plummet. Mr. Kamen, having foreseen this, and having sold short the stocks prior to publishing his blueprints, would naturally have made a killing.

In practice, of course, whatever Mr. Kamen's representations to venture capitalists might have been, the Segway has not revolutionized the transportation industry, nor was it likely to have done so, and shorting automobile stocks would have been a risky proposition. (Although in retrospect, it would have been a good decision for other reasons.) This is, after all, the way in which the billionaire turned social progressive George Soros made most of his money – by selling short the British pound in 1992 – only Soros' predictions were correct. But invention is a risky business in general, and the intellectual monopolist who has a valueless idea does not generally fare so well either. Indeed, even with the benefit of patent protection, Mr. Kamen has become less than immoderately wealthy by virtue of his innovation.

There are more obvious and more common advantages of being first mover. The primary advantage is simply that it takes time and money to reverse engineer a product. That is, in the example of this book mentioned previously, without copyright we would be in immediate competition with you as soon as we sold you a copy. Still, you would have to own a printing press and a distribution chain to start competing with us – well, with Cambridge University Press – and those things cost quite a bit. Still, there is a sense in which, if you were another university press, by purchasing a copy of this book you could, in a world without copyright, have a relatively inexpensive go at making copies of it. Of course, as we observed in the case of government documents, this does not take all the profit out of writing books. No matter, for books, music, and videos, reverse engineering appears to be relatively cheap; hence, the competitive solution lies somewhere else. Where? One can easily learn either by looking at what American publishers did around 1870 – flooding the market with lots of cheap copies of the book, thereby making life for anyone but the cheapest of the cheap imitators impossible – or by going back to the preceding theoretical diagram. When the innovator begins production with a very large capacity, the size of the residual competitive rent left for even the first imitator becomes very small, so small that, in general, it will not be profitable to imitate.

In most real-world cases, reproduction and reverse engineering are, in fact, expensive in the short run. Books, music, video, and copyrightable items can be encrypted, and it takes time and money to crack encryption schemes. New products, not to speak of new processes, are generally costly to reverse engineer. Moreover, the expertise that comes with being the innovator, and having been in production for longer than competitors, has substantial market value. The example of Boulton and Watt after the expiration of their patents is a case in point, but there are many others, such as the fact that patented drugs continue to command a substantial premium over their generic competitors, even long after the patent expires. In short, even without the benefit of legal protection, the innovator certainly will enjoy a short-term monopoly and can depend on such forces as reputation and consumer loyalty working to her advantage.

But how is the poor inventor, working in his basement, to profit against the large heartless corporations? Will they not take advantage of his lack of capital to steal his idea and put it into production themselves? Here we appeal to the clever scheme, explained by Anton and Yao in an article in the *American Economic Review*,[12] showing how the inventor can avoid this. To return to the example of the Ginger/Segway scooter, Mr. Kamen could have gone to one of the automobile companies, Ford, perhaps, and shown them his blueprint for free. He would then promise to keep it secret from their competitors, but only in exchange for a substantial share in Ford Motor Company. This creates what an economist would call an incentive-compatible mechanism, and what a pundit would call a win-win situation. The secret would have substantial value, as Ford would enjoy a first-mover advantage. As long as Mr. Kamen asked for less than the full value of the invention to Ford, Ford would be happy to pay, for if he were to reveal the secret to its competitors, Ford would lose its monopoly profits. On the other hand, Ford would understand that Mr. Kamen, sharing in the Ford stock, would not reveal the secret to the other companies – as this would reduce the value of his stock. Let us note, in passing, that this argument reveals that competition is double good for both society and inventors. First is for the reason exposed previously. Second is because Mr. Kamen's threat to Ford is credible if, and only if, there is at least one competitor to Ford in the production of cars. Absent competition in the production of cars, the genial innovator would have much less bargaining power with the only producer of cars. Hence, the moral: make sure to enforce competition, among innovators but also among not-so-innovative producers of old goods, such as cars – and shoes.

Quantifying the First-Mover Advantage

How strong the first-mover advantage is depends on whether profits are earned from venues in which duplication is difficult or venues in which profits can be earned quickly. When the first-mover advantage is strong, the economic rationale for protection is weak, because most worthwhile works will be produced in the absence of intellectual monopoly. Lobbyists from the book industry, such as the Authors Guild, the RIAA, speaking for the recording industry, and the MPAA, speaking for the movie industry, have been quite adamant about the need for protection of their intellectual property. So, it is worth taking a look at how strong the first-mover advantage is in these industries.

In the case of movies, prior to the advent of the VCR in the mid-1970s, the bulk of film revenue was from theatrical performances, with a small portion coming from television reruns. The bulk of profits are earned in initial theatrical releases, which typically last for several weeks to a month. Following the first-run theatrical release, there is a second run that begins one to two months after the end of the first. The striking feature about the second run is that ticket prices are typically much lower than for the first run. For example, in 2002, in Chicago, examining ticket prices on the Internet, we found that the typical first-run ticket cost $9, and the typical second-run ticket cost about $3. This high degree of impatience on the part of moviegoers is precisely the type of environment in which the case for intellectual monopoly is weak – especially because theatrical performances certainly are bounded by capacity (theatrical seat capacity, in this case) even in the absence of copyright.

We can also estimate the willingness to pay for earlier delivery through the examination of express delivery charges. On October 1, 2002, Amazon.com, for example, charged $0.99 per book delivered in three to seven days, $1.99 per book delivered in two days, and $2.99 per book delivered in one day. So, some consumers at least are willing to pay $1 extra to have a book delivered twenty-four hours sooner. This is obviously a substantial first-mover advantage.

Indeed, for books, we do find that up-front profits are typically the most important. Eric Flint reports that the "standard experience is that 80% of a book's sales happens in the first three months."[13] In the same page he also provides, among other things, the following data for his own novel cowritten with David Drake, *Oblique Approach*:

Royalty period	Sales
July–December 1998	30,431
Janurary–June 1999	5,546
July–December 1999	835
January–June 2000	795

Our own data on a much broader base of fiction novels shows a decrease in sales over the initial four months of roughly a factor of six.[14] The book industry, at least for paperback novels, is an industry in which the cost of creation is relatively small. Flint reports that the "average paperback sells, traditionally, about 15,000 copies" which, with a royalty of $2 per copy, would work out to about $30,000, also consistent with our broader database.

In the case of recorded music, we have the benefit of a natural experiment. Prior to 1999, recorded music was effectively protected by copyright law and technology. With the ability of computers to rip tracks from CDs and convert them into MP3 format, the advent of the peer-to-peer network Napster in May 1999 effectively eliminated copyright for music – so much so that the complete elimination of intellectual monopoly is now sometimes called "Napsterization." The impact of Napsterization on CD sales has been studied by Stan Liebowitz of the University of Texas. According to Liebowitz, Napsterization had little or no impact on CD sales through the end of 2001. In 2002, a decline in CD sales that began in 2001 became more severe, and Liebowitz estimates that in the long-run sales will fall by 20 percent.[15]

Complementary Sales

Another first-mover advantage, for creative works especially, is the well-documented and strong preference for originals, signed copies, and early versions that are in scarce supply over more widely available versions. Perhaps one of the most striking examples of the phenomenon is that of the J. Paul Getty Museum, in Los Angeles. The Getty bought, at astronomical prices, a large number of very good forgeries of famous works of art. These forgeries were sufficiently good that the experts of the museum believed that they were originals. However, additional subtle evidence and refined scientific testing established that indeed the works were fraudulent. Of course, from the functional point of view the works were unchanged – from the viewers perspective, the painting still looked exactly the same. But the market price, once the works were clearly established as unoriginal, plummeted by orders of magnitude. Similarly, authorized copies of a variety of fashion products, distinguishable from the original at most by the presence or absence of a label, sell for a vastly lower price than the original. So, while works of art may be currently protected by copyright, it is hard to make the case that there is any need to do so.

The preference for originals, signed or autographed copies, and so forth, is just a special example of a more general phenomenon: the complementary sale. That is, a creation, while not terribly scarce in some markets, is often quite scarce in other markets, and the innovator, by virtue of being the innovator, can generally command a premium for her services in areas not directly related to her idea. Examples of this abound. In music, live performances will remain scarce, no matter the price of electronic copies. Movies will be produced as long as first-run theatrical profits are sufficient to cover production costs, and no matter how many copies are given away over the Internet for free. Books will continue to be produced as long as initial hardcover sales are sufficient to cover production costs. Substantial money is to be earned by authors or inventors by going on the talk-show circuit. Even T-shirts signed by a famous author may be enough to pay for the opportunity cost of his labor in producing a great literary work – amazingly enough, a number of small online comic strips have found it a profitable business model to give their strip away for free and sell T-shirts.

Activities more mundane than great literary work may also suffice to make lots of money from complementary sales, as the Spanish soccer team Real Madrid has repeatedly proved by covering the large salaries of the "galactic" soccer stars who have played for the team (David Beckham, Michael Owen, Raúl González, Ronaldo, Zinedine Zidane) through the sale of clothing items bearing their names and numbers. Never mind if they never managed to win any serious competition, either in Spain or in Europe, during their galactic years: as innovators in the world-soccer circus they made plenty of money, plentiful imitators notwithstanding.

The greatest complementary sale of all is, of course, the sale of advertising. Those who doubt the possibility of making a profit from giving a product away for free would do well to look into the history of the radio and television industry. How many people became fabulously wealthy from an industry that for the first forty years of its existence had no choice but to provide its product for free? It is argued, of course, that, in the absence of copyright, people would simply redistribute the product with commercials removed. In the absence of technical means such as encryption, this might be possible. But, of course, there is nothing to prevent the creator from embedding the advertisement as an integral part of the story. Product placements are quite common in movies and television. If other advertising possibilities diminish, these will become correspondingly more valuable. There is no reason why this cannot extend to other works, such as books. In the old days, a remarkably large share of written work embodied some kind of advertising or another, as exemplified by Ludovico Ariosto's *Orlando furioso*.

> The first inscription there which meets the eye
> Recites at length Lucretia Borgia's fame,
> Whom Rome should place, for charms and chastity,
> Above that wife who whilom bore her name.[16]

Although Ian Fleming did not receive payment from Colt for equipping his spy with a gun of that manufacture, after the books became popular, he certainly could have made a profit by auctioning off the right to the James Bond gun. In fact, the Bond movies (in which he did not use a .38 Colt Police Positive) seem to have done exactly that.[17]

A similar possibility of complementary sales arises also in the market for patentable ideas. The inventor naturally has established special expertise in the ideas surrounding her invention. She will be in great demand as a consultant by those who wish to make use of the idea. Would not Watt have been in great demand from producers of steam engines even if he had no patent? He would; in fact, that is pretty much what he did until

1798 – he acted as an engineering consultant for those who wanted to build a steam engine. Indeed, the role of Boulton and Watt's patent was purely to prevent others from assembling steam engines, as most parts were produced by independent companies in any case. Would Transmeta have been willing to hire Linus Torvalds at a substantial salary had he not started the Linux project and written its first version? Despite having given his creation away for free, and despite an apparent reluctance to profit from his fame, such as by way of public appearances, Torvalds is nevertheless a millionaire today.

Ultimately, no academic work can do more than scratch the surface of the first-mover advantage: it is limited only by human ingenuity, an area in which academic economists have no special advantage. For example, profits can be made by escrowing contingent orders in advance, through serials and cliff-hangers, or even by selling tickets to a lottery involving innovation as one outcome. Looking back over history, we see the ingenious methods adopted by entrepreneurs in markets where indivisibilities have posed a problem. In the medieval period, the need for convoys created a substantial indivisibility for merchants that was overcome through the clever use of contingent contracts. In modern times, Asian immigrants (among others) have overcome the need for a minimum investment to start a small business by organizing small lottery clubs.

Ideas of Uncertain Value

Intellectual property supporters, such as Jack Valenti, former head of the MPAA, become extremely agitated about the fact that many innovations are risky. After all, it is bad enough that competitors should be allowed to "steal" "your" creation. But if the original project is risky, they will only choose to "steal" if you are successful: few illegal copies of such great flops as the 1987 *Ishtar* are widely distributed on the Internet. We have already mentioned elsewhere that such an argument makes little practical sense: there is only one way in which one can tell for sure if a movie or a book is a great success or a flop, and that always comes after the fact. If something is labeled a "great success," it means has sold lots of copies already, thereby allowing its original creator to make lots of money. That an imitator comes in after the fact to grab a few crumbs from the floor cannot make much of a difference.

In any case, it remains true that when a new product is launched it is with a high degree of uncertainty as to its actual market performances. What implication does the existence of uncertainty have for competition in the ideas sector? Does it make a difference that some ideas are revealed not to have any or little market value after the initial investment has already taken place, while others are hugely successful? It does not; it simply changes the algebra of computing profits. Imagine that producing an innovation has a given cost, which we label C. The amount earned in competition with many imitators we may label q. The social value of the innovation we may label v. When uncertainty is absent, the innovation is undertaken whenever $C < q$. However, if the project only succeeds with probability p, abstracting from risk aversion, the expected amount earned is only pq. So, the condition for innovation to be undertaken and profitable without intellectual monopoly becomes $C < pq$. Now think about the monopolist. Given the same fixed cost of creating the first copy of the idea, if the profit under monopoly is Q, the innovation will take place as long as $C < pQ$. Naturally, the lower the probability of success, the less likely the innovation is to occur – under either competition or monopoly. Of course, the social value of the innovation is pv and, if p is small enough, $C > pv$ and it is better from a social perspective that the innovation does not occur.

In short, the uncertainty surrounding the success of an innovation changes the specific calculations of how likely it is to take place; this is true with or without intellectual monopoly. But the basic theory of competitive innovation does not change on account of uncertainty – an uncertain outcome is equivalent to earning a lower rent or to having a higher cost.

The Social Value of Imitation

Imitation is a great thing. It is among the most powerful technologies humans have ever developed: there is a debate over the extent to which living beings other than *Homo sapiens* can actually learn through imitation. In spite of the miracles that our mimetic instinct has been performing for us over the millennia, imitation has received very bad press in the literature concerned with innovation and ideas. This is not a view that we share, as imitation is a powerful tool of economic development.

It should be clear, in fact, that acts of imitation, carried out while respecting ordinary private property rights and the rights to personal privacy, are key components of the competitive markets that benefit us on a daily basis. Imitation may or may not require reverse engineering; most times it does, as it is rather difficult to imitate a product without even looking at it and examining its internal components. But imitation is not limited to reverse engineering; it involves, and this is what makes it particularly valuable, leaping ahead of the pack.

On the one hand, imitation is a technology that allows us to increase productive capacity. Innovators increase productive capacity directly, while imitators increase productive capacity by purchasing one or more copies of the idea and then imitating it. Imitation, therefore, always requires an investment: not only do you need to purchase a copy of the idea (and if you try doing this shortly after the innovation has been released, it may be quite costly) but you also need to invest your time and other resources to carry out the imitation process. The output of the imitation process is additional productive capacity. As long as industry capacity is low enough that there are rents to be earned in selling copies of ideas at a price higher than marginal cost, people will make investment to increase capacity. Imitation is the main way in which such investments are implemented.

On the other hand, imitation is also a technology that allows further innovation. When you imitate you take as inputs a copy of the idea, various standard inputs available on the market, and your own skills; as output you get productive capacity for the idea. You do this because you are trying to collect as large a competitive rent as possible: making your copy of the idea a bit better, or cheaper, than the one the original innovators are selling is one way to increase your rents. Indeed, it is a very powerful way to increase your rents: it is the essence of competition. So, at the end, imitation is nothing else but an essential ingredient for competition, which may be characterized as imitation with lots of good imitators.

Intellectual monopoly greatly discourages imitation. For a monopolist, the worst possibility is losing the monopoly. If an imitator improves upon the product or learns how to produce it at cheaper cost, regardless of prior licensing agreements, your competitor now has the upper hand and is a threat to your monopoly. It is far more sensible simply to prevent imitation in the first place, by aggressive legal enforcement of patents and other forms of intellectual monopoly.

Notes

1. The tragic situation of Zimbabwe is too well documented in the daily press to require explicit references to be reported here. It got only worse and worse during the five years we spent finishing this book.
2. Somewhat less publicized than the Zimbabwean socioeconomic situation is the academic status of Michael Novak. According to the American Enterprise Institute's Web site (at http://www.aei.org/scholars/scholarID.44/scholar.asp) (accessed February 24, 2008), Michael Novak is the George Frederick Jewett Scholar in Religion, Philosophy, and Public Policy and "researches the three systems of the free society – the free polity, the free economy, and the culture of liberty – and their springs in religion and philosophy." It might be imagined that a degree in economics would be

a valuable prerequisite for such a position, but Mr. Novak's posted resume doesn't include one.

3. George J. Stigler was a great, if somewhat mordant, economist who, maybe because of his indefatigable free market position, has often been seen as tolerant of monopolies; nothing could be further from the truth. He not only had little sympathy for monopolies in general but also was one of the few academic economists writing overtly against the Schumpeterian view of innovation, which we shall later cover and criticize at length. In Stigler (1956), p. 269, he asks, "Is it monopoly or is it competition, that brings more rapid economic progress?" and his answer leaves no doubts: competition.

4. Kling (2003). Larry Jones pointed out to us first that, until the Plant Variety Protection Act of 1970 destroyed competition there too, markets for new plants and animal species were a perfect example of our abstract model. Many colleagues at agricultural economics departments around the country have since confirmed that what Larry had learned growing up in Sacramento, California, applied elsewhere as well.

5. That limited capacity is the source of economic rents even in competitive industries is scarcely our original idea. We both learned of it as undergraduates when cost curves were introduced and the partial equilibrium of an industry explained. We are not particularly knowledgeable in the history of economic thought, but our impression is that the first exposition of the concept is in the work of Alfred Marshall (1890, book V), who coined the term *quasi-rents* to, unnecessarily, distinguish them from the Ricardian rents accruing to inframarginal land. It was unnecessary because, in both cases, rents emerge from the existence of factors of production that are fixed at a point in time: land in one case and productive capacity in the other. In both cases, the rents accrue to the owners of the fixed factor. That land may, in general, not grow from one period to another, while productive capacity increases over time, only implies that the rent accruing to land may not vanish even in the long run, while rents accruing to the owner of productive capacity are eliminated, in the long run, by capacity expansion brought about by the forces of competition. Marshall appears to have also clearly understood that the ratio between the size of the market and the indivisibility plays a crucial role in the adoption of innovations: "In almost every trade many things are done by hand, though it is well known that they could easily be done by some adaptations of machines that are already in use in that or some other trade, and which are not made only because there would not as yet be enough employment for them to remunerate the trouble and expenses of making them" (1890, book IV, chapt IX, par 3, n1).

6. That competition is not a gala dinner follows directly from Comrade Mao Tse-tung's observation that the revolution is not a gala dinner either, and from the fact that competition is the source of an unending, but beneficial, revolution in our ways of producing the things we like.

7. That innovations do not, like Athena, spring out fully armored from the head of the innovator but are the products of painfully long processes of cumulative discovery to which hundreds, often thousands, of independent individuals contribute is well understood by actual innovators and repeated by an endless list of writers. The most recent discussion of this point we came across, in the business-related literature, is Berkun (2007), which contains plentiful, interesting examples and abundant reference to the many who argued this point before him, and us.

8. This criticism of our collaborative information-sharing argument is taken, verbatim, from an anonymous evaluator of the original book manuscript. This particular evaluator was incredibly helpful to us, and most of her or his criticisms were right to the point and most insightful. The serious intellectual debate with our position led us to substantially revise both the structure and the content of the book. Hopefully, he or she will find the final version more convincing than the original one.

9. Fudenberg and Tirole (1991).

10. From "The 'Mary Gloster'" by Rudyard Kipling; being out of copyright this is easily available at a number of Web sites, for example, http://www.poetryloverspage. com/poets/kipling/mary_gloster.html (accessed February 24, 2008). This was suggested by the same reviewer whom we thanked previously.

11. Hirshleifer (1971).

12. Anton and Yao (1994). More recent versions of models similar to that of Anton and Yao and Hirshleifer (1971) have different applications but the very same clear conclusion that competition and innovation go well together, while intellectual monopoly harms the second. See Baccara and Razin (2004) and Marimon and Quadrini (2006).

13. Flint (2002).

14. The broader database on book sales that we mention repeatedly is one we collected by using a variety of sources and that is illustrated in Boldrin and Levine (2005b).

15. Liebowitz (2004).

16. Also suggested by the reviewer. For curious readers, here are the original verses from stanza 83:

> *La prima iscrizion ch'agli occhi occorre,*
> *Con lungo onor Lucrezia Borgia noma*
> *La cui bellezza ed onestà preporre*
> *Debbe all'antiqua sua patria Roma.*

17. James Bond's brand of gun is described in Fleming (1953).

SEVEN

Defenses of Intellectual Monopoly

We focused at the outset on the many successful industries in which competition and innovation have gone and still go hand in hand. Then, we documented the many social evils that the presence of intellectual monopoly, in the form of either patents or copyrights, brings about. In Chapter 6, we introduced a theoretical framework capable of explaining the very same existence of innovative competitive industries, their evolution, and the call for intellectual monopoly arising from those industries once they mature and turn stagnant. Yet we have also learned that the same theoretical framework rationalizing competitive innovations also predicts that innovations of social value may fail to materialize under competition. This leaves open the theoretical possibility that intellectual monopoly increases overall innovation. If intellectual monopoly delivers substantially more innovation than competition, it might be a worthwhile system, despite the many costs we documented in Chapters 4 and 5. Hence, the issue is worthy of further investigation, which we pursue next in two steps. In this chapter, we examine the theoretical reasons – other than the indivisibility already discussed in Chapter 6 – adduced to support the existence of intellectual monopoly. In Chapter 8, we report on the extent to which patents and copyrights increase the social rate of creation and innovation.

We are keenly aware that there are many who argue in favor of intellectual monopoly. They often provide logically correct reasons why, all other things equal, intellectual monopoly would deliver more innovation than competition. After all, a monopoly is a good thing to have: holding out the prospect of getting a monopoly as a reward for innovating should, all other things equal, increase the incentive to innovate. But the fact that an argument is logically correct does not mean that it has practical importance for policy.

Consider the problem of automobiles and air pollution. When I drive my car, I do not have to pay you for the harm the poison in my exhaust does to your health. So, naturally, people drive more than is socially desirable and there is too much air pollution. Economists refer to this as a negative externality, and we all agree that it is a problem. Even conservative economists usually agree that government intervention of some sort is required.

We propose the following solution to the problem of automobile pollution: the government should grant us the exclusive right to sell automobiles. Naturally, as a monopolist, we will insist on charging a high price for automobiles, fewer automobiles will be sold, there will be less driving, and so less pollution. The fact that this will make us filthy rich is, of course, beside the point; the sole purpose of this policy is to reduce air pollution. This is all logically correct – but so far we don't think anyone has had the chutzpah to suggest that this is a good solution to the problem of air pollution.

If someone were to make a serious suggestion along these lines, we would simply point out that this "solution" has actually been tried. In Eastern Europe, under the old Communist governments, each country did in fact have a government monopoly over the production of automobiles. As the theory predicts, this did indeed result in expensive automobiles, fewer automobiles sold, and less driving. It is not so clear, however, that it actually resulted in less pollution. Sadly, the automobiles produced by the Eastern European monopolists were of such miserably bad quality that, for each mile they were driven, they created vastly more pollution than the automobiles driven in the competitive West. And, despite their absolute power, the monopolies of Eastern Europe managed to produce a lot more pollution per capita than the West did.

Arguments in favor of intellectual monopoly often have a similar flavor. They may be logically correct, but they tend to defy common sense. Ed Felten suggests applying what he calls the "pizzaright" test. The pizzaright is the exclusive right to sell pizza and makes it illegal to make or serve pizza without a license from the pizzaright owner.[1] We all recognize, of course, that this would be a terrible policy and that we should allow the market to decide who can make and sell pizza. The pizzaright test says that when evaluating an argument in favor of intellectual monopoly, if your argument serves equally well as an argument for a pizzaright, then your argument is defective – it proves too much. Whatever your argument is, it had better not apply to pizza.

Three things stand out in the case of arguments in favor of intellectual monopoly. First, all other things are never equal. A system of intellectual monopoly may well increase the amount of money that an innovator can make by selling his idea, but it also raises the cost of producing that idea. The innovator must pay all the other monopolists more to use their ideas to create his own. The system also creates a variety of other costs – innovators must engage in costly patent searches to make sure that they are not infringing existing patents – and the substantial legal and court fees earned by lawyers are all part of the cost of operating a system of intellectual monopoly. Because of all these costs, a system of intellectual monopoly may well lead to less innovation than a competitive system does. Second, monopoly is not widely viewed as the friend of innovation – the Eastern European state monopolies are only the most extreme of many examples. So, we may well wonder whether creating monopolies is really a good way to increase innovation. Finally – the bottom line. If intellectual monopoly is a good idea then it *must be* because it increases innovation and – given all the costs we have documented – it must increase innovation substantially over the competitive system. As we shall see, when we turn to the facts in the next chapter, there is no evidence that it does so.

Before returning to data and historical facts, we nevertheless choose, in this chapter, to entertain our readers with a few more theoretical debates. Probing critically the many theories explaining why intellectual monopoly is a socially valuable institutions – theories other than the large indivisibility–cum–small demand discussed in Chapter 6 – need not be a waste of time; rather, it serves three purposes. First, to debunk phony arguments widely used by lobbying groups, making clear to everyone that intellectual monopoly is not "obviously" or "logically" good. Second, to point at data that should be collected and empirical evidence that should be examined to assess whether patents and copyrights serve any useful social purpose. Third, understanding why most theories that support intellectual monopoly are jumbled is instrumental to obstruct policies meant to "improve" the func-tioning of the intellectual property system, and that are grounded upon such theories.

Private Property and Public Goods

A traditional argument in favor of intellectual monopoly is that the owner-ship of ideas is no different from the ownership of houses, cars, and other forms of private property. Certainly we agree – and not all opponents of intellectual property do – that private property can be a good thing. As an example of what goes wrong without private property in land and houses, we previously pointed to the situation in Zimbabwe. To elaborate:

"Last Saturday morning, a war veteran named Wind, accompanied by a bunch of young men, arrived on my farm in the morning. He gave my tenants and their young children two days to get off the farm and out of the house as he says it now belongs to him. Wind then went over the road and issued a verbal eviction order to my neighbors and then to the family living in their cottage," Buckle said. "These eviction orders were all non-negotiable and backed up by threats of violence. One of the threats was to throw a 4-year-old deaf child into a silage pit. Wind and his men then went to the houses of all the people who live and work on these farms. All the men, women and children were also ordered out. Wind closed the trading store on my farm and said it was now his. He ordered that all the dairy cows on one of the farms and all the laying hens on the other farm were not to be moved as they now belong to him."[2]

What are the consequences of the massive expropriation of private property that has been taking place in Zimbabwe for years? The following news item from the *Zimbabwe Independent* shows the economic devastation that occurs when there is no incentive to work your land because it may be seized by thugs at any moment:

GDP to decline by 11.5

The statistics released last week show that real GDP declined by 5% in 2000, 7.5% in 2001, and 11.9% in 2002. They are forecast to decline by a further 11.5% this year. [3]

So, one may be tempted to conclude, if the incentive to work and develop your land depends on your exclusive right to it, should not exclusive ownership of your idea be granted to you to provide for the appropriate incentives to develop it? Unfortunately, this analogy between idea and land is not a good one.

Consider the exclusive right to sell cars. From a legal point of view, there is nothing to prevent the government from giving me this as a property right. As with any property, I could sell or license the right – I could authorize General Motors and Ford to sell cars in exchange for fees; I could sell my exclusive franchise to Donald Trump; I could create a shrink-wrap agreement that anyone who purchased a car would have to agree to get off the road whenever I drove my car down the street. Pretty obviously this is a terrible idea, but the analogy between the exclusive right to sell cars and land is no different from the analogy between property of idea and property of land.

All property, then, is not created equal. There is good property – property of land and cars – which leads to competition. And there is bad property – property of ideas – which leads to monopoly. The difference between the two is not so difficult to see: granting me the exclusive right to sell cars gives me a property right over customers. That is, it gives me the right to tell my customers that they cannot do business with someone else. Economists agree that this is a terrible idea. Once upon a time, even *The Economist* thought so:

The granting [of] patents "inflames cupidity", excites fraud, stimulates men to run after schemes that may enable them to levy a tax on the public, begets disputes and quarrels betwixt inventors, provokes endless lawsuits.... The principle of the law from which such consequences flow cannot be just.[4]

These are, as we have come to learn during the century and a half in between, exactly the effects of intellectual "property."

A critical confusion in the case of ideas is the difference between an abstract idea and a concrete copy of it.[5] Owning an abstract idea means that you have the right to control all copies of that idea; owning a copy of an idea means that you have the right to control only the copy of that idea. We favor the latter but not the former right of property. The geometric idea of a circle and Piccadilly Circle are not the same thing, and it does not follow that if ownership of the second is good, so is ownership of the first. This is not some metaphysical quibble about Plato being right and George Berkeley being wrong, or about which came first the idea, the egg, or its implementation, the chicken. Quite the opposite, the difference is practical, economically relevant, and a matter of mere common sense.

Take, for example, the idea of antigravity. Imagine that you have just figured out how to reverse gravity. An embodiment of this abstract idea now exists in your mind. It has economic value: you can use it to construct flying saucers or you can teach it to other people interested in traveling to Mars. From an economic viewpoint, your knowledge of antigravity is as much a private good as the chair upon which you are sitting. In fact, your copy of antigravity is even more private than your chair. If you died without writing down or telling anyone of your idea, it would be as if your idea of antigravity had never been conceived, while your chair will probably survive you. If, on the other hand, you communicate your idea to me, then my copy of the idea of antigravity leads an existence entirely independent of your copy. You teaching me how antigravity works is a production process through which your idea, your time, and my time produce as output my knowledge of antigravity. If you were to die, my copy of the idea of antigravity would continue to exist and would be at least just as useful as it would have been had you remained alive. My copy of the idea of antigravity possesses, therefore, economic value. Similarly, your copy of the idea of antigravity also possesses economic value.

By way of contrast, abstract, disembodied ideas have no value. Borges makes this point clear in his short story "The Library of Babel." "When it was proclaimed that the Library contained all books, the first impression was one of extravagant happiness." But, of course, it is the embodied copies of ideas that have economic value, not their abstract existence, so, "As was natural, this inordinate hope was followed by an excessive depression. The certitude that some shelf in some hexagon held precious books and that these precious books were inaccessible, seemed almost intolerable."[6] Abstract ideas not yet embodied in someone or something are like the books in "The Library of Babel," socially useless because they are inaccessible. My working knowledge of antigravity or a textbook explaining antigravity have economic value, but the abstract idea has no value.

This may sound like we are making up unrealistic examples to build straw men that can easily catch fire. Nothing is further from truth. Consider the following discussion of some of the theoretical implications of the 1714–73 saga of John Harrison, his clocks, and the Board of Longitude prize.

What Parliament had solicited was knowledge. What it got were four clocks, all different. Compare Harrison's clocks with the astronomical algorithm that the board had hoped for. Such an algorithm did, in fact, materialize. The so-called lunar method used observations of distance between the moon and the stars to infer longitude. The lunar method had the essential feature of a pure public good: the tables that linked the observations to longitude were costly to compile in the first place, involving countless calculations, but once this was done, anyone could use the template at only the additional cost of owning the tables. The knowledge was nonrival.[7]

Was it? A nonrival, pure, public good means that we can all make use of the same knowledge without interfering with one another. Which knowledge was nonrival here? The clocks were certainly not, and the tables embodying the calculations were not either. If I were to take your clock or your table of calculations, that would certainly make it difficult for you to make use of the same. It is true that the tables were eventually made public together with the template of how to build the clock. This, however, is a consequence of the existence of the prize set by Parliament and administered by the Board of Longitude. The tables were "sold to the public" in exchange for the 10,000 pound prize, or at least for the promise of it, as it took a while for the prize to be awarded to Harrison. Absent the prize, Harrison would have most likely sold the clocks to skippers or shipowners in the most common of all private transactions: money for goods. To acquire usable knowledge, the buyers would have had to learn enough about astronomical laws, algebra, clock-making, and so on, to understand the tables and the template, and would have had to pay the requested price to the owner of the tables – the owner, that is, of the embodied knowledge.

To us, this story sounds like spending real resources to produce and acquire copies of usable knowledge: where is the public good hiding? No *usable* nonrival knowledge ever came into existence. The only two things that came into existence after Harrison completed his R&D investment were (1) the first copy of the new usable knowledge about marine chronometers, embodied in his brain, his tables, his templates; and (2) a "copying" technology, which produced replicas of such usable knowledge at a unit cost much lower than the one Harrison had to pay through his initial R&D investment. The example fits perfectly the theoretical model of competitive innovation we described in Chapter 6. Contrary to the quoted text's assertion, there is absolutely no public good or economically usable nonrivalrous knowledge, either here or elsewhere.

What does this have to do with property? A lot: because the usable knowledge is completely embodied in objects the inventor controls, and is reproducible through a production process that he also controls, ordinary property in embodied objects is enough to allow for appropriation of value by the innovator via competitive rents. There is no obvious need for additional rights, in particular for monopolistic rights such as those afforded by patents.

Ordinary property such as land and cars can be sold with contracts that place limitations such as easements or covenants on the new owner; it can also be rented on a temporary basis with a variety of restrictions placed on the user. How is this different from the owner of an abstract idea placing restrictions on the users of that idea? As we said, there is good property (the kind that enhances competition) and there is bad property (the kind that leads to monopoly). The law generally distinguishes between the two when it comes to writing contracts. If I sell you a portion of my land, and create an easement whereby you allow my cattle to cross your land to get to the nearby stream, the law recognizes this as a legitimate interest on my part, and such a contract is easily enforced, as there is no sense in which it implies an impediment to competition. If one car manufacturer sells another a part and requires that any car produced with that part must be sold at a very high price, that contract – promoting, as it does, monopoly and not competition – not only would not be enforceable but also would be a violation of antitrust law and would probably result in a substantial fine. The easement allowing cattle to cross the land is good because it is instrumental to the creation of additional economic value – raising the cattle. The prohibition on making copies of a legally acquired book not only does not facilitate the creation of additional economic value but, in fact, prevents it. Property in copies of ideas is good property, enhancing competition. Property in abstract copies of ideas is bad property, leading to monopoly.

There is a more sophisticated version of the argument that intellectual property is like any other kind of property, which is popular among economists rather than lawyers and politicians. It asserts that without intellectual monopoly ideas are nonrivalrous so that, once the first copy of an idea is produced, it becomes a public good. A good is nonrivalrous, or a public good, if one person's consumption does not limit the ability of others to consume it. For example, national defense is a public good. My enjoyment of the benefits of my country being defended does not limit your ability to enjoy the same benefit, so national defense is nonrivalrous. Put a different way, national defense is a public good, because we all share equally in its benefits. Economists argue that some form of government intervention is needed for the provision of public goods: because you will benefit from my contribution to the public good, there is a tendency for you to free ride off of my contribution and for me to undercontribute. This is sometimes called the tragedy of the commons – when something is commonly owned but privately enjoyed, everyone tries to consume without contributing. Ideas, it is argued, are nonrivalrous like public defense or the beauty of a sunset in Capri – your use of the fundamental theorem of calculus in no way interferes with my use of it. Ideas, it is argued, are prone to suffer the tragedy of the commons: everyone trying to use common ideas without ever contributing to the common pool. However, this same line of reasoning goes, ideas, unlike sunsets, are "excludable," meaning that we do not have to share ideas with other people if we do not choose to. We can therefore solve the problem of free riding on ideas by "protecting" them with intellectual monopoly.

To make sense, the argument that ideas are a public good must refer to abstract ideas, because only abstract ideas are nonrivalrous. Once we recognize that the relevant economic entities over which property should be exercised are not abstract ideas but copies of ideas, our perspective on intellectual property changes. Copies of ideas are obviously both rivalrous and excludable – they are not a public good. To put this in perspective, it is obvious that my drinking from my cup of coffee does not affect your use of your cup of coffee. No one would go on to suggest from this fact that coffee is nonrivalrous or a public good and that special laws and subsidies are needed in the coffee market. It is true that there is legal protection for cups of coffee – if you drink my cup of coffee without my permission, this would be an act of theft, and you would be subject to various civil and criminal penalties. Economists regard these good property rights in the usual fashion as securing the fruits of labor and providing incentive to care for valuable assets. But notice that less legal protection is needed for your copy of your idea than is needed for your cup of coffee – while it may be relatively easy for me to steal your cup of coffee by threat or when you are not looking, it is fairly difficult for me to learn your idea without your active assistance. Indeed, it would seem that the legal protection needed is no more than the legal right not to be subject to physical torture or coercion – a right that we enjoy (or according to recent U.S. legal developments, perhaps not) regardless of the state of copyright and patent law. Be this as it may, there is no serious challenge to intellectual property in the sense of your right to determine to whom, under what circumstances, and at what price you will transfer copies of your idea.

All of this brings us to what intellectual property law is really about – a reality that is often obscured by analogies to other types of property. Intellectual property law is not about your right to control your copy of your idea – this is a right that, as we have just pointed out, does not need a great deal of protection. What intellectual property law is really about is my right to control your copy of my idea.

To return to the Zimbabwean example, suppose that Wind, instead of seizing Buckle's farm, had purchased some unused land belonging to Buckle. If he then started his own farm on that land and entered into competition with Buckle, maybe imitating Buckle's selection of crops and farming techniques, Buckle might not much like that. But we would scarcely use derogatory words such as *pirate* to describe Wind's behavior in this case. Yet this is exactly what proponents of intellectual monopoly do. When I buy from you a copy of your idea and reproduce or improve it, I enter into competition with you. You might not much like that, but you still have the money I paid you for the price you set as well as your original copy of your idea, which you are free to use or sell or do with as you please.

To summarize then, it is copies of ideas that have economic value. Copies of ideas should have the usual protection afforded to all kinds of property: they should not be taken away without permission, and the owner should have the legal right to sell them. However, intellectual property in the form of patents and copyrights is not about property rights in this sense. It is about the right to control other people's copies of ideas and by doing so establish a legal monopoly over all copies of an idea. Because it makes this fact transparent, we prefer the term *intellectual monopoly* to the usual term *intellectual property*.

Economic Arguments for Intellectual Monopoly

Economists – ourselves included – think that it is important that the creators of ideas be compensated for their effort in adding to our stock of knowledge.[8] Although the economics literature generally acknowledges that intellectual property leads to undesirable intellectual monopoly, it also argues that this might be a good thing – because creators of new ideas may not be adequately compensated otherwise, and this is one way to provide additional compensation. As Joseph Schumpeter, in the words of Jean Tirole, puts it, "If one wants to induce firms to undertake R&D one must accept the creation of monopolies as a necessary evil."[9] This view is as commonly held among economists today as it was in the past. In their recent textbook, Robert Barro and Xavier Sala-i-Martin argue:

> In order to motivate research, successful innovators have to be compensated in some manner. The basic problem is that the creation of a new idea or design . . . is costly. . . . It would be efficient ex post to make the existing discoveries freely available to all producers, but this practice fails to provide the ex ante incentives for further inventions. A tradeoff arises . . . between restrictions on the use of existing ideas and the rewards to inventive activity.[10]

Fixed Cost and Constant Marginal Cost

The economic argument, then, for intellectual monopoly is that without it there will not be incentives to produce ideas. The traditional logic is one of fixed cost and constant marginal cost. The cost of innovation is a fixed cost – ideas are expensive to produce. Once discovered, ideas are distributed at a constant marginal cost. As we learn in Econ 101, perfect competition forces prices to marginal cost, so profits are forced to zero. This means that the fixed cost of producing the idea cannot be recouped. Consequently, without intellectual monopoly, there will be no innovation.

    The idea that monopoly is necessary for innovation forms the foundation for a wide variety of economic models, ranging from general equilibrium models of monopolistic competition to micromodels of patents and patent races. The original theoretical argument was sketched by Allyn Young before the Second World War and developed in greater detail by Joseph Schumpeter during the war. The first formal treatment of the idea that competitive markets are intrinsically incapable of handling innovations can be found in writings by Kenneth Arrow and subsequently Karl Shell, published in the early and middle 1960s. In the second half of the 1980s, Robert Lucas, Paul Romer, and many followers used new analytical instruments to apply this point of view to the problem of economic development, creating a theory now known as the new growth theory.

Leaving aside the, possibly too theoretical, observation that the logical argument works only if the marginal cost is truly constant and fails in the more generally accepted case in which it is increasing, the fixed cost plus constant marginal cost argument fails along two more substantive dimensions. First, as a matter of theory, perfect competition forces goods to be priced at marginal cost only in the absence of capacity constraints – and, as we just argued at length, the rents generated by capacity constraints along with other first-mover advantages can and do lead to thriving innovation. Pricing at marginal cost is a prediction for the long run, which applies only once capacity constraints are no longer binding. Erecting a theory of economic growth on the flimsy assumption that productive capacity always builds costlessly and instantaneously seems like a risky proposition, at least in a world where scarcity still reigns supreme. Second, as a practical matter, in most industries and for most innovations the short run is what matters to make money; when the long run comes, your innovation has probably already given way to an even newer one. Focusing the attention of the theory on the long-run equilibrium and bypassing the study of the short-run dynamics when capacity constraints are binding yields a formally elegant model with, unfortunately, little or no practical relevance. In spite of our dislike of Keynesian monetary economics, John Maynard Keynes's dictum, "in the long run we are all dead," does seem to apply to new growth theory.

There is an additional and important reason why the theoretical foundations of the new growth theory are shaky. A key element of new growth theory is the assumption that after an imitator enters, price will be driven down to cost, and there will be no profits to pay for the original innovation. A moment of reflection shows that if there is any cost at all to imitation, then there will be no imitation, and the innovator will enjoy an unfettered monopoly. For the imitators correctly understand that if they were to enter, they would lose their fixed cost of imitation. That is, if we take seriously the argument as to why there should be no innovation without intellectual property, we find that it means instead that there will not be imitation without intellectual property, thereby undermining the first argument.[11]

Now, strictly speaking, new growth theory assumes that imitation is in fact costless. Amazingly enough, this does not suffice to save the argument. For in this case imitators are indifferent to imitating, as there is no profit in it. So there is a perfectly good equilibrium in which innovators get monopoly profits and imitators choose not to enter. And there is also a – fairly implausible – equilibrium in which there is no innovation for fear that the imitators, although indifferent, will choose to enter. For some reason that completely escapes us, the scholars working in the new growth theory tradition take the least plausible equilibrium under the least plausible set of assumptions and act as though it is a dead certainty in the real world. Go figure.

Unpriced Spillover Externalities

A variation on the fixed cost plus constant marginal cost theme is that ideas are subject to unpriced spillover externalities – technical jargon hiding a simple idea that is easily illustrated through the example of the wheelbarrow. After the wheelbarrow is invented, to make productive use of it by moving sand, dirt, and dung around, it must be used in plain sight. Any passersby will see the wheelbarrow in use, and by doing so will get the idea of a wheelbarrow for free, thereby rushing home to build their own wheelbarrows. Hence, the valuable knowledge of the wheelbarrow is transmitted without the permission of, and without payment to, the inventor.

There is no point in denying that a number of valuable innovations are like the wheelbarrow; in these cases, imitation is relatively cheap and, what is more important, imitation can be carried out without having to purchase a copy of the idea from the original innovator. If looking and studying what the other person has done is enough to produce a good imitation, and very little compensation accrues to the innovator for the act of looking, then we say that there is an unpriced externality. Once you recognize that such cases exist, three questions become important. First, how widespread are they? That is, how many inventions are like the wheelbarrow? Second, for those that are like the wheelbarrow, are the externalities so large that, absent intellectual monopoly, the original innovator would have never invented the wheelbarrow? Third, and finally, is intellectual monopoly the socially smart way to address this potential inefficiency?

Young, Schumpeter, Arrow, and their more recent followers seem convinced that most ideas are like the idea of the wheelbarrow, spreading freely and costlessly. When we are reminded by our Mexican friends that the Mayas had the wheel but, partly for religious reasons and partly because the rough terrain made its use unbeneficial in the short run, used it only for children's toys, calendars, and other ritual purposes, but never for carts or other practical uses, or when we learn that the "idea" of agriculture spread from the Fertile Crescent at the amazing speed of roughly one kilometer per year, we tend to doubt that most ideas spread as fast as many economic theorists theorize. Not to speak of the ability of making espresso coffee properly, which seems to still remain secluded within the boundaries of Italy, or of Naples as a mutual friend of ours insistently and reasonably argues.

These may seem strange examples, but they are not: they are examples of ideas that, at least in principle, should spread fast and costlessly, as all they require is learning by looking. That most technologies do not spread all that fast – why are people in rural China or in large areas of Italy still not using wireless Internet? – is not surprising, as they require lots of human and physical capital, which are costly to accumulate. But why is the bidet not widespread in the United States, and why are the kitchen sinks of most European houses not equipped with a garbage disposal? Thousands of examples of "costless" ideas spreading painfully slow cast serious doubts on the alleged commonness of imitative externalities. Why is it taking so long for economists to realize that intellectual monopoly is a needless evil?

As for the other two questions, they either did not ask them or their answers were ambiguous. Arrow, for example, clearly thought that "yes" was the right answer to the second question, on the size of the externality, but that public support for research and innovation was the solution, thereby answering the third question in the negative. These are indeed complex questions, which can be seriously addressed only with substantial patience; no quick and ready answer is available. We will try to address the first and second questions here, while the last chapter tentatively addresses the third question and the policies we believe would result in socially beneficial outcomes.

The Imitative Externality

It is certainly true that imitation is everywhere, from sports to business, from dancing to dressing, from driving to singing. In fact, imitation is at the heart of competitive behavior and of almost any kind of social interaction. Like the fixed cost–cum–marginal cost argument that, as we pointed out earlier, is so powerful that it can be applied to any and every thing, imitation is so widespread that, when taken literally, it is also everywhere. By this token, one should see unpriced externalities in every market where producers imitate one another, and thereby conclude that all kinds of economic activities should be allowed some form of monopoly power. Restaurants imitate one another, as coffee shops, athletes, real estate agents, car salespeople, and even bricklayers do, but we would certainly find it crazy to attribute to a firm in each of these businesses a monopoly power on one technique or another. This suggests that equating imitation with unpriced externalities leads us into a dark night in which all cows are gray; this is not a pleasant situation; hence, we better turn on a few lights.

Although the view that ideas, once discovered, can be imitated for free by anybody is pervasive, it is far from the truth. Although it may occasionally be the case that an idea is acquired at no cost, ideas are generally difficult to communicate, and the resources for doing so are limited. It is rather ironic that a group of economists, who are also college professors and earn a substantial living teaching old ideas because their transmission is neither simple nor cheap, would argue otherwise in their scientific work. Most of the time imitation requires effort and, what is more important, imitation requires purchasing either some products or some teaching services from the original innovator, meaning that most spillovers are priced.

There are certainly informational spillovers as ideas move from person to person, but it is hard to see why in most instances they are not priced. Although it is possible to imagine examples such as the wheelbarrow where an idea cannot be used without revealing the secret, relatively few ideas are of this type. For copyrightable creations such as books, music, plays, movies, and art, unpriced spillovers obviously play little role. A book, a CD, or a work of art must be purchased before it can be used, and the creator is free to make use of his creation in the privacy of his home without revealing the secret to the public at large – similarly with movies or plays. In all cases, the creation must effectively be purchased before the "secret" is revealed.

In the case of patentable ideas such as the wheelbarrow, the idea of unpriced spillovers is more plausible. Yet there is no reason to believe that it is of practical importance. Indeed, there is a modern example of the wheelbarrow – that of Travelpro – the inventor of the modern wheeled roll-on suitcase with a retractable handle. Obviously, such an idea cannot both be useful and be secret – and once you see a wheeled roll-on suitcase it is not difficult to figure out how to make one of your own. Needless to say, Travelpro was quickly imitated – and you probably have never even heard of the company. Nevertheless – despite Travelpro's inability to garner an intellectual monopoly over its invention – it found it worthwhile to innovate, and it still does a lucrative business today, claiming "425,000 Flight Crew Members Worldwide Choose Travelpro Luggage."[12]

Quantifying Unpriced Spillovers

The widespread belief in the free availability of ideas is sometime due to poor inspection of data and historical documents, but most often it is the consequence of a common cognitive bias. Every day we are surrounded, one might say bombarded, by references to and the effects of so many ideas that we often feel as if we knew them all or could know and use them all if we only wanted to. But that is just a pious illusion, as we should have all learned when our seven-year-old child asked for an explanation of how the chip in our wondrous cellular phone *really* worked. For most ideas, we may have heard about them, we may even know where to find a manual or an expert who could teach us about them, but we are very far from being able to put them into productive economic usage. Take, for example, the famous idea $E = mc^2$. This is commonly known, in the sense that many people can quote the formula. But how many people actually know what it means or can put it to any productive use? The two of us, for starters, have no idea of what to do with it.

Most productive ideas these days especially, but certainly since at least the times of the Renaissance, are much more complicated and less self-evident than the wheelbarrow or the wheeled suitcase. One does not learn the formula for a new drug by staring at the pill, and while the formula may be divined in a chemical lab, the procedure for producing it may not be. Billions of people have drunk billions of gallons of Coca-Cola, but the formula is still famously a well-kept secret. Even the steam engine invented by this book's designated scoundrel, James Watt, was not easy to copy: twenty or thirty years after it had been introduced, purchasers still needed the expertise of Mr. Watt and his assistants to erect and operate it. More to the point, almost forty years after Honda and Toyota invaded the U.S. market, General Motors and Ford, not to speak of Fiat and Rover, are still incapable of producing cars with the same quality, reliability, and fuel consumption. Millions of books have described the recipe for *tortelloni di zucca* to millions of people around the world for decades, but we are sorry to inform you that those they make in the area between Mantua and Modena are still unbeatable, not to speak of those that the mother-in-law of one of us cooks, yearly, on December 24.

The point should be clear by now: when one looks at the world of productive ideas, there is little prima facie evidence of spillover externalities from economically valuable innovations. This makes the fact that little justification for the assumption is given in the economics literature rather suspicious. If we take the role of devil's advocate in support of the spillover theory, the most likely culprit would seem to be employees moving from firm to firm, carrying trade secrets with them as they move. However, as Gary Becker astutely observed: "Firms introducing innovations are alleged to be forced to share their knowledge with competitors through the bidding away of employees who are privy to their secrets. This may well be a common practice, but if employees benefit from access to salable information about secrets, they would be willing to work more cheaply than otherwise."[13] Plenty of supporting evidence, from apprentices' wages to the practice of pricing the academic quality of a department into the salary of new assistant professors, makes Becker's observation compelling.

The empirical justification for the idea of unpriced spillovers seems to come largely from the notion of agglomeration – that similar firms locate near one another to take advantage of positive externalities in the form of ideas that are "in the air." But notice that firms would have incentive to locate nearby even if spillovers were priced, provided that information transfer from nearby firms is less costly than it is from distant firms. Did Silicon Valley form so that employees might overhear valuable ideas in bars, or because it made it relatively easy for firms to interact with one another contractually? Certainly, evidence supporting the idea that large unpriced spillovers take place among innovating firms is scarce at best. Ellison and Glaeser provide the most careful analysis, finding only very weak evidence that agglomeration is due to spillovers.[14] Other studies find even weaker or no evidence for the allegedly pervasive unpriced spillovers. Acemoglu and Angrist, for example, estimate average schooling externalities at the U.S. state level and find no evidence of significant externalities.[15] Ciccone and Peri examine local labor markets to test whether productivity increases with the average human capital of the workforce in the area where firms are located; their data reject the hypothesis.[16] Castiglionesi and Ornaghi look carefully for external effects in a large panel of Spanish manufacturing firms data and conclude that they cannot find any.[17] Most anecdotal evidence about industrial agglomeration, from Silicon Valley to the greenhouses of Almería, suggests that firms do price informational and technological spillovers into the wages of their employees.

If unpriced spillovers are indeed important, it must be that ideas are so inexpensive to transmit that mere observation is enough to convey the essential core of the idea. Here the evidence is overwhelmingly against: there is a large literature on technology transfer strongly indicating that – even with the active help of the innovator – ideas are difficult and costly to transmit. Several examples of technology diffusion illustrate the point.

One of the earliest known examples of the diffusion of technology is the spread of agriculture during the Neolithic period. Work by Cavalli-Sforza and others has documented that the average speed of diffusion of agriculture was of about one kilometer a year, over a period of many thousands of years. Transportation available at the time – walking – could carry the ideas many thousands of kilometers per year, so there is a difference of three orders of magnitude between the rate at which ideas could physically move from one location to another and the rate at which the idea actually was transmitted and became useful.[18]

Of course, part of the reason for the slow diffusion of agriculture was the need to adopt crop strains to local circumstances, not merely the need to get "the idea" of agriculture. But the adaptation of ideas to local circumstances is important for most ideas – books printed in English, for example, are not of terrifically great value in China. As we argue elsewhere, competition, and not monopoly, generally provides the collaborative advantage that speeds diffusion. If copyright laws were enforced in China so that English books could not easily be pirated into Chinese translations, is it likely that this would increase the speed with which translations became available?

Another good example is that of seventeenth-century silk production:

In 1607 Vittorio Zonca published in Padova his Nuovo Teatro di Machine et Edificii, which included, among numerous engraving of various contraptions, the description of an intricate water-powered machine for throwing silk in a large factory. Zonca's book went into second edition in 1621 and a third in 1656. . . . G. N. Clark has shown that a copy of the first edition of Zonca's book had been on the open-access shelves of the Bodleian Library from at least as early as 1620.[19]

Yet despite the fact that the blueprint for a silk factory was readily available, it was not until one hundred years later that "the English succeeded in building a mill for the throwing of silk." This occurred only after "John Lombe, during two years of industrial espionage in Italy, found means to see this engine so often that he made himself a master of the whole invention and of all the different parts and motions."[20]

Other examples from the past also show the difficulties involved in transferring knowledge. There are many cases of individuals migrating to find out about technologies and inventions. To learn to work the dockyards, to make the pendulum clock, or to make woolens, you moved to Holland. To learn to cast ordnance, you moved to England. To make spectacles or to work glass, you moved to Venice.

Indeed, we find that knowledge is so embodied that craftsmen were bribed, and sometimes kidnapped and taken to an area where their skills were lacking:

An inquiry by the Bergskollegium in the 1660s into the emigration of Swedish iron masters revealed that a number of workers sailed from Nykoping believing that they were being taken to some other part of Sweden. Instead they were brought to Lubeck, from there to Hamburg, and finally to France, where Colbert was determined to start an iron industry on the Swedish model.[21]

Yet another example of the slow spread of knowledge is the use of double-entry bookkeeping. This was invented in Italy at the end of the fourteenth century, and widely used in Venice in the fifteenth century. It did not reach the Hanseatic League cities in northern Europe until well into the sixteenth century.

However, one does not have to turn to the Middle Ages to find examples of the difficulty in transferring ideas. *The Economist* of December 22, 2001, ran an amusing piece on the "search for a perfect cup" of espresso coffee. The point of the article is that, in spite of all its centuries of age and of the apparent simplicity of its very publicly available formula, most bartenders in the world outside Italy have no idea how to make a good espresso. What is especially interesting is the embodiment of information in espresso machines, in different varieties of coffee beans, and in different human beings.

Finally, let us go back from where we started and admit once again that very mild unpriced spillover externalities are endemic to everyday life. For example, when a beautifully dressed woman walks past one of the two of us, his utility is substantially increased, although there is no reason to believe that the woman gains from this admiration. Because beautifully dressed women cannot easily charge their male admirers, this is an unpriced spillover externality. To our knowledge, no public policy suggestion has been put forward that public monopolies should be awarded to solve this particular externality, nor many other similar minor externalities we encounter every day.

Secrecy and Patents

A common argument in favor of patent law is that to get a patent you must reveal the secret of your invention.[22] Are patent laws a cure for trade secrecy? Granting a legal monopoly in exchange for revealing the secret of the innovation is one way to make innovations more widely available in the long run. However, as a number of economists have pointed out, in the simplest case this argument fails.

Suppose that each innovation can be kept secret for some period of time, with the actual length varying from innovation to innovation, and that the length of legal patent protection is twenty years. Then the innovator will choose secrecy in those cases where it is possible to keep the secret for longer than twenty years, and will choose patent protection in those cases where the secret can be kept only for less than twenty years. In this case, patent protection has a socially damaging effect. Secrets that can be kept for more than twenty years are still kept for the maximum length of time, while those that without patent would have been monopolized for a shorter time are now monopolized for twenty years. Indeed, it is important to realize that outside the pharmaceutical industry, where the regulatory system effectively forces revelation, trade secrecy is considerably more important than patent. Repeatedly, in surveys of R&D lab and company managers, only 23 percent to 35 percent indicate that patents are effective as a means of appropriating returns. By way of contrast, 51 percent argue that trade secrecy is effective.[23]

Although in the simplest case patent law does not have an impact on trade secrecy, in cases where it is possible to expend real resources to make secrets less accessible, the innovator faces a real trade-off between private rent seeking through secrecy and public rent seeking through patents. This is true also in the case of copyright, as publicly enforced copyright is potentially an alternative to socially undesirable methods such as encryption and digital rights management that are designed to limit reproduction. There is a small literature in economics on this trade-off.[24]

One issue is how information that changes rival firm beliefs may work to the advantage of the firm releasing the information. Okuno-Fujiwara, Postlewaite, and Suzumura put focus on the fact the innovators may have strategic reasons to reveal secrets as well as to keep them: by revealing secrets they may induce R&D from competitors that they will benefit from in turn.[25] Ponce considers the possibility that under existing patent law, by disclosing a secret, a rival might be prevented from patenting the idea.[26] Boldrin and Levine show that an innovator who does not have the option of using a legal monopoly will invest less in productive capacity than an innovator who has access to patents, as less capacity increases profitability after the secret is lost.[27]

However, patents, which are meant to reduce secrecy, may lead to the opposite result. If imitation is possible early in the life cycle of the industry, an innovator has little reason to enforce a patent, as there is no reason to restrict capacity when industry capacity is low anyway. For this reason, an innovator with the option of a legal monopoly may have greater incentive for secrecy than one without – to make sure that imitation cannot take place until it is profitable for him to make use of the patent. By way of contrast, we have pointed out that under competition there is a strong incentive to make public small intermediate steps – by doing so, competitors are encouraged to make additional advances that the original innovator will benefit from. If instead there is a race for a patent, the incentive is to keep intermediate results secret so as to keep competitors from winning the race.

In fact there is much evidence that secrecy and legal monopoly are complementary rather than alternatives. Despite copyright, producers of books, music, and movies have aggressively attempted to encrypt their work with digital rights management, not only encrypting DVDs, but even going so far as to encrypt CDs using methods that are incompatible with many CD players and, in some cases, physically damaging to computers.

There is evidence that the possibility of legal monopoly does have an impact on the direction of R&D, if not on the amount of R&D. Recent research by Moser on countries with and without patents in the nineteenth century shows that those countries without patents did not innovate less, but tended to focus innovation in areas where secrecy is relatively easy, such as food processing and scientific instruments. Whether such innovations are more or less socially desirable than other innovations is difficult to say, as Moser stresses in her work.[28]

Although replacing secrecy with legal monopoly may have some impact on the direction of innovation, there is little reason to believe that it actually succeeds in making important secrets public and easily accessible to other innovators. For most innovations, it is the details that matter, not the rather vague descriptions required in patent applications. Take, for example, the controversial Amazon.com one-click patent, U.S. Patent No. 5,960,411. The actual idea is rather trivial, and there are a variety of ways in which one-click purchase can be implemented by computer, any one of which can be coded by a competent programmer given a modest investment of time and effort. For the record, here is the detailed description of the invention from the patent application:

The present invention provides a method and system for single-action ordering of items in a client/server environment. The single-action ordering system of the present invention reduces the number of purchaser interactions needed to place an order and reduces the amount of sensitive information that is transmitted between a client system and a server system. In one embodiment, the server system assigns a unique client identifier to each client system. The server system also stores purchaser-specific order information for various potential purchasers. The purchaser-specific order information may have been collected from a previous order placed by the purchaser. The server system maps each client identifier to a purchaser that may use that client system to place an order. The server system may map the client identifiers to the purchaser who last placed an order using that client system. When a purchaser wants to place an order, the purchaser uses a client system to send the request for information describing the item to be ordered along with its client identifier. The server system determines whether the client identifier for that client system is mapped to a purchaser. If so mapped, the server system determines whether single-action ordering is enabled for that purchaser at that client system. If enabled, the server system sends the requested information (e.g., via a Web page) to the client computer system along with an indication of the single action to perform to place the order for the item. When single-action ordering is enabled, the purchaser need only perform a single action (e.g., click a mouse button) to order the item. When the purchaser performs that single action, the client system notifies the server system. The server system then completes the order by adding the purchaser-specific order information for the purchaser that is mapped to that client identifier to the item order information (e.g., product identifier and quantity). Thus, once the description of an item is displayed, the purchaser need only take a single action to place the order to purchase that item. Also, since the client identifier identifies purchaser-specific order information already stored at the server system, there is no need for such sensitive information to be transmitted via the Internet or other communications medium.[29]

As can be seen, the "secret" that is revealed is, if anything, less informative than the simple observation that the purchaser buys something by means of a single click. Information that might actually be of use to a computer programmer – for example, the source code to the specific implementation used by Amazon – is not provided as part of the patent, nor is it required to be provided. In fact, the actual implementation of the one-click procedure consists of a complicated system of subcomponents and modules requiring a substantial amount of human capital and of specialized working time to be assembled. The generic idea revealed in the patent is easy to understand and copy, but it is of no practical value whatsoever. The useful ideas are neither revealed in the patent nor easy to imitate without reinventing them from scratch, which is what lots of other people beside Amazon's direct competitors (books are not the only thing sold on the Web, after all) would have done to everybody's else benefit, had U.S. Patent No. 5,960,411 not prevented them from actually doing so. Certainly it is hard to argue that the social cost of giving Amazon a monopoly over purchasing by clicking a single button is somehow offset by the social benefit of the information revealed in the patent application.

Schumpeterian Good Monopoly

Although originally not a mainstream view in economics, the Schumpeterian view is now close to becoming orthodoxy in most circles.[30] Schumpeter celebrates monopoly as the ultimate accomplishment of capitalism. He argues that, in a world in which intellectual property holders are monopolists, competition is a dynamic process that is implemented via the method of creative destruction. This idea remains widespread today; for example, Aghion and Howitt in 1992 developed a formal model based on Schumpeterian ideas. The critical principle is that competition is not in the market but for the market; while competition may be good at a given point in time, as it induces static efficiency, monopoly is good in the long run, these theorists argue, because it brings about dynamic efficiency, that is, innovation. The innovative winner takes all the market for a while, but threat of drastic innovation is strong enough to force dominant firms to continue innovating and to make monopolized markets effectively contestable. The idea is that drastic innovations are frequent, so that the monopolist is only a temporary one. Only monopolists who innovate as fast or faster than potential competitors remain viable; hence, the system is capable of generating a very high rate of innovation.

An example of how this might take place is given by Evans and Schmalensee.[31] They examine four cases of this "frequent policing" of monopolistic positions: (1) the 1990 leader in word processing, WordPerfect, is overtaken by Microsoft Word in 1997; (2) the 1988 leader of spreadsheets Lotus 1-2-3 is overtaken by Microsoft Excel by 1997; (3) the 1989 leader in personal finance, Managing your Money, is overtaken by Quicken by 1996; (4) the 1990 leader in desktop publishing, Adobe PageMaker, is overtaken by QuarkXPress by 1997.

There are, however, three features of this data that deserve note.

- Two of the four initial leaders are overtaken by the big monopoly, Microsoft, and since then ("then" was ten years ago) there has been no further overtaking. When the initial leaders are overtaken, they are far from being monopolists, either de facto or de jure.
- It takes about seven years for the first lead to change hands and, as far as we can tell, infinity for the second leader to be overtaken.
- All the reported examples of dynamic competition, either in the software industry or elsewhere, pertain to the early stages of a new industry, when intellectual property protection is low and imitation and competition are high. Had the spreadsheet been patented, would Lotus 1-2-3 have been overtaken by Excel?

As we have repeatedly insisted, once the industry matures and intellectual property rights are obtained, monopolies tend to become very long lasting. When was the last time that someone overtook the Hollywood studios or the Big Five in the movie and music industry? How long would have we waited for someone to overtake AT&T and free the telecommunication industry if its monopoly had not been torn apart by an antitrust action? More generally, we ask the reader to perform the following mental exercise: how many industries can you mention where the mechanism described in the Schumpeterian model has been at work, with innovators frequently supplanting the incumbent monopolist, becoming a monopolist in turn, to be killed shortly after by yet another innovator?

The basic Schumpeterian argument is oblivious to the fact that once monopolies are established, rather than allow themselves to be swept away by competition, they generally engage in rent-seeking behavior – using their size and political clout to get the government to protect their market position. How, for example, does the expenditure of money on lobbyists by drug companies that are fighting for extensions of their patents figure into the Schumpeterian picture?

Although Schumpeter's arguments were widely and broadly expounded in the industrial organization and growth literature forty to fifty years ago, they were swept away by the hard facts of the 1960s and 1970s when the monopolized sectors of the U.S. economy stagnated without innovating, while growth and innovation were flowing from small-sized firms, and everybody agreed that "small is beautiful." One should only thank our good luck, or the courts of the time, that Apple and IBM could not even conceive of patenting the PC and its crucial components back in the 1970s. Both the blossoming of the PC-hardware industry and the eventual demise of IBM and Apple as the dominant firms are due to the effective lack of patent protection on production processes and on most crucial components. Exactly the opposite of what the misleading Schumpeterian principles of drastic innovation and patents are beautiful would have predicted. Regrettably, such principles have made a comeback under the cover of "intellectual property is good for innovation": as usual, nothing is particularly new under the sun, at least in the land of economic fallacies. Even Schumpeter himself admitted, "It is certainly as conceivable that an all-pervading cartel system might sabotage all progress as it is that it might realize, with smaller social and private costs, all that perfect competition is supposed to realize."[32]

The Idea Economy

It is often suggested that ideas are becoming increasingly important as a component of the economy. Pundits and academics alike theorize about the new economy, the weightless economy, the global information economy, and so forth. They cast images of a world where machines, besides reproducing themselves, produce all kinds of material goods and services as well, while humans engage in creative activities and in the exchange of ideas. Although this sounds fascinating, like every utopia, it is mostly a pipedream: any reader of Karl Marx's *Grundrisse* would recognize his description of communism to match closely that of an idea economy.[33] The question is, which kind of institutional arrangements are advocated for travel to these gardens of utopia, and are the flowers of such gardens as enchanting as their advocates tell us?

Our suspicions are raised by the fact that, customarily, the visionary preacher of the idea economy is also a staunch supporter of intellectual monopoly, and of ever stronger and stricter intellectual monopoly laws. This seems to have the implication that either, eventually, we must reach a state where copyrights and patents, and the loss of freedom they entail, becomes ubiquitous, or we must somehow move beyond capitalism to some sort of socialistic world in which we no longer attempt to profit from our individual enterprises, but rather all agree to produce for some sort of common good, or perhaps even just for our own good with the hope that this somehow turns out to be the common good as well.

An example of this "modern" perspective can be found in DeLong and Froomkin's "deconstruct[ion of] Adam Smith's case for the market system."[34] To summarize their argument, excluding people from using an idea is difficult because digital data is too easy to copy, and in any case, digital goods are nonrivalrous, meaning that it is not a good idea from a social point of view to try, given that copies are so cheap. Then they argue that the value of digital goods is less apparent to the consumer than that of traditional goods. They conclude from this analysis that we are facing a massive market failure, and they look for remedies.

The reason why digital goods are complex goods about which consumers are badly informed seems to us more an assertion than a proven fact. Why a video game or a cellular phone service is any more complex than a recent BMW we do not know. Is a digital book more complex than a regular book? Is music in MP3 format more complex than a CD? Is purchasing underwear online from Victoria's Secret riskier than doing it by telephone from a catalog? As one starts to think of concrete examples, it is easy to realize that the additional complexity of digital goods with respect to the usual ones is just empty rhetoric. When our two children were, respectively, nineteen and fifteen years old, neither one seemed to have much of a problem purchasing digital or nondigital goods online. In fact, they did so much more easily and efficiently than by going to the local mall (among other things, because neither was yet allowed to drive around town). They seemed to be able to read the instructions online equally as well as on the piece of paper that comes with regularly wrapped goods.

As to the issue of whether digital data is too easy to copy, is it true that technological change – the Internet revolution – will lower the costs of copying and distributing ideas so much that competitive rents are no longer significant?

In a dynamic world in which capacity expands over time, such as that studied by Boldrin and Levine or Quah,[35] ideas may eventually become freely available to everyone. But time elapses before this happens, and in the interim, the idea sells for a positive price, with the rents going to the original innovator. What is the implication of technological change for these rents? Do competitive rents drop to zero, so that without strengthened intellectual monopoly, ideas will cease to be produced?

First, notice that for patentable ideas, this discussion is largely moot. The time required to transmit a blueprint or engineering diagram lies not in the difference between the several days it might take to deliver by mail and the several seconds by e-mail, but rather in the amount of time it takes for the receiver to read and understand the technical specifications. Indeed, in the case of many patentable ideas, the cost of redistribution may well be increasing over time. Certainly the idea of how to build a wheel is much easier to communicate than the idea of how to build an atomic bomb. Basically, inventions range from the trivial, such as the idea of a using a single click to buy an item on the Internet, to the complex, such as Karmarkar's algorithm for solving linear programming problems. Trivial ideas are cheap to communicate, but, of course, they are also cheap to create. Complex ideas are expensive to create, but they are also difficult to communicate, so they are scarce and will command a substantial premium for a long period of time. In both cases, the cost of producing the ideas and the competitive rents are commensurate, and some ideas will be produced without intellectual monopoly, while perhaps others will not.

In the case of copyrightable creations, it can be argued that technological change – computers and the Internet – are greatly lowering the cost of reproduction, and so the conventional model in which ideas trade instantly at zero price is relevant. However, it is cost relative to the amount of competitive rent that matters. If, indeed, the Internet is reducing competitive rents, bear in mind that the same computer technology is reducing the cost of producing copyrightable creations. Take music, for example. Music-editing capabilities that required millions of dollars of studio equipment ten years ago now require an investment in computer equipment of thousands of dollars. And long before the Internet swamps the markets with music and movies, authors will be able to create movies on their home computers with no greater difficulty than writing a book – and entirely without the assistance of actors, cinematographers, and all the other people who contribute to the high cost of moviemaking.[36]

Moreover, improving transmission and reproduction technology may increase, rather than decrease, competitive rents earned by the innovator. Simply put, the creator of the idea in competitive equilibrium can claim the present value of a share of all revenue generated by the idea. Whether price falling to zero implies revenue falling to zero depends on the elasticity of demand; the mathematics of infinity times zero is complicated at times and this is one of them. If, in fact, demand is elastic, then price falling to zero implies revenue increasing to infinity (because so many more units are sold). So, in this case, improved reproduction technology would increase rather than decrease the rents accruing to the competitive innovator.

The Global Economy

One often finds the argument that the increasingly freer trade, the growth of many Asian economies, and the lowering of transportation costs are creating a dangerous mix for our economic stability. In particular, it is argued, our ideas and products are increasingly being unrightfully copied, and this requires some kind of serious intervention by our governments. In other words, globalization is risky for our innovators, and we need to strengthen intellectual property protection and force emerging countries to do the same things we do. Free markets and free trade, we are lectured, are becoming a threat to our economic well-being, and Adam Smith's and David Ricardo's views that competition and comparative advantages will make all of us better off are too naive to be believed, and certainly not applicable to this complex and globalized economy.

In fact, as the economy expands, Smith and Ricardo, far from becoming irrelevant, as DeLong and Froomkin assert, become more relevant than ever, the rationale for intellectual monopoly fades away, and we may look forward to a future in which we earn our living by trading ideas and creations – but without the intervention of government-enforced intellectual monopolies. As the size of the market expands, both competitive rents and the profit from first-mover advantage will generally increase proportionally – meaning that most economically useful ideas will be produced even in the absence of intellectual monopoly.

The consequences of increasing market size are discussed extensively in technical work by the two of us and other researchers. Notice, first, an important commonsense fact: when the Indian and Chinese markets open up for, say, music or drugs produced in the United States or the European Union, no matter how much piracy there is over there, at least some slices of those markets are going to "legitimate" producers. Before India and China opened to trade, those same producers would have had to field the fixed costs of their innovations with the proceeds from sales in much smaller markets. Hence, even if "we" get, say, only 10 percent of the new markets (a ridiculously low number), that is still a lot more revenue, and hence profits, than we would have had without globalization. This, by itself, suggests that the equalization of globalization with the need for stronger intellectual property laws is just plain and simple rent-seeking propaganda from existing monopolies.

There is a second, maybe subtler but certainly not less relevant, argument. As market size increases, two things happen. More consumers are added for all those ideas you are already producing or you would have produced in any case. Let us call these good ideas, because they were good enough to be profitable even when the market was pretty small. Also, additional ideas from the new players getting into the game become available. Let us call these marginal ideas, because if they had been good ideas they would have been introduced even when the market was small. Now, lowering intellectual property protection decreases the monopoly distortions for all consumers of the good ideas. With a larger market, many more consumers benefit from the greater usefulness and availability of all these good ideas. Second, lowering intellectual property protection makes it harder for marginal ideas to make it into the market. But in a larger market, more of these marginal ideas are going to be produced anyway, as there are more consumers to pay for the cost of inventing them.

So, the bottom line is that as the size of the market increases, by lowering intellectual property protection, you can get a lot more use out of good ideas at the cost of not getting quite as many marginal ideas as you would have otherwise. If expanding the market meant only a few new people coming in, and there were lots of valuable marginal ideas to be produced if only they could earn a few dollars more, then maybe lowering intellectual property protection would not be such a good idea. Try, however, adding up China and India to your market, and then tell us if that gives you "a few people." If you also think that the world is full of great marginal ideas that would be produced if only they earned a few dollars more, then go ahead and insist that we trade with China and India only after they adopt our ever-increasing intellectual property terms. We looked at data, and we looked at theory, and then we looked at data again; we discovered that China and India are a lot of people, and that the great marginal ideas that do not get produced just because they do not make those few extra bucks are quite rare, at best. Hence, we concluded, we are a lot better off with lower intellectual property protection when the market size increases, not vice versa.

On the basis of a more technical analysis, we argue that a simple rule of thumb that allows for some additional marginal ideas to be created while reducing the overall monopoly distortion is to reduce the length of term of patents and copyrights in proportion to the scale of the market.[37] This simple rule of thumb would be that if the size of market grows by 4 percent, the length of protection should be cut by 1 percent.

Take, for example, the World Trade Organization. The G-7 nations account for about two-thirds of world gross domestic product. Adding the one-third from the rest of the world would increase the size of the market by about 50 percent. If we think of the intellectual property changes in the World Trade Organization as extending the protection that exists in the G-7 to the rest of the world, this suggests a reduction in the length of term by about one-twelfth. Similarly, as the world economy grows, copyright and patent terms should be reduced. If the world economy grows at a rate of 2 percent a year, our simple rule of thumb would be to reduce protection terms by 0.5 percent per year. Because the world economy has been growing for a while at around 4 percent to 5 percent a year, protection terms should have been decreasing at around 1 percent a year. Unfortunately, in the case of copyright, terms have been moving in the wrong direction; they have grown by a factor of about four, while world gross domestic product has grown by nearly two orders of magnitude. Hence, if the copyright term of twenty-eight years at the beginning of the twentieth century was socially optimal, the current term should be about a year rather than the current term of approximately one hundred years!

Notice that the conventional wisdom is quite different. As Hal Varian says, "One prominent feature of information goods is that they have large fixed costs of production and small variable costs of reproduction. Cost-based pricing makes little sense in this context; value-based pricing is much more appropriate."[38] In fact technological change is reducing the fixed cost for many creations, especially in music and movies, and value-based pricing here means a higher, and hence more distortionary, price. As the economy expands, there is less need for these price distortions, and we may hope that intellectual monopoly will eventually join communism on the scrap heap of history.

The Public Domain and the Commons

We are almost done with using our mallet to smash shiny myths, but an important one is still standing, which is quite popular among legal scholars and, more generally, people working in the law and economics tradition.

This is the myth that ideas in the public domain are like common pastures. Because of this, it is argued, the public domain suffers from congestion and overuse, and intellectual property rights are necessary to provide appropriate incentives to "maintain" existing works.

One reason for rights in ordinary property is indeed to prevent congestion and overuse. For example, if a pasture is public, I do not take account of the negative effect my grazing sheep have on the availability of grass for your sheep. Because roads are public, I do not consider that my driving on the road makes it more difficult for you to get to work. Because the ocean is public, I do not consider that catching fish leaves fewer for you. This is known as the tragedy of the commons, and in each case it means that the pasture, road, or ocean will be overused.

Is the public domain for ideas like a common? Does my using ideas in the public domain have an adverse effect on your ability to use them? Certainly common sense suggests that "there can be no overgrazing of intellectual property... because intellectual property is not destroyed or even diminished by consumption. Once a work is created, its intellectual content is infinitely multipliable."[39] That I might make use of an idea does not make you less able to use it. Indeed, it seems obvious that welfare is increased when more people become cognizant of a useful idea, whereas overall productive capacity is not increased when more sheep try to eat from the same square foot of pasture.

Congress and the Supreme Court apparently do not agree, and recently William Landes and Richard Posner, rejecting exactly the statement by Karjala we just quoted, have claimed that "recognition of an 'overgrazing' problem in copyrightable works has lagged."[40] In fact it has not, because there is no coherent theory or evidence pointing to such a problem.

The overgrazing argument holds that just as by grazing my cows on your grass I reduce the grass available for your cows, so by selling copies of an idea, I reduce the profitability to you of selling the same idea. Notice first that the analogy with the cow and the grass has already been broken by its own proponents: they do not argue, as the analogy requires, that by selling my copies of an idea I reduce the availability of that same idea, or any other idea for that matter, to you. They claim, instead, that I am reducing your profitability in selling other copies of the same idea, and thereby is the fallacy. To see the fallacy, consider applying the reduced profitability argument to the case of food. If my restaurant sells Ricardo a large meal, he is not likely to go across the street to your restaurant and buy another; my selling him a large meal does not prevent you from using your food, but it does prevent you from selling it to Ricardo. So, too, with ideas. If I sell

Ricardo a copy of my Bible, I do not prevent you from making copies of your Bible, but I will reduce your profit because Ricardo will not buy from you. By way of contrast, by taking fish from the sea, I am not merely taking your customers but also taking an economically useful good or service.

Economists refer to the former as a pecuniary externality and the latter as a technological externality. Pecuniary externalities are a good thing – the incentive to steal customers is an essential part of the normal and efficient functioning of the competitive system. Technological externalities are a bad thing, leading to overuse. Hence, ideas in the public domain are like fish in the common pond only if, because they are in the public domain and because of people making copies of them, they generate technological externalities. Do they?

There are precious few examples of what the externalities might be that involve ideas. Landes and Posner express concern about Mickey Mouse: "If because copyright had expired anyone were free to incorporate the Mickey Mouse character in a book, movie, song, etc., the value of the character might plummet."[41] The value for whom? It cannot be the social value of the Mickey Mouse character that plummets – this increases when more people have access. Rather, it is the market price of copies of the Mickey Mouse character that plummets: normally, this is the socially good effect of an increase in output. Next they assert that "the public [would] rapidly tire of Mickey Mouse."[42] But this is in fact the ordinary consequence of an increase in output. If I eat a large meal, I am less hungry – the value to me of a meal is diminished, and restaurants will find that I am not willing to pay them much money. No externality is involved: as more of a good is consumed, the more tired people become of it. For there to be an externality, it would have to be the case that my consumption of copies of Mickey Mouse from the public domain made you more tired of it – an improbability, to say the least.

Landes and Posner continue on to quote from a book on Disney marketing

To avoid overkill, Disney manages its character portfolio with care. It has hundreds of characters on its books, many of them just waiting to be called out of retirement.... Disney practices good husbandry of its characters and extends the life of its brands by not overexposing them.... They avoid debasing the currency.[43]

This is of course exactly how we would expect a monopolist to behave. If Disney were to be given a monopoly on food, we can be sure that it would practice "good husbandry" of food, most likely leaving us all on the edge of starvation. This would be good for Disney, because we would all be willing to pay a high price for food. But the losses to the rest of us would far outweigh the gain to Disney. It is a relief to know that, after all, Mickey Mouse is not such an essential ingredient of the American diet.

Landes and Posner also express concern that Mickey Mouse's "image might also be blurred or even tarnished, as some authors portrayed him as a Casanova, others as catmeat, others as an animal rights advocate, still others as the henpecked husband of Minnie."[44] Because in common parlance calling something Mickey Mouse is not intended as a compliment, one might wonder how Mickey Mouse's reputation could be more tarnished than it is. Regardless, bear in mind that the only thing that matters are copies of the idea of Mickey Mouse. If Mickey Mouse falls into the public domain, someone might well use his or her copy of the idea of Mickey Mouse to produce, say, a pornographic film starring Mickey Mouse. But would this tarnish the copies of the idea of Mickey Mouse in the minds of millions of six-year-old children? It is hard to see how: ordinarily children of this age are not allowed to see pornographic films. Presumably those people who choose to see the film are those who benefit from this portrayal of Mickey Mouse. How does their doing so interfere in any way with anyone else's enjoyment of their vision of Mickey Mouse?

A more pernicious idea is that in the absence of intellectual property there would be inadequate incentive to promote ideas. For example:

Consider an old movie on which copyright had expired that a studio wanted to issue in a colorized version.... Promoting the colorized version might increase the demand for the black and white version, a close substitute.... [T]he studio would have to take into account, in deciding whether to colorize, the increase in demand for the black and white version.[45]

But in all competitive markets, producers lack incentives to promote the industry. Individual wheat producers do not have much incentive to promote the healthy virtues of wheat, fishermen do not have much incentive to promote the healthy virtues of fish, and so on. That is why promotional campaigns for milk, cereals, and fish are usually carried out by some industrywide association, and not by individual firms. It is hard to see why the problem with old movies, books, and music is different, either qualitatively or quantitatively, from the one in these other competitive markets. Yet, quite rightly, no one argues that we need to grant wheat or fish monopolies to solve the "problem" of underpromotion.

It is worth reflecting briefly on promotional activities in competitive industries. Surely information about, say, the health benefits of fish, is useful to consumers; equally surely no individual fisherman has much incentive to provide this information. Is this some form of market failure? No – in a private ownership economy consumers will have to pay for useful information rather than have it provided for free by producers. And pay they do – doctors, health advisers, magazine publishers, all provide this type of information for a fee. There is no evidence that competitive markets underprovide product information. Rather, in the case of monopolists, because the value of the product mostly goes to the monopolist rather than the consumer, the consumer has little incentive to acquire information, while the monopolist has a lot of incentive to see that the consumer has access to it. So, we expect different arrangement for information provision (that is, promotion) in competitive and noncompetitive markets. In the former, the consumer pays and competitive providers generate information. In the latter, firms subsidize the provision of information. Of course, the monopolist, unlike the competitive providers, will have no incentive to provide accurate information. We rarely see Disney advertising that, however true it might be, the new Mickey Mouse movie is a real dog, and we should go see the old Mickey Mouse movie instead.

Notes

1. Ed Felten's (2005) pizzarights are discussed at his blog, Freedom to Tinker.
2. From WorldNetDaily, May 7, 2002; article available (accessed February 24, 2008) at http://www.worldnetdaily.com/index.php?fa=PAGE.view&pageId=13805.
3. *Zimbabwe Independent* (2003).
4. The excerpt from *The Economist* is dated 1851: we found it quoted, with a tone of paternal dismissal, by the very same magazine, *The Economist* (2005), which on page 18 of the same survey states, "On an individual basis this may be true [that patents hurt instead of helping innovations]. But something changes when transactions increase in volume and value. Sharing . . . can add more value to an innovation than hoarding it might do. Yet effective sharing requires a property right that can be traded in a market."

   O tempora! O mores!

5. The embodiment controversy is interesting but rather academic in nature. The interested reader should consult Greenwood and Jovanovic (1990) for a survey of the classical literature. Theory has not evolved much since then.
6. Borges (1983), pp. 51–8.
7. Scotchmer (2004), p. 33. This is an otherwise excellent and extremely useful textbook on various aspects of the economics of innovation. Although Scotchmer does take the standard model as her point of departure for a large part of the book, in various parts her careful analysis comes quite close to some of the theoretical and policy positions we propose here. We quoted out of Scotchmer's textbook because it is an excellent and otherwise very coherent one; similar but much more confused arguments abound in the literature.

8. A number of authors are references in the brief overview of the history of economic research on innovation. The conventional notion that ideas are a nonrivalrous public good is a major theme of Romer's work (1986, 1990a, 1990b), and is reflected also in Lucas (1988). Variations on this theme in the setting of monopolistic competition can be found in the work of Grossman and Helpman (1991). These ideas build on the earlier ideas of Allyn Young (1928), and especially the work of Kenneth Arrow (1962), further developed by Karl Shell (1966, 1967).

   To give credit where it belongs, we should point out that Arrow's original argument was meant to lead to the conclusion that R&D, because it produced a public good (nonrivalrous knowledge), ought to be financed by public expenditure. There is nothing in Arrow's seminal paper, nor in his subsequent writings on the topic, that suggests he had in mind intellectual monopoly as a solution to the allocational inefficiency that he – in our view, incorrectly – detected in the production of knowledge. There is also an extensive microeconomics literature on patents that generally begins with the assumption that innovation will not take place without a patent and inquires into the optimal length and breadth of patent protection. Good examples can be found in the work of Gilbert and Shapiro (1990) and Gallini and Scotchmer (2001). In many cases, the assumption that patents are necessary for innovation is not intended as an empirical principle, but arises from the fact that studying optimal patents in a world where it would be better not to have patents at all is not terribly interesting.

9. Tirole (1988), p. 390.
10. Barro and Sala-i-Martin (1999), p. 290.
11. Boldrin and Levine (2007) show that, under twin assumptions of unbounded capacity and Bertrand pricing, when written as a sequential game between innovator and imitators, the standard model has a unique subgame perfect equilibrium. In such equilibrium, the innovator innovates and the imitators, facing a positive cost of imitating, do not enter and let the first be a monopolist. Apart for a few extraordinary circumstances, we do not claim that this is an interesting, let alone realistic, description of real markets. On the contrary: the outcome described is a patently absurd portrayal of the way innovators and imitators behave absent intellectual monopoly. Nevertheless, because it is the straightforward logical implication of the standard model's fundamental assumptions (unbounded capacity and marginal cost pricing), this analytical result strongly suggests that at least one of them should be thrown away. Personally, we believe both should be thrown away, which is what we have done in most of our research. In our quoted paper, we show that even getting rid of marginal cost pricing alone leads to much more consequential results. On a different note, this also suggests that users of the standard model never seriously bothered with their homework of finding out what their preferred assumptions imply.
12. Ivan P'ng showed us the wheeled suitcase example.
13. Becker (1971).
14. Ellison and Glaeser (1997, 1999).
15. Acemoglu and Angrist (2000).
16. Ciccone and Peri (2002).
17. Castiglionesi and Ornaghi (2004).
18. Cavalli-Sforza (1996).

19. Cipolla (1972), p. 48.
20. Cipolla (1976), p. 154.
21. Cipolla (1976), p. 158.
22. We complain extensively about the schizophrenic way in which academic economists, and their alumni in business, politics, and the media, keep treating information and its transmission. The following quotation from the textbook from Hirshleifer and Riley (1992), p. 276, shows we are not alone in stressing the very costly nature of information transmission. What remains puzzling is the little use economists are willing to make of this fact.

> Only rarely does mere "disclosure" suffice to convey a message; something more active is typically required of both sender and receiver. Teachers work hard preparing lectures and textbooks; students grind away trying to understand them. In our earlier analysis we treated information as a transparently valuable but fugitive commodity, always liable to escape unless closely guarded. But of at least equal importance are types of information whose nature and value are not transparent, that are hard to transmit even to desirous users, and hard for them to absorb even when offered freely.

23. The R&D surveys referred to are in Levin et al. (1987) and Cohen and Walsh (1998).
24. Information revelation in the strategic patent process is studied by Anton and Yao (2000), Battacharya and Ritter (1983), Horstmann, MacDonald, and Slivinski (1985), Okuno-Fujiwara, Postlewaite, and Suzumura (1990), and Ponce (2003). We discuss the effect of secrecy on capacity choice in Boldrin and Levine (2004a).
25. Okuno-Fujiwara et al. (1990).
26. Ponce (2003).
27. Boldrin and Levine (2004a).
28. Moser (2003, 2005).
29. Available at http://www.gnu.org/philosophy/amazonpatent.html (accessed February 24, 2008).
30. Schumpeter's celebration of monopoly can be found in his (1943) work. A modern elaboration is in Aghion and Howitt (1992).
31. Evans and Schmalensee (2001).
32. Schumpeter (1943), p. 90.
33. Karl Marx's description of communism can be found in Marx (1857).
34. DeLong and Froomkin (1999).
35. Boldrin and Levine (2005b); Quah (2002).
36. At the time we first wrote this chapter, around 2003, we privately estimated that it would be a decade before the quality of home-produced movies caught up to the studio variety. However, this estimate has subsequently turned out to be off by ten years. The production quality of the movie *Star Wreck*, available online at http://www.starwreck.com, is comparable to a $200 million special effect blockbuster from the studios. Because they thank six sponsors, one for "lend[ing] us a Pinnacle DV500 ed[i]ting card" that retails for about $800, we can safely assume they didn't spend $200 million making this movie. To quote from the Web site:

> Q: Damn, you must be very rich when you can afford a film like this. . . . Huge sets, studios, actors and render farms!

A: What sets? The bridge sets are all virtual. The on-location shoots were made at locations that didn't cost any money (schools, public places etc). The "bluescreen studio" is actually a small piece of blue linoleum in Samuli's living room.....

For Samuli this is a somewhat costly hobby, but as a movie it's still very close to a zero budget. The most expensive part of the production has been keeping the computer equipment up to date.

The photograph of their "render farm" – a computer stuck in the corner of a rather small apartment kitchen gives the flavor of the production cost.

37. Boldrin and Levine (2005b).
38. Varian (1997), p. 1.
39. Karjala (1998), p. 9. On availability of products in the public domain, see also Karjala (2004) and our own analysis earlier in this book.
40. Landes and Posner (2003), p. 223.
41. Landes and Posner (2002), p. 15. A similar argument is developed, almost verbatim, also in Landes and Posner (2003), pp. 487–8.
42. Landes and Posner (2002), p. 15.
43. Bill Britt, "International Marketing: Disney's Global Goals," *Marketing*, May 17, 1990, as quoted in Landes and Posner (2002), p. 13. Also in Landes and Posner (2003), p. 224.
44. Landes and Posner (2003), p. 225. A similar statement is in Landes and Posner (2002), p. 15.
45. Landes and Posner (2003), p. 229.

EIGHT

Does Intellectual Monopoly
Increase Innovation?

What we have argued so far may not sound altogether incredible to the alert observer of the economics of innovation. Theory aside, what have we shown, after all? That thriving innovation has been and still is commonplace in the absence of intellectual monopoly and that intellectual monopoly leads to substantial and well-documented reductions in economic freedom and general prosperity. However, while expounding the theory of competitive innovation, we also recognized that, under perfect competition, some socially desirable innovations would not be produced because the indivisibility involved with introducing the first copy or implementation of the new idea is too large, relative to the size of the underlying market. When this is the case, monopoly power may generate the necessary incentive for the putative innovator to introduce socially valuable goods. And the value for society of these goods could dwarf the social losses we have documented. In fact, were standard theory correct, so that most innovators gave up innovating in a world without intellectual property, the gains from patents and copyright would certainly dwarf those losses. Alas, as we noted, standard theory is not even internally coherent, and its predictions are flatly violated by the facts reported in Chapters 2 and 3.

Nevertheless, when in the previous chapter we argued against all kinds of theoretical reasons brought forward to justify intellectual monopoly on scientific grounds, we carefully avoided stating that it is never the case the fixed cost of innovation is too large to be paid for by competitive rents. We did not argue it as a matter of theory because, as a matter of theory, fixed costs can be so large as to prevent almost anything from being invented. So, by our own admission, it is a theoretical possibility that intellectual monopoly could, at the end of the day, be better than competition. But does intellectual monopoly actually lead to greater innovation than competition?

From a theoretical point of view the answer is murky. In the long run, intellectual monopoly provides increased revenues to those that innovate, but it also makes innovation more costly. Innovations generally build on existing innovations. Although each individual innovator may earn more revenue from innovating if he has an intellectual monopoly, he also faces a higher cost of innovating: he must pay off all those other monopolists owning rights to existing innovations. Indeed, in the extreme case when each new innovation requires the use of lots of previous ideas, the presence of intellectual monopoly may bring innovation to a screeching halt.[1]

Additionally, intellectual monopoly provides the incumbent with a dominant position that discourages competitors from entering, thereby reducing the incentive for the incumbent to innovate to keep ahead. In part, this is because innovations build on existing innovations; hence, the monopolist can use high prices to make new innovations too expensive for competitors. In part, this is because monopolists generally face lower costs of "matching" whatever improved new product entrants may come up with. Notice that, in both cases, it is the discouragement effect that matters: this implies less effective contestability, and hence less innovative effort.

Further, theoretical considerations also suggest that the response of innovation to the strengthening of intellectual monopoly is not uniform over time. In the short run – for example, immediately after the first introduction of legislation allowing for patents – we would expect innovation to increase, as the revenues from innovating go up, but costs will not increase until some time in the future when many ideas have been patented. Strikingly – from a theoretical point of view – it is possible that, in the short run, introducing patents leads to more innovation and eliminating patents after they have been in place for a while, by reducing the cost of innovation, increases innovation as well.

A similar paradox is likely to underlie the long-run experience of Western societies. A number of economic historians, Douglass North and his followers foremost among them, have argued that the great acceleration in innovation and productivity we associate with the Industrial Revolution was caused by the development of ways to protect the right of inventors, allowing them to profit from their innovations.[2] Central among such ways was the attribution of patents to inventors, and their upholding either by Parliament or by the courts. Relative to the very poorly defined contractual rights of pre-seventeenth-century Europe, plagued by royal and aristocratic abuses of property and contracts, there is no doubt that allowing individuals a temporary but well-defined monopoly over the fruits of their inventive effort was a major step forward. Even monopolistic property is much better than a system that allows arbitrary seizure by the rich and powerful. This does not, however, contradict our claim that widespread and ever-growing monopolistic rights are not as socially beneficial as well-defined competitive property rights.

To put it differently, about four centuries ago, as Western societies moved away from postmedieval absolutist regimes, the establishment of patents constituted a step forward for the creation of a system of property rights that favored entrepreneurship and free market interaction. By the force of the same reasoning, the abolition of patents and of the distortionary monopolistic rights they entail may well result, now, in an analogous boost to entrepreneurial effort and free competition.

By the same token, theory suggests that small countries with low intellectual property (or IP) protection should witness a surge in the inflow of IP-related investment after protection is increased, as they capture investments from other countries where intellectual monopoly is protected less. The latter, unfortunately, appears to have gone beyond a mere theoretical possibility. What is not obvious, once again, is what the outcome will be once every country adopts the same high degree of protection. Leave aside the more or less terrifying scenarios of escalation – in which countries outdo one another trying to allure IP-related investments by progressively increasing their local protection of intellectual monopoly. It is still worth asking whether a world where everyone has the same degree of IP protection as, say, the United States currently does, is a world with a higher or lower rate of innovation and a higher or lower social welfare than a world with much less protection.[3]

The issue, then, is the one we posed at the outset: does monopoly really lead to more innovation, on average, than competition? Theory gives an ambiguous answer, so, let us look at evidence, supported by a bit of statistical common sense.

What is the evidence? Given the continued extension of patent protection to new areas – business practices and computer software, for example – one might hope that there is strong evidence that the introduction of patent protection has led to a substantial increase in innovation in recent years. These hopes, alas, are not to be fulfilled: it is already apparent that the recent explosion of patents in the United States, the European Union, and Japan has not brought about anything comparable in terms of useful innovations and aggregate productivity. Nevertheless, one may claim that it is too early to judge and that the process of progressive extension of intellectual monopoly to almost every area of human endeavor has not yet run its full course. Beneficial results will come, but in due time, so be patient and let the tide of intellectual monopoly run its course. To us, as it should be clear by now, the tide of intellectual monopoly resembles more those of destructive tsunamis or hurricanes than the benevolent one that supposedly lifts all boats. Hence, instead of letting it run its malevolent course and then observe the devastation from some helicopter flying high over the scene, we would rather learn now from the past and begin erecting strong levees. Indeed, the historical evidence provides little or no support for the view that intellectual monopoly is an effective method of increasing innovation when compared to well-defined but altogether "standard" property rights in competitive markets.[4]

Copyright and Music in the Eighteenth Century

The effect of copyright is difficult to analyze because it is hard to get reliable data prior to the nineteenth century. Copyright was already fairly ubiquitous across Europe early in the nineteenth century, and its term there has changed little since then.

The one exception turns out to be in the case of classical music. Copyright was unknown in the world of music until around the end of the eighteenth century. As a result, a large proportion of classical music, which still today accounts for about 3 percent of all music sales but obviously for a much larger portion of music production until late in the nineteenth century, was produced without the benefit of copyright protection.

In this case, as in others, England was the path breaker. The Statute of Anne did not cover printed music until a case filed by Johann Christian Bach (the youngest son of the more famous Johann Sebastian) led, in 1777, to a ruling that, after a relatively long sequence of failed attempts by other composers, allowed for the extension. It took various additional decades for the copyright logic to spread to the rest of Europe, which provides us with an interesting natural experiment. Think for a moment of the history of European music between 1780 and 1850, as, by the latter date, music had become copyrightable all over Europe.

- Which countries would you list in the "top three" of producers of music during that period?
- Would the United Kingdom make that list?
- Would you agree or disagree with the following statement: "After 1780, the quality and quantity of music produced in the United Kingdom increased substantially"?
- Make up your personal list of the top ten music composers of that period. How many are British or worked in England?

Table 8.1. *Composers in the population, UK versus
control group*

	Pre	Post	Ratio
United Kingdom	0.348	0.140	0.40
Germany	0.493	0.361	0.73
Italy	0.527	0.186	0.35
Austria	0.713	0.678	0.95

By the way, while evaluating the results of this small experiment, do keep in mind that England was the most economically advanced country in Europe during that period, and that both general and musical literacy was more widespread there than in continental Europe. Here is a quotation about a similar experiment; it comes from an unsuspecting source: Professor Scherer is (or at least was) a strong supporter of intellectual property:

The evolution of copyright from an occasional grant of royal privilege to a for-mal and eventually widespread system of law should in principle have enhanced composers' income from publication. The evidence from our quantitative compar-ison of honoraria received by Beethoven, with no copyright law in his territory, and Robert Schumann, benefiting from nearly universal European copyright, provides at best questionable support for the hypothesis that copyright fundamentally changed composers' fortunes. From the qualitative evidence on Giuseppe Verdi, who was the first important composer to experience the new Italian copyright regime and devise strategies to derive maximum advantage, it is clear that copyright could make a sub-stantial difference. In the case of Verdi, greater remuneration through full exploita-tion of the copyright system led perceptibly to a lessening of composing effort.[5]

Professor Scherer also exploited the variations between European coun-tries' copyright law regarding music to conduct a third natural experiment. He compared the average number of composers born per million people per decade in various European countries. Turning first to England, he considers the precopyright period 1700–52 and the postcopyright period 1767–1849. As controls, he looks also at what happened in Germany, Austria, and Italy, where there was no change in copyright during this period. This is summarized in Table 8.1.

We see that the number of composers per million declined everywhere, but it declined considerably faster in the United Kingdom after the intro-duction of copyright than it did in Germany or Austria, and at about the same rate as it did Italy. So there is no evidence here that copyright increased musical output.

Table 8.2. *Composers in the population, France versus control group*

	Pre	Post	Ratio
France	0.126	0.194	1.54
Germany	0.527	0.340	0.65
Italy	0.587	0.153	0.31
Austria	0.847	0.740	0.86

However, the evidence is mixed, because the same experiment in France is more favorable to copyright. In France, the precopyright period is 1700–68, and the postcopyright period is 1783–1849. Scherer's data are in Table 8.2.

Here we find that, in France, when copyright was introduced the number of composers per million increased substantially more than in other countries. This should be noted, as it is pretty much the only piece of evidence supporting the idea that copyright increased classical music production that we have been able to find.

Looking more broadly at the entire European scene and at the careers of comparable composers living with or without copyright protection, Scherer finds it difficult to conclude that copyright law was a significant factor, either way, in determining the amount of musical composition taking place. It may not have reduced the incentive to compose music, but it certainly did not increase it either: whatever the mechanism affecting composers' incentives, copyright protection was not an important part of it.

Patents and Innovation in the Nineteenth Century

Kenneth Sokoloff, together with Naomi Lamoreaux and Zorina Khan, examined the role of patents in the United States in the nineteenth and early twentieth centuries. In 1836, the United States

instituted an examination system under which, before granting patents, technical experts scrutinized applications for novelty and for the appropriateness of claims about invention. This procedure made patent rights more secure by increasing the likelihood that a grant for a specified technology would survive a court challenge, and may also have provided some signal about the significance of the new technology. Thereafter, both patenting and sales of patent rights boomed.[6]

Subsequently, they document the development of an elaborate system of trading ideas. This includes both specialized intermediaries and journals advertising the existence of patents. Some of these intermediaries not only assisted inventors in obtaining patents but, in some cases, also seem to have acted as modern-day venture capitalists, providing start-up funding to put ideas into production.

As a study of innovation in the late nineteenth and early twentieth centuries, this research is of great interest. It does not, however, provide much evidence that the patent system promotes innovation relative to a competitive system where property rights for inventors and imitators are well defined and the right to sell voluntarily is enforced. The aim of this research is to show that the patent system introduced in the United States after the 1830s created a well-defined market for patents and technologies that did not exist previously, and that the creation of such market lead to an increase in the number of patents registered and traded. It should be observed that the institutional change that led to the booming of patenting and the sales of patent rights was to make it more difficult to get patents – quite the opposite of modern institutional changes. In addition, although this research makes it clear that the number of patent agents and inventors making use of their services boomed, it also documents that an important portion of the services were to assist inventors in getting patents and in navigating the thicket of existing patents – socially wasteful activities that would be unnecessary in the absence of a patent system.

One important difficulty is in determining the level of innovative activity. One measure is the number of patents, of course, but this is meaningless in a country that has no patents or when patent laws change. Petra Moser gets around this problem by examining the catalogs of innovations from nineteenth-century world's fairs. Of the cataloged innovations, some are patented, some are not, some are from countries with patent systems, and some are from countries without. Moser catalogs more than thirty thousand innovations from a variety of industries: "Mid-nineteenth century Switzerland [a country without patents], for example, had the second highest number of exhibits per capita among all countries that visited the Crystal Palace Exhibition. Moreover, exhibits from countries without patent laws received disproportionate shares of medals for outstanding innovations."[7] Moser does, however, find a significant impact of patent law on the direction of innovation:

The analysis of exhibition data suggests that patent laws may be an important factor in determining the direction of innovative activity. Exhibition data show that countries without patents share an exceptionally strong focus on innovations in two industries: scientific instruments and food processing. At the Crystal Palace, every fourth exhibit from a country without patent laws is a scientific instrument, while no more than one seventh of other countries innovations belong to this category. At the same time, the patentless countries have significantly smaller shares of innovation in machinery, especially in machinery for manufacturing and agricultural machinery. After the Netherlands abolished her patent system in 1869 for political reasons, the share of Dutch innovations that were devoted to food processing increased from 11 to 37 percent.[8]

Moser then goes on to say, "Nineteenth-century sources report that secrecy was particularly effective at protecting innovations in scientific instruments and in food processing. On the other hand, patenting was essential to protect and motivate innovations in machinery, especially for large-scale manufacturing."[9]

Evidence that secrecy was important for scientific instruments and food processing is provided, but no evidence is given that patenting was actually essential to protect and motivate innovations in machinery. Notice that in an environment in which some countries provide patent protection and others do not, bias caused by the existence of patent laws will be exaggerated. Countries with patent laws will tend to specialize in innovations for which secrecy is difficult, while those without will tend to specialize in innovations for which secrecy is easy. This means that variations of patent protection would have different effects in different countries.

It is interesting also that patent laws may reflect the state of industry and innovation in a country:

Anecdotal evidence for the late nineteenth and for the twentieth century suggests that a country's choice of patent laws was often influenced by the nature of her technologies. In the 1880s, for example, two of Switzerland's most important industries chemicals and textiles were strongly opposed to the introduction of a patent system, as it would restrict their use of processes developed abroad.[10]

The nineteenth-century type of innovation – small process innovations – are the type for which patents may be most socially beneficial. Despite this and the careful study of economic historians, it is difficult to conclude that patents played an important role in increasing the rate of nineteenth- and early–twentieth-century innovation.

More recent work by Moser, exploiting the same data set from two different angles, strengthens this finding – that is, that patents did not increase the level of innovation.[11] In her words, "Comparisons between Britain and the United States suggest that even the most fundamental differences in patent laws failed to raise the proportion of patented innovations."[12] Her work appears to confirm two of the stylized facts we have often repeated in this book. First, as we just mentioned in discussing the work of Sokoloff, Lamoreaux, and Khan, innovations that are patented tend to be traded more than those that are not, and therefore to disperse geographically farther away from the original area of invention. On the basis of data for the period 1841–1901, innovation for industries in which patents are widely used is not higher but more dispersed geographically than innovation in industries in which patents are not used or are scarcely used. Second, when the defensive patenting motive is absent, as it was in 1851, an extremely small percentage of inventors (fewer than one in five) choose patents as a method for maximizing revenues and protecting intellectual property.

To sum up, careful statistical analyses of the nineteenth century's available data, carried out by distinguished economic historians, uniformly shows two things. Patents neither increase the rate of innovation nor are the best instrument to maximize inventors' revenue. Patents create a market in patents and in the legal and technical services required to trade and enforce them.

Intellectual Property and Innovation in the Twentieth Century

A number of scientific studies have attempted to examine whether introducing or strengthening patent protection leads to greater innovation by using data from post–Second World War advanced economies. We have identified twenty-three economic studies that have examined this issue empirically (see the table herein).[13] The executive summary: these studies find weak or no evidence that strengthening patent regimes increases innovation; they find evidence that strengthening the patent regime increases ... patenting! They also find evidence that, in countries with initially weak IP regimes, strengthening IP increases the flow of foreign investment in sectors where patents are frequently used. The following table contains our compilation of the principal characteristics of the studies examined.

The studies by Arundel, Gallini, and Jaffe are actually surveys of earlier empirical work, each one of them focusing on particular issues, data sets, or methodological approaches. In the abstract of the first, we read, "The results suggest that there is little need to strengthen patent protection since alternative appropriation methods are available and widely preferred. Instead, stronger patent protection could be leading to undesirable 'second-order' effects such as the use of patents to block competitors."[14] After failing to find a single study claiming that innovation increased as a consequence of the strengthening of U.S. patent protection in the 1980s, Gallini writes:

Table 8.3. *Empirical Studies of patents' impact on innovation*

Authors	Years	Country	Industry
Arora, Ceccagnoli, and Cohen	1990–2002	U.S.	Many
Arundel	Many	Many	Many
Baldwin and Hanel	1993	Canada	Many
Bessen and Hunt	1980–96	U.S.	Software
Branstetter and Sakakibara	1988–98	Japan	Many
Gallini	1980s	U.S.	Many
Hall and Ham	1980–94	U.S.	Semiconductor
Hall and Ziedonis	1979–95	U.S.	Semiconductor
Jaffe	Many	Many	Many
Kanwar and Evenson	1981–90	Many	Aggregate
Kortum and Lerner	1980–2000	U.S.	Many
Lanjouw (1997, 2002)	1990s	India	Pharmaceutical
Lanjouw and Cockburn	1975–96	India	Pharmaceutical
Leger	1978–2000	Mexico	Agriculture
Lerner (1995)	1850–2000	Many	Many
Lerner (2002)	1971–2000	U.S.	Financial
Levine and Saunders	1981–2001	U.S.	Software
Licht and Zoz	1992	Germany	Many
Lo	c. 1986	Taiwan	Many
Mann (2004, 2005)	1900–2002	U.S.	Software
Park	1987–95	OECD members	Many
Qian	1979–99	Many	Pharmaceutical
Sakakibara and Branstetter	1988–95	Japan	Many
Scherer and Weisbrod	1970s	Italy	Pharmaceutical

Although it seems plausible that the strengthening of U.S. patents may have contributed to the rise in patent over the past decade and a half, the connection has proven difficult to verify.... The explanation more favorable toward patents is that recent reforms deserve some attribution for the dramatic rise in patents (and innovation), but sufficient time has not passed to capture this effect empirically.[15]

Pretty much for the same reason – that is to say, the absence of any empirical evidence that more intellectual property and more patents mean more innovations and higher productivity – Jaffe's opening punch line is as follows: "Despite the significance of the policy changes and the wide availability of detailed data relating to patenting, robust conclusions regarding the empirical consequences for technological innovations of changes in patent policy are few."[16] He adds in the conclusion that "There is widespread unease that the costs of stronger patent protection may exceed the benefits. Both theoretical and, to a lesser extent, empirical research suggest this possibility."[17]

Several of these studies examine or are influenced by the upswing in patenting that occurred in the United States in the mid-1980s. That upswing followed the establishment of a special patent court in the United States in 1982; it turned into an explosion in the roaring 1990s, paralleling the dot-com stock market bubble, but it did not stop after that bubble burst. In 1983 in the United States, 59,715 patents were issued against 105,704 applications; by 2003, 189,597 patents were issued against 355,418 applications. In twenty years, the flow of patents roughly tripled.

Kortum and Lerner focus specifically on the surge in U.S. patents, and make no claim as to whether this means more or less productivity growth. By examining how the composition of patent applications changed, they argue that this surge in patenting reflects increased innovation – not merely taking advantage of greater laxity in patent laws. They also argue, though, that this increased innovation was not due to changes in the structure of patent law and intellectual property protection, but rather to a better management of R&D expenditure at the firm level.

Other studies look at natural experiments in other countries to find evidence of a causal link between strengthening intellectual property rights and either R&D spending or the rate of innovation. The conclusion of Branstetter and Sakakibara is that the 1988 Japanese reform had no impact whatsoever on Japanese R&D expenditure and innovation rate; that of Baldwin and colleagues is that one can repeat for Canada what we have seen to be true for the United States: innovation may lead to more patenting, but more patents and stronger patent protection do not lead to more innovation. Similar conclusions are drawn by Arora, claiming that increasing the patent premium does not lead to more R&D expenditure, and by Levine and Saunders, suggesting that the introduction of software patents has lead mostly to more court litigation, not to more innovation. This is a hard statement to disagree with in the days where half a dozen legal battles are starting between companies involved in the voice over Internet protocol business: they all patented something pretty similar, and they all claim that their patent is being infringed by one of their competitors.

The authors who find the strongest effect on innovation of increased patent protection are Kanwar and Evenson, as well as Lo. The latter examines the 1986 reform in Taiwan, while the former use time-series data from a cross-section of countries to regress R&D as fraction of gross domestic product (GDP) on various variables, including a qualitative measure of IP protection. Both sets of results are worth examining a bit more closely than the rest.

Lo finds increased innovation by Taiwanese inventors as measured by R&D expenditure and by the number of U.S. patents they were awarded. However, given the worldwide surge in U.S. patents about this time and the fact that the number of Taiwanese patents awarded to these same inventors did not much increase, we cannot reliably conclude that the effect of the 1986 law was either an increase in innovation or a jump in aggregate or sector productivity. What the reform certainly did, and Lo documents convincingly, was an increase in the number of patents awarded to Taiwanese firms, especially in the United States, which is altogether not surprising. Lo himself points out that the main channel through which the Taiwanese reform had a positive effect was by fostering foreign direct investment in Taiwan, especially in those sectors in which patents are widely used.

This is an important point, which deserves a separate comment. In a world in which strong patent protection in some countries coexists with weak protection in others, a country that increases patent protection should observe an increase in the inflow of foreign investment, especially in those sectors where patented technologies are used. Profit-maximizing entrepreneurs always choose to operate in those legal environments where their rights are the strongest. In the United States, for example, economists and people with common sense alike have long argued that the policy of offering tax incentives and subsidies to companies that relocate in one state or another is not a good policy for the United States as a whole. Nobody denies that if you provide a company with high-enough subsidies and tax incentives, it will probably take them and relocate to your state, at least temporarily. The problem is that, after you do so, other states will respond by doing the same, or more. In the ensuing equilibrium, the total amount of investment is roughly the same as when no one was offering a subsidy, but everyone is now paying a distorting tax to finance the subsidy. When capital moves freely across countries, the very same logic applies to the international determination of IP rights. In what economists call the Nash equilibrium of this game, it is obvious that patent holders prefer to locate in countries with strong IP laws. This increases the stock of capital in the receiving country and reduces it everywhere else, especially in countries with low IP protection. Hence, absent international cooperation, there is a strong incentive for most countries to keep increasing patent protection, even in the absence of lobbying and bribing by intellectual monopolists.

As for the study by Kanwar and Evenson, they have data on thirty-one countries for the period 1981–90. Using two five-year averages, they find support for the idea that higher protection leads to higher R&D as a fraction

Table 8.4. *Residual from
cross-country regression of IP levels*

IP level	Average residual
0	−0.95
1	−0.46
2	0.20
3	0.20
4	0.10

of GDP. Their measures of IP protection do not always seem to make sense, but this is not the proper place to engage in a statistical diatribe. There are five levels of IP protection, and R&D as a fraction of GDP ranges from a ten-year average of .231 percent in Jordan to 2.822 percent in Sweden. They find that increasing protection by one level raises R&D as a fraction of GDP between 0.6 percent and 1 percent. As before, the most favorable interpretation of this result is that countries offering higher levels of IP protection also attract investments in those sectors in which R&D and patents are most relevant. A less favorable interpretation of this result, instead, points out that Kanwar and Evenson have forgotten to include a main determinant of the ratio of R&D to GDP: that is, market size as measured by GDP. The most elementary theory of innovation, either under competition or monopoly, shows that the innovative effort is increasing in the size of the market, and that large and rich countries will invest a larger share of their GDP in R&D than will small and poor countries. Putting Kanwar and Evenson's data together with GDP data from the 1990 *CIA World Fact Book*, we find that a 1 percent increase in the size of a country as measured by GDP increases the ratio of R&D to GDP by 0.34 percent.

It is interesting to look at the residual error that is left over after we predict the ratio of (or the logarithm of) R&D to GDP from (the logarithm of) GDP (see Table 8.4).

What does the table show? The question is whether increasing the IP protection level leads to an increase in the residual. Moving from level 0 to 1 and from level 1 to 2 this is true, but it is not true when moving from level 2 to 3 or level 3 to 4. In other words, once you control for market size, higher IP protection increases the ratio of R&D to GDP at the very low levels but becomes uncorrelated with that ratio at any level of IP protection equal to two or more in the Kanwar and Evenson scale. This reinforces the idea that what we are seeing is primarily the effect of foreign investment. Among poor countries with low IP protection, increases bring in more foreign investment and raise R&D. In richer countries with high IP levels, foreign investment is not an issue, and increases in IP have little or no effect on innovation.

The Scherer and Weisbrod study shows that it is perhaps not too wise for large and advanced countries to rely on strengthening patent protection to bring in foreign investment. This may explain why when Italy introduced pharmaceutical patents in 1979, the Italian pharmaceutical industry that had been thriving by making generic drugs largely disappeared. This is just one example, among the possible many, of the intellectual property miracle not materializing.

The Lerner study is especially notable because he examined all significant changes in patent law in all countries over the past 150 years. His conclusion?

Consider, for instance, policy changes that strengthen patent protection. Once overall trends in patenting are adjusted for, the changes in patents by residents of the country undertaking the policy change are negative, both in Great Britain and in the country itself. Subject to the caveats noted in the conclusion this evidence suggests that these policy changes did not spur innovation.[18]

The Leger study is also worth mentioning, as it is one of the very few concerned with agricultural patents, and the only one we are aware of that is based on actual data. After mentioning a few (negative) studies of the impact of patents on Latin American agricultural production, it reports the results of a case study of Mexican maize breeding. The bottom line "shows that stronger IPRs [Intellectual Property Rights] have had few impacts on the development of new breeds and that few Mexican breeders used IPRs to protect their innovations."[19]

Finally, the Mann study is worth reading because it is the only attempt we are aware of to turn around the empirical findings of Bessen. As we extensively reported in Chapter 4, in a sequence of studies, Bessen and collaborators show that software patents did not increase and most likely decreased the rate of innovation in the software industry. As Bessen himself correctly points out in an unpublished rejoinder:

The actual empirical findings in this paper point to rather different conclusions than those that Mann draws, namely: few software startups benefits from software patents and patents are not widely used by software firms to obtain venture financing. Indeed, among other things, the paper reports that 80% of venture-financed software startups had not acquired any patents within four years of receiving financing.[20]

The remaining studies, like Lerner, find little or negative evidence that increased patent protection lead to increased innovation:

We find evidence that patents substitute for R&D effort at the firm level; they are associated with lower R&D intensity.[21]

The results suggest that stronger patents may have facilitated entry by firms in niche product markets, while spawning "patent portfolio races" among capital-intensive firms.[22]

It is too soon to draw any conclusion about what the effects will be of India's upcoming introduction of product patents for pharmaceuticals.... Currently Indian firms are quite quick to bring imitations to markets.... [B]ecause of concern over global price regulations ... innovative pharmaceuticals may actually become available to Indian consumers more slowly.[23]

Small firms prefer other mechanisms (e.g. secrecy) to protect their innovation or distrust patents, maybe because of the large costs involved in defending a patent. Another explanation of this result would be that small firms – on average – are more engaged in incremental innovation which does not fulfill the novelty requirement of patents. Moreover, large firms more probably apply for patent due to institutional requirements.... In addition, firms apply for patents because patents are used in cross-licensing agreements with other firms.[24]

National patent protection alone does not stimulate domestic innovation, as estimated by changes in citation-weighted U.S. patent awards, domestic R&D, and pharmaceutical industry exports. However, domestic innovation accelerates in countries with higher levels of economic development, educational attainment, and economic freedom. Additionally, there appears to be an optimal level of intellectual property rights regulation above which further enhancement reduces innovative activities.[25]

However, econometric analysis using both Japanese and U.S. patent data on 307 Japanese firms finds no evidence of an increase in either R&D spending or innovative output that could plausibly be attributed to patent reform.[26]

Route 128 and Silicon Valley

We now take up the tale, not of traditional intellectual monopoly such as patents and copyright, but of restrictive noncompete labor contract clauses. Although these are not, strictly speaking, tantamount to patents and copyright, they serve a similar purpose – that of maintaining monopoly over an innovation – and they are often used in place of patents where the latter are not legally allowed or easily enforceable. As the remark by Gary Becker we quoted in the previous chapter makes clear, legally preventing workers from spreading the knowledge they acquired in previous occupations is an inefficient way to internalize knowledge spillovers, something that could much more efficiently be achieved by using prices and wages. Noncompete clauses in labor contracts are a very common example of such inefficient and monopoly-inducing legal means. Testing their impact on the rate of innovation should help our understanding of the extent to which intellectual monopoly serves a beneficial social purpose.

You have probably heard of Silicon Valley. Perhaps you have not heard of Route 128. Yet Route 128 in Boston has been a high-technology district since the 1940s, long before farmers were displaced from Santa Clara Valley, as

Silicon Valley was then known, to make space for computer firms. In 1965, both Silicon Valley and Route 128 were centers of technology employment of equal importance, and with similar potentials and aspirations for further growth:

Route 128 began the race well ahead. In 1965, total technology employment in the Route 128 area was roughly triple that of Silicon Valley. By 1975, Silicon Valley employment had increased fivefold, but it had not quite doubled in Route 128, putting Silicon Valley about fifteen percent ahead in total technology employment. Between 1975 and 1990, the gap substantially widened. Over this period, Silicon Valley created three times the number of new technology-related jobs as Route 128. By 1990, Silicon Valley exported twice the amount of electronic products as Route 128, a comparison that excludes fields like software and multimedia, in which Silicon Valley's growth has been strongest. In 1995, Silicon Valley reported the highest gains in export sales of any metropolitan area in the United States, an increase of thirty-five percent over 1994; the Boston area, which includes Route 128, was not in the top five.[27]

What explains this radical difference in growth of the two areas? Certainly both had access to important universities, which are instrumental in the computer revolution – Harvard and MIT in the case of Route 128 and Stanford in the case of Silicon Valley. A careful analysis by Ronald J. Gilson shows that the only significant difference between the two areas lay in a small but significant difference between Massachusetts and California labor laws. According to Gilson:

A postemployment covenant not to compete prevents knowledge spillover of an employer's proprietary knowledge not, as does trade secret law, by prohibiting its disclosure or use, but by blocking the mechanism by which the spillover occurs: employees leaving to take up employment with a competitor or to form a competing start-up. Such a covenant provides that, after the termination of employment for any reason, the employee will not compete with the employer in the employer's existing or contemplated businesses for a designated period of time – typically one to two years – in a specified geographical region that corresponds to the market in which the employer participates.[28]

In Massachusetts:

Massachusetts law is generally representative of the approach taken toward postemployment covenants not to compete by the great majority of states. United States law in this area largely derives from English law that developed the basic pattern of blanket enforcement of covenants not to compete given by the seller in connection with the sale of a business, and the application of a rule of reason to covenants associated with employment. Covenants not to compete would be enforced against a departing employee if the covenant's duration and geographic coverage were no greater than necessary to protect an employer's legitimate business interest, and not otherwise contrary to the public interest. This formulation is commonplace in Massachusetts covenant cases, and dates to the late nineteenth century.[29]

By way of contrast, in California:

California law governing covenants not to compete is both unusual and radically different from that of Massachusetts. California Business and Professions Code section 16600 provides that "every contract by which anyone is restrained from engaging in a lawful profession, trade, or business of any kind is to that extent void." The courts have interpreted section 16600 "as broadly as its language reads." . . . Indeed, California courts' application of choice of law rules underscores the seriousness with which they view section 16600. Even if the employment agreement which contains a postemployment covenant not to compete explicitly designates the law of another state, under which the covenant would be enforceable, as controlling, and even if that state has contacts with the contract, California courts nonetheless will apply section 16600 on behalf of California residents to invalidate the covenant.[30]

Contrary to many business pundits, the reader of this book will perhaps not be surprised at the beneficial consequences of the Silicon Valley competitive environment. However, Saxenian, in her otherwise-informative book, remarks, "The paradox of Silicon Valley was that competition demanded continuous innovation, which in turn required cooperation among firms."[31] We know that there are good economic reasons why it must be so: competition is the mechanism that breeds innovation, and sustained competitive innovation, paradoxical as that may sound to those that do not understand it, often is best implemented via cooperation among competing firms.

While Route 128 companies spent resources to keep knowledge secret – inhibiting and preventing the growth of the high-tech industry – in California this was not possible. And so, Silicon Valley – freed of the millstone of monopolization – grew by leaps and bounds as employees left to start new firms, rejoined old firms, and generally spread socially useful knowledge far and wide.

Databases

The case of databases is still an experiment in the making. Unusually enough, the United States is, at least for now, on the right side of the divide. Databases are compilations of facts, which is broad and generic enough to include your personal list of people to whom you send valentine cards, the human genome, the local Yellow Pages, and the mailing list of those damned spammers. Databases, it seems obvious, have become increasingly important for private individuals, businesses, academic researchers, industrial R&D, and unfortunately, also for national security.

The experiment-in-the-making and the intense debate accompanying it both began in 1996. On March 11, the European Union issued a directive requiring member states to provide statutory protection of databases on the basis of copyright, even if the database in question contained material that was not itself under copyright. The European Union also tried to force nonmember states to accept its directive. It did this by deciding that E.U. protection would be extended to their citizens only if the nonmember states provided similar protection. By 2001, all E.U. countries had fully implemented the directive.

How about the United States? Stephen Maurer and Suzanne Scotchmer summarize the situation here in the following terms: "Except for opposition from the scientific and engineering communities, the United States probably would have signed a database protection treaty in 1997 and adopted corresponding domestic legislation in 1998. A revised bill known as H.R. 354, the Collections of Information Antipiracy Act, is currently pending in Congress."[32] As far as we know, the revised bill has not yet been approved, and the discussion is still open. This means that in the United States, until now at least, databases are not the objects of intellectual monopoly.

Databases, if you think of it, come extremely close to the idealized pure information that intellectual monopoly supporters talk about and that, according to dominant economic theory, is expensive to produce but absolutely cheap to copy. Maurer and Scotchmer are aware of this, and of the puzzling fact that very expensive databases keep being produced and traded without intellectual property protection:

The usual argument for statutory protection sounds simple and compelling. Databases are expensive to make but cheap to copy. For this reason, private and commercial database owners cannot compete with copiers in an open market. If databases cannot earn a fair return under existing law, no rational business would invest in them until Congress changed the rules. Instead, databases flourish.[33]

Furthermore:

Finally, many of the most popular and powerful methods depend on the marketplace. If consumers want frequent updates, a would-be copier has little to gain by offering last month's database at a bargain price. Similarly, consumers may think that a particular database is more valuable if it comes with copyrighted search software. In either case, copiers can only compete by making substantial investments of their own. The resulting protection is particularly effective in the sciences, where up-to-date, searchable data sets are at a premium.[34]

It beats us as to why – after pointing out all this and convincingly documenting the dramatically negative impact that introducing protected coverage of databases would have on both academic research and business activity in the United States – Maurer and Scotchmer decide to open up the door to some amount of intellectual monopoly by adding that "Congress could strengthen these methods still further by protecting each update or correction for 1 to 2 years. Such legislation would be far less restrictive than H.R. 354's proposed 15-year period."[35] But that is a different debate, which we leave for later.

In the meanwhile, the experiment continues along another dimension. Which one do you think is higher: the rate of creation of databases in the European Union, where they are protected, or in the United States, where they are not? Well, you guessed it right: in the United States. In fact, it is not even a race; the United States wins hands down, as Block points out. After documenting in details the excellent state of the U.S. database industry, its amazing growth rate and productivity, and the fact that the adoption of the directive does not seem to have produced any sustained increase in the European Union's production of databases, he adds: "For the entire period measured, U.S. online database production outpaced all of Europe by a factor of nearly 2.5:1. . . . American dominance of database production cannot be explained by incentives given to creators because American protection of database rights is much weaker than the Directive."[36] To which we add only that, most probably, American dominance of the industry *can* be explained by economic incentives to creators as measured by the actual profits accruing to them and by the competitive environment in which they operate, and that, almost certainly, neither of them is increased much by the E.U. directive. Our conjecture is that, within a few years, some smart applied economist will write an interesting Ph.D. dissertation showing just this.

Simultaneous Discovery

Insofar as inventors have unique ideas, it may make sense to reward them with monopolies to make sure that we get advantage of their unusual talents. For example, if, in the absence of James Watt, the steam condenser would not have been invented until long after his patent expired, there is some justification for having awarded him a monopoly. Of course, if others were going to discover it in a few years anyway, then it scarcely made sense to give him a long-term monopoly. As it happens, simultaneous discoveries tend to be the rule rather than the exception, and, in the presence of a patent system, they almost always lead to some ugly story. Those that follow may not be the most remarkable from a social point of view; they are just, among those we happen to have learned about, those that we found most significant. Many more, most certainly, are sitting out there, just waiting to be told. Because, you see, simultaneous discovery is not the exception; it is the rule, and even that greatest of all the modern innovators, our beloved James Watt, stumbled on to it, as Carnegie reports: "His first discovery was that of latent heat. When communicating this to Professor Black he found that his friend had anticipated him, and had been teaching it in lectures to his students for some years past."[37]

Since then, things have changed little along this dimension – if anything, simultaneous discovery has become more and more the rule, not the exception, nowadays. Academics, playing all kinds of tricks to "plant their flag first" and striving to publish that little working paper three days earlier than their colleagues who have reached the same result, are well aware of this fundamental fact. But patents on (very) basic research are not available yet – hence, the race to be first, until now, has affected only individual prestige and salaries. In those areas where patents are available, the impact has been much more dramatic, both for the individuals involved and for society at large.

Radio Waves

The radio, according to popular history, was invented by the great inventor Guglielmo Marconi. Indeed, some authors, such as Hong, go to great pains to argue the originality of Marconi relative to that of his contemporaries and the various other people that, between 1896 and 1898, claimed to have reached, or to be poised to reach, wireless transmission of radio signals at a substantial distance.[38]

Abundant evidence, including the very same evidence reported by Hong himself in his passionate defense of Marconi, suggests otherwise. There are many competitors, which is to say that many people who have claimed to have invented the radio in a form slightly different form, but functionally equivalent, to that of Marconi. They range from the most official ones, the British physicist Oliver Lodge in the United Kingdom and the forgotten genius Nikola Tesla in the United States, to the least loved one, the Russian Aleksander Popov – who, it is now clearly documented, described his findings in a paper published in 1895 and demonstrated the functioning of his apparatus in front of the St. Petersburg Physical Society in March 1896 – to the most relevant but least visible one, Henry B. Jackson, an engineer working for the Royal Navy.

The latter, who never complained about Marconi's patent and was in fact a friend of Marconi's, writes in an official report of May 2, 1897:

Comparing my experiments with those of Mr. Marconi, I would observe that before I heard of his results, I had succeeded with the instruments at my disposal in transmitting Morse signals with my apparatus about 100 yards, which I gradually increased to one-third of a mile, but could not improve upon till I obtained a more powerful induction coil last month, with which I have obtained my present results, using Marconi's system wires insulated in the air attached to transmitter and receiver.... With this exception, the details of my apparatus, which so closely resembles his, have been worked out quite.[39]

Talk about understatement and gentlemanliness! The fact is that Marconi was using established science at the time: long-run detection of Hertz waves was a widely studied topic. Marconi's box was frontier engineering, certainly, but there is no real scientific discovery in his black box. Similar experiments were carried out by Ernest Rutherford at Cambridge's Cavendish Laboratory as early as 1895–96. In describing Marconi's equipment, which is extremely similar to that of Rutherford and Jackson, even in terms of the size of many parts, Hong concludes: "There was an element of 'non-obviousness' in Marconi's solutions: his grounding[40] of one pole of the transmitter and one pole of the receiver." So, Marconi's contribution to solving the puzzle was the grounding of antenna and transmitter.

Trotter, Threlfall, and Crookes were all anticipators of Marconi's findings. Lodge's lecture to the August 1894 meeting of the British Association for the Advancement of Sciences at Oxford on using Hertzian waves to transmit signals also anticipated Marconi. Marconi started work on this in 1895. As it is clear from his first filing for a patent on June 2, 1896, he does not really understand Hertzian waves yet:

In his patent for wireless telegraphy, Marconi claimed almost everything about the use of the coherer (*which had been invented by Branly and improved by FitzGerald and Lodge*) in wireless telegraphy. In May 1897, Lodge had applied a patent for a system of wireless telegraphy of his own ... but he had had to withdraw his claims on the coherer and the tapper because they had been so thoroughly covered by Marconi.[41]

Marconi's final specification for the patent in 1897 is a "different kind of document entirely" from the initial one, thanks to the contribution of J. Fletcher Moulton and others, and it successfully manages to patent pretty much everything that goes into a radio, a radio transmitter, and a radio receiver. Not bad for a guy whose contribution was to ground the antenna!

Because Marconi came from an aristocratic family and had very good connections in London, he was able to patent first and to get away with patenting under his name lots of components that had been invented by others. Also because of his family connections in the city's financial circles, the Marconi Wireless Telegraph Company Ltd. was readily established and handsomely financed in 1897; it began thriving right away – its stock soaring from \$3 to \$22 in less than a year. The American Marconi Co. was formed in 1899, attracting investments from local big guns of the size of Thomas Edison and Andrew Carnegie. Then, on December 12, 1901, Marconi for the first time transmitted and received signals across the Atlantic Ocean. By 1903, the Marconi Company was carrying regular transatlantic news transmissions. End of story. Well, not quite.

Marconi may have been a glamorous and successful aristocrat, but he was an Italian aristocrat, and his patent was so broad that it left everybody else in England out in the cold. Furthermore, he was clearly appropriating rights over instruments that he had not invented and that were already widely used. All of this generated a strong reaction. Although this reaction did not affect Marconi's financial fortunes, nor allow those left out in the cold into the competition, it did at least leave enough documentation and bad feelings that we can now learn something from this experience.

To complete our learning, let us summarize what happened on the other side of the Atlantic. Nikola Tesla, the forgotten genius who has only recently come to renewed attention, filed for various radio patents in 1897. They were granted in 1900. This led to a repeated rejection of Marconi's application for a radio patent in the United States on the ground that Tesla's invention preceded his. We learned that the Patent Office, in 1903, pointed out the following while rejecting yet another Marconi application:

Many of the claims are not patentable over Tesla patent numbers 645,576 and 649,621, of record, the amendment to overcome said references as well as Marconi's pretended ignorance of the nature of a "Tesla oscillator" being little short of absurd.... [T]he term "Tesla oscillator" has become a household word on both continents.[42]

So, why didn't N. Tesla Broadcasting Co. hold a complete monopoly over radio communications in the United States until late in the 1920s? Why did Nikola Tesla die poor while Marconi enriched himself, on his way to a Nobel Prize? Because, you see, now like then, the game of patenting and intellectual monopoly is not all that democratic and open to the little guys as Ms. Khan's recent and altogether interesting book would like us to believe. So, it is the case that Marconi, supported by the likes of Edison and Carnegie, kept hammering the U.S. Patent Office until, in 1904, it reversed course and gave Marconi a patent for the invention of radio: "The reasons for this have never been fully explained, but the powerful financial backing for Marconi in the United States suggests one possible explanation."[43] We will spare you the sad story of Nikola Tesla's hapless fight against Marconi, you can figure that out by yourself. In fact, we are also sparing you the stories of the many other fights poor Tesla lost against some of the great "inventors" and "entrepreneurial geniuses" of the time, Edison foremost. The bottom line is that Tesla never got to see the rewards of his genius.

We beg you to note that the issue here is not whether Tesla or Marconi was the rightful monopolist of radio. Rather, the moral of this story is that simultaneous inventions are frequent; they are the rule and not the exception. The moral is that the patent system prevents simultaneous inventions from being recognized and used by society. And the moral, finally, is that the patent system destroys productive capacity, generates useless and damaging monopoly, and, last but not least, humiliates and destroys decent and humble geniuses like Aleksander Popov and Nikola Tesla.

The story of injustice to Nikola Tesla has a tragicomic ending: in 1943, the U.S. Supreme Court upheld Tesla's radio patent, reversing the earlier decision of the U.S. Patent Office. Of course, Tesla was dead by this time – and indeed that is why he was awarded the patent. The U.S. government had been sued by the Marconi Company for use of its patents during the First World War. By awarding the patent to Tesla, the government eliminated the claim by Marconi – and faced no similar claim from Tesla, who, being dead, was unable to sue.

Locking and Unlocking the Skies

As the radio was invented by the great inventor Marconi, so was the airplane invented by the great Wright Brothers.[44]

Again, the popular history turns out to be rather misleading. At the beginning of the nineteenth century, Sir George Cayley (1773–1857), a British engineer, had already written down and detailed the necessary specifications for the design of a successful airplane. The main difficulties were the lack of a lightweight power source and the control of flight, especially changing direction and altitude. Otto Lilienthal (1848–96), a German follower of Cayley, had made many successful flights on a hang gliders built by himself, thereby learning a number of crucial things about the management of flying. It is to Lilienthal, in fact, that the idea of wing warping is to be attributed. However, he killed himself in the tentative beginning of applying power to the hang glider. When the Wright brothers applied for the first patent in 1902, it was for the system of flight control obtained by the combined uses of warping and the rudder – that is, a very marginal improvement over the existing technology.

It should be noted as well that modern airplanes are not controlled by wing warping, but rather by movable control surfaces – elevators and ailerons. These were invented not by the Wright brothers, but by Glenn Curtiss – a fact that did not prevent the Wright brothers from suing Glenn Curtiss on the basis of their patent for wing warping.

Indeed, the story of the Wright brothers is not so terribly different from those of James Watt and Marconi: like Watt and Marconi, they made a marginal improvement to an existing technology and then used the patent system in an effort to monopolize an entire industry. The Wright brothers were merely less successful – perhaps lacking a politically connected partner such as Boulton's or Marconi's aristocratic connections – and were also unable to prevent innovation from taking place in France, where most serious airplane development took place beginning around 1907. Because we have probably tired you with the details of Marconi's story, we will spare you that of the Wrights.

But at least the Wright brothers were the undisputed first, were they not? Well, maybe. When you are done reading this book – or this paragraph, if you are impatient – go to the omnipresent Google, and enter "Mad Pearse, also known as Bamboo Dick" and then hit the "I'm Feeling Lucky" button.

Tele-things

Similar stories could and should be told, in sequence, for the many "tele-things" that, since the middle of the nineteenth century, have revolutionized our way of living: the telegraph, the telephone, and the television.[45] Nothing really new would be added, though, to the lessons learned so far, and some of those stories, in particular the one about the telephone and the growth of the Bell monopoly, do not make for a simple and entertaining summary.

In a nutshell, the telegraph, the telephone, and the television are clear cases of simultaneous invention and cumulative discovery by a number of more or less disconnected inventors. In all three cases, one of the inventors participating in the cumulative effort – generally the one with the smallest contribution but the best connections and the most cunning instinct for the monopoly game – won the patent, the glory, and the monopoly profits. Thanks to the patent system, the other innovators were left out in the cold, without economic reward, without the right to make copies of their own invention, without the right to compete in the market, and without any fame. Of course, it may be that the 2002 declaration by the U.S. Congress that Antonio Meucci invented the telephone was a suitable form of compensation for his invention. Given that, at the time of the ruling, Meucci had been dead for many decades, we very much doubt that he would have felt that this was the case.

The Moral

The moral of these and dozens of other stories – calculus, clipper ship, bicycles, motion pictures, magnetic resonance imaging, automobiles, duct tape – is simple. Most great inventions are cumulative and simultaneous; most great inventions could have been introduced simultaneously, or almost so by many different inventors and companies, competing among themselves to improve the product and sell it to consumers at a price as low as possible; most great inventions could have spread more rapidly and improved more quickly if the social productive capacity that simultaneous inventions generate had been usable. All of us, but for a dozen monopolists, would have been better off. None of this has happened, and none of this is happening, because the system of intellectual monopoly blocks it. Intellectual monopoly has historically given and still gives all the rewards to a lucky and often-undeserving person who manages, in one way or other, to get the patent and grab the monopoly power. As the stories we have told show, intellectual monopoly is absolutely not necessary for great inventions to take place. It is damaging for society, as valuable productive capacity is literally destroyed and thrown away. Finally, if you allow us, it is also awfully unfair.

Notes

1. The advantages and disadvantages of intellectual monopoly when innovations build on previous innovations is discussed in Scotchmer (1991) and Boldrin and Levine (1999), who construct examples in which competition achieves advantages best, while intellectual monopoly fails to innovate at all. More elaborate modeling and a more exhaustive analysis of the negative role intellectual monopoly plays when the complexity of innovations increases can be found in Boldrin and Levine (2005a, 2006). A detailed analysis of the problem, with implications for merger and acquisition patterns in industries where intellectual monopoly is widespread, is in Llanes and Trento (2006).
2. A starting point for Douglass North's views of the role that well-defined property rights, and patents in particular, played in the Industrial Revolution are his 1981 and 1991 works. It should be noted that North does not subscribe to a naive view of the evolution of property rights according to which they become progressively more efficient or just simply better as time goes on and the economy develops. Being aware of the fact they are, more often than not, determined by rent-seeking agents within a political game, North is careful at pointing out that the system of property rights one often faces is substantially inefficient, or inefficiency inducing, along more than one dimension.

3. Writing about the use of patents to lure investments away from other countries tempted us to engage in a, possibly not irrelevant, digression on the role that patents played in Europe, roughly, between 1400 and 1800. We resisted the temptation, but here are some hints for further reading. The original purpose of patents was to attract specific groups of artisans and highly skilled professionals who were, for one reason or another, lacking in the country or city promising the patent. Monopoly was the carrot offered by most Italian and northern European cities to inventors who agreed to immigrate and set up shop there. In England, during the seventeenth, eighteenth, and most of the nineteenth centuries, a royal patent privilege was awarded to those citizens who would travel abroad and be the first to bring back new goods and technologies. United States patent laws were less inclined to provide incentives to pirate foreign innovators, but they still discriminated heavily against foreign citizens and innovations until the 1861 reform; pirating of foreign inventions, especially British ones, was thriving. Notice the interesting fact: all these practices just amounted to imitation, or piracy, in modern jargon, rewarded with local monopoly! This is something worth keeping in mind in light of current sermons against Indian, Chinese, Mexican, and Brazilian people pirating "our" inventions. Our reading of historical records is that all this "reciprocal stealing" had no effect on the total amount of inventions.

4. If you care to read more, a few good books from where to start are Epstein and Maarten (2005), Khan (2005), esp. Chapter 2, and Landes (1969, 1998). A recent and fairly unbiased synthesis of the historical literature concerned with the impact of patents on the Industrial Revolution and inventive activity during the eighteenth and nineteenth centuries, MacLeod and Nuvolari (2006) p. 22, concludes:

> However, it would be wrong to assume that the emergence of patent systems played a critical or determinant role in such a transition. The evidence discussed in this paper has shown that the institutional arrangements supporting inventive activities in this historical phase were extremely variegated and sophisticated. . . . In other words, the roots of western industrialization seem to have been wider and deeper than the emergence of modern patent systems.

5. Scherer (2004), p. 191. It should be apparent that everything we know about the impact of copyright on classical music we have learned from Scherer (2004), and his sources. An additional valuable reference for the details relative to the extension of the Statute of Anne to musical compositions is Carroll (2005).

6. Lamoreaux and Sokoloff (2002), pp. 7–8. The research work of Khan, Lamoreux, and Sokoloff we mention is covered in a variety of articles and books, including the book by Khan (2005), which contains a very broad bibliography. On the growth of intermediaries and their role, see Lamoreaux and Sokoloff (2002).

7. Moser (2003), p. 3.

8. Ibid., p. 6.

9. Ibid., p. 6.

10. Moser (2003), pp. 34–35. Petra Moser's dissertation, which won the 2003 Gerschenkron Prize awarded by the Economic History Association to the best dissertation in the field, is a mine of valuable information on the role of patents in

determining innovative activity during the nineteenth and early twentieth centuries. The main findings are summarized in Moser (2003).

11. Moser (2005, 2006).
12. Moser (2006), abstract.
13. All the empirical studies listed in the long table can be found in the references at the end. The data about patents come from the 2003 Annual Report of the U.S. Patent and Trademark Office, which can be found online at http://www.uspto.gov/web/offices/com/annual. Additional basic data is from http://www.cms.hhs.gov.
14. Arundel (2001).
15. Gallini (2002), p. 139.
16. Jaffe (2000), abstract.
17. Ibid., p. 555.
18. Lerner (2002), p. 2.
19. Leger (2004), p. 9.
20. Bessen (2005), abstract.
21. Bessen and Hunt (2003), abstract.
22. Hall and Ham (1999), abstract.
23. Lanjouw (1997), p. 32.
24. Licht and Zoz (1996), p. 1.
25. Qian (2007), abstract.
26. Sakakibara and Branstetter (2001), abstract.
27. Gilson (1999). We quote from p. 16 of the original version (Working Paper 163, Stanford Law School, John M. Olin Program in Law and Economics, August 1998).
28. Ibid., p. 35.
29. Ibid., p. 36.
30. Ibid., p. 40. Kenney and von Burg (2000) also provide a great deal of information on the Route 128 versus Silicon Valley story.
31. Saxenian (1994), p. 46.
32. Maurer and Scotchmer (1999), p. 1129.
33. Ibid.
34. Ibid., p. 1130.
35. Maurer and Scotchmer (1999), p. 1129. A great deal of additional information about databases can be found in Block (2000), David (2001), Maurer (1999), Maurer, Firestone, and Scriver (2000).
36. Block (2000), p. 7.
37. Carnegie (1905), Chapter 3, p. 50.
38. To learn about Marconi and his contested invention, we started with Hong (2001), if anything because he tries harder than most to show that there was no simultaneous invention. On the Web, one can find lots of well-structured sites; we have made use of Marconi's page at Wikipedia – where we learned about Popov, in particular: that he was not a fraud, as one of us had been taught in junior high, and that he "died in 1905 and his claim was not pressed by the Russian government until 40 years later." No-longer-controversial facts about Tesla are reported in various places, including Johnston (1982) and Lomas (1999), and then continuing on with http://www.pbs.org/tesla/ll/ll_whoradio.html (accessed February 24, 2008) and the many other sites that in recent years have rediscovered Tesla, the genius that the patent system ignored.

39. Jackson (1897), quoted in Hong (2001), p. 17; it is also referenced in Burns (2004).
40. Hong (2001), p. 23.
41. Hong (2001), p. 13, emphasis added.
42. As reported at http://www.pbs.org/tesla/ll/ll_whoradio.html.
43. Ibid.
44. The details of the story of Glenn Curtiss and the Wright brothers can be found in the excellent book by Shulman (2003).
45. Brock (1981) provides a detailed and certainly unbiased (better said, biased, but on the other side) history of both the telegraph and the telephone industries that make up the telecommunications industry in the title. As the author seems to believe that monopoly pricing, cartels, stealing of inventions, political favors, and all the legal tricks that come with them, are business tools that any good entrepreneur should master and possibly adopt, he does not spare us the gory details. The book was written before U.S. Congress ruled that Bell had stolen the telephone invention from Antonio Meucci; hence, Brock reports only that Bell's patent was filed two hours earlier of an equivalent one by Elisha Gray that described the same invention. This, obviously, makes the whole thing even more entertaining in retrospect, as it proves once again that big simultaneous inventions are more the rule than the exception, and that big simultaneous stealing is also part of the feasible set (on the latter, see http://www.esanet.it/chez_basilio/meucci_faq.htm, accessed February 24, 2008). Historical details about Antonio Meucci can now be found everywhere; for the U.S. Congress resolution, passed on June 16, 2002, see http://www.guardian.co.uk/international/story/0,3604,738675,00.html (accessed February 24, 2008).

   As for the television, another "business is business" description can be found in the paper by Maclaurin (1950). Maclaurin somehow recognizes that television was a classical case of simultaneous invention, which was solved partly by forcibly pushing out of the playing field some of the inventors, and partly by building a monopolistic cartel among the survivors. Like every good follower of Schumpeter, though, Maclaurin concludes that the waste of productive capacity this involved, and the monopolistic pricing it generated, were good things. What is good for RCA is good for America, it seems. For different renditions of Philo T. Farnsworth's contribution to the invention of television, see the sharp booklet by Roberts (2003) or the longer and more romanticized biography by Schwartz (2003).

NINE

The Pharmaceutical Industry

It is often argued that the best case for the existence of patents is in the pharmaceutical industry. The fixed cost of innovation is large, with estimates of the average cost of bringing a single new drug to market as high as $800 million in year 2000 dollars.[1] Patent protection is more limited in the pharmaceutical industry than in other industries: because of the lengthy gap between discovery and approval of a new drug, the effective monopoly protection is estimated to last only twelve years – plus the three- to five-year extensions as allowed by the Drug Price Competition and Patent Term Restoration Act (known as the Hatch-Waxman Act) of September 1984.[2] Indeed, according to the industry surveys mentioned in earlier chapters, the only industry in which patents are thought to play an important role in bringing new products to market is the pharmaceutical industry.

The pharmaceutical industry is worthy of special consideration also for another complementary reason. The technology operated by the pharmaceutical industry – the chemical and industrial processes through which medicines are produced, packaged, and shipped – seems to fit the hypothesis of constant returns to scale almost perfectly. That is, the cost of shipping the ten-millionth container of medicine is about the same as that of shipping the first. From that come the many complaints about the pharmaceutical companies not shipping medicines to poor countries – even poor African consumers would be willing to pay the few additional cents needed to produce the additional medicine.

Also, and again, since the Hatch-Waxman Act of 1984, producers of generic drugs have found it easier to enter the market, so much so that, according to the Congressional Budget Office, in the United States, generic drugs reached 43 percent of the prescription segment in 1996, compared to 19 percent twenty-two years earlier. The Pharmaceutical Research and Manufacturers of America (PhRMA) reported their share to be in the interval of 42 percent to 58 percent in 2006.[3] In areas such as Latin America, Europe, India, and other Asian countries, the portion of the drug market occupied by generics is even higher. Consequently, as soon as the patent expires, the incumbent monopolist may expect to face competition from a growing number of generic producers that sell at prices a lot closer to marginal cost than the patented medicine did. In the United States, generic drugs are available at prices that are between 30 percent and 80 percent lower than that of the originally patented product.[4]

Finally, the global drug market is geographically concentrated, with sales in the United States accounting for about 48 percent of the total, followed by Europe's 29 percent and Japan's 11 percent. Why is this? The fixed cost of creating a new medicine is very high, it is argued; as a consequence, new drugs are expensive and only consumers in rich countries can afford them. Nevertheless, other markets are growing, and the economic development of China and India will soon lead to a substantial change in the world distribution of market shares.

Large fixed cost, small and constant marginal cost, innovation as the main competitive tool, and the market concentrated in rich countries where pirating is practically absent – this sounds like the textbook description of a traditional Schumpeterian industry. The model we have been criticizing as unrealistic and misguided until now seems to fit almost perfectly the situation of the pharmaceutical industry. Under these circumstances, the traditional model predicts that there should be many potential producers of a medicine, that the industry should be dynamically competitive and therefore highly innovative, with newcomers frequently challenging incumbents by means of innovative superior drugs. In some sense, this describes the global pharmaceutical industry. But in some other, equally if not more important sense, it does not.

Some people love the pharmaceutical industry and some people despise it: there is little middle ground. The pharmaceutical industry is the poster child of every intellectual monopoly supporter. It is the vivid example that, without the sheltering patents provided to inventors, the outpouring of new wonder drugs we have grown accustomed to would not have materialized, our life expectancies would be a lot shorter, and millions of people would have died of the diseases Big Pharma has instead managed to cure. In the opposite camp, Big Pharma is the scourge of humanity: a club of oligopolistic white men who, by controlling medicine around the globe and refusing to sell drugs at their marginal cost, are letting millions of poor people die. Withdrawal of supply by the big pharmaceutical companies is as close to economic crime as anything can be, we are told. The wonders of contemporary medicine and biotechnology are the fruits of intellectual property, it is countered.

This sounds utterly complicated, so let us handle it with care and, for once, play the role of the wise fellows: *in media stat virtus, et sanitas* [Virtue is in the middle, and so is health]. In fact, we will move (instead of jump) into this issue so carefully that, by the end of the chapter, the reader may feel we managed just to check the water's temperature and, maybe, salinity. The pharmaceutical industry is a complicated beast to vivisect, one that can be approached from many contradictory angles and viewpoints. We will stick to ours, narrow that it may be, and ask, How strong is the case for patents in pharmaceuticals? Is there substantial evidence that without patents we would not have the medicines we have, or at least that we would have many fewer and worse medicines? Would the industry shut down and talent move to some other, more rewarding enterprise if patents on drugs were more or less abolished; that is, if the world became like Switzerland until 1978 or Italy until a year later?

In fact, we shall see that although Big Pharma is not necessarily the monster some depict, the case for patents in pharmaceuticals is a lot weaker than most people think – and so, apparently, even under the most favorable circumstances, patents are not necessarily good for society, for consumers, or in this case, for sick people. Patents are good for monopolists, but that much we knew already.

World Shortest History of Pharmaceutical Patents

Pharmaceuticals are a significant industry and of growing significance. The industry's market size is approaching $700 billion worldwide and is growing at annual rates between 5 percent and 8 percent. In the United States, where drug sales ran at $275 billion in 2006,[5] the share of prescription drugs in total national health-care expenditure increased from 4.9 percent in 1980 to 10 percent in 2004, which corresponds to 1.6 percent of gross national product. New drugs are extremely costly to develop. Hansen, Grabowski, and Lasagna provide the following estimates of the cost in millions of 1987 dollars of bringing a new chemical entity to market, assuming a success rate of 23 percent for patented drugs.[6] The costs due to preclinical testing research amount to $66 million, which become $142 million when compounded at an interest rate of 8 percent. The clinical testing costs are $48 million, which compound to $72 million at the same interest rate. Added up, this gives $114 million at a zero interest rate and $214 million at an 8 percent interest rate.

Notice that the preclinical component of cost is large, and especially so when the interest rate is taken into account, as the preclinical costs must be paid before going to clinical trials. More recent estimates by Di Masi, Grabowski, and Hansen place the total cost of bringing a new drug to market at around $800 million, in year 2000 dollars.[7] Even if a number of researchers have questioned their methodology, this figure suggests a spectacular increase in the cost of innovating. This increase is due, mostly, to the capitalization of the longer and more expensive clinical trials that the U.S. Food and Drug Administration (FDA) requires. In a recent and much publicized case, Pfizer announced the write-off of almost $1 billion of expenditures sunk into the development of a new drug, Torcetrapib, which failed dramatically short of its expectations.[8] Of the $1 billion dollars involved, $800 million went to pay for clinical trials, while the Irish plant where the drug was supposed to be produced cost just $90 million.[9] With research and development (R&D) costs of such magnitude, it seems impossible to even dream of a pharmaceutical industry that could properly function and innovate in the absence of very strong patent protection. It was not always this way.

Historically, intellectual monopoly in pharmaceuticals has varied enormously over time and space. The summary story: the modern pharmaceutical industry developed faster in those countries where patents were fewer and weaker. Since the Second World War, and the upheaval of the worldwide distribution of power within the chemical industry that the war brought about, patent lobbyists have lobbied long and successfully to increase patent protection for pharmaceutical products. Here are the details of their accomplishments.

In the United States, drugs have been patentable since the beginning, for the very simple reason that chemical products have always been patentable. The United States recognizes two distinct forms of patent: the process by which a drug is produced may be patented independently of the chemical formula for the drug. Until 1984, U.S. patent law treated medical discoveries in the same way as other innovations, and no special treatment was reserved for drugs. In more recent years, longer and more frequent extensions for drug patents have been allowed than for other patents. As we already mentioned, the Hatch-Waxman Act of 1984 was designed to compensate for regulatory requirements that delay the introduction of new drugs. It is estimated that the act increased effective length of patent protection for pharmaceuticals by about three to five years.

In most of continental Europe, until recent years, only the process of producing a drug could be patented, so once a drug was discovered, a second producer could also produce it provided that it found a different way of doing so. The rationale behind process versus product patents is given by the German Association of the Chemical Industry in a memorandum to the Reichstag.[10] The association points out that the same chemical product can be obtained by different processes and methods, and even by starting from initially different materials and components. Hence, there is social value in patenting a new process, as it rewards the innovator without preventing further innovation. There is negative social value in patenting a specific product, as this would exclude all others from producing it, even through different processes. It should be noted, though, that this did not prevent German chemical companies from patenting their products where possible, in the United Kingdom and the United States especially.[11]

In France, under a law of July 5, 1844, pharmaceutical inventions could not be patented. Legislation then evolved to keep the prohibition for patenting products but to allow patents for processes. The executive order of February 4, 1959, and then the law of January 2, 1966, finally introduced limited patents for pharmaceutical products in France; the ban on patenting drugs was completely lifted only in 1978. In Germany, the law of May 25, 1877, introduced patents for both chemical and pharmaceutical processes, but products were explicitly excluded. The law of April 4, 1891, extended patent protection to products obtained via a patented process. Finally, the law of September 4, 1967, introduced general patentability of chemical and pharmaceutical products also in Germany.

In Switzerland, patents for chemical and pharmaceutical products were explicitly prohibited by the Swiss constitution. The Swiss pharmaceutical industry, whose strength does not need to be recalled, has, however, been a historically important competitor for the German pharmaceutical industry. Constant German pressure, both political and legal, eventually led to the adoption of patents for chemical processes with the Swiss law of June 21, 1907, which was nevertheless quite restrictive. The law of June 25, 1954, continued to apply only to processes but extended the length of patents from ten to eighteen years. Patents for products were introduced in Switzerland only in 1977.

In Italy, pharmaceutical patents were prohibited until 1978, when the Supreme Court ruled in favor of eighteen pharmaceutical companies, all foreign, requesting the enforcement of foreign patents on medical products in Italy. Despite this complete lack of any patent protection, Italy had developed a strong pharmaceutical industry: by the end of the 1970s, it was the fifth-largest world producer of pharmaceuticals and the seventh-largest exporter.

In Spain, the Ley de Patentes introduced patents for products in 1986, as a consequence of the country's entrance in the European Economic Community. The law began to be applied only in 1992. Before that date, regulations dating back to 1931 explicitly prohibited the patenting of any substance and, particularly, of any pharmaceutical substance. Patenting of processes was instead allowed.[12]

Pharmaceuticals are also covered by a variety of international agreements. The contemporary era of patenting began with the Convention of the Union of Paris in 1883 following the Vienna Conference of 1873. More recently, the Patent Cooperation Treaty was signed in Washington on June 19, 1970, which started a process of international extension of stronger patent protection for medical products. The Munich Convention of October 3, 1973, implemented on October 7, 1978, defines the notion of a European patent. Further revisions and modifications of the original basic agreement led, eventually, to the definition of the Community Patent Convention, which was signed in Luxembourg on December 15, 1975. The latter was not ratified by various countries (Denmark, Ireland, Greece, Portugal, and Spain) and the overall project eventually failed.

Nevertheless, the core idea of a unified European patent system was not abandoned and continued to be pursued in various forms, first under the leadership of the European Commission and then under that of the European Union. In 2000, the Community Patent Regulation proposal was approved, which was considered a major step toward the final establishment of a European patent. Things, nevertheless, did not proceed as expeditiously as the supporters of a European patent had expected. As of 2007, the project is still, in the words of European Union Commissioner Charlie McCreevy, "stuck in the mud" and far from being finalized.[13] Interestingly, the obstacles are neither technical nor due to a particularly strong political opposition to the establishment of a continent-wide form of intellectual monopoly. The obstacles are purely due to rent seeking by interest groups in the various countries involved, the number of which notoriously keeps growing. Current intellectual monopolists (and their national lawyers) would rather remain monopolists (legal specialists) for a bit longer in their own smaller markets than risk the chance of losing everything to a more powerful monopolist (or to a foreign firm with more skilled lawyers) in the bigger continental market.

It is worth pointing out that under EU patent law, programs for computers together with scientific discoveries and theories, mathematical methods, aesthetic creations, programs, rules and methods for performing mental acts, playing games or doing business, and presentations of information are expressly not regarded as inventions and therefore cannot be patented. Because there is a large degree of ambiguity as to what a scientific theory or discovery is, the extent to which a new medicine, or a new biologically engineered product, is or is not independent of the underlying chemical and biological model that explains it is not clear. As a result of this ambiguity, medical products and treatments have been increasingly patented in the European Union in ways similar to the United States.

Finally, in more recent years and within the framework of the World Trade Organization's Trade-related Aspects of Intellectual Property Rights agreement (known as the WTO-TRIPS agreement) that came into effect on January 1, 1995, a steady process of worldwide harmonization of patent rules in the pharmaceutical and other industries has been undertaken. Widespread controversies, both political and judicial, surrounding the modification of the Indian system of pharmaceutical patents in a direction favorable to intellectual monopoly, or the even more recent decision by the Brazilian government to "bypass" a number of foreign patents covering the production and distribution of AIDS-related drugs, are just two of the most visible aspects of this ongoing process, to which we return later and in Chapter 10.

Now, you may be wondering, why are we boring you with all these details about specific countries, patenting of chemical processes, pharmaceutical products, and so forth? For a very simple reason: if patents were a necessary requirement for pharmaceutical innovation, as claimed by their supporters, the large historical and cross-country variations in the patent protection of medical products should have had a dramatic impact on national pharmaceutical industries. In particular, at least between 1850 and 1980, most drugs and medical products should have been invented and produced in the United States and the United Kingdom, and very little if anything produced in continental Europe. Further, countries such as Italy, Switzerland, and, to a lesser extent, Germany, should have been the poor, sick laggards of the pharmaceutical industry until recently. Instead, the opposite was true for longer than a century.

Chemicals without Patents

Prior to the rise of the pharmaceutical industry, the most important form of chemical production was the paint and coloring industry. At its inception, the dye industry was a French and British business the same way that almost any industry was a French and British business until the second half of the nineteenth century. In both countries, patent protection applied for all kinds of industrial products. In 1862, British firms controlled about

50 percent of the world market and French firms another 40 percent, with Swiss and German companies as marginal players. By 1873, German companies had 50 percent of the market, while French, Swiss, and British firms controlled between 13 percent and 17 percent each. In 1913, German firms had a market share of more than 80 percent, the Swiss had about 8 percent, and the rest of the world had disappeared. During this entire period, there was no patent protection at all in Switzerland, while in Germany processes become patentable in 1877 but products did not. In France, the United Kingdom, and the United States, both products and processes had been patentable all along. Indeed, the strong patent protection for this industry in France and its absence in Switzerland was largely responsible for the development of the important Swiss chemical, and then pharmaceutical, industry after 1864.

In that year, a judicial sentence favoring the French company La Fuchsine, in a fight over the scope of patents it held on the colorant of the same name, established its almost complete grip on the French dye industry. This put the many French companies constituting the paint and coloring industry on notice, resulting in a large movement of firms to Switzerland, where patents were instead illegal. From 1864 onward and for about two decades, La Fuchsine (or Poirrer, after the 1868 acquisition) dominated the French market thanks to its patents. During the same period it innovated little, if at all, while its Swiss and German competitors, unprotected by patents, did. La Fuchsine was therefore completely unable to compete outside of France and, once its patents expired, it disappeared into oblivion, together with its analogous patent holders in Britain (among which Perkin was the most well known). In case this reminds you of how the Hollywood movie industry was created by migrating entrepreneurs running away from Edison's patents, you have begun to see the pattern. The migrating French firms located in and around Basel were rapidly followed by other chemical companies. The movement was so dramatic that just before the First World War, Haber observes that in France there was no production of chemical products, either organic or inorganic.[14]

Haber explicitly attributes the absence of a French chemical industry to the presence of patents stifling competition and making innovation impossible. He points out that, in a similar way, the slow growth of the coloring industry in the United States before the First World War was largely due to patent protection: most patents were held by the large German companies, such as Bayer, BASF, Hoechst, and IG Farben. The chemical industry in the United States was so underdeveloped that during the First World War the United States was forced to import dyes from Germany via submarines to bypass the British blockade.

This would be humorous, if it were not sad: German chemical companies competed heavily at home and across most European markets, where chemical products could not be patented. This situation forced them to innovate frequently and to develop production processes able to guarantee very high productivity. Such intense competition already gave them a competitive edge relative to the Anglo-Saxon companies living in a world of generalized patenting. To this initial advantage was added the opportunity to patent products in the United Kingdom and the United States, allowing the German chemical companies to erect insurmountable barriers to entry in the chemical market. Do not get us wrong here; we are not claiming that the German companies did not use patents in building up their worldwide dominance. They did, and there is no doubt whatsoever that the chemical industry worldwide was an assemblage of more or less loosely held together cartels until the late 1930s, cartels in which the big German chemical companies played a major leading and coordinating role. Still, the fact that they wiped out their French and Anglo-Saxon counterparts in the worldwide market, and that they did so in spite of having a lot less patent protection, speaks volumes in regard to the specific issue that concerns us in this chapter.[15]

So, before the First World War, medicines and other chemical products were scarce and expensive in England. This led, in 1919, to the modification of the English Patents Act of 1907 and the addition of Section 38A, which introduced mandatory licenses for medicines. Again, the report of the Sargent Committee of 1937 pointed out the shortage of medicines and its relationship to strong patents in England. In the Patents Act of 1949, Section 41, No. 2, a new special procedure was introduced to favor mandatory licensing of food and drug products. The British government spent about forty years fiddling around with its patent laws, without ever abolishing them, in the vain hope of lowering the prices of medicines and creating incentives for its pharmaceutical industry to catch up with that of the Germans. It did not succeed, as we all know: the German companies kept innovating, even if their new products were not protected by patents at home and the British pharmaceutical industry never came close to being competitive. Aspirin, that wonder drug, was a German invention, not a British one and, while it was patented in the United States, Britain, and France, it could not be patented in Germany. Bayer was forced to relinquish its patent on aspirin in the rest of the world by the Treaty of Versailles.[16]

Here is how Murmann summarizes the main findings from his historical study of the European synthetic dye industries during the 1857–1914 period:

British and French synthetic dye firms that initially dominated the synthetic dye industry because of their patent positions but later lost their leadership positions are important cases in point. It appears that these firms failed to develop superior capabilities in production, marketing and management precisely because patents initially sheltered them from competition. German and Swiss firms, on the other hand, could not file for patents in their home markets and only those firms that developed superior capabilities survived the competitive home market. When the initial French and British patents expired, the leading German and Swiss firms entered the British and French market, capturing large portions of sales at the expense of the former leaders.[17]

It is only with the end of the two world wars and the de facto expropriation of German chemical know-how, first by the French and British and then by the victorious Allies, that a degree of competition was restored in the chemical industry for a few decades. Indeed, in the end, the First World War blockade did work – allowing DuPont to enter the dyestuff market by pirating German products. The British government provided DuPont with access to the industrial secrets found in a Hoechst plant in the United Kingdom that had been confiscated at the start of the First World War; the U.S government allowed DuPont free access in 1919 to all German chemical patents, as these were confiscated at the end of the war.

From a theoretical point of view, it is not hard to understand the devastating impact of patents, especially of product patents, on innovation in the chemical industry. The chemical industry is a classic case of the innovation chains – new compounds and processes are built on the knowledge of existing ones. As we observed, patents are particularly harmful in this case, as the increased incentive to innovate that they may generate is, as in the chemical industry, more than offset by the increased difficulty of doing so.

It could be, and sometimes is, argued that the modern pharmaceutical industry is substantially different from the chemical industry of the past century. In particular, it is argued that the most significant cost of developing new drugs lies in testing numerous compounds to see which ones work. Insofar as this is true, it would seem that the development of new drugs is not so dependent on the usage and knowledge of old drugs. However, this is not the case according to the chief scientific officer at Bristol-Myers Squibb, Peter Ringrose, who "told *The New York Times* that there were 'more than 50 proteins possibly involved in cancer that the company was not working on because the patent holders either would not allow it or were demanding unreasonable royalties."[18]

Truth-telling remarks by pharmaceutical executives aside, there is a deeper reason why the pharmaceutical industry of the future will be more and more characterized by complex innovation chains: biotechnology. As of 2004, already more than half of the research projects carried out in the pharmaceutical industry had some biomedical foundation. In biomedical research, gene fragments are, in more than a metaphorical sense, the initial link of any valuable innovation chain. Successful innovation chains depart from, and then combine, very many gene fragments and cannot do without at least some of them. As gene fragments are finite in number, patenting them is equivalent to artificially fabricating what scientists in this area have labeled an "anticommons" problem. So, it seems that the impact of patent law in either promoting or inhibiting research remains, even in the modern pharmaceutical industry.[19]

Medicines without Patents

Patents for medicines were introduced in Italy, under pressure from foreign multinationals, in 1978. Today India, China, and Brazil are, reluctantly, caving in to U.S. pressure to do the same. Proponents of intellectual property argue that this will increase pharmaceutical innovation in those countries. So, we may ask, Did the strengthening of intellectual property protection trigger a golden age of innovation in the Italian pharmaceutical industry?

During the period 1961–80, a total of 1,282 new active chemical compounds were discovered around the world. Of these, a total of 119 came from Italy (9.28 percent). During the period 1980–83, a total of 108 compounds were discovered. Of these, eight came from Italy (7.5 percent).[20] Although we do not have data covering the most recent decades, the very clear impression of the informed observer is that things have become worse, not better. Professors Scherer and Weisburst, in fact, took the pain of carefully studying the evolution of the Italian pharmaceutical industry after the adoption of patents. Here is the summary verdict, in Scherer's own words: "Research by Sandy Weisburst and mentored by me showed, for example, that Italy, with a vibrant generic drug industry, did not achieve any significant increase in the discovery of innovative drugs during the first decade after the Italian Supreme Court mandated the issue of pharmaceutical product patents."[21]

A number of historical and empirical studies make evident that, absent patents, the Italian pharmaceutical industry did not suffer particularly until 1978. On the one hand, foreign companies holding patents abroad entered the Italian market, via direct investment and the establishment of local production units, in order to protect the market share of their own products. On the other hand, the possibility of freely imitating products patented elsewhere favored the creation of a large number of Italian imitative firms, which improved upon existing products and, at the same time, allowed for their diffusion at much lower prices. In spite of this, the forty largest Italian firms (out of about five hundred, until the late 1970s) did not simply imitate but also developed their own products and innovated extensively, either by using existing products as ingredients (25 percent of products developed) or by using products that were not patentable or with expired patents (31 percent of products developed).[22]

In other words, a thriving pharmaceutical industry had existed in Italy for more than a century in the complete absence of patents. That is point one. Point two is that neither the size nor the innovative output nor the economic performances of that industry have improved, to any measurable extent, during the thirty years since patents were adopted. Every indicator one can look at suggests that, if anything, the Italian pharmaceutical industry was hurt, not helped, by the adoption of patents, and every expert who has looked at it has come up with this same conclusion.

Since 1978, India has taken over as the primary center of pharmaceutical production without patent protection. The growth and vitality of the Indian industry is similar to that of the pre-1978 industry in Italy. In fact it is much more so, as the sheer size of the national market has turned Indian generic drug producers into big players in the global pharmaceutical industry. Within the framework of the WTO-TRIPS agreements, India has now been forced to introduce product patents on pharmaceutical products, which have become progressively more stringent (2005 was the formal deadline for complete compliance). Although a variety of researchers have speculated, partly on the ground of the Italian experience, about the consequences of this legislative shift for the Indian pharmaceutical industry, we are aware of very few studies that directly address the Indian situation.[23] Only one study focuses directly on India and asks the important welfare question: are Indian consumers going to be better or worse off after pharmaceutical patents are fully adopted in their country? By concentrating on the market for a specific drug – quinolones, for which very good micro time-series data are available – Chaudhuri, Goldberger, and Jia reach the following conclusion (apologies for the jargon; sometimes it is unavoidable):

We ... carry out counterfactual simulations of what prices, profits and consumer welfare would have been, had the fluoroquinolone molecules we study been under patent in India as they were in the U.S. at the time. ... We estimate that in the presence of price regulation the total annual welfare losses to the Indian economy from the withdrawal of the four domestic product groups in the fluoroquinolone sub-segment would be on the order of U.S. $305 million, or about 50% of the sales of the entire systemic anti-bacterials segment in 2000. Of this amount, foregone profits of domestic producers constitute roughly $50 million. The overwhelming portion of the total welfare loss therefore derives from the loss of consumer welfare. In contrast, the profit gains to foreign producers in the presence of price regulation are estimated to be only around $19.6 million per year.[24]

Other observers, looking at the big picture, are less negative. Interestingly, though, we have not been able to find a single independent analyst claiming that the additional amount of pharmaceutical innovation patents may stimulate in the Indian industry will be substantial and large enough to compensate for the other social costs. More to the point, the positive consequence of patent adoption in countries like India is, according to most analysts, a consequence of beneficial price discrimination. The argument goes as follows: monopoly power allows price discrimination – that is, the sale of the same good for a high price to people valuing it a lot (usually people richer than average) and for a low price to people valuing it little (usually people poorer than average). As a result of the absence of patent protection, there are very many new drugs that are not marketed in poor countries by their original producer, as the latter is not protected by reliable patents in that country. If it were, the profit-maximizing monopolist would have an incentive to quickly introduce those drugs, at prices lower than in rich countries, also in poor countries. This would increase the welfare of the poor country's residents, as they would receive the medicine earlier rather than later.

Although the argument sounds perfectly logical (leave aside the issue of how large the gains from this earlier marketing of new medicines would be), there are two points its advocates either do not notice or underplay. The first has to do with retrading, otherwise known as "parallel import" or free trade, if you like. If a drug is sold more cheaply in country X than in country Y, there is an incentive to set up a firm shipping the drug from X to Y, as many Americans and Canadians have recently discovered. Hence, the full requirement for poor countries is not just to adopt Western-style patents, so that price discrimination by the monopolist can benefit them, but also to restrict free trade. An interesting twist, given that the idea comes from the World Trade Organization, an international organization erected and financed to support and expand free trade worldwide! The second doubt comes from the following observation: if it were really true that imitating and pirating new drugs were that easy, absent patent protection, local firms would be already producing and marketing such drugs in the country in question. Hence, the arrival of the foreign patent holder's output could not really increase the welfare of local consumers, as it would purely replace that of existing local suppliers. This conclusion seems unavoidable, unless one is willing to argue that the marginal cost of producing drugs is not constant, or that imitation and reverse engineering are not all that cheap, or that the initial inventor has some cost advantages over its imitators. But then, once either of the last three points is admitted, the whole argument for patent protection fails in the first place, and we are back to square zero: *qui prodest?*

The Pharmaceutical Industry Today

In spite of the fact that between 1985 and 2005 a long string of almost fifty mergers and acquisitions led to a progressively more concentrated pharmaceutical industry, it is still hard to argue, from a worldwide perspective, that the pharmaceutical is a monopolized industry. True, a few large companies – about fifteen and possibly shrinking soon – hold a dominant position throughout the world, all of them based in the United States, Germany, the United Kingdom, Switzerland, and France. Still, the distance in sales between the companies ranked No. 15 and No. 16 in 2004 was $600 million, out of about $10 billion, and the list of the top fifty pharmaceutical and biomedical company looks more like a smooth continuum, starting at $52 billion with Pfizer and ending at $1.5 billion with Tanabe Seiyaku, with the two biggest percentage drops in sales between No. 2 (Johnson & Johnson) and No. 3 (GlaxoSmithKline), of about −21 percent, and No. 12 (Eli Lilly) and No. 13 (Bayer), of about −27 percent. Furthermore, the post-1985 merger wave runs parallel to the emergence of new biotech companies and, as documented earlier, of a growing number of generic drugs producers. These two factors have prevented monopolistic concentration in the industry; the combined worldwide market share of the top thirty pharmaceutical and biotechnology firms is just over 50 percent. The sales of the two largest ones covered about 15 percent of the global market for drugs in 2004. Relative size and market share are not the sources of monopoly power, if there is any, in this industry. Furthermore, although the wave of mergers may have erected substantial barriers for reaching the top, it would be a stretch to claim that there are substantial barriers to entry into the industry per se. In every country we have considered there are often hundreds of competing pharmaceutical firms, and new biomedical startups are appearing and being financed, especially in the United States, on a monthly basis.[25]

A few additional symptoms may help the reader get a better understanding of why, at the end, we reach the diagnosis we do. Sales are growing, fast; at about 12 percent a year for most of the 1990s, and still now at around 8 percent a year; R&D expenditures during the same period have been rising only 6 percent. A company such as Novartis (a big R&D player relative to industry averages) spends about 33 percent of sales on promotion and

19 percent on R&D. The industry average for the ratio of R&D expenditures to sales seems to be around 16 percent to 17 percent, while according to a 1998 Congressional Budget Office report, the same percentage was approximately 18 percent for American pharmaceuticals in 1994; according to a 2007 PhRMA report it was 19 percent in 2006. The point here is not that the pharmaceutical companies are spending too little on R&D – no one has managed (and we doubt anyone could manage) to calculate what the socially optimal amount of pharmaceutical R&D is. The point here is that the top thirty representative firm spends about twice as much on promotion and advertising as it does on R&D; and the top thirty is where private R&D expenditure is carried out, in the pharmaceutical industry.

Next, we note that no more than one-third – more likely one-quarter – of new drug approvals are considered by the FDA to have therapeutic benefit over existing treatments, implying that, under the most generous hypotheses, only 25 percent to 30 percent of the total R&D expenditure goes toward new drugs. The rest, as we will see better in a moment, goes toward the so-called me-too drugs. Related to this is the more and more obvious fact that the amount of price discrimination carried out by the top thirty among North America, Europe, and Japan is dramatically increasing, with price ratios for identical drugs reaching values as high as two or three. The designated victims, in this particular scheme, are apparently U.S. consumers and, to a lesser extent, northern European and Swiss consumers. At the same time, operating margins in the pharmaceutical industry run at about 25 percent against 15 percent or less for other consumer goods, with peaks, for U.S. market–based firms, as high as 35 percent. The U.S. pharmaceutical industry has been topping the list of the most profitable sectors in the U.S. economy for almost two decades, never dropping below third place, an accomplishment unmatched by any other manufacturing sector. Price discrimination, made possible by monopoly power, does have its rewards.

Summing up and moving forward, here are the symptoms of the malaise we should investigate further.

- There is innovation, but not as much as one might think there is, given what we spend.
- Pharmaceutical innovation seems to cost a lot and marketing new drugs even more, which makes the final price for consumers very high and increasing.
- Some consumers are hurt more than others, even after the worldwide extension of patent protection.

Where Do Useful Drugs Come From?

For starters, useful new drugs seem to come in a growing percentage from small firms, start-ups, and university laboratories. But this is not an indictment of the patent system, as, probably, such small firms and university labs would not have put in all the efforts they did in coming up with the new compounds if the prospective of a patent to be sold to a big pharmaceutical company were not in the cards.

Next there is the not-so-small detail that most of those university laboratories are actually financed by public money, mostly federal money flowing through the National Institutes of Health. The pharmaceutical industry is much less essential to medical research than its lobbyists might have you believe. In 1995, according to a study by two well-reputed University of Chicago economists, the United States spent about $25 billion on biomedical research. About $11.5 billion came from the federal government, with another $3.6 billion of academic research not funded by the feds. Industry spent about $10 billion.[26] However, industry R&D is eligible for a tax credit of about 20 percent, so the government also picked up about $2 billion of the cost of "industry" research. That was then, but now are things different? It does not look that way. According to industry sources, total research expenditure by the industry was, in 2006, about $57 billion, while the National Institutes of Health budget in the same year (the largest but by no means the only source of public funding for biomedical research) reached $28.5 billion.[27] So, it seems things are not changing: private industry pays for only about one-third of biomedical R&D. By way of contrast, outside of the biomedical area, private industry pays for more than two-thirds of R&D.

Many people infected with HIV can still recall the 1980s, when no effective treatment for AIDS was available, and being HIV-positive was a slow death sentence. Not unnaturally, many of these individuals are grateful to the pharmaceutical industry for bringing to market drugs that – if they do not eliminate HIV – make life livable:

> The "evil" pharmaceutical companies are, in fact, among the most beneficent organizations in the history of mankind and their research in the last couple of decades will one day be recognized as the revolution it truly is. Yes, they're motivated by profits. Duh. That's the genius of capitalism – to harness human improvement to the always-reliable yoke of human greed. Long may those companies prosper. I owe them literally my life.[28]

But it is wise to remember that the modern drug cocktail that is used to treat HIV was not invented by a large pharmaceutical company. It was invented by an academic researcher, Dr. David Ho.

Still, one may say, the issue we are debating here is patents and whether, in particular, medical patents are socially beneficial or not. Lots of, even most, important medical discoveries may come from publicly sponsored research laboratories, but it is a fact that, without the strong incentive that the prospect of a successful patent induces, those researchers would not be working as hard as they do. That is true, so let us think the issue through once again. We observe that, while the incentive to patent and commercialize their findings should have been increased by the Bayh-Dole Act allowing patentability of such research results, there is no evidence whatsoever that, since 1980 when the act was passed, major medical scientific discoveries have been pouring out of American universities' laboratories at an unprecedented rate. Good research was done before; good research is done now. Medical and biological scientists comparing then and now may complain, more often than not, about the direction of research (more commercially oriented now, and less directed toward big problems and pure scientific discovery than it was then), but they are not claiming that the quality went visibly down. At the same time, we are not aware of anybody claiming, let alone documenting, that after the Bayh-Dole Act took effect, the quality of biomedical research in U.S. universities and federally sponsored laboratories visibly increased. It just remained roughly where it was, meaning that patentability made no difference as far as general incentives are concerned.

Let us proceed, though. There are not just general incentives; there are also specific ones, and it may be that patents have biased biomedical research in a more socially valuable direction. The substantive findings emerging from Petra Moser's research (discussed in Chapter 8) suggest that the opportunity patents offer to achieve large private gains may push innovation in a certain direction instead of another. As interesting as this question may sound, apparently it has not been investigated, or at least we could not find any trace of an answer to it. It therefore remains an open question: did patentability of basic biomedical innovations create an incentive to engage in more socially valuable research projects and investigations?

Even worse, we also could not find anything in the field of health economics addressing what, in our view, is an even more basic question: where do medical and pharmaceutical discoveries of high social value come from? This left us on our own, trying to figure out what a fundamental medical discovery or a truly innovative medicine was, a topic we know nothing about. Being two theoretical economists, we appealed to the law of comparative advantages to figure out whom to ask: doctors, medical doctors more precisely. Consulting a large number of medical journals leads to the pleasant discovery that the *British Medical Journal*, a most distinguished publication, had decided to inaugurate its new series by helping us out. The editors of the *BMJ* asked their colleagues and readers something very close to our fundamental question: which medical and pharmaceutical discoveries are truly fundamental and where do they come from? In their own words:

We asked readers to nominate milestones, which you did in good numbers. A panel of editors and advisers narrowed the field down from more than 70 to 15. We invited champions to write on each one; their contributions make up the commemorative supplement we are publishing on 20 January. And we are now inviting readers to vote for which you think is the most important of these medical milestones (see *bmj.com*). The result will be announced on 18 January [2006].[29]

In no particular order, here come the selected fifteen (we could not get hold of the group of seventy, which, we suspect, would have not moved the bottom line an iota): penicillin, X-rays, tissue culture, ether (anesthetic), chlorpromazine, public sanitation, germ theory, evidence-based medicine, vaccines, the Pill, computers, oral rehydration therapy, DNA structure, monoclonal antibody technology, smoking health risk.[30]

How many entries in this list were patented or due to some previous patent or were obtained during a research project motivated by the desire to obtain a patent? Two: chlorpromazine and the Pill. Is this a fluke? We do not think so. In the same issue of the *BMJ* you can find references to other similar lists. A particularly interesting one was compiled since 1999–2000 by the U.S. Centers for Disease Control and Prevention: a top-ten list of public health achievements of the twentieth century in the United States. How do medical patents score on this one? A nice and round zero. The editor of the *BMJ*, recognizing the intrinsic arbitrariness of any top-*N* list, somewhere in the editorial presentation names her three beloved ones among the excluded: "Where are aspirin, *Helicobacter pylori*, and Medline?" Good point, and we ask, Do they owe anything to patents? Not a chance.

Even if one tries to stack the odds in favor of patents as much as possible, the bottom line changes only slightly. To do this we went to the Web site of *Chemical and Engineering News* magazine,[31] where a "List of Top Pharmaceuticals," divided by therapeutic categories, can be found.[32] These were the pharmaceutical products selling the most worldwide at the time of the survey (2005), and there are forty-six of them. Why forty-six and not fifty or one hundred? We have no idea; we did not compile the list. Each entry in the list links to a well-documented page telling the story of the drug and a number of other scientific and commercial details related to it. Using this abundant information, we went out and counted how many of these

wonder drugs of today do not owe their existence to patents in any mean-
ingful sense, either because they were never patented and those inventing
them did not have a patent as their aim or because they were discovered by
companies operating in countries where drugs could not be patented at all.
One would expect that pretty much all the entries in this list were patented
at one point in time or another. Well, here is the summary of our daylong
reading about all kinds of modern medicines.

Patents had pretty much nothing to do with the development of
twenty of the forty-six top-selling drugs (aspirin, AZT, cyclosporine, di-
goxin, ether, fluoride, insulin, isoniazid, medical marijuana, methadone,
morphine, oxytocin, penicillin, phenobarbital, prontosil, quinine, Ritalin
(methylphenidate), Salvarsan, vaccines, vitamins). The remaining twenty-
six products somehow owe their existence to the availability of drug patents
(Allegra, Botox, cisplatin, Crixivan, erythropoietin, fentanyl, Fosamax,
hydrocortisone, ivermectin, L-dopa, Librium, lovastatin, oral contracep-
tives, Premarin, Prozac, Rituxan, salbutamol, Tagamet, Taxol, thalidomide,
Thorazin, thyroxine, Viagra, Vioxx, RU-486, 6-mercaptopurine). Notice,
though, that of these twenty-six, four were discovered completely by chance
and then patented (cisplatin, Librium, Taxol, Thorazin,), two were discovered in university labs much before the Bayh-Dole Act was even conceived
(cisplatin and Taxol). Further, a few of them were also simultaneously discovered by more than one company, leading to long and expensive legal
battles, but we will spare you those three or four sad stories.

The bottom line is rather simple: even today, more than thirty years after
Germany, Italy, and Switzerland adopted patents on drugs and a good half
a century after pharmaceutical companies adopted the policy of patenting
anything they could put their hands on, more than half of the top-selling
medicines around the world do not owe their existence to pharmaceutical
patents. Are we still so certain that valuable medicines would stop being
invented if drug patents were either abolished or drastically curtailed?

This is not particularly original news, though. Older American readers may remember the Kefauver Committee of 1961, which investigated
monopolistic practices in the pharmaceutical industry.[33] Among the many
interesting things reported, the study showed that ten times as many basic
drug inventions were made in countries without product patents as were
made in countries with them. It also found that countries that did grant
product patents had higher prices than those that did not – again something
we seem to be well aware of.

The next question, then, is, if not to fundamental new medical discoveries,
where does all that pharmaceutical R&D money go?

Rent Seeking and Redundancy

There is much evidence of redundant research on pharmaceuticals. The National Institute of Health Care Management reveals that over the period 1989–2000, 54 percent of FDA-approved drug applications involved drugs that contained active ingredients already in the market. Hence, the novelty was in dosage form, route of administration, or combination with other ingredients. Of the new drug approvals, 35 percent were products with new active ingredients, but only a portion of these drugs were judged to have sufficient clinical improvements over existing treatments to be granted priority status. In fact, only 238 out of 1,035 drugs approved by the FDA contained new active ingredients and were given priority ratings on the basis of their clinical performances. In other words, about 77 percent of what the FDA approves is redundant from the strictly medical point of view.[34] *The New Republic*, commenting on these facts, pointedly continues:

If the report doesn't convince you, just turn on your television and note which drugs are being marketed most aggressively. Ads for Celebrex may imply that it will enable arthritics to jump rope, but the drug actually relieves pain no better than basic ibuprofen; its principal supposed benefit is causing fewer ulcers, but the FDA recently rejected even that claim. Clarinex is a differently packaged version of Claritin, which is of questionable efficacy in the first place and is sold over the counter abroad for vastly less. Promoted as though it must be some sort of elixir, the ubiquitous "purple pill," Nexium, is essentially AstraZeneca's old heartburn drug Prilosec with a minor chemical twist that allowed the company to extend its patent. (Perhaps not coincidentally researchers have found that purple is a particularly good pill color for inducing placebo effects.)[35]

Sad but ironically true, me-too or copycat drugs are pretty much the only available tool capable of inducing some kind of competition in an otherwise monopolized market. Because patent protection lasts long enough to make future entry by generics nearly irrelevant, the limited degree of substitutability and price competition that copycat drugs bring about is actually valuable. We are not kidding here, and this is a point that many commentators are often missing in their anti–Big Pharma crusade. Given the institutional environment pharmaceutical companies are currently operating in, me-too drugs are the obvious profit-maximizing tools, and there is nothing wrong with firms maximizing profits. Me-too drugs also increase the welfare of consumers, if ever so slightly, by offering more variety of choice and slightly lower prices. Again, they are an anemic and pathetic version of the market competition that would take place without patents, but competition they are. The sad and ironic aspect of me-too drugs, obviously, is that they are very expensive because of patent protection, and this cost we have brought upon ourselves for no good reason.

This expensive creation of redundancy also has two implications relevant to our final argument. As in the case of the computer software industry, it suggests that the indivisibility is not such a significant factor in the innovation process; in other words, the true fixed cost to be recouped via monopoly profits is probably small. Before you think we are crazy because of the $800 million figure we quoted earlier, make a note that says *clinical trials*, and give us a few more pages of your patience. Second, it suggests the presence of a substantial amount of socially inefficient rent-seeking, artificially created by the patent system itself. One often finds, in the public debate over the rising cost of health care, a misplaced insistence on the huge profits of Big Pharma. Yes, those profits are abnormally large and persistently so. A signal, we agree, of a highly monopolistic industry. But they are not the main cause of the rising cost of health care, because at the very end they are just 10 percent of the whole pie. The much larger amount of resources the patent system forces us to waste in the me-too drugs business, its advertising and its legal support, *that* is a sizable share of the pie. When you add them up together, the research cost, the legal cost, and the advertising and promotion cost get you to more than 50 percent of the whole pie!

Now consider this: assume we can cut Big Pharma's profits to the average level in the manufacturing sector. As a percentage of sales that would be about 5 percent, meaning 5 percent off the cost of drugs. Make the pharmaceutical industry a competitive one, and get rid of the resources insanely wasted in the monopolistic competition monkey business. Well, that is a beefy 50 percent off the cost of your drugs. Also, like the proverbial cherry on top of the sundae, making the pharmaceutical industry a competitive one will probably reduce its profit margins too more common level, giving you an extra 5 percent cost reduction for free. Next time, tell that to your congressperson, please.

Insofar as new drugs are replacements for drugs that already exist, they have little or no economic value in a world without patents – yet cost on the order of $800 million to bring to market because the existence of patents forces the producers to "invent something" that the U.S. Patent and Trademark Office can pretend to be sufficiently different from the original, patented drug. Where does that money go? What are the social gains from this kind of investment? None: the only social gain from introducing a me-too drug is that the supply of the beneficial active ingredient increases, and average prices possibly decrease somewhat. But this could be achieved, much more rapidly and at a cost orders of magnitude smaller, by simply copying the old drug and improving upon it. Money spent in obtaining a me-too drug that can be patented is money wasted for society that will be charged to consumers: rent seeking and monopoly profits can be very costly for all of us, indeed.

Redundancy and Bribing

A different way of looking at the same problem emphasizes the marketing of drugs over the R&D to search for new ones:

A better explanation for the pharmaceutical slump is a shift in priorities toward marketing, particularly since the FDA first allowed companies to directly target consumers five years ago. According to data collected by Alan Sager, a professor at the Boston University School of Public Health, the number of research and development (R&D) employees at companies making patented drugs declined slightly between 1995 and 2000, while the number of people working in marketing shot up 59 percent. "Drug companies trumpet the value of breakthrough research, but they seem to be devoting far fewer resources than their press releases suggest," says Sager.[36]

Libraries have been written on the obvious connection between marketing and the lack of competition. The pharmaceutical industry is no exception to this rule, and the evidence Professor Sager, and many others, point at has a simple and clear explanation: because of generalized and ever-extended patenting, large pharmaceutical companies have grown accustomed to operating like monopolies. Monopolies innovate as little as possible and only when forced to; in general, they would rather spend time seeking rents via political protection while trying to sell at a high price their old refurbished products to the powerless consumers, via massive doses of advertising: "[Pharmaceutical] Companies today have found that the return on investment for legal tactics is a lot higher than the return on investment for R&D," says Sharon Levine, the associate executive director of the HMO Kaiser Permanente. "Consumers today are paying an inordinate premium under the guise of the creating the stream of innovation in the future. But it's actually funding lawyers."[37]

Economists call this socially inefficient rent seeking. It is ugly, but the polite academic jargon *rent seeking* means "corruption" and all that comes with it. We have already mentioned the music industry, where corruption has become the standard marketing practice, as exemplified by the sorry story of payola. In industries that are highly monopolized and in which the returns from capturing the main distribution and information channels are enormous, the temptation to bend and then break the rules is too strong to resist, as public choice theory and economic common sense suggest. In the pharmaceutical industry, the main distribution and information channels are not the radio and television stations, but the medical profession. Hence, the unavoidable and continued temptation to capture the doctors, to make them promote the drug, and to be silent over the other drugs. This is why we have started to learn, more and more frequently, that "As Doctors Write Prescriptions, Drug Companies Write Checks," as Gardiner Harris aptly titled his report on how drug companies mail nice, fat checks to doctors in exchange for "consulting activities" that amount to – doing absolutely nothing, just keep prescribing our drugs, thank you.

In Boston, federal prosecutors have been attempting to crack down on these marketing practices. From the cases they have brought, it appears that this is not just the usual story of the few rotten apples:

Last month, Pfizer agreed to pay $430 million and pleaded guilty to criminal charges involving the marketing of the pain drug Neurontin by the company's Warner-Lambert unit. AstraZeneca paid $355 million last year and TAP Pharmaceuticals paid $875 million in 2001; each pleaded guilty to criminal charges of fraud for inducing physicians to bill the government for some drugs that the company gave the doctors free.

Over the last two years, Schering-Plough, which had sales of $8.33 billion last year, has set aside a total of $500 million to cover its legal problems – mainly for expected fines from the Boston investigation and from a separate inquiry by federal prosecutors in Philadelphia who are investigating whether Schering-Plough overcharged Medicaid.[38]

The case is overwhelming, and there is not much value added in repeating further stories of this kind, either older or more recent.[39] Now, you may wonder, what is the point of bringing this kind of scandal into an otherwise serious debate? We are not trying to score some cheap moral points here – even if, it should be said, the fact that business is business cannot be used to put up with every kind of conceivable immorality. We are stressing, instead, a dramatically poignant policy implication: a monopolized industry, where patents are the core and foundation of the business method adopted, must end up practicing rent seeking and bribery, it must conceal or suppress relevant research findings, it must monitor doctors' prescription behavior, it must employ a sales force three times the size of its research team, and it must, finally, become one of the top donors of political campaign contributions.

If this were the radio industry and the bribery affected the quality of the tunes played on this station or another, there would be only a very mild case for social concern. But this is the health industry, and the bribery is affecting the medicine you take.

How Steep Is the Trade-off, Then?

A relatively recent National Bureau of Economic Research paper, by Hughes, Moore, and Snyder and sponsored by Aventis Pharmaceuticals [now Sanofi-Aventis], attacks directly the costs and the benefits of drug patents.[40] They conclude that if the appropriate rate of interest for discounting the social benefits of new drugs is greater than about 5 percent, then the social benefit of eliminating patents is greater than the cost. Because the social benefits of pharmaceuticals are risky, and indeed in this study they are assumed to be perfectly correlated with private risk, an appropriate interest rate is the rate of return in the pharmaceutical industry. Indeed, the interest rates used for cost-benefit calculations for government projects are usually around 15 percent, which is the same as the rate of return Hughes, Moore, and Snyder assume for pharmaceutical R&D. This is substantially in excess of 5 percent for eliminating patents.

Because Hughes, Moore, and Snyder are among the few who have attempted to quantify the costs and benefits of intellectual monopoly, it is worth reviewing their calculations. They assume that demand for pharmaceuticals is linear. From the perspective of cost-benefit analysis, this assumes that as output expands past the monopoly level, demand falls off at a constant rate. If demand falls abruptly, then the loss of consumer surplus is much smaller than would be estimated by a linear demand function, and we would get a more favorable case for patents. However, there is some reason to think that demand for pharmaceuticals depends upon income, and if this is the case, the linear demand assumption is a reasonable one. Other parameters of the Hughes, Moore, and Snyder model are calibrated to the data. They assume that 75 percent of pharmaceutical revenue is generated by drugs still under patent, that market exclusivity lasts nine years, and that the lifetime of a new drug is twenty-five years. They assume that it will take generic manufacturers one year to enter after innovation. Also on the basis of data about competition between generic and nongeneric drugs after patent expiration, they attribute a first-mover advantage to the innovator by assuming that the innovator will be able to charge the monopoly price and still serve 20 percent of the market. In fact, evidence from India suggests that it takes closer to four years for generics to enter; and relatively unbiased sources such as the Congressional Budget Office suggest that market share after the entry of generics is substantially greater than 20 percent.

Finally, a critical assumption is the connection between producer surplus and the number of new drugs discovered. That is, higher expectations of profit due to monopoly lead to more pharmaceutical research, and consequently to more drugs. Notice, however, that this effect can be negative, as the monopolization of existing drugs may also make it harder to discover new drugs, and we saw that this was empirically important in the history of the chemical industry. Hughes, Moore, and Snyder assume that the number of new drugs discovered is proportional to producer surplus. That is, because they estimate that, without a patent, profits are about 25 percent of what they would be with a patent, they assume that there will be 25 percent as many drugs discovered without patents. Even without the problem of innovation chains and the cost of inventing around existing patents discussed earlier, this assumption is very favorable to the patent system. The number of discoveries is scarcely likely to drop 75 percent if profits are reduced by 75 percent. On the basis of survey data from industry interviews (which, in turn, probably understate the number of drugs that would be developed without patents), a figure of 40 percent would appear to be closer to the mark. We should also note that our own estimate is that, without patents, firms would earn closer to 80 percent of what they earn with patents, rather than 25 percent.[41] Despite these apparent biases, Hughes, Moore, and Snyder still find that, even with an interest rate as low as 5 percent, the immediate benefit of wider drug availability exceeds the long-term cost of having fewer new drugs.

How steep is the trade-off society faces, then? Not too steep, apparently, if a 5 percent discount rate is high enough for even a pharmaceutical industry sponsored study to conclude we would be better off without patents.

The Cost of New Drugs, Revisited

Much of the case for drug patents rests on the high cost of bringing drugs to market. Most studies have been sponsored by the pharmaceutical industry and are so quite suspect. In our previous analysis, we have already seen one huge reason for suspicion: the cost of new drugs includes not only the cost of failed projects; that would be reasonable. It includes also the R&D cost for me-too drugs, which is about 75 percent of all R&D cost; and that is a lot less reasonable. The story does not end here, though, so let us proceed with the accounting.

The Consumer Project on Technology examined the cost of clinical trials for orphan drugs – good data are available for these drugs because they are eligible for special government benefits.[42] A pharmaceutical industry–sponsored study estimated the average cost of clinical trials for a drug at about $24.5 million 1995 dollars. However, for orphan drugs where better data are available, the average cost of clinical trials was only about $6.5 million 1995 dollars – yet there is no reason to believe that these clinical trials are in any way atypical.[43]

A 2002 report of the Center for Economic and Policy Research also estimates costs orders of magnitude less than those claimed by the pharmaceutical companies.[44] It also finds that, holding output of pharmaceutical products constant, private companies tend to spend twice as much as public medical research centers to come up with new drugs. As one might suspect, the report documents that the additional costs of the private drug monopolists are mostly legal and advertising costs: the first to get patents and defend them, and the second to convince doctors to prescribe "their" drug instead of the alternative, most often a generic and cheaper alternative.

Last, but not least, are clinical trials: the forbearance we asked of you a few pages ago may now be redeemed. Even after accounting for the money wasted in me-too drugs, and the resources thrown into the legal and marketing costs the patent system induces, it is still a fact that, on December 5, 2006, Pfizer had to write off $800 million of clinical trials expenses when it gave up on the production and commercialization of Torcetrapib. Somehow, somewhere, the pharmaceutical industry must recoup such costs. By common admission, from both pharmaceutical firms and outside observers, the cost of clinical trials now amounts to about 80 percent or more of the total cost of developing a new drug. Although clinical trials related to imitative drugs are almost a complete waste from a social point of view, those related to truly innovative and therapeutically beneficial drugs are not so. On the contrary, they are socially very valuable and need to be recouped. Are pharmaceutical patents necessary to accomplish this?

No, they are not. And because this chapter is already long enough, we will be brief and leave the details of this argument for the next, final chapter, in which we address a few proposals for reform. Clinical trials are the step in the process of developing a new drug during which information is produced about the effect of a given chemical compound on a large sample of humans. The cost of distributing and absorbing this information being low, and the cost of acquiring it being high, it has a strong public good component. There is also no reason, by way of either economic efficiency or equity, why this should be paid for by the pharmaceutical firms developing the new drug – indeed, as they will be first to market they have a strong conflict of interest. The cost of clinical trials cost would better paid from the public purse, for example, by competitive and peer-reviewed National Institutes of Health grants – at which point patents on drugs would no longer have any reason to exist.

The Ultimate Virus

The pharmaceutical malaise has many ingredients – the FDA system of regulation, the entire idea that some drugs should be available by prescription only, and the broader problems of health insurance and who pays for drugs. To argue that the system could be fixed by eliminating patents on pharmaceuticals would be foolish. It would be foolish also to think that it would make sense to abolish patents on pharmaceuticals without also reforming the infrastructure – such as the way clinical trials are paid for and made available – at the same time.

That said, we have seen that patents do not play a helpful role in pharmaceutical innovation. Far from encouraging great new health and life-saving products, the system instead produces too much innovation and expense of the wrong kind – me-too drugs to get around the other guy's patents and get a share of a lucrative monopoly, and all the advertising and marketing expenses attendant upon monopoly power.[45] In the play that is life, health is the ultimate commodity – we all want to live longer and stay healthier. As we have just seen, patents do not have a useful role in this play.

Comments

The point of view we take here is a very narrow one, and this chapter should not be read as an overall evaluation of the current functioning of the pharmaceutical industry and of the impact that reducing patentability of new drugs would have on it. In particular, it does not ask, as a complete analysis instead should, whether, under an alternative system, doctors, medical researchers, and shareholders of Big Pharma would be better or worse off than they are now.

Notes

1. Hansen, Grabowski, and Lasagna (1991) report on the 1987 cost of developing a new drug. The Department of Commerce reports an implicit gross domestic product price deflator in the first quarter of 1987 of 72.487 and in 2000 of 99.317, which is used to convert the $200 million year 1987 dollars of the earlier estimate to year 2000 dollars.
2. The estimate length of medical patent protection is from Grabowski (2002), while the impact on it of the Hatch-Waxman Act is from Grabowski and Vernon (1986, 1996).
3. PhRMA (2007), p. 2.
4. Basic information about the current structure of the drug industry and its economic performance is widely available online. The specific data we quote are taken from

El Feki (2005), http://healthguideusa.org/NationalCosts.htm, and various online reports freely available at http://www.imshealth.com.

5. Up from $253.7 billion in 2005, as reported by IMS Health at its Web site http://www.imshealth.com. The top ten drugs accounted for about $41 billion.

6. Hansen et al. (1991).

7. Di Masi, Grabowski, and Hansen (2003). This study also explains the interest rates used in capitalizing and discounting costs and benefits in the pharmaceutical industry.

8. For the FDA's official announcement, visit http://www.fda.gov/bbs/topics/NEWS/2006/NEW01514.html.

9. These figures are from Pfizer's press report on December 3, 2006, and are still available online from the many Web sites that reported the announcement, e.g. The New York Times of December 4, 2006, available on line at http://www.nytimes.com/2006/12/04/health/04pfizer.html [accessed February 24, 2008].

10. Dutfield (2003), p. 78.

11. In fact, a number of large chemical companies wanted to leave the industry completely free of any patent protection to avoid the fate of the French dye industry (see note 14 herein) and favor its development. Apart from Dutfield (2003), see also Seckelmann (2001) for additional details about the German patent system at the end of the nineteenth century, and Arora, Landau, and Rosenberg (1998) for various historical studies on the growth of the chemical industry.

12. Again, Dutfield (2003), especially Chapters 4 and 5, is our main source of information. Zorina Kahn's online history of patent laws, at http://eh.net/encyclopedia/article/khan.patents, provides a useful and easy-to-access summary of the main facts.

13. Quoted [as of February 24, 2008] in http://en.wikipedia.org/wiki/Community_patent, on the basis of various media sources, such as http://www.eupolitix.com/EN/News/200702/7be97fa5-3cb6-403f-aadf-103ad99a9950.htm.

14. To begin learning about the history of the dye industry and the crucial, if not necessarily positive, role patents played in it, see Morris and Travis (1992) and the plenty of references therein. For why patents and monopoly did not allow La Fuchsine to thrive, see Van den Belt (1992). For similar stories of not-so-useful patents in other sectors and countries, such as in the United States, see Murmann (2004), where the initial stages of the dye industry are also carefully analyzed. If you are curious about the nature of the mysterious dye fuchsine, Wikipedia can tell you about its chemical composition.

15. Meyer-Thurow (1982) provides additional information about both the dye industry and the development of the German chemical industry. The absence of both organic and inorganic chemical production in France is noted by Haber (1958, 1971), from which other details about the history of the chemical industry are also drawn. The demise of the British coloring industry is also discussed by Penrose (1951), pp. 102–5.

16. As confirmed by any of the hundreds Web sites reporting the history of aspirin, e.g. http://www.medicine.mcgill.ca/mjm/v02n02/aspirin.html, accessed February 24, 2008.

17. Murmann (2004), p. 3.

18. Pollack (2001).

19. Together with its label, the anticommons problem in medical research was pointed out first in a much-debated article by Heller and Eisenberg (1998). More recent appraisals are in Scherer (2002) and Epstein and Kuhlik (2004), who argue that patents on gene fragments are still growing and that patent holders will want to make money (hence, there should be no anticommons problem at all); Benkler (2004) and Clark et al. (2000), who argue that patent pools, as in the software industry, will solve the problem (an oligopoly is better than a monopoly, after all); and the dozens of references that these articles contain. A conference at the University of Illinois College of Law, "The Future of the Commons and the Anticommons", http://home.law.uiuc.edu/iple/conferenceJune06.html, provides a good picture of where the debate stands as of 2006. Information about the growing number of scientists and medical or biological research labs willing to share their results can be found in a variety of journalistic sources, among which are Begley (2006), Leaf (2005), Maurer, Rai, and Sali (2004).
20. Information and data about the Italian pharmaceutical industry are mostly from Campanella (1979), Ferraguto, Lucioni, and Onida (1983), and Paci (1990).
21. Scherer (2003), p. 122. This is Scherer's study of the welfare impact that worldwide drug patents may have, the conclusion of which is, in case you are wondering, that medical patents are bad for our health.
22. One may wonder why we did not look more carefully at the Swiss pharmaceutical industry, which also grew without patents in its home country to become more successful than the Italian, and still is, even if patents were adopted in Switzerland just one year earlier than in Italy. That would have been more than mildly unfair, though equally so to both sides of the debate, as the Swiss did exceedingly well both without and with patents. Although it is quite true, as pointed out in this chapter, that the Swiss chemical industry was created by French firms running away from French patents, the size of the internal Swiss market is too small to be relevant. That the chemical, first, and then pharmaceutical Swiss firms could not use either process or product patents to protect their home turf is of little relevance, given that they could use patents, and use them they did, in most other countries the market size of which dwarfed that of Switzerland. In this sense, and apart for its inception, the successful Swiss pharmaceutical industry – championed today by Novartis and Hoffman-La Roche sitting at Nos. 5 and 6 respectively of the world scale, but also by Alcon (No. 29) and Serono (No. 35) – is neither a pro- nor a counter-patent story. It is nevertheless significant that from Mr. Alexander Clavel and his fellow French patent runners there came great firms such as CIBA-Geigy and Hoffman-La Roche. That until the late 1960s the leading pharmaceutical countries were Germany, Switzerland, and Italy (that is, those either without patents or with weak patents) is recognized even by Wikipedia in its entry "pharmaceutical company."
23. Readers interested in quickly learning more about the Indian pharmaceutical industry and how it grew without patents may consult the Wikipedia's entry "Pharmaceuticals in India." As of February 24, 2008, it is particularly informative, well written, and reports abundant references and data sources. The late Jean Lanjouw was probably the leading world expert on the impact that the adoption of patents may have on India's drug industry. In her (1997, 2002, 2005) papers, she casts a very balanced view of the pros and cons faced by low- and middle-income countries

adopting pharmaceutical patents. As far as our limited question is concerned, though, the answer coming from her empirical work is fairly clear, if technically phrased:

There is some evidence that high levels of protection might encourage more frequent entry of innovative products in the short term, particularly in countries where multinationals might otherwise hesitate because local technical capacity might create competitive pressures. On the other hand, in the longer term that same domestic capacity could be an alternative source of entry, and we find that a country offering extensive patent protection may lose the benefits of that activity and have fewer new products in the market overall as a result. (2005, p. 25)

Admittedly, Lanjouw is one of the analysts who, albeit in a very tentative form, has advanced the idea that patent adoption may help poor countries by making price discrimination more effective. A substantially more robust statement in this direction can be found in Maskus (2001). The paper focuses mostly on parallel imports and advocates the strange charity argument, according to which rich countries should be allowed to export drugs to poor ones when the prices are higher in the poorer than in the richer countries, or at best equal, but not vice versa. Which piece of economic logic and which social welfare function support this asymmetrical free-trade rule escapes us, but maybe we missed the whole point. Why this would be benevolent to poor countries is even more mysterious. To see why we say so, try applying the same logic to agricultural products. Oops! That is exactly what the EU agricultural trade policy amounts to.

24. Chaudhuri, Goldberg, and Jia (2003), abstract.
25. Our general information about the status of the pharmaceutical industry comes from various sources: Commission on Intellectual Property Rights (2002), El Feki (2005), International Federation of Pharmaceutical Manufacturers (2004, and subsequent years), Maskus (2001), National Institute for Health Care Management (NIHCM; 2002), Wikipedia, and the *Chemical & Engineering News* special issue, available at http://pubs.acs.org/cen/coverstory/83/8325/index.html.
26. Murphy and Topel (1999).
27. PhRMA (2007), "Key Facts."
28. As reported in Andrew Sullivan's blog, on July 1, 2005. This text is no longer directly available, but it referred to and quoted in various other blogs and internet discussion groups.
29. Godlee (2007), p. 1.
30. Godlee (2007), p. 1. The special issue of the *BMJ* in which this editorial piece appears lists the top fifteen medical milestones and is available at http://www.bmj.com.
31. http://pubs.acs.org/cen/.
32. http://pubs.acs.org/cen/coverstory/83/8325/8325list.html.
33. Information about the 1959–61 Kefauver Committee leading, among other things to the Kefauver-Harris or Drug Efficacy Amendment of 1962, is abundantly available online. This committee is not to be confused with the more famous one by the same name, but of 1950–51, which investigated organized crime in the USA. For an introduction to some of its economic aspects, see Comanor (1966) or the more recent survery Comanor (1986).
34. NIHCM (2002).

35. This and the following most amusing string of quotations on me-too drugs and their distinctive purple color, on the ratio between R&D and marketing employees in pharmaceutical companies, and on what consumers are financing with the outrageous prices they are forced to pay for drugs are all from the same *The New Republic* piece, but you will need a subscription to access the article. The link is http://www.thenewrepublic.com/docprint.mhtml?i=20021007&s=thompson100702.
36. Ibid.
37. Ibid.
38. Harris (2004).
39. A long, if incomplete, list of rent-seeking practices bordering the highly improper, if not the strictly illegal, is in Baker and Chatani (2002). Additional information on the development and patenting of imitative drugs are in Hubbard and Love (2004) and references therein, whereas more details about marketing to the medical profession are in Angell and Relman (2002).
40. Hughes, Moore, and Snyder (2002). We should note that their stated conclusion is the opposite of ours: they conclude that drug patents should not be abolished. The reason is that they apparently believe that the relevant interest rate is less than 5%.
41. The 40 percent estimate of the fraction of drugs that would be developed without patent is from the Levin et al. (1987) survey. Information about generics in India is from Lanjouw (1997); information about market share after generic entry is from Congressional Budget Office (1998), and our own calculations are in Boldrin and Levine (2005b).
42. http://www.cptech.org/.
43. The orphan drug study is Love (1997).
44. http://www.cepr.net/. The CEPR study comparing the cost of inventing new drugs for private and public research centers is Baker and Chatani (2002).
45. Excessive me-too imitation is explored theoretically in the market for textbooks by Boldrin and Levine (2002), where we show that under certain circumstances – not dissimilar from those in the pharmaceutical industry – the result can be the Pareto worst outcome. This idea is not very distant from that advanced in the, apparently now forgotten, literature on patent races and excess R&D spending; see, for example, Fudenberg and Tirole (1991).

TEN

The Bad, the Good, and the Ugly

In a famous 1958 study on the economics of the patent system, the distinguished economist Fritz Machlup, paraphrasing an earlier statement by his longtime coauthor Edith Penrose, concluded[1]

> If we did not have a patent system, it would be irresponsible, on the basis of our present knowledge of its economic consequences, to recommend instituting one. But since we have had a patent system for a long time, it would be irresponsible, on the basis of our present knowledge, to recommend abolishing it.

Almost fifty years later, the first half of this illustrious sentence is more valid than it has ever been. Sadly, the recommendation has not been followed: far from maintaining the status quo, the patent system has been enormously extended, and there is no sign of the end of the expansion of intellectual monopoly to every corner of our economic system. Moreover, the fifty years since have turned up no evidence that patents serve to increase innovation. It is time to reconsider the second recommendation.

Defenders of intellectual monopoly like to portray intellectual property as a powerful and beneficial medicine. If a medicine has serious side effects and scientific studies have found at best weak evidence of temporary benefits, would you employ such a drug on an otherwise healthy patient? Probably not, unless the illness was life threatening. Yet we have documented that innovation thrives in the absence of intellectual monopoly (the patient is healthy), that the latter has serious side effects (the evils of intellectual monopoly), and that a series of scientific studies have found weak or no evidence that it increases innovation (the proposed beneficial effect is probably absent). The case against intellectual monopoly is decisive, and we must conclude that the second half of Machlup's policy advice is now obsolete.

"On the basis of the present knowledge," progressively but effectively abolishing intellectual property protection is the only socially responsible thing to do. Evidence has accumulated during the past fifty years leaving little doubt about the damaging effects of current intellectual property laws. At the same time, legal, economic, and business know-how has also accumulated about how markets for innovation operate without intellectual monopoly. To rule out abolition a priori would be as silly now as it would have been to rule out the abolition of tariffs and trade barriers fifty years ago, when the trade liberalization process that has given us prosperity and globalization began. For a long time, the individuals and firms that profited from trade barriers argued that these increased the wealth of the nation and defended homeland companies and jobs, and that abolishing them would lead to a disaster for many sectors of our economy. It took a while to realize that this was not true, and that trade barriers were nothing more than rent-seeking devices, favoring a minority and dramatically hurting the overall economy and everyone else, beginning with low-income consumers. The same is now true of patents and copyright.

A realistic view of intellectual monopoly is that it is a disease rather than a cure. It arises not from a principled effort to increase innovation, but from an obnoxious combination of medieval institutions – guilds, royal licenses, trade restrictions, religious and political censorship – and the rent-seeking behavior of would-be monopolists seeking to fatten their purse at the expense of public prosperity. We may debate whether, say, Social Security is worth keeping given the current demographic and financial markets evolution, but no one would doubt that it was designed to provide old-age insurance that financial markets were not always capable of providing. Patents and copyright, by way of contrast, were never designed to efficiently foster innovation.

Essentially all scientific studies of the current system agree that it is badly broken. So getting rid of it may not be such a bad idea. Still, one should pause. Realizing that intellectual monopoly is a kind of cancer, we recognize that simply cutting it all out at once may not be a good idea. Because intellectual property laws have been around for a long while, we have learned to live with them. Myriad other legal and informal institutions, business practices, and professional skills have grown up around them and in symbiosis with them. Consequently, a sudden elimination of intellectual property laws may bring about collateral damages of an intolerable magnitude.

Take, for example, the case of pharmaceuticals. Drugs not only are patented but also are regulated by the government in myriad ways. Under the current system, achieving FDA approval in the United States requires costly clinical trials – and the results of those trials must be made freely available to competitors. Certainly, abolishing patents and simultaneously requiring firms that conduct expensive clinical trials to make their results freely available to competitors cannot be a good reform. Here patents can be sensibly eliminated only by simultaneously changing the process by which the results of clinical trials are obtained, first, and then made available to the public and to competitors in particular. We will come back to the specifics of the pharmaceutical industry later, when listing some of the good things one can reasonably consider doable even in the short run.

What this example suggests is that abolition must be approached by smaller steps, and that the sequencing of steps matters. Gradual reform is necessary both because of the need for other institutions, such as the FDA, to reform in parallel and because it is a political necessity. The number of people prospering thanks to intellectual monopoly is large and growing. Although some of them have accrued so much wealth that one should not really worry about Tom Cruise's pauperization in the wake of intellectual monopoly abolition, for many others this is not the case. For many ordinary people intellectual monopoly has become another way of earning a living and, while most of them would be able to earn an equally good or even better living without it, many others need time to adjust. Further, and again in analogy with trade barriers, although the number of people who would benefit from the elimination of intellectual monopoly is large and growing, the gain each one of them expects as likely is small. In spite of the big brouhaha surrounding the pirating of popular music and movies, the direct personal savings from copyright reduction or even abolition would not be substantial, as music, movies, and books are a tiny share of household consumption. In the case of medicines and software, consumers' potential savings may be more substantial but harder to perceive. Finally, and most important, if in the 1950s or 1960s the average citizen of the world could hardly forecast the tremendous improvement in her standard of living that free trade would have brought about within thirty years, even harder it is now to perceive the incremental technological advances that a progressive elimination of intellectual monopoly could bring about in a couple of decades.

In summary, dismantling our intellectual property system faces a set of circumstances that the literature on collective action has identified as major barriers to reform. A few well-organized and coordinated monopolists are on the one side, bound to lose a lot if the protective barriers are lifted. A very large number of uncoordinated consumers are on the other side, expecting very small personal gains from the adoption of freer competition. For a long time then, the battleground is going to be one of competing ideas and theories aimed at convincing the public opinion that substantial gains are possible from the elimination of intellectual monopoly. In the mean time, there is a vast clutter of ideas both for greatly expanding intellectual property and, in the opposite direction, for useful reform. In this, our concluding chapter, we try to sort these proposals into the bad, the good, and the just plain ugly.

The Bad

Despite the fact that our system of intellectual property is badly broken, there are those who seek to break it even further. The first priority must be to stem the tide of rent seekers demanding ever-greater privilege. Domestically, within the United States and Europe, there is a continued effort to expand the scope of innovations subject to patent, to extend the length of copyright, and to impose ever more draconian penalties for intellectual property violation. Internationally, the United States – as a net exporter of ideas – has been negotiating dramatic increases in the protection of U.S. intellectual monopolists as part of free trade agreements; the recent Central American – Dominican Republic Free Trade Agreement is an outstanding example of this bad practice.

There seems to be no end to the list of bad proposals for strengthening intellectual monopoly. To give a partial list starting with the least significant:

- Extend the scope of patent to include sports moves and plays.[2]
- Extend the scope of copyright to include news clips, press releases, and so forth.[3]
- Allow for patenting of story lines – something the U.S. Patent Office just did by awarding a patent to Mr. Andrew Knight for his "The Zombie Stare" invention.[4]
- Extend the level of protection copyright offers to databases, along the lines of the 1996 E.U. Database Directive and the subsequent World Intellectual Property Organization (WIPO) treaty proposal.[5]
- Extend the scope of copyright and patents to the results of scientific research, including that financed by public funds, something that was already partially achieved with the Bayh-Dole Act.[6]
- Extend the length of copyright in Europe to match that in the United States – which is most ironic, as the sponsors of the Copyright Term Extension Act (CTEA) and the Digital Millennium Copyright Act (DMCA) in the United States claimed they were necessary to match new and longer European copyright terms.[7]

- Extend the set of circumstances in which refusal to license is allowed and enforced by antitrust authorities. More generally, turn around the 1970s Antitrust Division wisdom that lead to the so-called nine no-no's to licensing practices. Previous wisdom correctly saw such practices as anticompetitive restraints of trade in the licensing business. Persistent and successful lobbying from the beneficiaries of intellectual monopoly has managed to turn the table around, portraying such monopolistic practices as necessary or even vital ingredients for a well-functioning patent licensing market.[8]
- Establish, as a relatively recent U.S. Supreme Court ruling in the case of *Verizon v. Trinko* did, that legally acquired monopoly power and its use to charge higher prices not only is admissible but "is an important element of the free-market system" because "it induces innovation and economic growth."[9]
- Impose legal restrictions on the design of computers, forcing them to protect intellectual property.[10]
- Make producers of software used in peer-to-peer exchanges directly liable for any copyright violation carried out with the use of their software, something that may well be in the making after the Supreme Court ruling in the *Grokster* case.[11]
- Allow the patenting of computer software in Europe – this we escaped, momentarily, due to a sudden spark of rationality by the European Parliament.[12]
- Allow the patenting of any kind of plant variety outside of the United States where it is already allowed.[13]
- Allow for generalized patenting of genomic products outside of the United States where it is already allowed.[14]
- Force other countries, especially developing countries, to impose the same draconian intellectual property laws as the United States, the European Union, and Japan.[15]

All of these are bad ideas – why they are bad should be self-evident by now – and all should be rejected.

Developing countries in particular should be wary of negotiating away their intellectual freedom in exchange for greater access to U.S. and EU markets. Developing countries are, slowly but surely, giving in to U.S. and EU pressure and modifying their national legislation in accordance with the requirements imposed by TRIPS and the WIPO. This is partly the effect of sheer lobbying and political pressure by Western governments and large multinationals. Partly, this is also due to the lack of a workable and coherent alternative to the overreaching redesign of world intellectual property rights underlying TRIPS and its ideology. This makes an open and critical debate on such themes in developing countries even more urgent and valuable than it would be in any case.

The Good

There are a great many things that can be done to make modest improvements in the current system of both patents and copyrights. In the case of patents, there are a variety of proposals to make the patent system less vulnerable to submarine patenting, and generally to tighten up the system so that a patent has some real connection to innovation and is not merely a claim to someone else's invention. In the case of copyright, a major priority is to make sure that all the abandoned and orphaned works do not forever remain unusable because they are under copyright, and the copyright holder is dead, has disappeared, or is in any case untraceable.

For both patents and copyright, a fundamental priority is to prevent the public domain from shrinking further and, when possible, to push back the tight fences that are progressively enclosing it. This means, on the one hand, opposing new proposals for the extension of copyright term and coverage beyond those established by the 1998 DMCA and CTEA. On the other hand, it also means taking proactive actions to defend from rapacious hands what is growing in the public domain and needs to be nurtured. Private economic initiative can be extremely useful along this dimension, and the recent Open Innovation Network initiative, led by none other than IBM, is a wonderful case in point.[16]

Briefly described, the Open Innovation Network has been formed by IBM, Philips, Sony, and two large Linux resellers, Red Hat (a Linux distributor we discussed in an earlier chapter) and Novell (another successful Linux distributor, which we forgot to mention). The Open Innovation Network has been set up as a foundation that aims to buy Linux-related patents from holders and to create a pool of intellectual property it can then license for free. Probably more important, though, is the commitment, which is part of the Open Innovation Network's charter, to sue anyone who tries either to attack Linux, claiming some parts of it violate an outstanding patent, or to dismember it by attempting to patent bits and pieces of it. Patents controlled by the Open Innovation Network will be freely available to anyone agreeing not to assert their own patents against other users who have signed a license with Open Innovation Network when using software related to Linux. That a hundred such networks blossom should be the motto!

Let us continue looking into other short-run improvements to the burden of intellectual monopoly. Jaffe and Lerner document in great detail how the patent system, as it is currently implemented in the United States, is broken.[17] They make numerous proposals to make frivolous patents more difficult to get and enforce. We support these proposals in principle – and while we might disagree over some of the details, we expect that were we to debate the matter, they would convince us on some points and we would convince them on others.

One proposal in particular is to allow patents to be challenged before they are granted. This would allow real evidence to be brought to bear on the issue of prior art – something the U.S. Patent and Trademark Office seems to know little about, as the thousands of patents on how to swing a swing and peanut butter and jelly sandwiches suggest.[18] Realistically, however, few individuals or firms would be likely to monitor the patent system carefully enough to identify bad patents, or to incur the expense of providing the public good of challenging bad patents. Quillen, Webster, and Eichmann examine the rigor with which the U.S. Patent and Trademark Office carries out its examining activities and compare it to those of the European and Japanese patent offices.[19] They take the opposite approach from Lerner and Jaffe, suggesting that the patent office is not the appropriate place to reach decisions concerning patentability. They conclude by asking this:

Why should we not go to a registration system and avoid the expenses of operating an examination system. . . . [S]houldn't we abolish continuing applications so that the USPTO will be able to obtain final decisions as to the patentability of subject matter presented in patent applications and avoid having rework imposed upon it. Finally, so long as the USPTO grants a patent for virtually every application filed, are the courts justified in adhering to the clear and convincing evidence standard for overcoming the statutory presumption of validity?[20]

It is striking but true that either of these proposals, although they go in opposite directions, would be an improvement over the current system. That speaks volumes about how bad the current system is: mathematicians call a global minimum a position such that any movement away from it, in any direction, improves things!

Also of great significance is the proposal of Gallini and Scotchmer to allow the independent invention defense to patent claims.[21] That is, they would allow proof that an invention was independently derived and not obtained directly or indirectly as a consequence of a similar invention that was patented first as a defense against patent infringement. For example, if you patented the "one click" with the mouse to paste text into a word processor, and then sued me because my word processor also pasted text with just one click, I could defend myself by showing that I had written my word processor in my spare time and had never read your patent or seen a copy of your word processor. This would not only relieve the innovator from concern that in his ignorance he would run afoul of some existing patent but also make it substantially more difficult to engage in submarine warfare, as the inventor who is torpedoed by the submarine could argue, and prove, that his invention was independent. This reform, alone, would be of great social value and would enormously reduce the burden of intellectual monopoly. As we have illustrated repeatedly, simultaneous or independent inventions are almost the rule, rather than the exception, and for many great inventions of the last century – the radio, the television, the airplane, the telephone – having allowed the two or more independent and simultaneous inventors to both exploit their invention commercially would have greatly benefited consumers and economic progress in general. This is even more true and more relevant today, as the number of judicial disputes over practically identical and simultaneous innovations skyrocket, especially in the fields of software, biomedical products, and telecommunications, and for business practices in general.

An alternative reform would be to require mandatory licensing at fees based on estimates of R&D costs. The principle is the following: if it costs $100 to invent a gadget, 10 percent is a reasonable rate of return on this type of investment, and expected demand for licensing is on the order of one hundred units, then a net present value fee of $1.10 would be right. Toss in an extra $0.05 for the uncertainty and set mandatory licensing at a fee of $1.15 for this particular patent. William Kingston takes a more serious look at how this might work in practice, particularly figuring a multiple to account for the many failed innovations needed to produce a successful one. Kingston points out that cost estimates are already widely used in patent litigation and are not so difficult to produce and document. He estimates that, for most of the cases he studied, the total revenue from licensing products that are successfully patented and licensed should be about eight times their R&D cost, if the license is taken immediately; for licenses issued as the products actually go to market, a multiple of four would be more appropriate. In the case of pharmaceuticals, he suggests a multiple of two would be sufficient, noting, "If three such licenses were taken, the payments would [already] put the product into the most profitable decile (the home of the blockbuster drugs)."[22]

A backdoor to reducing the term of patent, and making it less easy to accidentally run afoul of long-standing but meaningless patents, would be to reintroduce patent renewal – for example, keeping the term of patent fixed while splitting the twenty-year term into smaller increments, with a renewal required at each stage. This is discussed by Cornelli and Schankerman and by Scotchmer.[23]

In copyright, the most immediate problem is that of a Congress and Supreme Court that are "bought and paid for." Sorry, but after reading both the congressional hearings on the DMCA and the Supreme Court decision in *Eldred* either they are bought and paid for or we have a dramatic case of total IQs dropping to the double-digit level.[24] The triple whammy of giving automatic copyright to every work, whether or not it is registered, eliminating the need for renewal, and extending the term of copyright to be essentially infinite means that, over time, virtually everything written will become inaccessible. Lessig, among others, documents in great detail the problems caused by these "ugly reforms."[25] He proposes that some of the ill effect could be undone by a modest renewal fee. Landes and Posner suggest that the legal principle of abandonment could be applied to copyright holders who do not actively make it clear that they are maintaining their copyright.[26] Either or both of these proposals – however politically naive they might be – would be a great improvement over the current untenable situation.

The debacle we currently face in copyright is that as more and more draconian laws concerning copyright are introduced, less and less real copyright protection is possible, as it has proved impossible to police the peer-to-peer networks in any realistic sense. Many have suggested that the way out of this dilemma is through mandatory licensing – much as radio broadcasters simply pay a fixed fee but require no particular permission to broadcast a song, so payments to copyright holders could be based on the number of times a song is downloaded – and the downloads would be made legal. This is not a perfect proposal – the possibility of manipulating the download ratings comes to mind, and the mandatory licensing fee for Internet radio was set ridiculously high – but on balance, would probably serve to improve the current situation.

The recent, and widely advertised if limited, decisions by Apple and EMI to renounce policing peer-to-peer file sharing via technological means (that is, by giving up on digital rights management) is also a positive step. It signals that at least a few among the big players are realizing that the technological police approach is a losing business proposition, and that plenty of money can be made by selling downloadable music that consumers can then share and redistribute more or less freely.[27]

Deregulation

An intermediate position between abolition and the current system would be to get the government out of the copyright and patent business all together but to allow the use of private contracts to enforce intellectual property. What this means, basically, is that copyright and patents will be no longer regulated by laws, and that the government would no longer act as a costless third-party enforcer of such laws. Violations of private arrangements about patents and copyright by one of the subscribing parties will be brought to a court of law by the offended party and treated as any other breach-of-contract case.

This is a delicate point and deserves some clarification. Beyond copyright and patent, there are also downstream licensing agreements through private contract. That is, before I sell you my book or show you my idea, I can require you to sign a contract agreeing not to resell it. Or these contracts can be included as shrink-wrap agreements implicitly agreed to when the package is opened, as is the case with much computer software. Strict abolition of intellectual property would require that the government commit to not enforcing these types of agreements. An intermediate step to abolition would allow the enforcement of these types of contracts while abolishing legislated copyright terms altogether. Relative to alternatives, this proposal has both pluses and minuses.

In the case of copyright, deregulation would have some negative effects, because fair use and time limits could be eliminated altogether by abusive private contracts. But because the time limit is effectively gone anyway, and because the courts are moving in the direction of allowing contracts limiting fair use to supersede copyright law, the negative effect would not be so great. On the positive side, third parties would be out of the picture. Once a copyrighted item was leaked on to the Internet, there would be no obligation on my part to figure out whether someone else had violated their contract by putting it there. In effect, while the leaker could be sued, the work would nevertheless enter the public domain as a matter of fact. An additional drawback, though, is that this may increase the litigation rate dramatically, with the obvious social costs this implies. Intellectual property lawyers would shift their byzantine skills from the current aim of copyrighting everything to writing more and more complicated copyright contracts and then suing either side for violation of said contracts.

In the case of patents, deregulation would solve a great many problems within a few minuses. It would put an end to submarines – as the submarine pirate would not be as able to get me to sign a contract agreeing to pay him for his useless piece of patent paper. And, of course, independent invention would be protected – the independent inventor would simply avoid signing any licensing contracts. The risk of soaring litigation costs would remain, though, especially when it comes to independent inventions: if you are sitting on a valuable monopoly and someone comes in that has invented the same thing independently, even a miniscule chance that she may not be able to prove it convincingly in front of a court provides a very big incentive to hire some lawyers and go to court to retain monopoly power.

Lack of public disclosure would not be much of a problem either. The amount of effective disclosure that current patents allow is miniscule, if positive at all, as amply documented and easily verifiable by visiting the U.S. Patent and Trademark Office site and by going through a few patents.

Increasing secrecy would probably be the worst drawback of privately contractable patents and/or licenses, especially under the independent invention provision: how can tell if I just reverse engineered your idea from a copy you licensed someone else or I discovered by myself? This may entail a non-negligible waste of resources relative to current conditions, especially for inventions that are now patented but would be hard to keep secret once access to the product embodying the invention is allowed.

Abolition

Beyond deregulation is outright abolition. In other words, in addition to eliminating patents and copyrights, we would not have the government enforce collusive contracts such as downstream licensing agreements. Because economists generally argue in favor of the enforcement of private contracts, it may be a surprise that we argue against some of them in the name of free markets and competition. However, there are two key elements of the usual argument in favor of private contracts that are missing in the case of downstream licensing.

First, downstream licensing restrictions negatively affect people who are not party to the agreement. That is, if I purchase a book by signing a private agreement not to resell copies, this agreement impinges on the right of other people to buy the book from me. These kinds of agreements, in which a group of people (the seller and the first buyer) agree to limit their provision of some good or service, are usually called cartels and are generally illegal under antitrust law. If you and I, as owners of bakeries, get together and sign a contract agreeing to limit the number of loaves of bread we will sell, not only will the courts not enforce that contract, but we will be subject to criminal prosecution as well. The same is true if the same contract is entered into by a bakery and, say, a client restaurant or even a private citizen.

Second, economists recognize the important element of transaction costs in determining which contracts should be enforced. "Possession is nine-tenths of the law" is a truth in economics as well as in common parlance. Take the case of slavery. Why should people not be allowed to sign private contracts binding them to slavery? In fact economists have consistently argued against slavery – during the nineteenth century David Ricardo and John Stuart Mill engaged in a heated public debate with literary luminaries such as Charles Dickens, with the economists opposing slavery and the literary giants arguing in favor.[28] The fact is that our labor cannot be separated from ourselves. For someone else to own our labor requires them to engage in intrusive and costly supervision of our personal behavior. Selling our labor is not tantamount to selling our house, which is why even renting it – that is, becoming an employee – is quite complicated and subject to a variety of regulations and transaction costs. The transaction costs implied by slavery are socially damaging, as they imply violation of privacy and of essential civil liberties. Hence, they are commonly rejected on economic, not just moral, grounds. Moreover, there is no economic reason to allow slavery. With well-functioning markets, renting labor is a good substitute for owning it. And so we allow the rental of labor but not its permanent sale.

For intellectual property, the reverse is the socially beneficial arrangement: allow the permanent sale but ban the rental. Again, this is efficient because it minimizes transaction costs. For, with intellectual property, possession belongs to the buyer and not to the seller. If you sell me a copy of an idea, I now have that idea embodied either in me or in an object I own. For you to control the idea requires intrusive and costly supervision of my private sphere – similarly, if you sell me a book, a CD, or a computer file. In each case, I have physical control of the item, and you can control its use only through intrusive measures. Moreover, in the case of well-functioning markets, owning is a good substitute for renting. Our basic argument against intellectual monopoly is that markets will function well in its absence, and so there is no need for a rental market as the latter only effectuates intellectual monopoly.

We emphasize that it is not rental versus sale that is the crucial distinction, but the presence of restrictions on the use made of an idea. Rental agreements over intellectual property that implied no restrictions on the use of the idea during the period for which rental was agreed would be consistent with our proposal but would offer little advantages over sale. In the case of an idea, such as an invention or mathematical formula, once you have passed the idea to me, rental has little meaning because I can neither return my copy of the idea to you nor credibly promise to forget it after a fixed period of time. In the case of an object embodying an idea, such as a book or a CD, you may well rent the object to me for a fixed period of time. However, in the absence of intellectual monopoly effectuated by downstream licensing, I am free to make a copy of the book or CD, and that copy would remain my property even after the rental period expires. There is no economic objection to rental without downstream licensing; on the other hand, while we would not prohibit such rentals, we would not expect such rental markets to be widespread in the absence of intellectual monopoly.

More extreme forms of abolition are possible, even if it is not obvious how desirable they are or what their practical relevance might be. Still, the economic theorist living inside us must contemplate also these possibilities. Without government grants of monopoly or enforcement of monopolistic contracts, innovators by virtue of their first-mover advantage will generally have some monopoly power. There are government policies that can be used to combat even this ephemeral monopoly. For example, at the lesser end, trade secrecy, digital rights management, and encryption could be eliminated by a law requiring the publication of detailed information about an innovation as a condition of doing business. Of course, the transaction costs are probably large, as the definition of *innovation* would suddenly become blurred, and legal challenges could be mounted with relative ease.

Nevertheless, the idea is certainly practical. For example, to sell computer software, the seller would be required to make available the source code; to sell a drug, the manufacturer would have to publish the chemical formula. This latter example may convince you that, along certain dimensions, such a proposal is scarcely radical – to sell a drug now, the chemical formula must be published – pharmaceutical companies are not allowed trade secrecy over their products. Along other dimensions, though, the proposal is more radical. Consider the case in which a new production process or a new business method is adopted, and think about the complexity involved with full disclosure of its details. The very same facts that, in earlier chapters, allowed us to claim that, in the real world, imitation is costly and that innovations do not become public information just because they are implemented or because a technical paper is published describing them imply, in this case, that full disclosure may be nearly impossible and most certainly manipulated, leading to excessive legal and transaction costs. So – and rather uncharacteristically of us – we would drop the radical position in this particular case and vote for a system in which, if you are lucky to become a monopolist because you really got there first and the other have a hard time catching up with you, well, lucky you!

There is also the intermediate possibility of allowing the elimination of secrecy through private contract only – that is abolishing all copyright except the GNU public license, which serves to enhance rather than limit competition. This, in particular, is a form of copyright we would like to see preserved and extended to patents. Indeed, and limited to the Linux software area, this is pretty much what the Open Initiative Network mentioned earlier strives to achieve.

On the opposite side of the coin, economists often argue that, in the absence of government enforcement of contracts, a contracting black market may arise. An example is the prohibition of usurious lending contracts that limit the charging of high interest rates and limit also the penalties that can be contracted for in the case of failure to repay. Naturally, an illegal market has sprung up – and organized criminals are happy to lend you money without security at very high interest rates, and then come and break your knees if you fail to repay. From a social point of view, the contracts have not been eliminated – but simply pushed out of the civilized world and made the object of persecution by the law-and-order system. Would not something similar happen if the government were to stop enforcing shrink-wrap agreements? The answer is probably not. Antitrust law has not created much of a market for breaking the knees of competitors who fail to collude – and however much the RIAA and MPAA might like to break the knees of those who leak copyright material on to the Internet, they have not had much success in finding them.

Overall, we do not favor the extreme approach of the government actively trying to enforce competition – we favor abolition, including the government refusing to enforce collusive downstream licensing contracts. We would not oppose the private enforcement of licensing contracts, as long as knees and backbones are not allowed to become the channels of enforcement. For example, in the television and movie industry, authorship and profit share is established not according to copyright law, but according to a private contract between the studios and the writers' unions. Without intellectual property, such a contract could not be enforced in court – but it could be enforced, for example, by the writers going on strike or by the studios locking out the writers union. This is not necessarily a good thing from an economic perspective. However, it is very costly for the government to become involved in preventing private contract enforcement; hence, private, nondisruptive enforcement may be the lesser of the two evils. Moreover, this type of enforcement, unlike government enforcement, is self-limiting. That is, the studios can always accept the strike and find replacement authors, and the authors can always start studios of their own. Because some downstream monopoly may serve a good social purpose, it seems a poor idea to try to control this type of self-limiting enforcement.

Pharmaceuticals

Handling properly the pharmaceutical industry constitutes the litmus test for the reform process we are advocating. Simple abolition, or even a progressive scaling down of patent terms, would not work in this sector for the obvious reasons outlined in the previous chapter. Reforming the system of intellectual property in the pharmaceutical industry is a daunting task that involves multiple dimensions of government intervention and regulation of the medical sector. Although we are perfectly aware that knowledgeable readers and practitioners of the pharmaceutical and medical industry will probably find the statements that follow utterly simplistic, when not arrogantly preposterous, we try nevertheless. That this is just a two-page subsection in a book is, we understand, a paltry excuse but a true one nevertheless. In sequential order, here is our list of desiderata.

- Free the pharmaceutical industry of the stage 2 and 3 clinical trials costs, which are the really heavy ones. Have them financed by the National Institutes of Health (NIH) on a competitive basis: pharmaceutical companies that have completed stage 1 trials submit applications to the NIH to have stages 2 and 3 financed. In parallel, medical clinics and university hospitals submit competitive bids to the NIH to have the approved trials assigned to them. Match the winning drugs to the best bids, and use public-choice common sense to minimize the most obvious risks of capture. Clinical trial results become public goods and are available, possibly for a fee covering administrative and maintenance costs, to all who request them. This would not prevent drug companies from deciding that, for whatever reason, they carry out their clinical trials privately and pay for them; that is their choice. Nevertheless, allowing the public financing of stages 2 and 3 of clinical trials – by far the largest component of the private fixed cost associated with the development of new drugs – would remove the biggest (nay, the only) rationale for allowing drugs' patents to last longer than a handful of years.
- Begin reducing the term of pharmaceutical patents proportionally. Should we take pharmaceuticals' claims at their face value, our reform

eliminates between 70 percent and 80 percent of the private fixed cost. Hence, a patent's length should be lowered to four years, instead of the current twenty, without extension. Recall that, again according to the industry, effective patent terms are currently around twelve years from the first day the drug is commercialized; hence, we propose to cut them down by two-thirds, which is less than the proportional cost reduction. To compensate for the fact that NIH-related inefficiencies may slow down the clinical trial process, start patent terms from the first day in which commercialization of the drug is authorized. A ten-year transition period would allow enough time to prepare for the new regulatory environment.

- Sizably reduce the number of drugs that cannot be sold without medical prescription. For many drugs, this is less a protection of otherwise well-informed consumers than a way to enforce monopolistic control over doctors' prescription patterns and to artificially increase distribution costs, with rents accruing partly to pharmaceutical companies and partly to the inefficient local monopolies called pharmacies.
- Allow for simultaneous or independent discovery, along the lines of Gallini and Scotchmer.[29] Further, because patent terms should be running from the start of commercialization, but applications should be filed (without being disclosed) earlier, mandatory licensing of idle or unused active chemical component and drugs should be introduced. In other words, make certain that the following monopolistic tactic becomes unfeasible: file a patent application for entire families of compounds, and then develop them sequentially over a long period of time, postponing clinical trials and production of some compounds until patents on earlier members of the same family have been fully exploited.

This sequence of reform may not be a panacea – nothing is – but we are willing to bet that a pharmaceutical industry organized along these lines will produce no fewer valuable drugs than the current one, at a much lower cost for consumers. Should any congressperson or senator be interested in working out the details that are necessary to make this operational, we hereby volunteer our time and expertise to the enterprise, for free.

Next we examine the issue of poor countries, with Africa and the AIDS epidemic at center stage. From a global perspective, this is a more dramatic and urgent problem than the high cost of drugs in more advanced countries. Here positions oscillate between the *dura sed lex* of TRIPS (forcing the introduction of medical patents in India, South Africa, China, and so on) to requests for a temporary but long-lasting suspension of patents rights for poor countries.[30] Even if our road map for reform were to be implemented – we are theorists; do not forget that detail – the transition time of about ten years is long enough to make the current situation in Africa degenerate much further. There is no doubt, therefore, that a ten- or fifteen-year suspension of drugs' patents for developing countries would be an improvement over the current situation. Recent unilateral actions along these lines, taken by Brazil in relation to AIDS drugs, suggest that this theoretical possibility is becoming a political possibility and its economic and social implications seriously waged. Because it is especially the fear of parallel import of cheap medicines from those countries to the rich ones that fosters the strong opposition of Big Pharma to such a proposal, tem- porarily suspending free trade in medicines may even be worth considering. In other words, a parallel temporary suspension of medical patents in poor countries and of medicines' trade from them to the rest of the world may, in the end, increase social welfare in those areas. This is not an obvious call, though, and we must admit having found very little technical and quanti- tative analysis of the pros and cons of such a policy shift in the literature advocating it.

Furthermore, we cannot help but notice the obvious, if cynical, economic point: only when the worldwide gains from price discrimination are low enough will large pharmaceutical companies find it attractive to get seri- ously involved in the development and production of new drugs specifically targeted to the many diseases plaguing the poor countries of Africa, Latin America, and so on. What this means is that reforming the pharmaceutical markets of the United States, Europe, and Japan in the direction we indicate is, in fact, almost a prerequisite to make sure that we can effectively address the health problems of the less developed countries in a systematic and not purely charitable way. Charity is commendable, useful, and valuable, but history has taught us, over and again, that charity has never eradicated and never will eradicate either poverty or widespread plaguelike diseases. Free competitive markets and the technological innovation they foster are a much more effective and well-tested medicine than any, temporary and charitable, partial reform of the global system of pharmaceutical patents.

Trademarks
We have given little attention to trademarks – which serve to identify rather than to monopolize. Strangely, trademarks have attracted lots of attention in the antiglobalization and antimarket movement, with a variety of antilogo, antitrademark, anti–big corporation rallies, books, movies, and pamphlets

being produced. This, we are afraid, is due more to the double desire of the leading figures in that movement to become a recognizable logo themselves and to the frustration of many youngsters of not owning enough "logoized" items than it is to any serious social loss from the crocodiles stitched onto colorful cotton T-shirts.

In the eventuality, however, that copyright and patents are significantly weakened, there would be a temptation to substitute trademark for other forms of intellectual property protection. For example, if Disney were to lose the copyright over Mickey Mouse, they would have a strong temptation to trademark Mickey Mouse and so prevent the use of Mickey Mouse images. So any effort toward legal reform of copyright and patent law will necessarily have to consider how to limit the use of trademarks for purposes of identification, and how prevent their use as a substitute for copyright and patents.

Subsides for Innovation and Creation

It is theoretically possible that the competitive market alone provides insufficient incentive to innovate – although there is no evidence that this is the case. Suppose that we succeed in abolishing intellectual monopoly and discover, after a few years, that there is less innovation than would be socially desirable. Unlikely as this event may be, the little theorist in us insists that we nevertheless consider it. Hence, should we reintroduce intellectual monopoly in this case?

Intellectual property law is about the government enforcing private monopolies. In countries without effective tax-collection mechanisms, both historically and currently, government grants of monopolies were and are commonplace; we all have seen some old label for a tea or chocolate brand reporting "By Appointment of Her Majesty This or That." As nations develop, more effective tax-collection infrastructures have been replacing such revenue devices as the salt monopoly or the grant of exclusive import rights to the brother-in-law of the president. Hence, the sale by government officials of exclusive rights to carry out this or other commercial activity or to produce and commercialize certain goods and services have progressively disappeared in almost all advanced market economies. Intellectual property is one of the few remaining anachronisms from the prehistory of modern tax collection; worse, indeed, it is a distorted anachronism that is now being exploited for rent-seeking purposes that are opposite to those for which it was originally established. So, the answer is that, if there is indeed a need for extra incentives, it should be done through subsidization and not through government grants of monopoly.

A first question might be, What level of subsidy would replace the profits of the current monopolists?[31] Schankerman makes the calculation that a subsidy to R&D of 15 percent to 35 percent would be enough to provide an incentive equivalent to that currently provided by patents – ironically, subsidies of nearly this level are already available in addition to patents, especially in the pharmaceutical industry, as we documented in the previous chapter.[32] Indeed, the offensive sight of the government using taxpayers' money to subsidize research and then awarding it a private monopoly reaches absurd heights in academia, where in recent years the mantra of private-public partnership has taken hold. A more ridiculous form of public subsidy for private monopolies is hard to imagine.

Like monopolies, subsidies can lead to rent seeking and have distortionary effects, so they should scarcely be a first resort. Some economists, such as Paul Romer, painfully aware of these negative side effects, have proposed to avoid some of these distortions by narrowly targeted subsidies – for example, to graduate students, who, the evidence suggests, are key instruments in the process of innovation. Others, such as Andreas Irmen and Martin Hellwig, suggest that broad subsides to investment in general – interest-rate subsidies, for example – are likely to be the least distortionary. Yet others, such as Michael Kremer, suggest that prizes awarded after the fact create greater incentives to innovate. Nancy Gallini and Suzanne Scotchmer go further and compare various subsidization methods in their recent work. Their technical analysis is beyond the scope of this book, but the bottom line remains: various intelligent forms of subsidizing basic research and even applied invention exist, and an appropriate mix can be found that would greatly improve upon patents and copyright.[33]

Social Norms

Social norms are not a topic in which we are especially expert. Still, it is a relevant topic: property rights are never enforced only by the law-and-order system, or even by costly private monitoring of other people's behavior. Broadly accepted and well-functioning property right systems rest also, one is tempted to write *primarily*, on a commonly shared sense of morality. I do not litter my neighbors' yard with all kinds of small pieces of garbage, not just because they may yell at me or prosecute me, but, first and foremost, because I would be ashamed of myself for doing so. The same is clearly true for the day-to-day enforcement of the "small" aspects of intellectual monopoly, such as copying books, movies, and music, downloading materials from the Internet, making copies of movies we own for friends to watch at home, and so on and so forth. Plainly, enforcement of current intellectual monopoly standards is, to a large extent, a matter of which social norms are accepted and will be accepted, and what is considered, by the average citizen, morally acceptable or not.

Eric Rasmusen has thought quite a bit, and quite originally, about the issue of social norms and intellectual property. Consider one of his not-so-paradoxical paradoxes:

> Video rental stores and libraries, of course, reduce originator profits and hurt innovation, but that is a utilitarian concern. What is of more ethical concern is that whenever, for example, someone borrows a book from the public library instead of buying a book, he has deprived the author of the fruits of his labor and participated in reducing the author's power to control his self-expression. Thus, if it is immoral to violate a book's copyright, so too it would seem to be immoral to use public libraries. Libraries are not illegal, but the law's injustice would be no reason for a moral person to do unjust things. The existence of children's sections would be particularly heinous, as encouraging children to steal.[34]

By following the same commonsense logic, he comes to the following sensible conclusion:

> To entirely deter copying would require a norm inflicting a considerable amount of guilt on copiers, since legal enforcement of copying by individuals is so difficult. To partially deter it would be undesirable for two reasons. First, it would generate a large amount of disutility while failing to deter the target misbehavior. Second, it would reduce the effectiveness of guilt in other situations, by pushing so many people over the threshold of being moral reprobates. At the same time, the benefit from deterring copying by individuals, the increased incentive for creation of new products, is relatively small. I thus conclude that people should not feel guilty about copying.[35]

That, even at the very personal level of our own daily moral judgment, we agree with such evaluation – as, apparently, do tens of millions of Americans and other people around the world – should be quite clear, by now. That a much more explicit and transparent public debate about such moral issues is long overdue seems to us obvious exactly because of the contradiction that not just the two of us but everyone we know faces daily. Although the law and official public morality sternly state that it is wrong, people repeatedly copy digital and nondigital copyrighted materials for noncommercial uses – and without guilt.

It is somewhat comforting, therefore, that a growing number of European judges appear to be coming to the same conclusion as the laypeople. Recent rulings in Denmark and Spain first, and in Italy just recently, asserted that copying for private use and with no intention of extracting commercial profit does not violate fair use and should not be punished.

The Ugly

Whether Walt Disney will get to continue its monopoly of Mickey Mouse does not seem like an issue that should lead either to revolt or nonviolent insurrection. But have no doubt: intellectual monopoly threatens both our prosperity and our freedom – it threatens to kill the goose that laid the golden eggs – to strangle innovation all together.

This might seem an exaggerated statement, made only to stir controversy – and to sell a few more copies of our copyrighted book. Yet, despite the fact that by 1433 the great Chinese explorer Cheng Ho's fleets had explored Africa and the Middle East, in the subsequent centuries the world was colonized by Europeans and not by the Chinese.[36] The monopolists of the Ming Dynasty saw a threat to their monopoly – which was then a monopoly of intellectual and administrative power – in the innovative explorations of Cheng Ho and forced him to stop. This lead to a static, inward-looking, and regressive regime, where emperors ruled under mottos such as "Stay the Course" and "Do Nothing," and where innovation and progress not only faltered but were progressively replaced by obsolescence, regression, and, eventually, poverty. And so it is that in the United States we celebrate Christopher Columbus Day rather than Cheng Ho Day.

"Stay the Course," Forbidden City, Beijing. Photo by authors, 2004.

On a smaller scale, but with a no less real impact on world history, we find that intellectual property has delayed the development of the steam engine, the automobile, the airplane, and innumerable other useful things. This took place at a time before the United States became the sole dominant world power, and before a system nearly as noxious as the current system in the United States and the European Union was in place. It took place during a time when very many countries were still competing for world primacy, and the collusive pact among intellectual monopolists that our modern trade agreements have been built to enforce was not in the cards. If the Wright brothers preferred litigation to invention, at least the French were free to develop the airplane. If Gottlieb Daimler and Karl Benz were the first to build a practical automobile powered by an internal-combustion engine, their German patent did not prevent John Lambert, only six years later, from developing America's first gasoline-powered automobile. Nor did it prevent the Duryea brothers, shortly after, from founding America's first company to manufacture and sell gasoline-powered vehicles.[37]

Where, today, is a software innovator to find safe haven from Microsoft's lawyers? Where, tomorrow, will the pharmaceutical companies be that will challenge the patents of Big Pharma and produce drugs and vaccines for the millions dying in Africa and elsewhere? Where, today, are courageous publishers, committed to the idea that accumulated knowledge should be widely available, defending the Google Book Search initiative? Nowhere, as far as we can tell, and this is a bad omen for the times to come. The legal and political war between the innovators and the monopolists is a real one, and the innovators may not win, as the forces of "Stay the Course" and "Do Nothing" are powerful and on the rise.

Certainly, the basic threat to prosperity and liberty can be resolved through sensible reform. But intellectual property is a cancer. The goal must be not merely to make the cancer more benign but ultimately to get rid of it entirely. So, although we are skeptical of the idea of immediately and permanently eliminating intellectual monopoly, the long-term goal should be no less than a complete elimination. A phased reduction in the length of terms of both patents and copyrights would be the right place to start. By gradually reducing terms, it becomes possible to make the necessary adjustments – for example, to FDA regulations, publishing techniques and practices, software development and distribution methods – while at the same time making a commitment to eventual elimination.

Given that it may well be the case that some modest degree of intellectual monopoly is superior to complete abolition, why do we set as a goal complete elimination of intellectual property? Our position on intellectual monopoly is not different than the position most economists take on trade restrictions: although some modest amount of protection might be desirable in special cases, it is more practical and useful to focus on the elimination of restrictions as a general rule. Similarly, although some modest amount of intellectual monopoly might be desirable in very special cases, it is more practical and useful to focus on the elimination of intellectual monopoly as a general rule. In innovation as in trade, a modest degree of monopoly is not sustainable. Once the lobbyist's nose is inside the tent, the entire lobby is sure to follow, and we will once again face a broken patent system and absurdly long copyright terms. To secure our prosperity and freedom, we must abolish intellectual monopoly from the tent entirely. To do so, we must develop the very same patient determination with which we have been after trade restrictions for more than half a century, and we are not done yet.

This analogy between intellectual property and trade restrictions is not a purely rhetorical tool nor a random comparison. For centuries, human innovative activity took the form of creating new consumption goods, new machines, and new staples of food. But the transmission of ideas from one producer to another and across countries was not nearly as fast, standardized, or routinized as it is today. Creative human activity was focused on the creation and reproduction of physical goods and not on the creation and reproduction of ideas. Free trade of commodities was therefore key to the fostering of progress: the more competitors came in with shoes like yours, the more you had to improve on your shoes to keep selling them.

This dialectic we used to call economic progress, and, after a few centuries of intellectual debate and numerous wars, Western societies came to understand that restricting international trade was damaging because protectionism prevents economic progress and fosters international tensions leading to conflict. Since at least the late Middle Ages, the battle has been between the forces of progress, individual freedom, competition, and free trade and the forces of stagnation, regulation of individual actions, monopoly, and trade protection. Now that the intellectual and political battle over free trade of physical goods seems won, and an increasing number of less advanced countries are joining the progressive ranks of free-trading nations, pressure to make intellectual property protection stronger is mounting in those very same countries that advocate free trade. This is not coincidence.

Most physical goods already are and, in the decades to come, will increasingly be, produced in less developed countries. Most innovations and creations are taking place in the advanced world, and the information technology and bioengineering revolutions suggest that this will continue

for a while at least. It is not surprising, then, that a new version of the
eternal parasite of economic progress – mercantilism – is emerging in the
rich countries of North America, Europe, and Asia.

Economic progress springs from having things produced as efficiently
as possible so that they can sell at the lowest price. This wisdom applies
to both the things we *buy* and to those we *sell*, and therein lies the trap of
mercantilism. Most of us have learned that the surest way to make a profit is
to buy cheap and sell dear. When there is adequate competition and everyone
tries to buy cheap and sell dear, then the *only* way I can buy cheap and sell
dear is if I am more efficient than you are. This generates incentives for
innovation and progress. The trap and tragedy of mercantilism is when this
individually correct philosophy is transformed into a national policy: that
we are all better off when our country as a whole buys cheap and sells dear. It
was this myopic and distorted view of the way in which markets function that
Smith, Ricardo, and the classic economists were fighting against 250 years
ago. At that time, wheat producers in England wanted to restrict free trade in
wheat so English producers could sell it dear. That meant English consumers
could not buy it cheap. Now, before moving to the next paragraph, consider
the current debate about preventing parallel imports of medicines, CDs,
DVDs, and other products covered by intellectual monopoly. Do you see
parallelism? That is our point.

The contemporary variation of this economic pest is one in which our
collective interest is, allegedly, best served if we buy goods cheap and sell ideas
dear. In the mind of those who preach this new version of the mercantilist
credo, the World Trade Organization should enforce as much free trade as
possible, so we can buy "their" products at a low price. It should also protect
our intellectual property as much as possible, so we can sell "our" movies,
software, and medicines at a high price. What this folly misses is that, now,
like three centuries ago, although it is good to buy their food cheap, if they
buy movies and medicines at high prices, so do "we." In fact, as the case
of medicines and DVDs proves, the monopolist sells to "us" at even higher
prices than to "them." This has dramatic consequences for the incentives to
progress: when someone can sell at high prices because of legal protection
from imitators, he or she will not expend much effort looking for better and
cheaper ways to do things.

For centuries, the cause of economic progress has identified with that
of free trade. In the decades to come, sustaining economic progress will
depend, more and more, on our ability to progressively reduce and eventually eliminate intellectual monopoly. As in the battle for free trade, the first
step must consist in destroying the intellectual foundations of the obscu-
rantist position. Back then the mercantilist fallacy taught that, to become

wealthy, a country must regulate trade and strive for trade surpluses. Today, the same fallacy teaches that, without intellectual monopoly, innovations would be impossible and that our governments should prohibit parallel import and enforce draconian intellectual monopoly rules. We hope that we have made some progress in demolishing that glass house.

Notes

1. Machlup (1958), p. 80. It appears that Machlup was, in fact, paraphrasing Penrose (1951), which we learned from a talk by Bronwyn Hall, who apparently learned it from Joshua Lerner.
2. To the best of our knowledge, the first published statement of this proposal is in Kukkonen (1998), but a quick search on Google shows the idea is receiving lots of attention from interested lawyers and law firms, see Das (2000) and http://www.mofo.com/news/updates/files/update1022.html (accessed February 24, 2008).
3. As in the Spanish case of Gedeprensa, which we discussed in Chapter 2.
4. The recent extension of patents to story lines is discussed at http://www.emediawire.com/releases/2005/11/emw303435.htm (accessed February 24, 2008). For a more than sympathetic, but highly revealing in its bias, legal analysis of the whole idea of patenting plots, visit http://www.plotpatents.com/legal_analysis.htm (accessed February 24, 2008), which comes directly from the law firm that worked hard to patent fictional plots.
5. As we discussed in Chapter 8 and references therein.
6. There is no need for references here; still, here is one to an old and rather interesting case of university research patenting: Apple (1989).
7. Again, material abounds on the Web and in the regular press about the ongoing debate to extend the E.U. copyright term to match the U.S. one, post–Sonny Bono Act. To start, see http://news.bbc.co.uk/1/hi/entertainment/music/3547788.stm (accessed February 24, 2008). For a piece by Dennis Karjala on European Union–United States harmonization, see http://homepages.law.asu.edu/~dkarjala/Opposing CopyrightExtension/legmats/HarmonizationChartDSK.html (accessed February 24, 2008).
8. See http://www.usdoj.gov/atr/public/hearings/ip/chapter_1.pdf (accessed February 24, 2008) for a relatively technical discussion of the issues involved in the unilateral refusal to license practice. For a list of the nine no-no's, and a not-unbiased discussion of the opportunity to dispose of them, clearly favoring the disposal option, see Gilbert and Shapiro (1997). For a very different view, cogently applied to the two recent Microsoft antitrust cases, see First (2006).
9. Information about the *Verizon v. Trinko* case can be found widely on the Internet, for example, Evans (2004), available at http://www.aei-brookings.org/policy/page.php?id=174, or the summary by George Hay at http://www.accessmylibrary.com/coms2/summary_0286-25484663_ITM, (both accessed on February 24, 2008). With a bit of patience the Supreme Court ruling can be found online at its Web-site, http://www.supremecourtus.gov, or (as of February 24, 2008) at http://www.law.cornell.edu/supct/html/02-682.ZO.html for those in a hurry.
10. Information and news about the digital rights management initiative (in its multiple versions) and its very controversial nature are widespread on the Web and in other

media. The curious reader may want to begin with the Wikipedia entry and then continue from there.

11. For detailed information about the *Grokster* case, Wikipedia is again a good starting point, and additional info can be found at the Electronic Frontier Foundation page on *MGM v. Grokster*. A middle-of-the-road legal assessment is in Samuelson (2004). For the sad effect of the Supreme Court ruling on economic innovation, just go to http://www.grokster.com and read the scary message welcoming you, even on February 24, 2008.

12. On July 2, 2005, the European Parliament voted 648 to 14 (with 18 abstentions) to scrap the so-called Directive on the Patentability of Computer Implemented Inventions. Although this was good news, the battle on software patents in Europe is far from over. The vote is attributable more to a general fight with the EU Commission, which tends to ignore whatever the Parliament suggests, than to a widespread opposition to software patents within the latter body. In the meanwhile, though, grassroots opposition has grown and, especially within the business community, a variety of action groups have sprung up that oppose software patents along pro-business lines and on the basis of pro–free market arguments such as those exposed in this book.

13. News and information on this topic are widespread through all kinds of media. The Food and Agriculture Organization of the United Nations' online Forum on Biotechnology in Food and Agriculture, at http://www.fao.org/biotech/forum.asp (accessed February 24, 2008), is a particularly informative starting point for the interested reader. A number of very reasonable reforms that would improve developing countries' situation in the agricultural sector can be found at http://issues.org/17.4/barton.htm (accessed February 24, 2008).

14. Having abundantly clarified why genomic patents are a pretty bad idea, here are a couple of references to people who like them for all the wrong reasons: Putnam (2004) and Hale, Tolleri, and Telford (2006).

15. This is the main, if not the only, reason behind the existence of WTO-TRIPS, as is easily verified from the documents contained on its Web page, http://www.wto.org/english/tratop_e/trips_e/trips_e.htm (accessed February 24, 2008).

16. Information about the IBM and other companies' protective patent pool on Linux is widespread on the Web and other media. Visit Wikipedia under "OSDL" and "Free Standards group" to learn more, or go directly to http://www.openinventionnetwork.com and http://www.linux-foundation.org/en/Main_Page, (both accessed on February 24, 2008).

17. A detailed discussion of possible, and all very reasonable, reforms can be found in Jaffe and Lerner (2004).

18. Obviously, the "how to swing a swing" patent (U.S. Patent No. 6,368,227) is here just a label for a gigantic and ever-growing class of patents that are so crazy and unbelievable that one may think we fabricated the whole thing. Well, we must admit that we do not have the level of insane imagination needed to reach the heights achieved by the U.S. Patent and Trademark Office in cooperation with the most shameless rent seekers of the world. For entertaining surveys of this modern zoo of legal monstrosities, out of an almost endless list of sites are the following few: http://www.freepatentsonline.com/crazy.html, http://www.crazypatents.com, http://www.totallyabsurd.com, and http://www.patentlysilly.com (all accessed February 24, 2008) should keep you amused if not frightened.

19. Quillen, Webster, and Eichmann (2002).
20. Ibid., pp. 50–51.
21. Gallini and Scotchmer (2001).
22. Kingston (2001) p. 32.
23. Patent renewal schemes are discussed in Cornelli and Schankerman (1999) and Scotchmer (1999).
24. See http://www.supremecourtus.gov/opinions/02pdf/01–618.pdf (accessed February 24, 2008).
25. Lessig (2004). See especially the chapter "Registration and Renewal" in the public domain version at http://www.authorama.com (accessed February 24, 2008).
26. Landes and Posner (2003).
27. Mildly good legal news seem also to be coming from the European courts, which have started to rule against some of the most preposterous requests to treat any form of music downloading as theft, even when intended only for personal use and with no commercial purposes. For the Spanish and Italian court rulings see, for example, http://www.theregister.co.uk/2006/11/03/spanish_judge_says_downloading_legal/ (accessed February 24, 2008), and http://www.repubblica.it/2006/10/sezioni/cronaca/cassazione-3/lecito-scaricare-file/lecito-scaricare-file.html (accessed February 24, 2008).
28. The debate between economists and others over slavery is discussed at some length in Levy and Peart (2001). In addition to defending slavery, Dickens was a strong proponent of copyright law and was extremely incensed that his works could be legally distributed in the United States without his permission. Ironically, a limited form of slavery is still allowed in the music and sports industries, where long-term contracts binding the artist or the athlete to a particular studio or team are commonplace.
29. Gallini and Scotchmer (2001).
30. Condon and Sinha (2004), among others, have studied criteria for suspension of patents in developing countries.
31. Schankerman and Pakes (1986) have studied patent returns in various European countries. Using their data, Kingston (2001, p. 18) estimates the subsidies that would be required to replace the current patent system:

    Schankerman and Pakes reported that for patents in Britain, France and Germany, the returns appear to be only a small fraction of the domestic R&D expenditure of the business enterprises. The means of the discounted sum of rewards from patent age 5 were about $7,000 in Britain and France and $19,000 in Germany. The value of patents as a proportion of total national R&D expenditure was 0.057 in France, 0.068 in Britain and 0.056 in Germany (1986, pp. 1068, 1074). Schankerman subsequently estimated that a subsidy to R&D of 15%–35% would be enough to provide an equivalent incentive to patents (1988, p. 95).

32. Schankerman (1998). Notice that this is the same paper referred to by Kingston in the quotation reported in the previous note; 1988 is clearly a typo in Kingston's working paper.
33. See, respectively, Romer (1996), Hellwig and Irmen (2001), Kremer (2001a, 2001b) and Glennerster, Kremer, and Williams (2006), and Gallini and Scotchmer (2001).
34. Rasmusen (2005), p. 6.
35. Rasmusen (2005), p. 21.

36. To start learning about Cheng Ho, see, for example, http://famousmuslims.muslimonline.org/zheng-he-cheng-ho.html (accessed February 24, 2008).
37. Apart for two small entries on Wikipedia and a few other small sites, there is little on the Web about either John Lambert or the Duryea brothers. Still, by searching wisely and reading carefully, their stories and their achievements come out slowly but surely. Neither of them took out a patent, but their innovative actions started the American automobile industry nevertheless. See Scharchburg (1993).

References

Acemoglu, D. and J. Angrist (2000), "How Large are the Social Returns to Education? Evidence from Compulsory Schooling Laws," in *NBER Macroeconomic Annual 2000*, ed. B. S. Bernanke and K. Rogoff, 9–59. Cambridge: MA: MIT Press.

Acemoglu, D. and J. Linn (2003), "Market Size in Innovation: Theory and Evidence from the Pharmaceutical Industry," NBER Working Paper No. 10038, June.

Adams, W. and J. B. Dirlam (1966), "Big Steel, Invention and Innovation," *Quarterly Journal of Economics* **80**, 167–89.

Aghion, P. and P. Howitt (1992), "A Model of Growth through Creative Destruction," *Econometrica* **60**, 323–51.

Akerloff, G. A., K. J. Arrow, T. F. Bresnahan, J. M. Buchanan, R. H. Coase, L. R. Cohen, M. Friedman, J. R. Green, R. W. Hahn, T. W. Hazlett, C. S. Hemphill, R. E. Litan, R. G. Noll, R. Schmalensee, S. Shavell, H. R. Varian, and R. J. Zeckhauser (2002), "Amicus Curiae Brief in Support of Petitioners in the Supreme Court of the United States *Eric Eldred et al v. John D. Ashcroft, Attorney General.*"

Allen, R. C. (1983), "Collective Invention," *Journal of Economic Behavior and Organization* **4**, 1–24.

Alston, J. M. and R. J. Venner (2000), "The Effects of the U.S. Plant Variety Protection Act on Wheat Genetic Improvement," D.P. No. 62, International Food Policy Research Institute, May.

Angell, M. and A. S. Relman (2002), "Patents, Profits, and American Medicine: Conflicts of Interest in the Marketing and Testing of New Drugs," *Daedalus* (Spring), 102–11.

Anton, J. J. and D. A. Yao (1994), "Expropriation and Inventions: Appropriable Rents in the Absence of Property Rights," *American Economic Review* **84**, 190–209.

Anton, J. J. and D. A. Yao (2000), "Little Patents and Big Secrets: Managing Intellectual Property," mimeo, Wharton Graduate School of Business, University of Pennsylvania.

Apple, R. (1989), "Patenting University Research: Harry Steenbock and the Wisconsin Alumni Research Foundation," *Isis* **80** (3), 374–94.

Arewa, O. B. (2006), "Copyright on Catfish Row: Musical Borrowing, Porgy & Bess and Unfair Use," ExpressO Preprint Series, Paper 1116, Berkeley Electronic Press, available at http://law.bepress.com/expresso/eps/1116.

Arora, A., M. Ceccagnoli, and W. Cohen (2003), "R&D and the Patent Premium," NBER Working Paper No. W9431.

Arora, A., R. Landau, and N. Rosenberg (1998), *Chemicals and Long-Term Economic Growth: Insights from the Chemical Industry*. New York: John Wiley & Sons.

Arrow, K. (1962), "Economic Welfare and the Allocation of Resources for Invention," in *Rate and Direction of Inventive Activity: Economic and Social Factors*, ed. National Bureau of Economic Research, 609, 617. Princeton, NJ: Princeton University Press.

Arundel, A. (2001), "Patents in the Knowledge-Based Economy," *Beleidsstudies Technologie Economie* **37**, 67–88.

Associated Press (2005), "Publisher of 9/11 Report to Make Donation," July 21.

Baccara, M. G. and R. Razin (2004), "Curb Your Innovation: Corporate Conservatism in the Presence of Imperfect Intellectual Property Rights," mimeo, New York University.

Baker, D. and N. Chatani (2002), "Promoting Good Ideas on Drugs: Are Patents the Best Way? The Relative Efficiency of Patent and Public Support for Bio-medical Research," briefing paper, Center for Economic and Policy Research.

Baldwin, J. M. and P. Hanel (2003), *Innovation and Knowledge Creation in an Open Economy: Canadian Industry and International Implications*. Cambridge: Cambridge University Press.

Barragan Arce, J. (2005), "The Apples of Competition: A Study of Plants Innovation in Nineteenth and Twentieth Century USA," Ph.D. dissertation, University of Minnesota, in progress.

Barro, R. J. and X. Sala-i-Martin (1995), *Economic Growth*. Cambridge, MA: MIT Press.

Battacharya, S. and J. R. Ritter (1983), "Innovation and Communication: Signalling with Partial Disclosure," *Review of Economic Studies* **50**, 331–46.

Becker, G. (1971), *Economic Theory*. New York: Knopf.

Begley, S. (2006), "In Switch, Scientists Share Data to Develop Useful Drug Therapies," *Wall Street Journal*, January 20.

Benkler, Y. (2004), "Commons-Based Strategies and the Problems of Patents," *Science* **305**, 1110–11.

Bercovitz, A. (1974), "La protección jurídica de las invenciones y la industria quimicofarmacéutica." Paper presented at a colloquium organized by the Business Law Department of the University of Salamanca, Madrid.

Berkun S. (2007), *The Myths of Innovation*. Sebastopol, CA: O'Reilly Media.

Bessen, J. (2003), "Patent Thickets: Strategic Patenting of Complex Technologies," mimeo, School of Law, Boston University, March.

Bessen, J. (2005), "A Comment on 'Do Patents Facilitate Financing in the Software Industry?'" Boston University School of Law and Research on Innovation, available at http://www.researchoninnovation.org/comment on Mann.pdf.

Bessen, J. and R. M. Hunt (2003), "An Empirical Look at Software Patents," mimeo, Massachusetts Institute of Technology, May, available at http://opensource.mit.edu/papers/bessen.pdf. Abridged version published in *Journal of Economics & Management Strategy* **16**, no. 1 (2007), 157–89.

Biddle, P., P. England, M. Peinado, and B. Willman (n.d.), "The Darknet and the Future of Content Distribution," mimeo, Microsoft Corporation.

Block, M. (2000), "The Empirical Basis for Statutory Database Protection after the European Database Directive," mimeo, Duke Law School, available at www.law.duke.edu/cspd/papers/empirical.doc.

Boldrin, M. and D. K. Levine (1999), "Perfectly Competitive Innovation," mimeo, University of Minnesota and UCLA, available at http://dklevine.com and http://www.econ.umn.edu/~mboldrin.

Boldrin, M. and D. K. Levine (2002), "The Case Against Intellectual Property," *The American Economic Review: Papers and Proceedings* 92, 209–12.

Boldrin, M. and D. K. Levine (2004a), "Rent Seeking and Innovation," *Journal of Monetary Economics* 51, 127–60.

Boldrin, M. and D. K. Levine (2004b), "2003 Lawrence Klein Lecture: The Case Against Intellectual Monopoly," *International Economic Review* 45, 327–50.

Boldrin, M. and D. K. Levine (2005a), "The Economics of Ideas and Intellectual Property," *Proceedings of the National Academy of Sciences* 102, 1252–56.

Boldrin, M. and D. K. Levine (2005b), "IP and Market Size," mimeo, available at http://www.econ.umn.edu/~mboldrin//Research/Current_Research/innovation.html.

Boldrin, M. and D. K. Levine (2006), "Standing on Giants' Shoulders. The Economics of Innovation in a Complex Economy," working paper, Washington University in St. Louis.

Boldrin, M. and D. K. Levine (2007), "Full Appropriation and Intellectual Property," mimeo, Washington University in St. Louis, February.

Borges, J. L. (1983), *Labyrinths: Selected Stories and Other Writings.* New York: Modern Library.

Boynton, R. S. (2004), "The Tyranny of Copyright?" *New York Times*, January 25.

Braguinsky, S., S. Gabdrakhmanov, and A. Ohyama (2007), "A Theory of Industry Dynamics With Innovation and Imitation," mimeo, Department of Economics, SUNY Buffalo, forthcoming in *Review of Economic Dynamics*.

Branstetter, L. and M. Sakakibara (2001), "Do Stronger Patents Induce More Innovation? Evidence from the 1988 Japanese Patent Law Reforms," *Rand Journal of Economics* 32, 77–100.

Breyer, S. (1970), "The Uneasy Case for Copyright. A Study of Copyright in Books, Photocopies, and Computer Programs," *Harvard Law Review* 84, 281–351.

Britt, B. (1990), "International Marketing: Disney's Global Goals," *Marketing*, May 17.

Brock, G. W. (1981), *The Telecommunications Industry: The Dynamics of Market Structure.* Cambridge, MA: Harvard University Press.

Brown, K. (2005), *Samizdat*, unpublished manuscript, Alexis de Tocqueville Institute, discussion of the manuscript is available at http://www.adti.net/samizdat/samizdat.updatesold.html.

Burns, R. W. (2004), *Communications: An International History of the Formative Years*, IEE History of Technology Series 32.

Butler L. J. and B. Marion (1985), *The Impact of Patent Protection on the U.S. Seed Industry and Public Breeding.* Madison: University of Wisconsin Press.

Campanella, L. (1979), "La politica dei farmaci in Italia con particolare riferimento ai problemi della ricerca scientifica," in *La concentrazione industriale: Problemi teorici e considerazioni empiriche con particolare riferimento all'industria farmaceutica*, ed. G. Querini. Franco Angeli.

Campbell, B. and M. Overton (1991), *Land, Labour and Livestock: Historical Studies in European Agricultural Productivity. Manchester*, UK: Manchester University Press.

Carnegie, A. (1905), *James Watt*. Doubleday, Page & Co.

Carr, D. (2002), "Cybersmut and Debt Undermine Penthouse," *New York Times*, April 8.

Carroll, M. W. (2005), "The Struggle for Music Copyright," *Florida Law Review* **57**, 907–61.

Castiglionesi, F. and C. Ornaghi (2004), "An Empirical Assessment of the Determinants of TFP Growth," mimeo, Universidad Carlos III, Madrid.

Cavalli-Sforza, L. L. (1996), "The Spread of Agriculture and Nomadic Pastoralism: Insights from Genetics, Linguistics, and Archaeology," in *The Origins and Spread of Agriculture and Pastoralism in Eurasia*, ed. D. Harris, 51–69. London: University College London Press.

Caves, R. E., M. D. Whinston, and M. A. Hurwitz (1991), "Patent Expiration, Entry and Competition in the U.S. Pharmaceutical Industry: An Exploratory Analysis," Brookings Papers on Economic Activity: Microeconomics, 1–48.

Chaudhuri, S., P. Goldberg, and P. Jia (2003), "The Effects of Extending Intellectual Property Rights Protection to Developing Countries: A Case Study of the Indian Pharmaceutical Market," NBER Working Paper No. 10159, forthcoming in *The American Economic Review*.

Chien, R. I., ed. (1979), *Issues in Pharmaceutical Economics*. Lanham, MD: Lexington Books.

Ciccone, A. and G. Peri (2002), "Identifying Human Capital Externalities: Theory with an Application to US Cities," IZA Discussion Papers No. 488, Institute for the Study of Labor.

Cipolla, C. M. (1969), *Literacy and Development in the West*. Harmondsworth, UK: Penguin Books.

Cipolla, C. M. (1972), "The Diffusion of Innovations in Early Modern Europe," *Comparative Studies in Society and History* **14**, 46–52.

Cipolla, C. M. (1976), *Before the Industrial Revolution: European Society and Economy, 1000–1700*. New York: W. W. Norton.

Clark, G. (2007), *A Farewell to Alms: A Brief Economic History of the World*. Princeton, NJ: Princeton University Press.

Clark, J., J. Piccolo, B. Stanton, and K. Tyson (2000), "Patent Pools: A Solution to the Problem of Access in Biotechnology Patents?" mimeo, U.S. Patent and Trademark Office, Washington, DC.

Cohen, W. M., A. Arora, M. Ceccagnoli, A. Goto, A. Nagata, R. R. Nelson, and J. P. Walsh (2002), "Patents: Their Effectiveness and Role," mimeo, Carnegie-Mellon University.

Cohen, W. M., R. R. Nelson, and J. P. Walsh (2000), "Protecting Their Intellectual Assets: Appropriability Conditions and Why U.S. Manufacturing Firms Patent (or Not)," NBER Working Paper No. 7552, February.

Cohen, W. M. and J. Walsh (1998), "R&D Spillovers, Appropriability and R&D Intensity: A Survey Based Approach," mimeo, Carnegie-Mellon University.

Colyvas, J., M. Crow, A. Gelijns, R. Mazzoleni, R. Nelson, N. Rosenberg, and B. N. Sampat (2002), "How Do University Inventions Get into Practice?" *Management Science* **48**, 61–72.

Comanor, W. S. (1966), "The Drug Industry and Medical Research: The Economics of the Kefauver Committee Investigations," *The Journal of Business* **39**, 12–18.

Comanor, W. S. (1986), "The Political Economy of the Pharmaceutical Industry," *Journal of Economic Literature* **24**, 1178–1217.

Commission on Intellectual Property Rights (2002), "Integrating Intellectual Property Right and Development Policy," final report of the commission, available at http://www.iprcommission.org/papers/pdfs/final_report/CIPRfullfinal.pdf.

Condon, B. and T. Sinha (2004), "Global Diseases, Global Patents, and Differential Treatment in WTO Law: Criteria for Suspending Patent Obligations in Developing Countries," mimeo, Instituto Tecnológico Autónomo de México, Mexico City, forthcoming in *Journal of International Law and Business.*

Congressional Budget Office (1998), *How Increased Competition from Generic Drugs Has Affected Prices and Returns in the Pharmaceuticals Industry.* Washington, DC: Congressional Budget Office, available at http://www.cbo.gov/showdoc.cfm?index=655& sequence=0.

Coover, J. (1985), *Music Publishing: Copyright and Piracy in Victorian England.* London: Mansell Publishing.

Cornelli, F. and M. D. Schankerman (1999), "Patent Renewal and R&D Incentives," *Rand Journal of Economics* **30**, 197–213.

Costas, J. M. and E. Heuvelink, eds. (2000), *Greenhouse Horticulture in Almería (Spain): Report on a Study Tour.*

Das, P. K. (2000), "Offensive Protection: The Potential Application of Intellectual Property Law to Scripted Sports Plays," *Indiana Law Journal* **75**, 1073–1100.

David, P. A. (2001), "Tragedy of the Public Knowledge 'Commons'? Global Science, Intellectual Property and the Digital Technology Boomerang," MERIT Research Memoranda 003, http://econwpa.wustl.edu/eps/dev/papers/0502/0502010.pdf.

DeLong, B. and M. Froomkin (1999). *Speculative Microeconomics for Tomorrow's Economy,* available at http://personal.law.miami.edu/~froomkin/articles/spec.htm.

Derry, T. K. and T. I. Williams (1960), *A Short History of Technology.* Oxford, UK: Clarendon Press.

DiMasi, J., R. W. Hansen, and H. G. Grabowski (2003), "The Price of Innovation: New Estimates of Drug Development Costs," *Journal of Health Economics* **22**, 151–85.

Dunlap, D. W. (2005), "Copyright Suit over Tower Design Can Proceed, Judge Says," *New York Times,* August 11, C19.

Dutfield, G. (2003), *Intellectual Property Rights and the Life Science Industries: A Twentieth Century History.* Aldershot, UK: Ashgate.

The Economist (2005), "A Market for Ideas: A Survey of Patents and Technologies," October 22, 1–20.

Electronic Frontier Foundation (2003), "DMCA Archives," available at http://www.eff.org/IP/DMCA/.

El Feki, S. (2005), "Prescription for Change: A Survey of Pharmaceuticals," *The Economist,* June 18.

Ellison, G. and E. Glaeser (1997), "Geographic Concentration in U.S. Manufacturing Industries: A Dartboard Approach," *Journal of Political Economy* **105**, 889–927.

Ellison, G. and E. Glaeser (1999), "The Geographic Concentration of Industry: Does Natural Advantage Explain Agglomeration?" *The American Economic Review, Papers and Proceedings* **89**, 311–16.

Epstein, R. A. and B. N. Kuhlik (2004), "Is There a Biomedical Anticommons?" *Regulation Magazine* **27**, 54–58.

Epstein, S. R. and P. Maarten, eds. (2005), *Guilds, Technology and the Economy in Europe, 1400–1800.* London: Routledge.

Evans, D. S. (2004), "What's Yours is Mine," *Wall Street Journal*, February 2.

Evans, D. S. and R. Schmalensee (2001), "Some Economic Aspects of Antitrust Analysis in Dynamically Competitive Industries," NBER Working Paper No. 8268.

Federal Trade Commission (2002), "Complaint 0110017: In the Matter of Rambus Incorporated, A Corporation," Docket No. 9302, available at http://www.ftc.gov/os/adjpro/d9302/020618admincmp.pdf.

Felten, E. (2005), "The Pizzaright Principle," Freedom to Tinker, September 28, available at http://www.freedom-to-tinker.com/?p=902.

Ferraguto, G., C. Lucioni, and F. Onida (1983), *L'industria farmaceutica italiana: L'innovazione tecnologica*. Il Mulino.

First, H. (2006), "Microsoft and the Evolution of the Intellectual Property Concept," New York University Law and Economics Working Papers No. 74.

Fleming, I. (1953), *Casino Royale*. London: Jonathan Cape.

Flint, E. (2002), "Prime Palaver #6," April 15, available at http://www.baen.com/library/palaver6.htm.

Flynn, L. J. and S. Lohr (2006), "Two Giants in a Deal over Linux," *New York Times*, November 3.

Fox, S. P. (2002), "Opening Statements of Stephen P. Fox Associate General Counsel, Director of Intellectual Property Hewlett-Packard Company," FTC/DOJ Hearings on Competition and Intellectual Property Law and Policy in the Knowledge-Based Economy, February 28.

Fudenberg, D. and J. Tirole (1991), *Game Theory*. Cambridge, MA: MIT Press.

Gall, B. W. (2000), "What is 'Fair Use' in Copyright Law?" available at http://www.gigalaw.com/articles/2000-all/gall-2000–12-all.html.

Gallini, N. (2002), "The Economics of Patents: Lessons from Recent U.S. Patent Reform," *Journal of Economic Perspective* 16, 131–54.

Gallini, N. and S. Scotchmer (2001), "Intellectual Property: When Is It the Best Incentive System?" in *Innovation Policy and the Economy*, Vol. 2, ed. A. Jaffe, J. Lerner, and S. Stern. Cambridge, MA: MIT Press.

Gans, J. S., D. H. Hsu, and S. Stern (2000), "When Does Start Up Innovation Spur the Gale of Creative Destruction?" NBER Working Paper No. 7851, August.

Gardner, W. M. (1915), *The British Coal-Tar Industry*. Manchester, NH: Ayer Publishing. Reprint, London: Williams and Norgate, 1981.

Gates, B. (1991), "Microsoft Challenges and Strategy Memo," May 16. Quoted online at http://www.nytimes.com/2007/06/09/opinion/09lee.html?ex=1339041600&en=a2f3d8f1f3cfcb61&ei=5090.

Gilbert, A. (2005), "Red Hat Revenues Jump 46%," *Web Design & Technology News*, July 2.

Gilbert, R. and C. Shapiro (1990), "Optimal Patent Length and Breadth," *Rand Journal of Economics* 21, 106–12.

Gilbert, R. and C. Shapiro (1997), "Antitrust Issues in the Licensing of Intellectual Property: The Nine No-No's Meet the Nineties," Brookings Papers on Economic Activity: Microeconomics, 283–336.

Gilbert, R. J. and D. M. G. Newbery (1982), "Preemptive Patenting and the Persistence of Monopoly," *The American Economic Review* 72, 514–26.

Gilson, R. (1999), "The Legal Infrastructure of High Technology Industrial Districts: Silicon Valley, Route 128, and Covenants not to Compete," *New York University Law Review* 74, 575–629.

Glennerster, R., M. Kremer, and H. Williams (2006), "Creating Markets for Vaccines," *Innovations* **1** (1), 67–79.

Godlee, F. (2007), "Milestones on the Long Road to Knowledge," *British Medical Journal* (**334**, suppl.), available at http://www.bmj.com/cgi/content/full/334/suppl_1/s2.

Grabowski, H. G. (2002), "Patents, Innovation and Access to New Pharmaceuticals," *Journal of International Economics Law* **5**, 849–60.

Grabowski, H. G. and J. M. Vernon (1986), "Longer Patent for Lower Imitation Barriers: The 1984 Drug Act," *The American Economic Review, Papers and Proceedings* **76**, 195–98.

Grabowski H. G. and J. M. Vernon (1996), "Longer Patents for Increased Generic Competition in the US," *PharmacoEconomics* **10**, 110–23.

Graham, S. H. (2002), "Secrecy in the Shadow's of Patenting: Firms' Use of Continuation Patents: 1975–1994," Ph.D. dissertation chapter, Haas School of Business, University of California, Berkeley.

Green, J. (2006), "Exit, Pursued by a Lawyer," *New York Times*, January 29.

Greenwood, J. and B. Jovanovic (1990), "Financial Development, Growth, and the Distribution of Income," *Journal of Political Economy* **98**, 1076–1107.

Griliches, Z. (1957), "Hybrid Corn: An Exploration in the Economics of Technological Change," *Econometrica* **25**, 501–22.

Griliches, Z. (1960), "Hybrid Corn and the Economics of Innovation," *Science* **132** (July).

Grossman, G. and E. Helpman (1991), "Quality Ladders in the Theory of Growth," *Review of Economic Studies* **58**, 43–61.

Haber, L. F. (1958), The *Chemical Industry During the Nineteenth Century*. Cambridge, UK: Clarendon Press.

Haber, L.F. (1971), *The Chemical Industry: 1900–1930*. Oxford: Clarendon Press.

Hale, R., L. Tolleri, and J. L. Telford (2006), "The Evolution and Impact of Genome Patents and Patent Applications," *Expert Opinion on Therapeutic Patents* **16** (3), 231–5.

Hall, B. H. and R. H. Ziedonis (2001), "The Patent Paradox Revisited: An Empirical Study of Patenting in the U.S. Semiconductor Industry, 1979–1995," *Rand Journal of Economics* **32**, 101–28.

Hall, G. and R.-M. Ham (1999), "The Patents Paradox Revisited: Determinants of Patenting in the U.S. Semiconductor Industry, 1980–94," mimeo, University of California at Berkley, April.

Hansen, R. W., H. G. Grabowski, and L. Lasagna (1991), "Cost of Innovation in the Pharmaceutical Industry," *Journal of Health Economics* **10**, 107–42.

Harris, G. (2004), "As Doctors Write Prescriptions, Drug Companies Write Checks," *New York Times*, June 27.

Hayek, F. (1960), "Free Enterprise and Competitive Order," in *Individualism and Economic Order*. Chicago: University of Chicago Press.

Heinlein, R. (1939), "Life Line," in *Astounding Science Fiction*.

Heller, M. A. and R. S. Eisenberg (1998), "Can Patents Deter Innovation? The Anticommons in Biomedical Research," *Science* **280**, 698–701.

Hellwig, M. and C. Irmen (2001), "Endogenous Technical Change in a Competitive Economy," *Journal of Economic Theory* **101**, 1–39.

Herrera, H. and E. Schroth (2004), "Developer's Expertise and the Dynamics of Financial Innovation: Theory and Evidence," FAME Research Paper No. 124, University of Lausanne, October.

Hesse, C. (2002), "The rise of intellectual property, 700 BC–AD 2000: An Idea in the Balance," *Daedalus* (Spring), 26–45.

Hirshleifer, J. (1971), "The Private and Social Value of Information and the Reward to Inventive Activity," *American Economic Review* **61**, 561–74.

Hirshleifer, J. and J. G. Riley (1992), *The Analytics of Uncertainty and Information*. Cambridge: Cambridge University Press.

Hong, S. (2001), *Wireless: From Marconi's Black-Box to the Audion*. Cambridge, MA: MIT Press.

Horstmann, I., G. M. MacDonald, and A. Slivinski (1985), "Patents as Information Transfer Mechanisms: To Patent or (Maybe) Not to Patent," *Journal of Political Economy* **93**, 837–58.

Hubbard, T. and J. Love (2004), "A New Trade Framework for Global Healthcare R&D," *PLoS Biology* **2** (2), E52, available at http://0-biology.plosjournals.org.ilsprod.lib.neu.edu/perlserv/?SESSID=58f35c0e6f50f2af6fca8736674f75c6&request=get-document&doi=10.1371%2Fjournal.pbio.0020052.

Hughes, J. W., M. J. More, and E. A. Snyder (2002), "'Napsterizing' Pharmaceuticals: Access, Innovation, and Consumer Welfare," NBER Working Paper No. 9229, October.

International Federation of Pharmaceutical Manufacturers (2004), *The Pharmaceutical Innovation Platform*. Geneva: International Federation of Pharmaceutical Manufacturers.

Jackson, H. B. (1897), "Report of Captain Jackson," May 22, 1897, ADM 116/523, U.K. Public Records Office, Kew.

Jaffe, A. B. (2000), "The U.S. Patent System in Transition: Policy Innovation and the Innovation Process," *Research Policy* **29**, 531–57.

Jaffe, A. B. and J. Lerner (2004), *Innovation and Its Discontents*. Princeton, NJ: Princeton University Press.

Johns, A. (2002), "Pop Music Pirate Hunters," *Daedalus* (Spring), 67–77.

Johnston, B. (1982), *My Inventions: The Autobiography of Nikola Tesla*. Williston, VT: Hart Brothers Publishing.

Kanefsky, J. W. (1979), "The Diffusion of Power Technology in British Industry, 1760–1870," Ph.D. dissertation, University of Exeter.

Kanefsky, J. W. and J. Robey (1980), "Steam Engines in 18th Century Britain: A Quantitative Assessment," *Technology and Culture* **21**, 161–86.

Kanwar, S. and R. Evenson (2003), "Does Intellectual Property Protection Spur Technological Change?" *Oxford Economic Papers* **55**, 235–64.

Karjala, D. S. (1998), "Statement of Copyright and Intellectual Law Professors in Opposition to H.R. 604, H.R. 2589 and S. 505, The Copyright Term Extension Act, Submitted to the Joint Committees of the Judiciary," January 28, available at http://www.public.asu.edu/~dkarjala/legmats/1998Statement.html.

Karjala, D. S. (2004), "Opposing Copyright Extension," available at http://www.public.asu.edu/~dkarjala/legmats/hatch95.html.

Kaufer, E. (2002), *The Economics of the Patent System*, Routledge.

Kenney, M. and von Burg, U. (2000), "Institutions and Economies: Creating Silicon Valley", in *Understanding Silicon Valley: Anatomy of an Entrepreneurial Region*, ed. M. Kenney. Palo Alto, CA: Stanford University Press.

Kevles, D. J. (2001), "Patenting Life. A Historical Overview of Law, Interests, and Ethics," mimeo, Legal Theory Workshop, Yale Law School, December 20.

Khan, Z. (2005), *The Democratization of Invention: Patents and Copyrights in American Development, 1790–1920*. New York: Cambridge University Press.

Kingston, W. (1984), *The Political Economy of Innovation*. The Hague: Martinus Nijhoff, 1989.

Kingston, W. (2001), "Meeting Nelson's Concerns about Intellectual Property," paper presented at the Nelson and Winter Conference, Danish Research Unit for Industrial Dynamics, Aalborg, June 12–15, available at http://www.druid.dk/conferences/nw/.

Klein, J. I. (1997), "Cross-Licensing and Antitrust Law," paper presented at the conference of the American Intellectual Property Law Association, available at http://www.usdoj.gov/atr/public/speeches/1118.htm.

Klevorick, A. K., R. C. Levin, R. R. Nelson, and S. G. Winter (1995), "On the Sources and Significance of Interindustry Differences in Technological Opportunities," *Research Policy* **25**, 185–205.

Kling, A. (2003), "A Metaphor's Metaphor," Tech Central Station, available at http://www.techcentralstation.com/030303B.html.

Kloppenburg, J. R., Jr., (1988), *First the Seed: The Political Economy of Plant Biotechnology, 1492–2000*. London: Cambridge University Press.

Koerner, B. J. (2004), "Who Gets the 9/11 Report Profits?" *Slate*, July 27, available at http://slate.msn.com/id/2104431.

Kortum, S. and Lerner, J. (1998), "Stronger Protection or Technological Revolution: What Is Behind the Recent Surge in Patenting?" *Carnegie-Rochester Conference Series on Public Policy* **48**, 247–304.

Kremer, M. (2001a), "Creating Markets for New Vaccines: Part I: Rationale," in *Innovation Policy and the Economy*, Vol. 1, ed. A. B. Jaffe, J. Lerner, and S. Stern. Cambridge, MA: MIT Press.

Kremer, M. (2001b), "Creating Markets for New Vaccines: Part II: Design Issues," in *Innovation Policy and the Economy*, Vol. 1, ed. A. B. Jaffe, J. Lerner, and S. Stern. Cambridge, MA: MIT Press.

Krugman, P. (1980), "Scale Economies, Product Differentiation, and the Pattern of Trade," *American Economic Review* **70**, 950–9.

Kukkonen, C. A. (1998), "Be a Good Sport and Refrain from Using My Patented Putt: Intellectual Property Protection for Sports Related Movements," *Journal of the Patent and Trademark Office Society* **80**, 808.

Ladas and Parry LLP (2003), "A Brief History of Patent Law in the United States," The Patent System: Historical Articles and Introductory Information, available at http://www.ladas.com/Patents/IntroductoryIndex.html.

Lamberti, M. J. (2001), "An Industry in Evolution," CenterWatch, available at http://www.centerwatch.com.

Lamoreaux, N. R. and K. L. Sokoloff (2002), "Intermediaries in the U.S. Market for Technology, 1870–1920," NBER Working Paper No. 9016.

Landes, D. S. (1969), *The Unbound Prometheus: Technological Change and Industrial Development in Western Europe from 1750 to Present*. New York: Cambridge University Press.

Landes, D. S. (1998), *The Wealth and Poverty of Nations: Why Are Some So Rich and Others So Poor?* New York: W. W. Norton.

Landes, W. M. and R. Posner (2002), "Indefinitely Renewable Copyright," working paper, Olin Center for Law and Economics, University of Chicago, available at http://www.law.uchicago.edu/Lawecon/WkngPprs_151–175/154.wml-rap.copyright.new.pdf.

Landes, W. M. and R. A. Posner (2003), *The Economic Structure of Intellectual Property Law*. Cambridge, MA: Harvard University Press.

Lanjouw, J. O. (1997), "The Introduction of Pharmaceutical Product Patents in India: Heartless Exploitation of the Poor and Suffering?" NBER Working Paper No. 6366.

Lanjouw, J. O. (2002), "Intellectual Property and the Availability of Pharmaceutical in Poor Countries," Center for Global Development Working Paper No. 5.

Lanjouw, J. O. (2005), "Patents, Price Controls and Access to New Drugs: How Policy Affects Global Market Entry," Center for Global Development Working Paper No. 61.

Lanjouw, J. and I. Cockburn (2002), "New Pills For Poor People? Empirical Evidence after GATT," *World Development* **29**, 265–89.

Lanjouw, J. O. and J. Lerner (1996), "Preliminary Injunctive Relief: Theory and Evidence from Patent Litigation," NBER Working Paper No. 5689.

Leaf, C. (2005), "The Law of Unintended Consequences," *Fortune*, September 19.

Leger, A. (2004), "Strenghtening of Intellectual Property Rights in Mexico: A Case Study of Maize Breeding," working paper, Unisfera International Center, June, available at http://www.unisfera.org.

Lemley, M. A. (2004), "Ex Ante versus Ex Post Justifications for Intellectual Property," mimeo, University of California, Berkeley.

Lerner, J. (1995), "Patenting in the Shadow of Competitors," *Journal of Law and Economics* **38**, 563–95.

Lerner, J. (2002), "Patent Protection and Innovation over 150 Years," available at http://www.epip.eu/papers/20030424/epip/papers/cd/papers_speakers/Lerner_Paper_EPIP_210403.pdf. Abridged version published as "150 Years of Patent Office Protection," *American Economic Review, Papers and Proceedings* **92**, 221–25.

Lessig, L. (2004), *Free Culture*. New York: Penguin Press.

Levin, R. C., A. K. Klevorick, R. R. Nelson, and S. G. Winter (1987), "Appropriating the Returns from Industrial Research and Development," Brookings Papers on Economic Activity No. 3, 783–820.

Levine, L. and K. M. Saunders (2004), "Software Patents: Innovation or Litigation?" paper presented at the IFIP 8.6 Working Conference: IT Innovation for Adaptiveness and Competitive Advantage, Leixlip, Ireland.

Levy, D. M. and S. J. Peart (2001), "The Secret History of the Dismal Science," available at http://www.econlib.org/library/Columns/LevyPeartdismal.html.

Lewis, M. (1989), *Liar's Poker*. New York: W. W. Norton.

Licht, G. and K. Zoz (1996), "Patents and R&D: An Econometric Investigation Using Applications for German, European and US Patents by German Companies," Discussion Paper No. 96–19, ZEW-Mannheim, June.

Liebowitz, S. (2004), "Will MP3 Downloads Annihilate the Record Industry? The Evidence So Far," *Advances in the Study of Entrepreneurship, Innovation, and Economic Growth* **15**, 229–60.

Lindsey, B. (2001), *Against the Dead Hand: The Uncertain Struggle for Global Capitalism*. New York: John Wiley & Sons.

Llanes, G. and S. Trento (2006), "Complex Sequential Innovation," mimeo, Universidad Carlos III de Madrid, October.

Lo, S.-T. (2004), "Strenghtening Intellectual Property Rights: Experience from the 1986 Taiwanese Patent Reforms," mimeo, Department of Economics, UCLA, available at http://www.international.ucla.edu/article.asp?parentid=10985.

Lomas, R. (1999), *The Man Who Invented the Twentieth Century: Nikola Tesla, Forgotten Genius of Electricity.* London: Headline.

Lord, J. (1923), *Capital and Steam Power.* London: P. S. King & Son.

Love, J. (1997), "Call for More Reliable Costs Data on Clinical Trials," January 13, available at http://www.cptech.org/pharm/marketletter.html.

Lucas, R. E. (1988), "On the Mechanics of Economic Development," *Journal of Monetary Economics* **22**, 3–42.

Machlup, F. (1958), "An Economic Review of the Patent System," Study of the Sub-Committee on Patents, Trademarks, and Copyrights of the Committee on the Judiciary. U.S. Senate, 85th Congress, 2d sess. Pursuant to S. Res. 236, Study No. 15.

Maclaurin, R. W. (1950), "Patents and Technical Progress: A Study of Television," *Journal of Political Economy* **58**, 142–57.

MacLeod, C. and A. Nuvolari (2006), "Inventive Activities, Patents and Early Industrialization: A Synthesis of Research Issues," Danish Research Unit for Industrial Dynamics Working Paper No. 06–28.

Mallory, J. (1992), "Camera Makers Pay Honeywell $124M in Patent Settlement: Kodak, Konica, Kyocera, Canon, Matsushita, Nikon, Premier," Newsbytes News Network, August 24.

Manes, S. (2004), "The Trouble with Larry," *Forbes Magazine*, March 29, available at http://www.forbes.com/columnists/business/free_forbes/2004/0329/084.html.

Mann, C. C. (2000), "The Heavenly Jukebox," *Atlantic Monthly* **286** (3).

Mann, R. (2004), "The Myth of the Software Patent Thicket: An Empirical Investigation of the Relationship between Intellectual Property and Innovation in Software Firms," University of Texas School of Law, Law and Economics Working Paper No. 022, February.

Mann, R. (2005), "Do Patents Facilitate Financing in the Software Industry?" *Texas Law Review* **83**, 961–1030.

Mantoux, P. (1905), *La revolution industrielle au XVIII siecle.* Paris: Aguillar. Reprint, 1962.

Marimon, R. and V. Quadrini (2006), "Competition, Innovation and Growth with Limited Commitment," mimeo, Universitat Pompeu Fabra and University of South Carolina, July.

Marsden, B. (2004), *Watt's Perfect Engine: Steam and the Age of Invention.* New York : Columbia University Press.

Marshall, A. (1920), *Principles of Economics*, 8th ed. New York: Macmillan.

Marx, K. (1857), *Grundrisse der Kritik der Politischen Oekonomie.* Berlin: Dietz.

Maskus, K. E. (2001), "Parallel Imports in Pharmaceuticals: Implications for Competition and Prices in Developing Countries," final report to World Intellectual Property Organization, April.

Maurer, S. M. (1999), "Raw Knowledge: Protecting Technical Databases for Science and Technology," Committee on Promoting Access to Scientific and Technical Knowledge, National Research Council, National Academy of Sciences.

Maurer, S. M., R. B. Firestone, and C. R. Scriver (2000), "Science's Neglected Legacy," *Nature* **405**, 117–20.

Maurer, S. M., A. Rai, and A. Sali (2004), "Finding Cures for Tropical Diseases: Is Open Source an Answer?" *PLoS Medicine* **1** (3): e56.

Maurer, S. M. and S. Scotchmer (1999) "Database Protection: Is It Broken and Should We Fix It?" *Science* **284**, 1129–30.

May, E. R. (2005), "When Government Writes History: The 9–11 Commission Report," History News Network, available at http://hnn.us/articles/11972.html.

McClelland, P. D. (1997), *Sowing Modernity: America's First Agricultural Revolution*. Ithaca, NY: Cornell University Press.

McKenzie, L. W. (1981), "The Classical Theorem on Existence of Competitive Equilibrium," *Econometrica* **49**, 819–41.

Meyer-Thurow, G. (1982), "The Industrialization of Invention: A Case Study from the German Chemical Industry," *Isis* **73** (3), 363–81.

Morris, P. J. and A. S. Travis (1992), "A History of the International Dyestuff Industry," *American Dyestuff Reporter* **81** (11), available at http://colorantshistory.org/HistoryInternationalDyeIndustry.html.

Moser, P. (2003), "How Do Patent Laws Influence Innovation? Evidence from Nineteenth-Century World Fairs," NBER Working Paper No. 9909. Abridged version published in American Economic Review **95**, 1215–36.

Moser, P. (2005), "Do Patents Facilitate Knowledge Spillovers? Evidence from the Economic Geography of Innovations in 1851," mimeo, National Bureau of Economic Research and Massachusetts Institute of Technology, available at http://web.mit.edu/moser/www/loc507nber.pdf.

Moser, P. (2006), "What Do Inventors Patent?" mimeo, National Bureau of Economic Research and Massachusetts Institute of Technology, available at http://web.mit.edu/moser/www/patrat603.pdf.

Mowery, D. C. (1990), "The Economic History of Technology: The Development of Industrial Research in U.S. Manufacturing," *American Economic Review* **80** (May), 345–9.

Mowery, D. C. and N. Rosenberg (1998), *Paths of Innovation: Technological Change in 20th Century America*. New York: Cambridge University Press.

Murmann, J. P. (2004), "Patents and Technological Competencies: A Cross National Study of Intellectual Property Right Strategies in the Synthetic Dye Industry, 1857–1914," paper presented at the 2004 Economic History Association Meetings, San Jose, CA.

Murphy, K. M. and R. Topel (1999), "The Economic Value of Medical Research," mimeo, University of Chicago, September.

National Institute for Health Care Management (2002), "Changing Patterns of Pharmaceutical Innovation," available at http://www.nihcm.org/innovations.pdf.

North, D. (1991), *Institutions, Institutional Change and Economic Performance*. New York: Cambridge University Press.

North, D. C. (1981), *Structure and Change in Economic History*. New York: W. W. Norton.

Novak, M. (1996), *The Fire of Invention, the Fuel of Interest*. Washington, DC: American Enterprise Institute Press.

Nuvolari, A. (2004a), "Collective Invention during the British Industrial Revolution: The Case of the Cornish Pumping Engine," *Cambridge Journal of Economics* **28**, 347–63.

Nuvolari, A. (2004b), "The Making of Steam Power Technology," Ph.D. dissertation, Eindhoven Centre for Innovation Studies.

Nuvolari, A. (2005), "Open Source Software Development: Some Historical Perspectives," *First Monday. Peer-reviewed Journal on the Internet* **10** (10), available at http://www.firstmonday.org/issues/issue10_10/nuvolari/index.html.

Nwokeaba, H. (2002), "Why Industrial Revolution Missed Africa: A 'traditional knowledge' Perspective," United Nations Economic Commission for Africa Paper No. 01/02.

Oberholzer, F. and K. Strumpf (2004), "The Effect of File Sharing on Record Sale: An Empirical Analysis," mimeo, Harvard Business School, March.

Okuno-Fujiwara, M., A. Postlewaite, and K. Suzumura (1990), "Strategic Information Revelation," *Review of Economic Studies* **57**, 25–47.

Olmstead, A. L. and P. W. Rhode (2002), "The Red Queen and the Hard Reds: Productivity Growth in American Wheat, 1800–1940," *Journal of Economic History* **62**, 929–66.

Olmstead, A. L. and P. W. Rhode (2003), "Hog-Round Marketing, Seed Quality, and Government Policy: Institutional Change in U.S. Cotton Production, 1920–1960," *Journal of Economic History* **63**, 447–88.

Paci, R. (1990), *Innovazione tecnologica e intervento pubblico nell'industria farmaceutica*. Milan: Franco Angeli.

Park, W. G. (2001), "R&D, Spillovers, and Intellectual Property Rights," mimeo, Department of Economics, American University, December.

Penrose, E. (1951), *The Economics of the International Patent System*. Baltimore: John Hopkins University Press.

Perelman, M. (2002), *Steal This Idea: Intellectual Property Rights and the Corporate Confiscation of Creativity*. New York: Palgrave Macmillan.

Pesendorfer, W. (1995). "Design Innovation and Fashion Cycles," *American Economic Review* **85**, 771–92.

Pharmaceutical Research and Manufacturers of America (2007), *Pharmaceutical Industry Profile: 2007*. Washington, DC: Pharmaceutical Research and Manufacturers of America.

Plant, A. (1934), "The Economic Aspect of Copyright in Books," *Economica* **1**, n.s., 167–95.

Plant, A. (1953), *The New Commerce in Ideas and Intellectual Property*. London: Athlone Press.

Pofeldt, E. (2003). "Patent (Lawsuits) Pending, Small E-tailers Get Squeezed by Questionable IP Claims," *Fortune Small Business*, March 1.

Pollack, A. (2001), "Bristol-Myers and Athersys Make Deal on Gene Patents," *New York Times*, January 8.

Ponce, C. (2003), "Knowledge Disclosure as Optimal Intellectual Property Protection," mimeo, Department of Economics, UCLA.

Posner, R. A. (2002), "The Law and Economics of Intellectual Property," *Daedalus* (Spring), 5–12.

Posner, R. A. (2004), "Posner Responds to 'Why Mickey Mouse Is Not Subject to Congestion,' by Michele Boldrin and David Levine," *The Economists' Voice* **1**, 2.

Price, W. H. (2006), *The English Patents of Monopolies: A History*. Clark, NJ: Lawbook Exchange.

Putnam, J. D. (2004), "Cost and Benefits of Genomic Patents," *American Journal of Pharmacogenomics* **4** (5), 277–92.

Qian, Y. (2007), "Do National Patent Laws Stimulate Domestic Innovation in a Global Patenting Environment? A Cross-Country Analysis of Pharmaceutical Patent Protection, 1978–2002," *Review of Economics and Statistics* **89**, 436–53.

Quah, D. (2002), "24/7 Competitive Innovation," mimeo, London School of Economics, available at http://econ.lse.ac.uk/staff/dquah/currmnu1.html.

Quillen, C. D., Jr., O. H. Webster, and R. Eichmann (2002), "Continuing Patent Applications and Performance of the U.S. Patent and Trademark Office: Extended," *Federal Circuit Court Bar Journal* **12** (1), 35–55.

Rasmusen, E. B. (2005), "An Economic Approach to the Ethics of Copyright Violation," American Law & Economics Association 15th Annual Meeting Working Paper No. 61, available at http://law.bepress.com/alea/15th/art61.

Raustiala, K. and C. Sprigman (2006), "The Piracy Paradox: Innovation and Intellectual Property in Fashion Design," working paper, UCLA School of Law.

Rich E. E. and C. H. Wilson eds. (1965), *The Cambridge Economic History of Europe*, Vol. 4. New York: Cambridge University Press, 1965.

Roberts, R. (2003), *Philo T. Farnsworth: The Life of Television's Forgotten Inventor (Unlocking the Secrets of Science)*. Bear, DE: Mitchell Lane Publishers.

Romer, P. (1986), "Increasing Returns and Long Run Growth," *Journal of Political Economy* **94**, 1002–3.

Romer, P. (1990a), "Are Nonconvexities Important for Understanding Growth?" *American Economic Review* **80**, 97–103.

Romer, P. (1990b), "Endogenous Technological Change," *Journal of Political Economy* **98**, S71–S102.

Romer, P. (1996), "Science, Economic Growth and Public Policy," in *Technology, R&D, and the Economy*, ed. B. Smith and C. Barfield. Washington, DC: Brookings Institution and American Enterprise Institute.

Rowe, J. (1953), *Cornwall in the Age of the Industrial Revolution*. Liverpool, UK: Liverpool University Press.

Sadeghi, Y. (2004), "Alum Alleges Stolen Design: Shine Files Suit over Freedom Tower Design," *Yale Daily News*, November 10, available at http://www.yaledailynews.com/Article.aspx?ArticleID = 27255.

Sakakibara, M. and L. Branstetter (2001), "Do Stronger Patents Induce More Innovation? Evidence from the 1988 Japanese Patent Law Reforms," *Rand Journal of Economics* **32**, 77–100.

Samuelson, P. (2004), "What's at Stake in *MGM vs. Grokster*?" *Communications of the ACM* **47** (2), 15–20.

Saunders, K. M. (2002), "Patent Nonuse and the Role of Public Interest as a Deterrent to Technology Suppression," *Harvard Journal of Law and Technology* **15**, 1–64.

Saxenian, A.-L. (1994), *Regional Advantage: Culture and Competition in Silicon Valley and Route 128*. Cambridge, MA: Harvard University Press.

Schankerman, M. (1998), "How Valuable Is Patent Protection? Estimates by Technology Field," *Rand Journal of Economics* **29**, 77–107.

Schankerman, M. and A. Pakes (1986), "Estimates of the Value of Patent Rights in European Countries During the Post-1950 Period," *Economic Journal* **96** (384), 1052–77.

Scharchburg, R. P. (1993), *Carriages without Horses: J. Frank Duryea and the Birth of the American Automobile Industry*. Warrendale, PA: Society of Automotive Engineers.

Scherer, F. M. (1965), "Innovation and Invention in the Watt-Boulton Steam Engine Venture," *Technology and Culture* **6**, 165–87.

Scherer, F. M. (1984), *Innovation and Growth: Schumpeterian Perspective.* Cambridge, MA: MIT Press.

Scherer, F. M. (2002), "The Economics of Human Gene Patents," *Academic Medicine* **77**.

Scherer, F. M. (2003), "Global Welfare in Pharmaceutical Patenting," mimeo Haverford College, December.

Scherer, F. M. (2004), *Quarter Notes and Bank Notes: The Economics of Music Composition in the Eighteenth and Nineteenth Centuries.* Princeton, NJ: Princeton University Press.

Scherer F. M. and S. Weisbrod (1995), "Economic Effects of Strengthening Pharmaceutical Patent Protection in Italy," *International Review of Industrial Property and Copyright Law* **26**, 1009–24.

Schumpeter, J. (1911), *The Theory of Economic Development.* New York: McGraw Hill.

Schumpeter, J. (1943), *Capitalism, Socialism and Democracy.* London: Unwin University Books.

Schwartz, E. I. (2003), *The Last Lone Inventor: A Tale of Genius, Deceit, and the Birth of Television.* New York: Harper Paperbacks.

Schwartzman, D. (1976), *Innovation in the Pharmaceutical Industry.* Baltimore: John Hopkins University Press.

Scotchmer, S. (1991), "Standing on the Shoulders of Giants: Cumulative Research and the Patent Law," *Journal of Economic Perspectives* **5**, 29–41.

Scotchmer, S. (1999), "On the Optimality of the Patent Renewal System," *Rand Journal of Economics* **30**, 181–96.

Scotchmer, S. (2004), *Innovation and Incentives.* Cambridge, MA: MIT Press.

Seabright, P. (2004), *The Company of Strangers: A Natural History of Economic Life.* Princeton, NJ: Princeton University Press.

Seckelmann, M. (2001), "The Quest for Legal Stability: Patent Protection within the German Empire, 1871–1903," working paper, Max Planck Institute for European Legal History, August.

Selgin, G. and J. Turner (2006), "James Watt as an Intellectual Monopolist: Comment on Boldrin and Levine," *International Economic Review* **47**, 1341–54.

Shapiro, C. (2001), "Navigating the Patent Thicket: Cross Licenses, Patent Pools and Standards Setting," in *Innovation and the Economy*, Vol. 1, ed. A. Jaffe, J. Lerner, and S. Stern. Cambridge, MA: MIT Press.

Shell, K. (1966), "Toward a Theory of Inventive Activity and Capital Accumulation," *American Economic Review* **56**, 62–68.

Shell, K. (1967), "A Model of Inventive Activity and Capital Accumulation," in *Essays on the Theory of Optimal Economic Growth*, ed. K. Shell, 67–85. Cambridge, MA: MIT Press.

Shulman, S. (2003), *Unlocking the Sky.* New York: Harper Perennial.

Smith, A. (1977–78), "Steam and the City: The Committee of Proprietors of the Invention for Raising Water by Fire, 1715–1735," *Transactions of the Newcomen Society* **49**, 5–20.

Smith, J. (1991), *Patenting the Sun: Polio and the Salk Vaccine.* New York: Anchor/Doubleday.

Sokoloff, K. L. and Z. Kahn (2000): "Intellectual Property Institutions in the United States: Early Development and Comparative Perspective," UCLA.

Sonobe, T., M. Kawakami, and K. Otsuka (2003), "Changing Roles of Innovation and Imitation in Industrial Development: The Case of the Machine Tool Industry in Taiwan," *Economic Development and Cultural Change* 52, 103–28.

Stigler, G. J. (1956), "Industrial Organization and Economic Progress," in *The State of the Social Science*, ed. L. D. White, 269–82. Chicago: University of Chicago Press.

Surowiecki, J. (2003), "Patent Bending," in 'The Financial Page', *The New Yorker*, July 14.

Swartz, J. (2004), "Porn Often Leads High-Tech Way," *USA Today*, September 3.

Takeyama, L. N. (1997), "The Intertemporal Consequences of Unauthorized Reproduction of Intellectual Property," *Journal of Law & Economics* 40, 511–22.

The Economist (2001), Issue of June 23.

Thompson, B. (1847), *Inventions, Improvements, and Practice of Benjamin Thompson, in the Combined Character of Colliery Engineer and General Manager*. Newcastle.

Thurston, R. (1878), "A History of the Growth of the Steam-Engine," in *The Cambridge History of Science*, Vol. 4, ed. R. Porter et al., 854. New York: Cambridge University Press.

Tirole, J. (1988), *The Theory of Industrial Organization*. Cambridge, MA: MIT Press.

Tufano, P. (1989), "First-Mover Advantages in Financial Innovation," *Journal of Financial Economics* 3, 350–70.

Tufano, P. (2003), "Financial Innovation," in *The Handbook of the Economics of Finance*, ed. G. Constantinides, M. Harris, and R. Stulz. Amsterdam: North Holland.

Urban, T. N. (2000), "Agricultural Biotechnology: Its History and Future," available at http://www.dieboldinstitute.org.

U.S. Patent and Trademark Office (1994), "USPTO Public Hearings," available at http://www.uspto.gov/web/offices/com/hearings/index.html.

Van den Belt, H. (1992), "Why Monopoly Failed: The Rise and Fall of Société La Fuchsine," *British Journal for the History of Science* 25 (84), 45–63.

Varian, H. R. (1997), "Versioning Information Goods," mimeo, University of California, Berkeley.

Varnedoe, K. (1990), *A Fine Disregard: What Makes Modern Art Modern*. New York: H. N. Abrams.

von Hippel, E. (1988), *The Sources of Innovation*. New York: Oxford University Press.

von Hippel, E. (2005), *Democratizing Innovation*. Cambridge, MA: MIT Press.

von Tunzelmann, G. N. (1978), *Steam Power and British Industrialization to 1860*. Oxford, UK: Clarendon Press.

Washington Post (2004), "Best Sellers," October 10.

Wyatt, E. (2004), "For Publisher of 9/11 Report, a Royalty-Free Windfall," *New York Times*, July 28.

Young, A. (1928), "Increasing Returns and Economic Progress", *Economic Journal* 38, 527–42.

Zimbabwe Independent (2003), "GDP to Decline by 11.5%", September 12.

Index

innovation (*cont.*)
  in fashion, 59
  in financial securities, 57–58
  and fixed cost, 158, 184
  found in World Fair catalogs, 190–191
  hampered by patents, 2, 4
  and imitation, 146
  impact of non-compete clauses on,
    199–200
  impact of patent law on direction of,
    190–191
  importance of details in, 168
  increase of in U.S., 194
  intellectual monopoly as necessary for,
    10, 158–159
  intellectual monopoly unnecessary for,
    15
  lack of under monopoly, 43, 151, 187
  limited by patents, 4, 42, 49–50, 83–84
  in newspapers, 29
  patent law as reflection of state of, 191
  patents and reduction of, 83–84
  and patents in software, 197
  possible under abolition of patents, 186
  reasons for, 62–63
  risk in, 144–145, 174
  and sharing of information, 136–137
  social value of, 57
  in software without patent protection, 16
  in steam engines, *See also* steam engines
  studies of patents and, 192, 198t,
  subsidies for, 260–261
  and Total Factor Productivity (TFP), 54
innovators. *See also* first-mover advantage;
    innovation; producers
  and promise of large initial rents, 132–133
  rents of compared to imitators, 133
  rewarding of, 6
insufficient rent, 135
intellectual colonization, 38
intellectual imperialism, 81
intellectual monopoly. *See also* copyright;
    intellectual property; non-compete
    clauses; patents
  and costs of innovation, 150–151
  discouragement of imitation by, 146
  discouragement of new entrants by, 185

economic argument for, 135–136
  as good, 158, 243
  and lack of increase in innovation, 11,
    151, 187
  as necessary for innovation, 10, 158–159
  "pizzaright" test, 150
  in private sector, 61
  purposes of debates on, 151
  as unnecessary for innovation, 15
  as unwelcome consequence of
    innovation, 17
  and vision of idea economy, 172
  voluntary relinquishment of, 17, 18
intellectual property. *See also* copyright;
    ideas; ideas, copies of; intellectual
    monopoly; non-compete clauses;
    patents
  abolition of, 253–257
  control of after sale, 8
  desirable features of world without,
    125–126
  duration of and market size, 175
  effect on world history, 263–264
  efforts to expand, 246–248
  elimination of government from,
    252–253
  goal of complete elimination, 264–265
  history of in Europe, 43–47
  as incentive, 6
  levels of and R&D/BDP ratio, 196t
  and monopoly profits, 6
  vs. ordinary property, 123–124
  overuse argument for, 177–179
  in poor and developing countries,
    247–248
  and R&D as fraction of GDP, 195–196
  reasons to abolish, 243–244
  recent vintage of, 15
  reform of, 244–245, 257–259
  strengthening of, 192, 194–196, 197–198
  suggestions for reform in, 248–262
  suggestions for short-run improvements
    in, 248–251
  threat of to freedom and prosperity, 97,
    264
  types of, 8
  as unnecessary evil, 6–7